JOHN WESLEY
The Last Phase

JOHN WESLEY

The Last Phase

By
JOHN S. SIMON, D.D.
Author of
The Manual of Methodist Law and Discipline, The Revival of Religion in England in the Eighteenth Century, John Wesley and the Religious Societies, John Wesley and the Methodist Societies, John Wesley and the Advance of Methodism, John Wesley the Master-Builder, &c.

WIPF & STOCK · Eugene, Oregon

Wipf and Stock Publishers
199 W 8th Ave, Suite 3
Eugene, OR 97401

John Wesley
The Last Phase
By Simon, John S.
Copyright©1934 Methodist Publishing - Epworth Press
ISBN 13: 978-1-4982-8048-8
Publication date 1/27/2016
Previously published by Epworth Press, 1934

Every effort has been made to trace the current copyright owner
of this publication but without success. If you have any information
or interest in the copyright, please contact the publishers.

CONTENTS

CHAP.		PAGE
	PREFACE. BY A. W. HARRISON - - -	7
	JOHN SMITH SIMON. BY G. ELSIE HARRISON	9
I.	ENGLAND AND AMERICA - - - -	19
II.	WAR CLOUDS - - - - - -	36
III.	THE OUTBREAK OF WAR - - - -	49
IV.	THE NEED FOR AN ORDAINED MINISTRY -	60
V.	MRS. JOHN WESLEY - - - - -	73
VI.	CITY ROAD CHAPEL - - - - -	80
VII.	BRISTOL AND THE WAR WITH AMERICA - -	96
VIII.	JOURNEYINGS OF 1777 - - - - -	102
IX.	THE EFFECTS OF THE WAR IN ENGLAND AND IRELAND - - - - - -	121
X.	A YEAR OF DIFFICULTIES - - - -	137
XI.	WESLEY'S ATTITUDE TO THE CHURCH OF ENGLAND AND THE ROMAN CATHOLICS IN 1780 - - - - - - -	150
XII.	A CROWDED YEAR - - - - -	167
XIII.	TOIL AND TROUBLE - - - - -	183
XIV.	PASSING CLOUDS - - - - - -	198
XV.	THE LEGAL HUNDRED - - - - -	208
XVI.	THE AMERICAN PROBLEM - - - -	220
XVII.	THE METHODIST EPISCOPAL CHURCH - -	235
XVIII.	A MEMORABLE YEAR - - - - -	245
XIX.	A WORLD EVANGELIST - - - -	259

CHAP.		PAGE
XX.	Advance	268
XXI.	The Channel Islands	280
XXII.	The Death of Charles Wesley	296
XXIII.	A Triumphal Progress	308
XXIV.	Problems and Difficulties	319
XXV.	A Peaceful Close	332
	Index	344

PREFACE

It is seven years since the fourth volume of Dr. Simon's study of Wesley's life and work appeared and some explanation of the delay in producing this fifth and final volume seems necessary. *John Wesley and the Religious Societies* and *John Wesley and the Methodist Societies*, which were published in 1921 and 1923 respectively, contained the most important part of the contribution Dr. Simon made to the origins of Methodism. At intervals of two years the third and fourth volumes followed, but here the pathway was more straightforward since Wesley had found his great mission and his own *Journal* marked the highway clearly enough. At the age of eighty-four Dr. Simon began to write the present volume. His own pace began to show signs of slackening and he was more inclined to quote from his authorities than to tell the story himself in his own characteristically vivid manner. At the end of three years he had got as far as the middle of Chapter xxii, but after that he seemed to find the work of composition beyond him. Possibly he was reluctant to bring his hero to the death-bed scene at City Road. He began to read the story over and over again, and his friends began to wonder whether his own length of days would exceed the long limits of John Wesley's life. He had lived with John Wesley nearly all his days and he seemed half-inclined to die with him. Actually he outlived his hero by more than two years, for he himself died three days after his ninetieth birthday. On the last night of his life he told his youngest daughter that he hoped and expected that her husband would finish his book.

Little editing was needed for that part which he had already written. He wrote with such scrupulous care that sharp critics seldom found him in error. Old age had, however, begun to impair his memory and a few repetitions had to be omitted and some faults of forgetfulness corrected. It was impossible, however, to bring to the task of describing the closing days of John Wesley, the same reverent affection ('a little this side idolatry') for the founder of Methodism that Dr. Simon always displayed. I was familiar with that atmosphere of veneration from my earliest youth, for my grandparents had preserved the traditional attitude of the old Methodists to 'Mr. Wesley' unimpaired. Our age is more critical. Nevertheless, I have done my best, and my wife has consented to write a short sketch of her father's career. Those who love John Simon's book will be glad to hear a little more of the author.

A. W. HARRISON.

Westminster College,
    August, 1934.

JOHN SMITH SIMON

John Simon was born in Scotland and owed almost all he was to a Scottish mother. She it was who taught him the 23rd Psalm and saw to it that he developed a bump of reverence. It was also through her that he fell heir to a Methodist inheritance, albeit in the sandy stretches of Montrose. She was the granddaughter of that William Saunderson, one of Wesley's preachers, who died in the old cathedral city of Brechin in the year 1810. As the sands of time were running low he called for a Bible, and by the aid of a flickering candle flame read the 23rd Psalm and 'bowed himself before the Lord.' Those who gathered in that poor little bedroom, furnished from the Scottish roups, remembered how he said: 'I have endeavoured for above thirty years to keep the hour of death constantly in view that it might be as easy as going out of one room into another, and, blessed be God, I find it as easy now.' More than one hundred years later his great grandson, still a Methodist preacher, was to tread the self-same way. He arose to go from his study to his bedroom, and then set out on that further journey quietly and without fear. He was fond of telling his children that he always slept on the 23rd Psalm and in that last night they thought that he could not have got further than the great ' yea ' verse for he was so comfortably and so soon asleep :—

> 'Yea, though I walk through the Valley of the Shadow of Death I will fear no evil.'

There was always this something of the north about John Simon's allegiance, something utterly loyal and final. It was a secret he carried in his heart through ninety years of pilgrim exile.

His father was a Welshman, a Methodist by conviction, not by birth. He had been cut off with a shilling by his Church of England family for joining the Methodists in the thoroughgoing fashion of those early days.

On his son's 'note to preach' the Rev. John Rattenbury wrote, 'may his father's God be with him,' but it was his mother's God in reality who kept covenant with him all those ninety years. It was the God of the Methodist ' to the manner born' who won him for ever at the time of his father's death. Conversion for such an one was a tremendous affair. It gathered to itself all the romance and rapture of the Renascence of Wonder. In the life of John Simon it came about in this way. He had travelled from England to the Channel Islands to be present at his father's funeral. At that time he was articled to a solicitor in Bristol and taking very good care not to be inveigled into any solemn league and covenant with God. In the presence of death, confronted with his mother's faith and a yawning gap in the ranks of the Methodist ministry, he partook himself to his bedroom in a highly uncomfortable frame of mind. The young man had made a tempestuous and dark crossing from England, had endured an old-fashioned funeral and Methodist oration in a crowded chapel amidst many tears, and now, drumming in his head with awful insistence were the words: 'Seek ye the Lord whilst He may be found; call ye upon Him whilst He is near.' He fell on his knees and there in that prosaic manse bedroom the miracle happened. He saw Christ lifted up for the sin of the world and the rapture of that knowledge broke his heart:

> O let me kiss Thy bleeding feet,
>   And bathe and wash them with my tears!
> The story of Thy love repeat
>   In every drooping sinner's ears,
> That all may hear the quickening sound,
> Since I, even I, have mercy found.

Providence, in the guise of the Stationing Committee, saw to it that the ardent recruit to the ranks of the ministry should make immediate contact with John Wesley. He was appointed as Dr. Jobson's assistant to live in Wesley's own old house in the City Road. There he moved about the little rooms and became familiar with the place where Wesley lived and where he died. There at the back of the house was Wesley's grave in the tangled grass of the only garden the house possessed. In the rooms looking towards City Road, Dr. Jobson entertained the leaders of the Methodism of his day, and the young man became familiar with the prophets on whom the mantle of Wesley had fallen. He was always amazed at the kindness they showed to him, the raw recruit, and he never forgot the magic of the brotherhood. It was in that old house, with Christ in his heart and Wesley at his elbow, that the whole cast of his own ministry was fashioned. Ever afterwards he seemed to have known John Wesley 'after the flesh,' and to have cherished for him that spirit, compounded of reverence, obedience and love, which was the hall-mark of Wesley's own preachers.

The whirligig of stations later deposited John Simon in the bewitching county of Dorset. How would the first love stand so drastic a change of atmosphere? The land was full of pixies, of ancient defeat, of black melancholy. The trees were bent and twisted in their patient bearing of the storms of life. The sheep were huddled under the lea of the hedge in sad resignation. The old faiths of stone circle and barrow mocked the young Methodist preacher with their whisper on the wings of the wind: 'I care for nothing—all shall go.' The surf on the Chesil Beach alike proclaimed 'the long withdrawing roar' of faith's defeat. There was another young man walking through that same country at the same time, who so saw and so heard. He noted the bent twig, the hopeless, meaningless coercion, the intolerable age of things and the pitiable marionettes dancing down the years at the bidding of the President of the Immortals. He painted Egdon Heath and humanity hand in hand with trouble. But it so happened that whilst Thomas Hardy mourned for the sorrows of Tess in Winchester gaol, John Simon stumbled on the tracks of the grandfather of the Wesleys, a prisoner for conscience sake in the gaol at Blandford. By accident or design the trail was blazed again, and the young preacher could defy all the demons of hell with head down against the wind. With good northern courage he strung his Scottish Psalm to his Methodist lyre and went on his way rejoicing:

> By Thine unerring Spirit led,
> We shall not in the desert stray;
> We shall not full direction need,
> Nor miss our providential way.

His journal shows that he preached the 23rd Psalm and 'Christ lifted up' all through Thomas Hardy's Wessex.

The most that the bewitching county could do was to shake the 'dour' in that stockish figure just enough to make him fall in love. It was in Dorset that he met the one who was to be his wife, and when he saw her 'passing by,' the prosaic pavements of Weymouth became as the shining streets of Paradise. She was the daughter of Thomas Adams, who spent many years as a missionary in the South Sea Islands. The family came from a Methodist farm house in Cornwall, and numbered amongst its sons John Couch Adams of Cambridge, and William Grylls Adams, of King's College, London. The discoverer of Neptune taught the missionary brother how to calculate the time of eclipses, for the benefit of Mr. Wesley's darker children of Tonga, and the old Methodist father was as proud of the missionary as of the astronomer.

The brothers came together again many years afterwards in Cambridge, and it was from the Cambridge Observatory that the wedding of Maria Adams and John Simon took place. Their first married home was in Welshpool, and through many faithful years they travelled on together in Doncaster, Birmingham, London, Scarborough and Bristol. For her the journey's end was Manchester. So do the Methodists wander and stay and pass by, but to John Simon in all the pilgrimage there was nothing ever again quite like Dorset. Years afterwards, when God was taking away the desire of his eyes, the lessons of Dorset were his salvation. His students at Didsbury College remember how he kept his appointment with them and with God at the Saturday morning Prayer Meeting with the look of one who had turned to flight armies of aliens. They knew the victory was never really in doubt by the tone of his voice as he gave out the first hymn:
> By Thine unerring Spirit led,
> We shall not in the desert stray.

It was in Dorset that John Simon really found himself. There he began those loves and enthusiasms which lasted all through his life. The cliffs of Lyme Regis caught his imagination with their story of the petrified monsters of the past. The stone circle held him breathless with the magic of old lost primitive man. His own Methodism gripped him as never before. Here he was working the organization of John

Wesley's own Society, and getting its laws into his very bones. Here he tried out his preaching and felt the rapture of the herald of the grace of God. The first book he ever wrote was entitled *Methodism in Dorset,* and that very title has a brave look about it. It reads so like 'saints in Sardis' to any one who remembers the spell of the Wessex novels. It seems to hint that the feeling of isolation which went right through John Simon's ministry was also born in Dorsetshire.

If the bewitching county was his first love, Bristol held a very warm place in his heart. He delighted to tell how he had·'travelled' for nine years in the same circuit which had sent him into the ministry, and how he would have completed the twelve had not Conference appointed him Governor of Didsbury College. He loved the Bristol people and walked about their city with joy, catching sight of John Wesley at so many turns and bends of the road. The roots in Lancashire could not go so deep, but he would allow that the folk of Manchester could sing. He would come posting back from London and Committees to emerge from the Central Station in gloom and mud, at top speed, if haply he might be in time for the Pastoral Symphony at the Free Trade Hall. He would stand contentedly for the rest of the evening in that packed gallery as though he were the only person in the place and *The Messiah* exclusively his own. He must have seen the bewitching county, and the folded sheep in that great symphony, and known the glory of victory in the 'Hallelujah' Chorus.

It was to Lancashire that he retired after fifty years in the active ranks of the ministry. His mother had had a school at Southport which still survives in Wintersdorf, the junior house of Trinity Hall, which is the school for ministers' daughters. The place held many memories of her. She had come there in her widowhood with her two daughters after a period of residence in Berlin. Southport must have been chosen for the scholastic venture because it was as sandy as Montrose and had the same record of sunshine. There, for twenty years in his house near the sandhills, her son lived, and there he did his work on the life and times of John Wesley.

John Simon seemed a lonely man but he was really never less alone than when alone. His isolation sprang partly from his Victorian turn of mind, and partly from his sense of integrity. He stood aside always from any sort of cabal, and to pull a string or manipulate a wire was anathema to him. Yet he loved his brethren, and in 1907 they elected him by a handsome majority to John Wesley's chair as President of the Conference. He served them all the days of his ministry, giving 'Counsel's Opinion' gratis, on all the points of Methodist Law which troubled them. He must have received and answered hundreds of letters with his careful and accurate solutions of their problems. He only failed two of his correspondents and was himself mystified and troubled by the failure, not realizing that Methodist Union had come and made a new heaven and a new earth. He answered every call of his own old Wesleyan Methodist Church until her own last day.

Of course the Victorian had his reward, for was he not quite sure that he was the only one after John Wesley who really understood Methodist Law? Also, had not John Wesley put Joseph Saunderson in the first Legal Hundred as he himself, his great-grand-nephew, was now in the last? The Victorian loved to remember all the way the Lord his God had led his own particular tribe. It brought a shattering sense of personal responsibility.

To the blasé modern, spoon-fed on psychology, the Victorian may seem pitifully deceived. We ask how they could maintain their sanity if they really thought that the Almighty dealt with them by 'the direct method.' Yet, in their robust day, they continued to keep their wits and at the same time believe

> God has a few of us whom
> He whispers in the ear.

They had received this stern legacy from Cromwell and Milton but they contrived to shoot it through and through with gleams of personality and emotion from the Evangelical Revival of John Wesley. It brought a superb concentration of energy and a vivid appreciation of the worthwhileness of being alive. So it was with John Simon. He seemed single-handed to have returned Bright, Muntz and Chamberlain to Parliament in those far off Birmingham days. He had stood alone with Gladstone when Home Rule first split the perennially splittable Liberal Party. At the age of eighty-eight he had precipitated the national landslide when he conceived the brilliant idea of 'Voting Tory' for the first time in his life. He was much amused at that election when a motor-car came to fetch him to the polling booth long after he had returned from recording his vote. Did they not know that no election could really begin at all until John Simon had put on his boots and walked to the Poll? It was the same with the affairs of the Kingdom of Heaven. Those Victorian boots were donned in as resolute a manner to carry the Methodist minister on the King's business. It all depended on John Smith Simon. There are memories of a Christmas Day at Blackheath in the '90's, when the family merrymaking was dramatically stayed by the father's summons to the bedside of some dying saint. That darkness of the open door, beyond the mirth and warmth of the family circle, and the sight of that hurrying figure head down against the blast are quite imperishable. To one young heart it brought a strong conviction that it was terribly exciting and important to be a minister of Christ.

There is another vivid picture belonging to the year of his Presidency when just before his Fernley Lecture he was surprised on his knees alone in Wesley's vestry. The family had 'breezed in' to wish him well, as families will, but there was instant withdrawal and confusion of spirit. That look of his face and his wrapt attitude of prayer brought an overpowering sense of what the whole thing meant to him. This matter of John Wesley and the Methodist Church was between himself and God alone.

That attitude of mind was the controlling force in all that John Simon wrote about Wesley. He had to wait until he was seventy before he could begin his life-work, then, with the abandon of a lover, he threw himself into the task which God had yet remaining for him to do.

He has been criticized for his use of the 'historic present' in his narrative, but that was just what it was to him. He toured the dear land of England with his hero and waited impatiently at many a ferry which held up the great worker in his journeys, or grieved over his plight in the mud of those terrible roads. The eighteenth century at last became more real than the twentieth. The biographer might mix up the generations in his own family, but he could remember the ramifications of Wesley's lineage without fault. He lived with Wesley, slept with him and almost literally died with him. But he began his darling theme too late. Four volumes he accomplished, but the fifth he never finished. He would try and try again to get up to the death of his hero, but the old loyal heart fainted, and the old hands faltered and crossed out and re-crossed out, and he could not come at it. He never had the heart to inter even Charles Wesley. The attempt to do so cost him dear.

To those who dismantled that quiet study at the end, it seemed like the place of the communion of saints, and it was not without its own stigmata. It was the scene of human effort and defeat—one thought of Captain Scott and his gallant failure. Here the South Pole was a little folded paper stuck in *Hill's Arrangement* on the study desk, and on it was written the record of Wesley's death and the concluding words of Southey's Life, *Soli deo gloria*. The camps which marked the pilgrimage were little bits of paper found all about the books, with jottings upon them of how long it had taken to write the chapters. He must have known it was hopeless when the separate entry of months added painfully up to six for Chapter xxii. But like the Polar Party he was not going to let any one know that he knew he was beaten. Under a load of ninety years, and afflicted as Browning's Grammarian, he toiled on and dropped in his tracks.

It was only on the day before his death that he suggested the possibility that he might not finish his book. He was conducting a family meal through its slow meandering with his habitual old time courtesy, when he asked quite suddenly if his son-in-law would finish 'John Wesley' for him. 'I shall never do it—I have every confidence in him,' he said. Then clearly and generously he discussed details whilst those with him felt they looked on things apocalyptic. They were dimly conscious of the lengthening shadows creeping up to surround their Venerable Bede. 'There is yet one sentence unwritten, dear master.' 'Write it quickly.' 'It's finished now.' 'You speak truth, all is finished now.' That evening at the family altar he rejoiced in prayer and praise. He read the 91st Psalm as well as ever in his life, ringing out its cadences and glorying in its confident trust: 'He that dwelleth in the secret place of the Most High shall abide under the shadow of the Almighty.' In prayer he exulted in the guiding hand of the Good Shepherd felt throughout world history, and more intimately and tenderly realized in the annals of family history. He looked for the triumph of the gospel and the coming of the Kingdom of God: 'Come, Lord of Hosts, the waves divide and land us all in heaven.' The rest of the evening he spent quietly in his study and went to bed at his usual hour, heavy with sleep. The Methodist was the Methodist to the end. All was in perfect order—shoes ready, watch wound up against the coming of the morning. But he never awoke again. He had no tryst remaining to be kept with John Wesley, and so he slipped quietly away. The travelling preacher had accomplished his last journey:

> Raised by the breath of Love divine,
>   We urge our way with strength renewed;
> The Church of the first-born to join,
>   We travel to the mount of God,
> With joy upon our heads arise,
> And meet our Captain in the skies.

G. Elsie Harrison.

JOHN WESLEY
THE LAST PHASE

I

ENGLAND AND AMERICA

In January, 1773, John Wesley reached the conclusion that it was necessary to make arrangements for the future government of the Methodist Societies. He was convinced that, when he had passed away, the Societies would still exist, and that, in them, there would be a large number of persons who had never been members of the Church of England. His open-air work had brought into the Societies a host of people who had been outside all the Churches. In addition, many Dissenters had joined the Societies. It is probable that the majority of the Methodists were members of the Established Church; but, in Scotland and Ireland, people who had never had any connexion with the Church of England had joined the Societies. Fixing our attention on the Church of England groups we must remember that, in many localities, their allegiance to the Established Church had been sorely tried. Mob violence, which in some districts had been excited and directed by clergymen, had produced a strong effect on the opinions of persons who had been accustomed to attend the services in the parish churches. They became habitual attendants at the Methodist Preaching-houses that were swiftly increasing in number in many parts of the country. Those 'houses,' in ever-increasing numbers, were protected by licences originally intended for Dissenters' Meeting-houses. Under such protection services were conducted in peace by preachers, many of whom held Dissenters' licences. The effect of persecution by Church of England mobs was evident in the change that was gradually coming over the opinions of Church people who had joined the Methodist Societies. When we consider all these facts we do not wonder that John Wesley began to see that his dream of a Methodist Society incorporated with the Church of England would not be realized. If he still halted between two opinions he must have been influenced by the problem that was arising in America, a country where the members of the Church of England were in a minority. Considering all the circumstances of the case we do not wonder that Wesley felt himself compelled to face the question of the future government of the Methodist Societies, and that he wrote the following letter to John Fletcher:

January, 1773.
DEAR SIR,
    What an amazing work has God wrought in these Kingdoms, in less than forty years! And it not only continues, but increases, throughout England, Scotland and Ireland; nay, it has lately spread into New York, Pennsylvania, Virginia, Maryland and Carolina. But the wise men of the world say, 'When Mr. Wesley drops, then all this is at an end.' And so it surely will unless, before God calls him hence, one is found to stand in his place. For it is not good that the supreme power should be lodged in many hands: Let there be one chief governor. [This sentence is written in Greek.] I see more and more, unless there be one person who presides over the rest [also written in Greek] the work can never be carried on. The body of the Preachers are not united: Nor will any part of them submit to the rest; so that either there must be one to preside over all, or the work will indeed come to an end.

But who is sufficient for these things? Qualified to preside both over the Preachers and people? He must be a man of faith and love, and one that has a single eye to the advancement of the Kingdom of God. He must have a clear understanding; a knowledge of men and things, particularly of the Methodist doctrine and discipline; a ready utterance; diligence and activity, with a tolerable share of health. There must be added to these, favour with the people, with the Methodists in general. For unless God turn their eyes and their hearts towards him, he will be quite incapable of the work. He must likewise have some degree of learning; because there are many adversaries, learned as well as unlearned, whose mouths must be stopped. But this cannot be done, unless he be able to meet them on their own ground.

But has God provided one so qualified? Who is he? Thou art the man! God has given you a measure of loving faith, and a single eye to His glory. He has given you some knowledge of men and things; particularly of the old plan of Methodism. You are blessed with some health, activity, and diligence; together with a degree of learning. And to all these, he has lately added, by a way none could have foreseen, favour both with the Preachers and the whole people. Come out, in the name of God! Come to the help of the Lord against the mighty! Come while I am alive and capable of labour. . . . Come while I am able, God assisting, to build you up in faith, to ripen your gifts, and to introduce you to the people. . . . What possible employment can you have, which is of so great importance?

But you will naturally say, 'I am not equal to the task; I have neither grace nor gifts for such an employment.' You say true; it is certain you have not. And who has? But do you not know Him who is able to give them? Perhaps not at once, but rather day by day: as each is, so shall your strength be. 'But this implies,' you may say, 'a thousand crosses, such as I feel I am not able to bear.' You are not able to bear them now; and they are not now come. Whenever they do come, will He not send them in due number, weight, and measure? And will they not all be for your profit, that you may be a partaker of His holiness?

Without conferring, therefore, with flesh and blood, come and strengthen the hands, comfort the heart, and share the labour, of
Your affectionate friend and brother,
JOHN WESLEY.[1]

In Henry Moore's *Life of John Wesley* light is cast on this letter to Fletcher. He says that the preachers pressed Wesley to apply to Fletcher; and, when he reported the reply he had received, they asked him to renew his application. We are especially indebted to Moore for rescuing Fletcher's reply from oblivion. We will extract a few paragraphs from his letter, which is dated February 6, 1773. He says:

I hope the Lord, who has so wonderfully stood by you hitherto, will preserve you to see many of your sheep, and *me* among the rest, enter into rest. Should Providence call you first, I shall do my best, by the Lord's assistance, to help *your brother* to gather the wreck, and keep together those who are not absolutely bent upon throwing away the Methodist doctrine or discipline, as soon as he that now letteth shall be removed out of their way. Every little help will then be necessary; and I hope I shall not be backward to throw in my mite.

In the meantime, you stand sometimes in need of an assistant to serve tables, and occasionally to fill up a gap. Providence visibly appointed me to that office many years ago: and though it no less evidently called me here, yet I have not been without doubt, especially for some years past, whether it would not be expedient that I should resume my place, as your Deacon; not with any view of presiding over the Methodists after you (God knows!), but to save you a little in your old age, and be in the way of receiving, and perhaps of doing, more good. I have sometimes considered how shameful it was that no clergyman should join you, to keep in the church the work which the Lord had enabled you to carry on therein; and, as the little estate I have in my native country is sufficient for my maintenance, I have thought I would, one day or other, offer you and the Methodists my *free* services. . . .

Nevertheless, I would not leave this place without a fuller persuasion that the time is quite come. Not that God uses me much now among

[1] Wesley's *Works*, Vol. XII, pp. 163-4; Moore's *Life of Wesley*, Vol. II, pp. 255-7.

my parishioners, but because I have not sufficiently cleared my conscience from the blood of all men, especially with regard to ferreting out the poor, and expostulating with the rich, who make it their business to fly from me. In the meantime, it shall be my employment to beg the Lord to give me light, to guide me by His counsel, and make me willing to go anywhere or nowhere, to be anything or nothing.[1]

Leaving the question of his successor in the government of the Societies in England to a future solution, Wesley faced the difficulty that was caused by the advance of Methodism in America. It was fortunate that Lieutenant Webb and the preachers who had been designated at the Leeds Conference for appointments in America, were still in England. Conversations with them were possible, and he was able to understand the exact position of affairs in the Colonies. It is clear that he suggested arrangements for the government of the Societies that had been formed in America. Those who have read the account of Lieutenant Webb's speech in the Leeds Conference of 1772 will remember that Thomas Rankin and George Shadford, lay preachers, offered to go to America 'in the next spring.' The time of their embarkation was approaching. On Good Friday, April 9, 1773, they went on board a ship that landed them in America after a passage of seven and a half weeks.[2] Lieutenant Webb and his wife were their travelling companions. The delay in the return of Webb to America is soon explained. When he landed in England he was a widower, but, on February 12, 1773, he was married to Grace Gilbert at Whitchurch, in Shropshire. Mr. Bretherton, who is an authority on all matters which concern the Gilbert family, has informed us that the wedding was conducted by John Fletcher, the Vicar of Madeley. He has sent us a true extract from the register of marriages, copied out of the book by the Rector, the Rev. W. H. Egerton, on January 4, 1896. The witnesses were Mary Gilbert and Thomas Hatton. It is clear that the bride was married from the house of Francis Gilbert, the brother of Nathaniel Gilbert, whose work in the island of Antigua stands out so prominently in the history of Methodist missions. There has been some difficulty in deciding the question of the exact relationship of Mrs. Webb to the Gilbert family.

Tyerman, writing to Mr. Lockwood, the author of *The*

---
[1] Moore's *Life of John Wesley*, II, 259-60.
[2] See *John Wesley the Master Builder*, 314-15.

Western Pioneers, says: 'I think there can be little doubt that Miss Gilbert was a member of the family of the West Indian Gilberts.' Mr. Bretherton, using later information, is of opinion that she was the sister of Francis Gilbert, and he has no doubt that Mary Gilbert, one of the witnesses, was the wife of Francis Gilbert. It may be of interest to note that Lieutenant Webb's name disappeared from the Army List of 1767. He retired on a pension, and was set free to give up much of his time to his work as a Methodist evangelist.

When Thomas Rankin and George Shadford sailed from England, John Wesley was in Ireland, where he continued until the beginning of July. On March 7, when he was in Birmingham, he saw Thomas Rankin and gave him his last instructions concerning his conduct in America. At the Conference held in 1772 Rankin had been appointed as the superintendent of 'the whole work' in America, and it was necessary to give him full instructions as to the way in which it should be conducted.[1]

There is much hidden meaning in Wesley's letter to George Shadford, which reached him about the time he sailed: 'I let you loose, George, on the great continent of America. Publish your message in the open face of the sun, and do all the good you can.' Those who are acquainted with the earliest stages of American Methodist history know that there was a tendency to concentrate the work of the preachers on a few of the big towns. When Asbury arrived he perceived the danger and struck out into the country. We must not forget that the pervasive work of the first Methodist preachers in America was hindered by the smallness of their number. That difficulty was gradually being overcome, and, in process of time, it disappeared.

Dr. Abel Stevens says that the first American Methodist Conference began its session in Philadelphia on Wednesday, July 14, 1773.[2] It had been summoned by Thomas Rankin, Wesley's duly appointed 'general assistant or superintendent' of the American Societies. Asbury was not present on the first day. When he arrived the Conference consisted of ten persons—all Europeans—Thomas Rankin, Richard Board-

---

[1] See *Early Methodist Preachers,* v. 184.
[2] Considerable confusion exists as to the date of its meeting; but there is no doubt that Dr. Stevens's statement is correct.

man, Joseph Pilmoor, Francis Asbury, Richard Wright, George Shadford, Thomas Webb, John King, Abraham Whitworth, and Joseph Yearbry.[1] Boardman and Pilmoor were on the eve of their return to England. Yearbry had accompanied Rankin and Shadford on their voyage to America.

In the Centenary Number of the *New York Christian Advocate*, dated September 9, 1926, there is a reproduction of the Minutes of this important Conference photographed from the original document. It shows the course and character of the business transacted, and we present it without any verbal alteration.

The following queries were proposed to every preacher:

1.—Ought not the authority of Mr. Wesley and that conference, to extend to the preachers and people in America, as well as in Great Britain and Ireland?

Answer. Yes.

2.—Ought not the doctrine and discipline of the Methodists, as contained in the Minutes, to be the sole rule of our conduct who labour, in the connexion with Mr. Wesley, in America?

Answer. Yes.

3.—If so, does it not follow that if any preachers deviate from the Minutes, we can have no fellowship with them till they change their conduct?

Answer. Yes.

The following rules were agreed to by all the preachers present.

1.—Every preacher who acts in connexion with Mr. Wesley and the brethren who labour in America, is strictly to avoid administering the ordinance of Baptism and the Lord's Supper.

2.—All the people among whom we labour to be earnestly exhorted to attend the church, and to receive the ordinances there; but in a particular manner to press the people in Maryland and Virginia, to the observance of this Minute.

3.—No person or persons to be admitted to our love-feasts oftener than twice or thrice, unless they become members; and none to be admitted to the Society Meetings more than thrice.

4.—None of the preachers in America to reprint any of Mr. Wesley's books without his authority (when it can be got) and the consent of their brethren.

5.—Robert Williams to sell the books he has already printed, but to print no more, unless under the above restriction.

[1] Dr. Abel Stevens' *History of American Methodism* in one Vol., p. 73.

6.—Every preacher who acts as an assistant, to send an account of the work once in six months to the General Assistant.

Question 1. How are the preachers stationed?
Answer.

New York. } Thomas Rankin.
Philadelphia. } George Shadford
to change in 4 months.

New Jersey. John King, William Waters.

Baltimore. Francis Asbury, Robert Strawbridge, Abraham Whitworth, Joseph Yearbry.

Norfolk. Richard Wright.

Petersburg. Robert Williams.

Question 2. What number are there in the Society?
Answer.

New York	180
Philadelphia	180
New Jersey	200
Maryland	500
Virginia	100
	1,160

The proceedings of the first Methodist Conference held in America arrest our attention and demand careful consideration. It must be remembered that Thomas Rankin was sent out by Wesley for a specific purpose. His conversations with Webb had given him some insight into the condition of the Methodist Societies in America and had convinced him that, in several respects, they needed careful supervision. Richard Boardman and Joseph Pilmoor were returning to England, and an opportunity of bringing the American Societies into line with those in Great Britain and Ireland presented itself. In his interviews with Rankin, Wesley gave him instructions, the effects of which are visible in the proceedings of the Philadelphia Conference. Dr. Stevens, in his *History of American Methodism,* emphasizes the fact that irregularities existed in the mode of managing the Societies in America. Dealing with the return of the number of members, he says that the aggregate returns represent only the members who met in classes; and that there were many more adherents who considered themselves of the Methodist Societies. In addition, he tells us that 'the preachers had formed Societies without classes,' and that 'the exact discipline of English Methodism had not, in fact, been introduced into America.' He goes on to say that Francis Asbury had laboured hard to conform the American Societies to Wesley's model, but had met with no little resistence from both the preachers and the people. After stating that Rankin had been sent out to conform the discipline of the Methodism of America to Wesley's 'model,' he declares that to Asbury and Rankin, those two thorough disciplinarians, America owes 'the effective organization of the incipient Methodism of the New World.'[1]

In glancing at the 'rules' adopted by the first American Conference we are impressed by the unanimity of consent which prevailed. The word 'yes' is appended to all the 'queries' which were proposed to all the preachers, and similar unanimity prevailed after the 'rules' had been considered. It will be noted that Robert Strawbridge and Robert Williams were not at the Conference. This fact may account for the unanimity that prevailed. Confining our attention to the 'rules' we pause in the presence of those which concern the administration of the Sacraments and the attendance at church. We have said that George Shadford had been empowered by Wesley to publish his message 'in the open face of the sun,' and had been 'let loose on the great continent of America.' He was not the only Methodist evangelist who was acting in the spirit of that commission. The backwoods' preacher was beginning to be conspicuous. When a man went into the backwoods and formed a little Society there, was he to exhort the members 'to attend the church and receive all the ordinances there' ? In many cases there might not be a Church of England within a hundred miles of the spot. As a matter of fact, the Church of England was far from being in a strong position in America at that time; its churches, save in Connecticut, Pennsylvania and Virginia, were few and far between. We are indebted to the late Bishop Samuel Wilberforce for inserting in his *History of the American Church* a return of the white population and of 'the various religious persuasions' on the continent of North America, which was transmitted to the Bishop of London in 1761. We reproduce it for the benefit of our readers.

[1] *History of American Methodism*, 68, English edition.

Numbers of the White Population and the Various Religious Persuasions.[1]

North American Continent.	Whites.	Church People.	Presbyterians and Independents.	Quakers, German and Dutch of various sects, Jews, Papists, &c.
Newfoundland and Nova Scotia	25,000	13,000	6,000	6,000
Four New England Colonies:				
New Hampshire ... 30,000				
Massachusetts ... 250,000				
Rhode Island ... 35,000				
Connecticut ... 120,000				
	435,000	40,000	250,000	145,000
New York	100,000	25,000	20,000	55,000
New Jersey	100,000	16,000	40,000	44,000
Pennsylvania	280,000	65,000*	45,000	170,000†
Maryland	60,000	36,000	6,000	18,000‡
Virgina	80,000	60,000	10,000	10,000
North Carolina	36,000	18,000	9,000	9,000
South Carolina	22,000	20,000	5,000	3,000
Georgia	6,000			
Total	1,144,000	293,000	391,000	460,000

* This includes 40,000 Swedes and German Lutherans, who reckon their service, &c., the same as that of the Church.

† About a third of these are Quakers, about 10,000 Papists, the rest Germans of various sects.

‡ Chiefly Papists.

It will be noted that in the return of Church people in Pennsylvania forty thousand Swedes and German Lutherans are included on the ground that their services were the same as those conducted in the English Church. That is scarcely a convincing reason for the inclusion. But, allowing it to stand, the result of the return was that of the white population in the States, in 1761, 293,000 belonged to the Church of England, and 851,000 to other religious denominations. In 1773 it is easy to hear the muttering of an approaching storm which, to the regret of thousands of Englishmen, was to inflict almost irreparable damage to the English Church in America. When the full force of that storm fell on the Church we think that many Methodists were grateful that the policy of the first Conference in respect of the Church of England had not been followed.

[1] See Wilberforce's *History of the American Church*, p. 133, 2nd edition, 1846.

There was another 'rule' of the first Conference which is of great importance. It referred to the administration of the ordinances of Baptism and the Lord's Supper. Every preacher who acted in connexion with Wesley and 'the brethren in America was strictly to avoid administering these ordinances.' Again we think of the backwoods' preachers and the people who were far removed from the clergy of the Church of England. They were condemned to allow their children to be unbaptized, and they themselves had to refrain from approaching the Table of the Lord. It is no wonder that such a condition of things could not last. It is not difficult to discover the reason that induced the Conference to utter its prohibition. Those who were present knew that Robert Strawbridge had administered the Sacraments under circumstances which are described by Dr. Stevens. He says:

> Robert Strawbridge contended sturdily for the right of the people to the Sacraments, and could not be deterred by Asbury or Rankin from administering them. He had founded the Church in the regions whence now nearly one-half of its members were reported; he had administered to them the Sacraments before any English itinerants appeared in the country; and being an Irishman, he shared not in the deferential sympathies of his English brethren for the Establishment: as for any other sentiments, the actual character of the representatives of the Establishment, clerical and lay, around him could claim none from him but pity or contempt. Its clergy were known chiefly as the heartiest card-players, horse-racers, and drinkers of the middle colonies. Strawbridge was doubtless imprudent in the Irish resolution with which he resisted the policy of the English itinerants; for the intuitive foresight with which he anticipated the necessity of the independent administration of the Sacraments, should have suggested to him the certainty of their concession in due time, and therefore the expediency of patient harmony in the infant Church till that time should come. Discord was extremely perilous at this early stage of the denomination. He was firm, however, and though the first 'rule' adopted by this Conference seems absolute, yet we learn from Asbury that it was adopted with the understanding that 'no preacher in our Connexion shall be permitted to administer the ordinances at this time except Mr. Strawbridge, and he under the particular direction of the assistant.' A concession so singular shows the extraordinary consideration in which Strawbridge was held, the influence he had obtained over the Societies of Maryland and Virginia, perhaps also the conscious necessity of the independent administration of the Sacraments in that chief field of the denomination.[1]

Dr. Stevens, in his defence of Strawbridge's action, mentions a fact which must be borne in mind when we are

[1] *History of American Methodism*, 70. English edition.

considering the question of the introduction of the Sacraments into the American Methodist Societies. This description of some of the clerical and lay members of the Church of England at that time is severe and correct. In his *History of the American Church,* Bishop Wilberforce deplores the moral condition of some of the clergy. In one place he says that in the State of Maryland 'the scandal of ill-living clergymen had risen to a fearful height'; and when dealing with the condition of the Church in Virginia he does not fail to point out the moral defects of its clergy and laymen. We can see that he makes his charges with deep regret. We do not wonder at that fact for he held that 'in the institutions of no separatists from the Church has the gift of enduring spiritual vitality been found,' and the collapse of men who had such an opportunity of displaying the highest virtue in his own Church must have disappointed him.[1] But, in our opinion, he reluctantly laid his hand on one of the principal causes of the separation of the Methodists from the American branch of the Church of England.

We must now return to John Wesley, and note some of the events which occurred about the time when the first Conference was held in America. After a visit to Ireland, which began on March 26 and ended on July 5, Wesley's evangelizing work was carried on in England. One incident connected with his Irish tour must be recorded. On Saturday, May 22, he was in Swanlinbar, where he seems to have had an interview with the curate of the parish, the Rev. James Creighton. In a note which appears in John Wesley's *Journal,* we find some interesting particulars about Creighton. A year before he was expecting that Wesley would visit Swanlinbar he 'meditated' a sermon that he would preach against him. He did not pursue this line of attack, but he sent Wesley a number of 'queries' without signing his name. Wesley guessed from whom they came and in reply forwarded to Creighton copies of his *Appeals.* Time went on. In 1775 he read Fletcher's *Appeal.* Gradually he found his way to the light. His name is familiar to all who are acquainted with early Methodist history. He joined the Methodist Society; and, in 1783, was invited to labour with Wesley in London. The 'note' writer says: 'For many years he served at City

[1] *History of the American Church,* 123, 139.

Road and West Street as an ordained minister of the Church of England and a minister in the London Circuit.'[1] We shall meet with him again.

After visiting Fletcher in Madeley, and preaching in the church, Wesley returned to London, arriving there on July 17. A few days later he received news of the death of his old friend Howell Harris. On July 21, after much suffering, he passed away at Trevecca 'rejoicing to the last that Death had lost its sting.' He died in the sixtieth year of his age. He was buried near the Communion Table in Talgarth church. In our book on *The Revival of Religion in England in the Eighteenth Century* we have described the great event that occurred there on Whit-Sunday, May 25, 1735, when the sacrament of the Lord's Supper was received by Howell Harris. In Talgarth church, in the presence of the emblems of the Saviour's sacrificial death, there shone out before the eyes of Howell Harris a vision of the crucified Christ. The great change took place, and he went out into the light of the new life. It was fitting that his resting place, when the toils of his life were over, should be near the spot where there came to him 'the peace that passeth understanding.'[2]

The 'passing' of his friend touched the heart of Wesley, but his faith in their eternal blessedness never wavered. He went on with his work. The time for holding the Conference in London was approaching. It was to assemble on Tuesday, August 3, and much thought had to be spent on one part of the business that was to be transacted. We have already referred to his attempt to secure Fletcher's consent to become his successor. He was conscious that when he died there would be danger of serious disruption not only in the Societies but among the preachers. The problem weighed on his mind. Its solution occupied his thoughts, year after year; in 1773 he was convinced that it was necessary to take a step in this important matter. So, before the Conference assembled, he thought out a scheme that might be considered by the preachers.

The Conference of 1773 proceeded on the usual lines. The business transacted is indicated in the published *Minutes*. There was a considerable increase in the number of the

---

[1] Wesley's *Journal*, v. 507.
[2] See *The Revival of Religion in England*, 140.

members in Society. Including those in America they amounted to 33,274. The debt which had caused Wesley considerable anxiety, was lessened, and twelve preachers were admitted on trial. Passing by the general business it is only necessary to draw attention to the question and answer which appear at the close of the records of this Conference.[1]

Q. 17. Can anything be done now, in order to lay a foundation for the future union? Would it not be well for any that are willing to sign some articles of agreement before God calls me hence?

A. We will do it.

Accordingly, the following paper was written and signed:—

We, whose names are underwritten, being thoroughly convinced of the necessity of a close union between those whom God is pleased to use as instruments in this glorious work, in order to preserve this union between ourselves, are resolved, God being our helper,

I. To devote ourselves entirely to God; denying ourselves, taking up our cross daily, steadily aiming at one thing, to save our own souls, and them that hear us.

II. To preach the old Methodist doctrines, and no other,[2] contained in the Minutes of the Conferences.

III. To observe and enforce the whole Methodist discipline laid down in the said Minutes.

At the Conference of 1773 forty-nine preachers signed this document. The plan was continued at the Conferences of 1774 and 1775. At these two Conferences fifty-three new names were added to the list; so that it may be said that more than a hundred of the preachers pledged themselves to this expression of loyalty to Methodism and to each other. It is clear that Wesley saw that the union of the preachers would secure the union of the Methodist people. As the years went by he discovered a still more excellent way of effecting his purpose. In 1784, acting on the advice of his solicitor, he adopted another plan of effecting his object. That plan has not only preserved the union of the preachers; it has

---

[1] *Minutes*, Vol. I, 110.
[2] A modern reader might easily misunderstand the second article in this pledge. By 'no other doctrines' Wesley meant doctrines opposed to those contained at that time in the *Minutes* of Conference.

secured the stability of the Wesleyan Methodist Societies in times of extreme peril.[1]

After the Conference Wesley spent the rest of the year in constant visitation of the Societies. He went to Bristol and then set out for Cornwall. He returned to Bristol on August 28, and stayed there until October. During this visit he was seriously ill, and was laid aside for several days. There is a note of pathos in his *Journal* entry on October 3. He says: ' I took a solemn leave of the Society at Bristol, now consisting of eight hundred members.' It seems as if one of those periods during which he thought that his work would soon be ended had returned. But he went to Shaftesbury and Salisbury, and, on October 6, he reached London in the evening. We find a record of a tour in Sussex in November; then on December 10 he returned to London. On Christmas Day, and on the following days, this is his record: ' We had many opportunities of celebrating the solemn feast days, according to the design of their institution. We concluded the year with a fast day, closed with a solemn watch-night.' [2]

During this busy year Wesley's thoughts must have frequently turned towards America. His visit to Ireland must have made him aware of the fact that the emigration to America was telling on his Societies. Crookshank, in his *History of Methodism in Ireland,* when dealing with the increase of the membership in the province of Ulster says: ' These statistics, as well as others already given, are not, however, to be regarded as presenting anything like an adequate idea of the results of the labours of the itinerants. It was computed that in this and five preceding years, the north of Ireland was drained of one-fourth of its population by emigration to the American settlements. These emigrants were chiefly from the agricultural districts, where Methodism had proved most successful.[3] It is no wonder that Wesley often longed to cross the Atlantic and see for himself the

[1] See John Wesley's *Deed of Declaration.* *Summary of Methodist Law and Discipline,* 373-80. Fifth edition.
[2] In 1773 Wesley published his *Works* in thirty-two volumes duodecimo. Myles says: ' Some of these were extracts from other writers, which he had long circulated among the people: others were written on the spur of the moment, and manifest the fertility of his mind; and others were composed in defence of the great doctrines of Christianity. They form a rich collection of the purest and most exalted divinity.' *Chronological History of the People called Methodists,* 135.
[3] Crookshank's *History of Methodism in Ireland,* Vol. I, 278.

country where many of his people had found a home. He was not the only man in England who would soon have to fix his thoughts on America. On Thursday, December 16, 1773, an event occurred in Boston, Massachusetts, that has left an enduring mark on the memory of Englishmen and Americans.

Readers of American history in the present day have reason to congratulate themselves on the change that has taken place in the spirit of the recorders and critics of the events of the American Revolution. That change is apparent in books written on both sides of the Atlantic. Fortunately our own course is clear. It is necessary that we should refer to some incidents, preceding and occurring during the war, that affected John Wesley, his preachers, and people. So far as possible we will confine ourselves to the limits indicated.

On Sunday, November 28, the ship *Dartmouth* finished her voyage from England and arrived off the harbour of Boston. She had on board a cargo of tea. It must be remembered that in 1765 the English Parliament had passed the Stamp Act which imposed duties on foreign commodities imported into America, and our colonial products exported therefrom, together with a heavy duty on molasses and sugar, which formed the principal articles of trade in New England. The passing of the Act roused fierce opposition. In Boston the feeling in opposition to it ran higher than in any other place. There were outbreaks of mob violence in the town. A public meeting was called which denounced these riots. But the lawful opposition went on more vigorously than ever, and was much more serious than the outbreaks of the mob.[1] The opposition was successful. On February 24, 1765, the House of Commons, under the leadership of Pitt, passed a Bill to repeal the Stamp Act, and on March 17 it received the sanction of the King. The people of America received the news with great joy. Lodge says: 'The people indeed were so overjoyed that they did not notice that the English ministry in repealing the Stamp Act had made the fatal blunder of joining to it a declaratory act, in which they asserted that Parliament had the power to legislate for America in all cases whatsoever, thus reiterating the principle, which was the real

---

[1] See Senator Henry Cabot Lodge's 'Boston' in Freeman and Hunt's *Historic Towns* series, 125-6.

thing at stake, while they gave up the practice, which was a merely temporary concession.' [1]

Time went on, and the consequence of the declarative principle was seen. Under Townshend's administration a Bill was passed which gave the English Parliament power to levy duty on glass, paper, painters' colours, and tea. It also established a board of customs at Boston to collect the American revenue. It can be easily imagined that when the news of the passing of the Bill arrived in Boston the town was stirred to opposition. On March 5, 1770, a fatal outbreak took place, the troops were called out, and rioting and bloodshed followed. Soldiers who had fired on the mob were put on their trial. Six of them, together with their captain, were acquitted, but two of the men who were found guilty were branded on the hand. On the day when this riot took place Lord North, in the English Parliament, brought in and carried a Bill to repeal the Revenue Act, to which we have alluded, with the exception of the preamble and the duty on tea. The relief in most of the colonies was great. Lodge says that 'even in Massachusetts the movement in opposition to the Crown seemed to subside.' [2] But Boston opposed the duty on tea. Town-meetings were held, and it was clear that Boston was determined that the cargo of tea should not be unloaded, but that the ship should be sent back to England. During the long discussions two other tea-ships arrived and were anchored near the *Dartmouth*, the three vessels being strongly guarded by Boston citizens. On December 16 a crowded meeting was held in the Old South Church. Lodge affirms that the people of Boston wanted to have the ships returned peaceably, and the consignees were quite willing to yield, but the governor would not give a permit. One of those present at the meeting was Rotch, the owner of the *Dartmouth*. He was asked to interview the governor once more; he did so, but failed to change the governor's determination. The result is well known. We will describe it in Lodge's words. He says:

'By the afternoon over seven thousand people were gathered in and about the church. The short winter day was drawing to a close, and the dimly-lighted church grew darker and darker, while the people waited, determined to know the end.

[1] *Historic Towns*, 128.   [2] *ibid*, 139.

At last Rotch appeared again, and reported that the governor would not give a pass. The moment he had concluded his report Samuel Adams arose and said, " This meeting can do nothing more to save the country." The words were of course a signal. A shout was heard in the street, and some forty or fifty men disguised as Indians rushed by the door and down toward the wharves, followed by the people. The ' Mohawks,' as they were called, rushed on board the tea-ships and threw the chests of tea into the bay. No violence was committed, and no tea was taken; the cargoes were simply destroyed so that they could never be landed. It was a picturesque refusal on the part of the people of Boston to pay the tax. It was the sudden appearance, in a world tired of existing systems of government, of the power of the people in action. The expression may have been rude, and the immediate result trivial, but the act was none the less of the gravest consequence. It was the small beginning of the great democratic movement which has gone forward ever since, and which it would have been well for English statesmen who were then concerned with it to have pondered deeply.'[1]

In reading Senator Lodge's book we always remember his strong leaning towards the American side of disputed questions. But we at once assent to his statement that the act of the ' Mohawks ' was of the gravest consequence. It led to the sending out of British troops from England to Boston to ' punish ' the town for the assault on the tea-ships; and that act was the prelude of the long war that ended in England's loss of the American colonies.

[1] ' Boston,' in *Historic Towns* series, 144-5.

II
WAR CLOUDS

EARLY in January, 1774, John Wesley found that he must no longer postpone the surgical operation which the Edinburgh doctors had advised in 1772. For nearly two years he had done his work at considerable inconvenience. At last he put himself into the hands of his London doctor, and the operation was skilfully performed. He was laid aside for a week. Then, on January 11, he started out on the visitation of the Society. He went 'from house to house' at the east end of London. He says: 'I know no branch of the pastoral office which is of greater importance than this. But it is so grievous to flesh and blood that I can prevail on few, even of our preachers, to undertake it.' In this, as in every other department of the work, he never imposed on others duties he was not prepared to perform himself. He was soon sketching the order of his spring journeys. In arranging them he was evidently impressed by a change that had taken place in recent years. In a letter to Miss Bosanquet, written on February 9, he says: 'We are little troubled at present with English mobs; and probably shall not while King George the Third lives.' So far as he himself was concerned violent assaults had subsided. Thinking of the districts he would visit on his northern journey, he felt that he might set out with confidence. He was going to Yorkshire where, at that time, there was no danger that he would be assailed; then he was to visit Scotland, where there had never been any danger of mob violence. So he took a cheerful view of his coming journeys. On March 15 he left London. It is only necessary to indicate the significant fact that, while in Yorkshire, he met with a hearty welcome from some of the clergy of the county, and preached in the churches at Halifax, Huddersfield, Heptonstall and Haworth. It was evident that the number of his friends among the Yorkshire clergy was increasing and the fact caused him great satisfaction.

On May 9 Wesley set out from Whitehaven for Scotland. He stayed there a month. On his return journey he visited Edinburgh, arriving there on June 1; and the next day he examined the Society 'one by one.' He was agreeably surprised with the change that had taken place in the spirit of the members since his last visit. He says that such a number of persons 'having sound Christian experience' he had never found in the Society before. That remark causes us to turn to the *Minutes of Conference*. We find that Joseph Benson had been stationed as the second preacher in Edinburgh for a year; and that, at the time of Wesley's visit, he was the superintendent of the circuit.[1]

We have said that in Scotland there was never any danger of mob violence; but during Wesley's visit to Edinburgh he had a disagreeable experience. The day after he had examined the Society he was walking home after preaching. He noticed that two men were following him. He stopped and let them overtake him. One of them said: 'Sir, you are my prisoner. I have a warrant from the sheriff to carry you to the Tolbooth.' Wesley thought that the man jested; but was soon convinced he was in earnest. Asking one or two of his friends to accompany him, he walked towards the prison. The man who had served the warrant seems to have had his wits about him; instead of lodging Wesley in prison he led him and his companions to a house adjoining the Tolbooth. Arriving there Wesley asked to see the warrant for his apprehension. When it was shown him he found that a man, who had been a member of the Methodist Society in Edinburgh, had sworn that Hugh Saunderson, one of the Methodist preachers, had taken from his wife one hundred pounds in money and upwards of thirty pounds in goods; and further, that he had terrified his wife into madness, so that through the want of her help and the loss of business he was damaged to the extent of five hundred pounds. It is difficult to see Wesley's connexion with this part of the deposition. But when the man appeared before the sheriff he had sworn that John Wesley and the accused preacher were preparing to 'fly the country'; he therefore desired a warrant 'to search for, seize, and incarcerate them in the Tolbooth till they should find security for their appearance at the trial.' To

---

[1] For Joseph Benson, see *John Wesley the Master Builder*, 286-89.

this request the sheriff had assented and had given his warrant for Wesley's arrest. The prosecutor, hearing that Wesley had been taken to a house 'near the Tolbooth,' was furious; he insisted that the warrant-officer should remove him to the prison without delay. However, the officer waited until some of Wesley's friends arrived who gave a bond for his appearance on June 24. When the case was tried Hugh Saunderson was present. The cause was heard. The prosecutor lost his case. He was fined; and the upshot was that his action against Wesley and Saunderson cost him a thousand pounds.

During this visit to Edinburgh Joseph Benson was often in company with Wesley. Benson had known all sorts of men, from University dons to poverty-stricken day-labourers in England and Wales. During this visit of Wesley to Edinburgh Benson watched him closely, and he gives us the result of their companionship and frank conversations. He says:

> I was constantly with him for a week. I had an opportunity of examining narrowly his spirit and conduct; and I assure you, I am more than ever persuaded, he is a none such. I know not his fellow, first, for abilities, natural and acquired; and, secondly, for his incomparable diligence in the application of those abilities to the best of employments. His lively fancy, tenacious memory, clear understanding, ready elocution, manly courage, indefatigable industry, really amaze me. I admire, but wish in vain to imitate, his diligent improvement of every moment of time; his wonderful exactness even in little things; the order and regularity wherewith he does and treats everything he takes in hand; together with his quick dispatch of business, and calm, cheerful serenity of soul. I ought not to omit to mention, what is very manifest to all who know him, his resolution, which no shocks of opposition can shake; his patience which no length of trials can weary; his zeal for the glory of God and the good of man, which no waters of persecution or tribulation have yet been able to quench. Happy man! Long hast thou borne the burden and heat of the day, amidst the insults of foes, and the base treachery of seeming friends; but thou shalt rest from thy labours and thy works shall follow thee!

We do not know a more accurate description of Wesley at the close of his seventy-first year than that which was written by the firm hand of Joseph Benson.[1]

On Friday, June 10, Wesley preached at Newcastle; and,

---

[1] See *Methodist Magazine* for 1825, 386; Tyerman's *Life and Times of Wesley*, iii. 168-9. For Alexander Knox's opinion of Wesley see *John Wesley the Master Builder*, 175-6.

the next day, he set out for the Dales. Two years before there had been, what he calls, 'a vast work of God' in that neighbourhood. Owing to causes, which he describes in his *Journal*, the great revival had rapidly subsided—'the fruitful field had become a wilderness.' He visited the villages; but all he could say about them was—'There is now a little revival; God grant it may increase!'[1] On June 14 he left Swaledale in company with some of his friends. They crossed over 'the enormous mountain into lovely Wensleydale, the largest by far of all the Dales, as well as the most beautiful.' Some years before many persons had been gathered into Benjamin Ingham's Societies; but disputes had arisen and 'the poor sheep had all been scattered.' The Methodist preachers had 'gleaned up and joined together' a considerable number of these people. In this journey Wesley reached Redmire. He knew the place well for thirty years before he had preached there. As he and his friends rode through the street the people stared at them as if they had been 'a company of monsters.' Wesley thought he would preach there once more; so he dismounted from his horse and began his service. Young and old soon ran together from every quarter. At first there seems to have been some disturbance, but Wesley says: 'I reminded the elder of their having seen me thirty years before, when I preached in Wensley church.' He took the same text that day at Redmire —'What shall I do to be saved? Believe on the Lord Jesus Christ, and thou shalt be saved.' We expect that some of the old people exchanged glances and woke up to the fact that the preacher was John Wesley. When the service closed and he rode back through the town, it wore a new face. He says: 'The people were profoundly civil; they were bowing and curtseying on every side. Such a change in two hours I have seldom seen.'[2]

He made his return to Newcastle and during this visit an event occurred which confirms Benson's opinion concerning his 'manly courage.' On June 20 he set out for Horsley, a village which lies a few miles west of Newcastle. William Smith, his step-son-in-law, and Christopher Hopper, were

---

[1] *Journal*, vi., 25.
[2] For Wesley's visits to Wensley and Redmire, see *John Wesley and the Methodist Societies*, 192-5.

mounted on horses; Mrs. Smith, who is known to some of us so well as Jenny Vazeille, and her two little girls were with Wesley in a chaise drawn by two horses. His adventure must be described in his own words :

> About two miles from the town, just on the brow of the hill, on a sudden both the horses set out, without any visible cause, and flew down the hill like an arrow out of a bow. In a minute John fell off the coach-box. The horses then went on full speed, sometimes to the edge of the ditch on the right, sometimes on the left. A cart came up against them; they avoided it as exactly as if the man had been on the box. A narrow bridge was at the foot of the hill; they went directly over the middle of it. They ran up the next hill with the same speed, many persons meeting us, but getting out of the way. Near the top of the hill was a gate, which led into a farmer's yard. It stood open. They turned short and ran through it, without touching the gate on one side or the post on the other. I thought, 'However, the gate which is on the other side of the yard, and is shut, will stop them.' But they rushed through it as if it had been a cobweb. and galloped on through the cornfield. The little girls cried out, 'Grandpa, save us!' I told them 'Nothing will hurt you; do not be afraid'; feeling no more fear or care (blessed be God!) than if I had been sitting in my study. The horses ran on till they came to the edge of a steep precipice. Just then Mr. Smith, who could not overtake us before, galloped in between. They stopped in a moment. Had they gone on ever so little he and we must have gone down together.[1]

On July 28, John Wesley entered on his seventy-second year. As was usual with him he gives us his birthday musings. He says : ' I was considering, How is this, that I find just the same strength as I did thirty years ago? That my sight is considerably better now, and my nerves firmer than they were then? That I have none of the infirmities of old age, and have lost several I had in my youth? The grand cause is the good pleasure of God, who doeth whatsoever pleaseth Him. The chief means are (1) my constantly rising at four for about fifty years; (2) my generally preaching at five in the morning—one of the most healthy exercises in the world; (3) my never travelling less, by sea or land, than four thousand five hundred miles in a year.' [2]

Journeying towards the south, and preaching at places in Yorkshire and Lincolnshire, Wesley, on Saturday, July 20, reached Madeley. There he had the joy of staying in the home of Fletcher and of talking with him on questions that concerned the condition of Methodism. The next day he

[1] *Journal*, vi., 27.   [2] *ibid*, vi., 29.

preached in the church. Then he turned his face towards the west. He made his way to Bristol, where he arrived on Saturday, August 6. He was in time for the Conference which was to be held during the following week. This Conference was held at a critical time in the history of England, but we look in vain for any recognition of that fact. The concluding sentence of Wesley's brief description may have some reference to national unrest; but it needs some ingenuity to discover it. Wesley says: 'We observed Friday, the 12th, as a day of fasting and prayer for the success of the gospel.' It is possible that America was not forgotten in the prayers that were offered. In footnotes in Wesley's *Journal* we get some light on the proceedings of this Conference. Thomas Taylor, who was well known for his downrightness, says, in his *MS. Journal*: 'Aug. 9.—Most of the day was taken up in temporal matters, which is dry business. Aug. 10.—This morning our characters were examined, and that closely. The afternoon was chiefly spent in taking in new preachers. In the evening Mr. Wesley gave us but an indifferent sermon. Aug. 11.—We spent this day pretty profitably in considering some things of importance, especially how to prevent levity, idleness, and evil speaking. At night Mr. Wesley gave us a profitable discourse on brotherly love.' Another footnote, which contains an extract from an unpublished letter written by Miss March, casts a quieter light on the proceedings. She says: 'Our Conference is now ended. I promised myself a jubilee, a time of holy rejoicing, but found it rather a season of hurry and dissipation. Mr. Wesley opened the Conference with a plan of great and necessary business. His preaching was chiefly to the preachers—of the searching reproving kind. The preachers said there was much concord amongst them; and one observed, Mr. Wesley seemed to do all the business himself. Friday was the best time, and the evening sermon, from Matt. vii. 24, was the prettiest and most simple discourse I ever heard on that text. Mr. Wesley left us on Monday for Wales. When he first came he looked worn down with care and sorrow; but he left us well and lively.'[1]

These side-lights on the Conference of 1774 are welcome. Turning to the published *Minutes* we see that although most

[1] Wesley's *Journal*, vi., 35, Note.

of the business ran along the usual lines there are certain items which will interest those who have watched the gradual growth of the constitutional system of Methodism. We note that, so far as England was concerned, every Assistant was directed to take care to attend the Conference. It was also declared that the General Assistant of Scotland and Ireland must always attend. The question of the leadership of class-meetings was raised. It was found that it was difficult, in some places, to secure suitable lay-leaders, and the Conference decided that, where such difficulty existed, 'the Preacher should constantly meet the Society as a class.' The 'Articles of Agreement' were again produced, and several new signatures were added to the list. We are especially interested in the return of the number of members in the Methodist Societies. At the previous Conference it was reported that there were one thousand members in America; in 1774 there were two thousand two hundred and four. In spite of the disturbed condition of the country the work in America had been carried on with cheering success. Dr. Stevens describes the great revival which took place towards the end of the year 1773 and in the spring of 1774.[1] Its effect in Virginia may be judged by the fact that the membership in the colony rose from less than three hundred to nearly a thousand.

Those who are familiar with the meetings of the Methodist Conference will agree with us that some of their most enduring memories come to them when the toils of the day are over. We can imagine that was the case at this Bristol Conference. We think of little groups of men gathered together and talking about an event which finds no record in the *Minutes*. On Monday, July 18, John Nelson was in Leeds. Struck with sudden sickness he passed away on that day. On Wednesday there was a great procession through the streets of Leeds. It was moving towards Birstall where Nelson was to be buried. An eye-witness describing the scene, says that thousands of people were in the procession. He noticed that ' they were either singing or weeping.' As we look back over the vanished years we share their sorrow. But the thought of John Nelson's work as one of the leaders in the great revival of religion in this country inspires us. On the tombstone which was erected in the long years ago, it was stated

[1] Stevens's *History of American Methodism*, 98-99. English edition.

that he died when he was sixty-seven years of age. There was a touch of pathos in another inscription on that stone. John Nelson, as we have said, died on July 18, 1774. His wife died on September 11 in the same year. Those who are acquainted with the valour and sufferings of husband and wife in the cause of Christ will find relief in the thought that in death 'they were not long divided.'[1]

Early in 1774 John Wesley had lost another of his pioneers. Nathaniel Gilbert died suddenly in Antigua. Mr. Bretherton says that 'he died in great Christian confidence, leaving behind him in St. John's, Antigua, a Methodist Society of sixty members.' The Society was not dispersed. Francis Gilbert, his brother, went out from England to the island and engaged in Christian work for a year. Then, acting on medical advice, he returned. He died on July 1, 1779. His widow sailed for Antigua in 1781 and spent ten years in the island 'being abundant in labours for the good of the people.'[2] We shall have to record events which led to the firm establishment of Methodism in Antigua.

Before laying aside the *Minutes* of the Conference held in 1774, it is necessary that we should note two entries which appear in the records of the business transacted. Under the question 'Who desist from travelling?' we note the name of Joseph Pilmoor; and, in the list of stations, we see that Richard Boardman was appointed to Londonderry in Ireland. The entries have an interesting background; but it will be enough to say that these preachers, who had rendered important service to Methodism in America,[3] left that country during the first week in January, 1774. The date of their arrival in England is uncertain. We know that, when John Wesley was suddenly re-called from Congleton to Bristol, Boardman supplied his place in Congleton and preached there on April 30. The appointment of Thomas Rankin as General Superintendent of the work in America, and the strong conviction of Francis Asbury concerning the missioning of places far away from large towns, are supposed, by some writers, to have influenced Boardman and Pilmoor in their determination to return to England. Lockwood, in his book on *The*

---

[1] D.N.B. article on John Nelson says, 'As a preacher he had a power and exercised an influence scarcely inferior to Wesley's.'
[2] See Bretherton's *Early Methodism in and around Chester*, 81.
[3] See *John Wesley the Master Builder*, 249-61, 298, 313.

Western Pioneers,[1] deals with this question and recognizes fully the value of the work that Boardman and Pilmoor had done in America.

On Monday, August 15, John Wesley left Bristol and spent a week in Wales. He returned to Bristol; then, on August 29, he started on his journey to Cornwall and did not arrive again in Bristol until the second week in September. He seems to have been restless in his movements and to have had reasons for making Bristol his special ' sphere of influence.' It is probable that he had learned much concerning the state of public affairs in America from Boardman and Pilmoor; it is certain that his mind was disturbed by events which had happened since they left the country. Those who are acquainted with the history of the American colonial war know that the English government resolved to ' punish ' Boston for the raid on the tea-ships. Warships were sent out; and, on June 1, Boston harbour was closed. Dr. Hunt describes the effect.[2] He says : ' The busy little town lay desolate, its wharfs were deserted, its warehouses shut up, its streets silent; its merchants were threatened with ruin, its seamen, shipwrights, and labourers and their families with starvation.' The effect of the blockade of Boston harbour was soon felt in London, Bristol, and Liverpool. The merchants there had carried on a profitable trade with Boston; but that ceased until the long war with America came to an end.

There was another reason for Wesley's presence in Bristol at this time. Although the British Parliament had not lasted seven years, which was then its full term, it was dissolved on September 30, 1774. It is probable that those who were watching the course of events were aware of the probability of a sudden appeal to the country, and were getting ready for the elections. It is certain that on Thursday, October 6, Wesley met the Methodist voters in Bristol. He gave them the following advice : ' To vote, without fee or reward, for the person they judged most worthy; to speak no evil of the person they voted against; and to take care their spirits were not sharpened against those that voted on the other side.' Wesley's influence in Bristol was great and we have no doubt

---

[1] Lockwood's *The Western Pioneers*, 178-81. In 1776 Pilmoor's name re-appears in the *Minutes of Conference*. He was appointed to London.
[2] *The Political History of England*, x., 132.

that the Methodists there accepted his counsels. In addition, it is probable that he also distributed among them his *Word to a Freeholder*, a tract that had done good service at elections since 1747, when it was written.

In Latimer's *Annals of Bristol in the Eighteenth Century* we have a profoundly interesting description of this Bristol election. It commenced on October 7 and ended on November 2. It lives in history as the election at which Henry Cruger, by birth an American, and Edmund Burke headed the poll. We have been accustomed to accept the story that Cruger was so incapable of public speaking as to be only able to cry, at the declaration of the poll, 'I say ditto to Mr. Burke.' Latimer says that the tale is 'a silly fiction.' He asserts that Cruger, as senior member, was the first to return thanks for his election, and that he made an appropriate address. He also declares that, subsequently, he spoke so ably in the House of Commons on American affairs as to be complimented by his party leaders.[1] But what a picture of an election in the olden time do we get as we turn over the pages of Latimer's book! He says: 'Upwards of four hundred freemen were brought from London; one came from Guernsey, two from Ireland, and one is recorded, as "John Lloyd, merchant, Charlestown, South Carolina." In addition to these, an immense number of men, more than two thousand, were placed on the freemen's roll, the fees being paid by the committees of the rival candidates. The right of no small portion of these persons was derived from their having summarily married the daughters of freemen for the mere purpose of obtaining a vote, the newly-united couples often separating for ever on leaving the church. One of the devices for divorce employed by such couples was to stand on each side of a grave in the churchyard, and to separate after repeating the words, "Death us do part." The fees of these weddings were of course defrayed by the election agents. As the constituency was also copiously regaled throughout the contest, the gross outlay of the contending parties must have been enormous. Burke, in a letter to his wife's sister, stated that he had been returned at no expense to himself; but six years later, in a letter to Joseph Harford, he referred with horror to the burden he had entailed on his friends.'[2] We

[1] Latimer's *Annals of Bristol*, 411.   [2] *ibid*, 411.

submit this picture to those who sigh for the return of 'the good, old days.'

The success achieved in Bristol encouraged people who were in favour of a policy of conciliation in the dispute that had arisen in America in connexion with the Boston blockade. But, as a matter of fact, when Parliament was opened on November 30, the weakness of the party opposed to the government was revealed. In both Houses an amendment to the Address was moved, and the voting showed the comparative strength of the two parties. In the Upper House, the amendment was defeated by sixty-three votes to thirteen; in the House of Commons, it was lost by two hundred and sixty-four votes to seventy-three. It is possible that these large majorities were influenced by news that had been received from America concerning the action of a Continental Congress which met at Philadelphia on September 5, 1774. At that Congress all the American colonies, with the exception of Georgia, were represented. Dr. William Hunt gives us an insight into the composition of the Congress and the business that was transacted. He says:

The delegates came with different instructions and different intentions, and even among delegates from the same province there was much difference of opinion. As a body the Congress did not meet with any predetermined revolutionary purpose. Many loyalists and indeed moderate men of both parties believed that it would be a means of arranging a reconciliation with Great Britain, and though the most decided loyalists would have nothing to do with it, even they hoped for a good result: one-third of the delegates, John Adams said, were whigs, one-third tories (loyalists), and the rest mongrel. A proposal for a new constitution with a president over all the colonies to be appointed by the crown, and a grand council to be elected by the several assemblies and to act in connexion with Parliament, was only negatived by the votes of six colonies to five. Yet the revolutionists gained a decided preponderance, largely through the skilful management of Samuel Adams, who persuaded the Congress to approve the 'resolves' passed at a meeting of Suffolk county, Massachusetts. These 'resolves' rejected the Act for the government of the province, required tax collectors not to pay money into the governor's treasury, and advised towns to appoint their own officers of militia. Besides endorsing a policy of armed resistance to government, Congress further demanded the revocation of a series of Acts of Parliament, including the Quebec Act and the late Penal Legislation, drew up a Declaration of Rights, agreed on non-exportation and non-importation, sent a petition to the King, and published an address to the English people. It arranged that a new Congress should meet the following May, and invited the Canadians to join in it, suggesting grounds of discontent with the English government and pretending a zeal for religious equality. But the Canadians were not to be caught.

Congress separated without having laid down any basis for conciliation save complete surrender on the part of Parliament, which was clearly impossible. It professed loyalty to the crown, and it is probable that certain eminent Americans, who, like George Washington, declared that they knew of no wish for independence, really desired to maintain the connexion with England, if they could bring affairs back to their condition before 1763, and actually believed that by cutting off commercial relations with her, they could compel her to consent to their demands without an appeal to arms. Like the vast majority of Englishmen, who did not believe that the Americans would fight, they failed to understand the situation.[1]

We are much indebted to Dr. Hunt for his clear description of the situation in America at the time when the new House of Commons assembled in England. It helps us to understand the impression that was produced on the King and the people of England by the proceedings of the Philadelphia Congress. On hearing the news concerning its decisions, the King expressed the opinion that the New England colonies were in a state of rebellion, and that 'blows must decide whether they are to be subject to this country or independent.' Although some of his ministers, and a few of their party, were averse from violent measures, and the merchants who traded with America were anxious for conciliation, Dr. Hunt is of opinion that King George expressed the feeling of by far the larger part of his people. But the whigs, as a body, strongly opposed the thought of war. It is important to notice that although John Wesley was a strong royalist he objected to the King's remedy.

During the remainder of the year Wesley continued his work in the Societies in the Midlands and the south of England. From time to time he visited London, where we find him at the close of December. After this eventful year it is a relief to see him enjoying an interval of rest. On Christmas Day we find this record in his *Journal*: 'During the twelve festival days we had the Lord's Supper daily; a little emblem of the Primitive Church. May we be followers of them in all things, as they were of Christ!' On December 28 we see him in his study writing to his old

---

[1] See *The Political History of England*, x., 132-3. Dr. Hunt refers to Jones's *History of New York*, and to Flick's *Loyalism in New York*, in support of his statements.

friend Charles Perronet. He seems to be weary of controversy, especially of doctrinal disputes. Putting these things aside, this is what he says in his letter: 'If we could once bring all our Preachers, itinerant and local, uniformly and steadily to insist on those two points, *Christ dying for us,* and *Christ reigning in us,* we should shake the trembling gates of hell. I think most of them are now exceeding clear herein, and the rest come nearer and nearer; especially since they have read Mr. Fletcher's *Checks,* which have removed many difficulties out of the way.' Wesley was evidently thinking of the old times when the first race of Methodist Preachers proclaimed the central doctrines of the Christian religion with overwhelming power. In the previous month he had lost one of them. John Downes is known to those who are familiar with the work of the Early Methodist Preachers. On Friday evening, November 4, he attempted to preach at West Street chapel. He took for his text, ' Come unto me all ye that labour and are heavy laden, and I will give you rest.' But he had over-estimated his strength. He felt that he could not finish his sermon. He gave out some lines of a hymn that is familiar to all Methodists:

> Father, I lift my hands to Thee,
> No other help I know.

But he sank down in the pulpit from which he was taken by a preacher who was present. He was carried to bed where he lay quiet and speechless till eight o'clock on the morning of the next day. John Wesley must have felt sad when he heard of his friend's sudden death. But one thought consoled him. His old comrade had answered to the call of the Master: ' Come unto Me! I will give you rest.'

III

THE OUTBREAK OF WAR

THE year 1775 occupies an exceptional position in the annals of Great Britain and America. During its opening months attempts were made to effect arrangements between the two countries which might have prevented the outbreak of war. On February 20, Lord North moved a noteworthy resolution in the House of Commons. It was to the effect that if any colony provided what Parliament considered its fair proportion towards the common defence and the expenses of its civil administration, no duty or tax should be imposed upon it, except for the regulation of trade. The proposal raised a great storm of opposition in the House; but it was carried. Dr. William Hunt, in the *Political History of England*, commenting on this fact, says: 'By accepting North's resolution Parliament showed a desire for pacification. The resolution proposed a compromise; while it maintained the authority of Parliament, it offered the Americans self-taxation. It was made with a sincere desire to end the quarrel. At one time it might have led to pacification, but it came too late.'[1] On March 22, Edmund Burke, the new member for Bristol, made a great speech in the House of Commons. Dr. Hunt, in describing it, says: 'He urged the House to return to its old policy, to respect the Americans' love of freedom, to look to the colonial assemblies to supply the expenses of their government and defence, to abandon the futile attempt to impose taxation, and to extend to Americans the privileges of Englishmen.' But the great majority on the government side of the House opposed Burke's suggestions, and they were defeated. It is well to recall these efforts to preserve peace. But the time for their calm consideration by all parties had passed. During these months of discussion troops were assembling in America. On April

[1] *The Political History of England*, x., 139.

19, the sound of gun-fire was heard at Concord and Lexington. It marked the beginning of the battles of the Revolution.

The news about the fight at Lexington did not reach England until nearly the end of May. On May 29 it was published in the English papers. It caused great excitement in this country. Turning from the discussions in Parliament we will attempt to ascertain the opinions of the English people of that time concerning the wisdom of imposing taxation on the Americans by force of arms. In the present day we are so accustomed to look to Parliament for the expression of the nation's will that we need to be reminded that its constitution has been greatly changed since the perilous years of the American war. At that time the members of the House of Commons were elected by a comparatively small minority of the people of England. It was not until August 7, 1832, that a Parliament which had been elected by a much enlarged constituency assembled at Westminster. We have seen the manner in which elections were conducted in the eighteenth century, and have noted some instances of the large sums of money that were employed in purchasing the votes of many of the men who possessed the franchise. Recent revelations have shed light on the tactics that were employed, in 1775, to secure the election of the majority that overwhelmed Edmund Burke and the little group of members who supported him in his opposition to the war with America. The more clearly we see the means by which the House of Commons was then elected the less likely is it that we shall admire the wisdom of its decisions.

When we try to ascertain the opinions of the nation it is possible to get a clearer idea of the condition of public opinion on the question of the resort to war. It is certain that until recent years many Americans have thought that the action of the King and Parliament, in 1775, had the approval of the whole British nation. But a welcome change of opinion is now taking place on the other side of the Atlantic. It has been brought about, to a large extent, by books that have been written by Professor Osgood and Professor Beer. They have rendered a great service by their clear and convincing statements of the facts of the case. At this stage of our inquiry into the difficult question of the condition of public opinion in England concerning the declaration of war against the Americans, we have been helped by a book recently written by Dr. Fred Junkin Hinkhouse, another American Professor of History. It is entitled, *The Preliminaries of the American Revolution as seen in the English Press, 1763-1775*. Dr. Hinkhouse was not satisfied with the opinions commonly held by Americans on the subject of the origin of the war. He therefore determined to go to England in order to ascertain the facts of the case. He came to the conclusion that he would get direct light on the condition of public opinion in this country concerning the beginning of the war if he fixed his attention on the reviews, magazines, and newspapers that were published during the years mentioned in the title page of his book. He gives a list of twenty documents he examined. It is clear that his examination of documents published during the period 1763-1775 was close and exhaustive.

We are only concerned, at this moment, with Dr. Hinkhouse's verdict on the condition of public opinion in England on the question of the declaration of war with America. In his last chapter he gives a summary of the conclusions he reached on the subject. We present them in an abbreviated form.

An analysis of sentiment among English social classes reveals that the landed interest was consistently for strong measures against the Americans. On the other hand the evidence examined just as clearly shows that the great merchants were almost always friendly to the American cause. The manufacturers also favoured reconciliation with the Americans, but their views were not quite so pronounced as those of the traders.

When we consider the ecclesiastical party in England we find the landed interest again. The Church of England was identified with the land-owning aristocracy. Their interests were the same, and their policy was the same. Only two members of the episcopal bench took a pro-American stand. They were Jonathan Shipley, Bishop of St. Asaph, a close friend to Benjamin Franklin, and Hinchliffe, Bishop of Peterborough. The former, on February 19, 1773, preached a strongly pro-American sermon before the Society for the Propagation of the Gospel, which was widely quoted and warmly approved by the friends of the American cause. The attitude of the Church of England was well displayed also in the Bishop controversy. The Church was clearly against the Americans.

Opposed to the Church by natural alignment was the non-conformist interest. Their attitude may have been prompted by a fellow-feeling for their non-conformist brethren in America, by their Puritan inheritance which set them against the Established Church, and by the very natural tendency to oppose a group over them that was often domineering and always aristocratic. The attitude of the Quakers displayed in 1775 shows them joined with the opponents of strong action against the colonists.

It is evident, therefore, that the friends of America in England were not limited to a few advocates in Parliament but included a large and very vocal group outside, and that the war of the American revolution was in a very real sense a civil war.[1]

We think it will be admitted that Dr. Hinkhouse's researches have established the fact that there was a considerable division of opinion in England, in 1775, on the question of war with America. We must now consider the action of John Wesley at this crisis of the nation's history. His mind often turned towards the men who were carrying on the work of Methodism in America. On March 1, 1775, he wrote a letter to Thomas Rankin in which he said that it was not unlikely that peace would be re-established between England and the colonies. He does not give the reason for his expectation. He was strongly opposed to the appeal to arms, and must have been influenced by his hopefulness. But he had to admit that affairs were in a doubtful situation, and so he enclosed in his letter to Rankin 'a line to all the preachers.' In this communication he says: 'You were never in your lives in so critical a situation as you are at this time. It is your part to be peace-makers; to be loving and tender to all; but to addict yourself to no party. In spite of all solicitations, of rough or smooth words, say not one word against one or other side. Keep yourselves pure; do all you can to help and soften all; but beware how you adopt another's jar. See that you act in full union with each other: this is of the utmost consequence. Not only let there be no bitterness or anger, but no shyness or coldness, between you. Mark all those that would set one of you against the other. Some such will never be wanting. But give them no countenance; rather ferret them out, and drag them into open day. The conduct of T. Rankin has been suitable to the Methodist plan: I hope all of you tread in his steps. Let your eye be single. Be in peace with each other, and the God of peace will be with you.'[2]

[1] See Hinkhouse's *The Preliminaries of the American Revolution*, 202-205. *The Colonial Background of the American Revolution*, by Charles M. Andrews, Farnam Professor of American History in Yale University, should be consulted.
[2] *Works*, xii., 308-309.

THE OUTBREAK OF WAR 53

Under the same date, March 1, Charles Wesley also wrote to Rankin. In his letter we find a paragraph which reveals his position in respect to the threatened war. He says: ' As to the public affairs, I wish you to be like-minded with me. I am of neither side, and yet of both; on the side of New England, and of old. Private Christians are excused, exempted, privileged, to take no part in civil troubles. We love all and pray for all, with a sincere and impartial love. Faults there may be on both sides; but such as neither you nor I can remedy; therefore, let us, and all our children, give ourselves unto prayer, and so stand still and see the salvation of God.'[1] A keen eye will detect a difference in the standpoints occupied by John and Charles Wesley.

In John Wesley's letter to Rankin, there is this postscript: ' To-morrow I intend to set out for Ireland.' After finishing his correspondence on Ash Wednesday, and taking a solemn leave of his friends in London, he set out, on March 2, on his journey. He visited several towns in England during the remainder of the month; but, on Sunday, April 2, he landed in Ireland at Dunleary.[2] A week later he attended a service at St. Patrick's Church, Dublin. He says: ' The good old Dean of St. Patrick's desired me to come within the rails and assist him at the Lord's Supper. This also was the means of removing much prejudice from those who were zealous for the Church.' On Monday, April 10, ' leaving just four hundred members in the Society,' he began his tour through Ireland. We note that, on April 19, he preached in the market-place at Clara.[3] The people flocked to hear him; there was no buying or selling till he concluded. He little thought that in Lexington the harsh note of the beginning of the American war was being sounded. On Monday, April 24, he was in Maryborough, where Mr. Jenkins invited him to preach in his church. He preached to a numerous congregation. Two days later he was in Waterford. He wished to hold a service in the open air but the rain drove him into the preaching-house. The next day he went into the open air, and a large congregation attended. We note that the major of the Highland Regiment quartered in the town stood behind him, with several

---
[1] John Wesley's *Works*, xii., 309, note.
[2] Kingstown, now named by the Irish Free State: *Dun Laughaire*.
[3] So Crookshank, *History of Methodism in Ireland*, i., p. 294, not Clare as in *Journal*.

of his officers; many soldiers were before him, and a sentinel was placed at the entrance of the court to prevent all disturbance. With soldiers about him he was in his element. He was so delighted with his congregation that he preached twice the next day in Waterford. On Sunday, April 30, he was in Cork. He preached there three times. At the evening service held 'in the room,' he was much charmed by the singing. He says: 'I could not but observe such singing as I have seldom heard in England. The women, in particular, sang so exactly that it seemed but one voice.' The next day he examined the Society, and found it in such order, so increased both in grace and number as he apprehended 'it had not been since the time of William Pennington.' On May 9, he reached Limerick. It was during this visit that he rode to Ballingarrane. He had a depressing experience. The men and women he had known so well in other days were far away in America. He says: 'Though I came to the town at the time appointed, I could find neither man, woman, nor child to direct me to the preaching-house. After gaping and staring some time, I judged it best to go to Newmarket, where I was to preach in the evening.'

We have no doubt that Wesley, during his fruitless visit to Ballingarrane, thought of the days when Philip Embury shepherded the Methodist Society in that place. We must pause for a few moments and pay our tribute to a man to whom Irish and American Methodism owes so much. Wakeley, in his *Lost Chapters recovered from the Early History of American Methodism,* has rescued facts from undeserved oblivion. He has thrown light on the closing years of Embury's life, and has enabled us to follow him as he continued his service of his Divine Master. Soon after Boardman and Pilmoor came from England to America he moved from New York city to Camden, in Washington County, New York State. Camden was a village about seven miles from Ashgrove, a town in which several emigrants from Ireland had settled. Among them was Mr. Ashton, the Dublin Methodist who paid the fare of Robert Williams when they left Ireland to settle in America.[1] Embury formed a class-meeting in Ashgrove, and acted as a local preacher in the neighbourhood. He worked at his trade, and earned the

---
[1] See *John Wesley the Master Builder,* 247.

respect of his neighbours. Then, in the summer of 1775, while mowing in his meadow at Camden, he so seriously injured himself that he suddenly died. Wakeley stirs our compassion when he describes his burial. He says: 'Mr. Embury died in the prime of manhood, at the early age of forty-five, and was buried in a lonely place on a neighbouring farm in Camden. No monument or tombstone or slab was erected over him; not a single line, rudely carved, to tell of his faith, toils, or success.' Here his body lay for fifty-seven years. Then it was disinterred and removed to the beautiful burying-ground in Ashgrove. Over the new grave a marble tablet was placed; it bore an inscription which fully recognized the value of his work.[1] We are not able to fix the exact date of Embury's death. We must be content to know it was in the summer of 1775, probably shortly after John Wesley's disappointing visit to Ballingarrane. Embury was not the only friend Mr. Ashton lost in 1775. On September 26 Robert Williams passed away. He is well known as 'the Apostle of Methodism in Virginia and North Carolina,' a distinction well earned by his fearless and successful work. Asbury preached his funeral sermon. In his *Journal*, he says: 'He has been a very useful laborious man, and the Lord gave him many souls to his ministry. Perhaps no one in America has been an instrument of awakening so many souls as God has awakened by him.'[2]

As we watch the journeys of John Wesley during the month of June, 1775, we follow him with sympathy. His mind was weighed down with anxiety concerning the progress of events in America. He moved about the country visiting the Societies and preaching to large congregations in several towns; but his strength was fading. He continued to travel and preach until, on Saturday, June 17, he yielded to the advice of others who persuaded him to send for Dr. Laws, whom he describes as 'a sensible and skilful physician.' The doctor told him that he was in a high fever, and advised him to 'lay by.' Instead of acting on this advice he informed the doctor that it could not be done as he had made appointments to preach at several places, 'and must preach as long as he could speak.' He went to Tanderagee, taking with him 'a

---

[1] See Wakeley's *Lost Chapters*, 131-140.
[2] Entry on September 28, 1775.

cooling draught which the doctor had prescribed.' When he got to the town he found that he was not able to preach, 'his understanding being quite confused and his strength entirely gone.' His friends persuaded him not to undertake a journey to Lisburn, or Dublin, as he proposed, but to go to Derryaghy, the seat of Edward Gayer, clerk to the Irish House of Lords. His wife and daughter were members of the Methodist Society at Lisburn. They became his nurses, and to them we are indebted for the continuance of Wesley's work in the world. It was not until July 10 that he resumed his regular course of preaching, morning and evening. At one stage of his illness a report of his death was circulated in London and caused great consternation.

We have said that before Wesley's sickness the progress of events in America weighed on his mind. Evidence of that fact is shown in the letter he wrote to Lord North, the Prime Minister, shortly before his illness. We reproduce it.

Armagh. June 15, 1775.

MY LORD,—I would not speak, as it may seem to be concerning myself with things that lie out of my province; but I dare not refrain from it any longer. I think silence in the present case would be a sin against God, against my country, and against my own soul. But what hope can I have of doing good, of making the least impression upon your lordship, when so many have spoken in vain, and those far better qualified to speak on so delicate a subject? They were better qualified in some respects; in others they were not. They had not less bias upon their minds; they were not free from worldly hopes and fears. Their passions were engaged; and how easily do those blind the eyes of their understanding! They were not more impartial; most of them were prejudiced in the highest degree. They neither loved the King nor his ministers; rather they hated them with a perfect hatred; and your lordship knows that you could not, if you were a man, avoid having some prejudice to them. In this case it would be hardly possible to feel the full force of their arguments. They had not better means of information, of knowing the real tempers and sentiments either of the Americans on the one hand, or the English, Irish, or Scots on the other. Above all, they trusted in themselves, in their own power of convincing and persuading; I trust only in the living God, who hath the hearts of all men in His hands. And whether my writing do any good or no, it need do no harm; for it rests within your lordship's breast whether any eye but your own shall see it.

I do not intend to enter upon the question whether the Americans are in the right or in the wrong. Here all my prejudices are against the Americans; for I am a High Churchman, the son of a High

THE OUTBREAK OF WAR

Churchman,[1] bred up from my childhood in the highest notions of passive obedience and non-resistance; and yet, in spite of all my long-rooted prejudices, I cannot avoid thinking, if I think at all, these, an oppressed people, asked for nothing more than their legal rights, and that in the most modest and inoffensive manner that the nature of the thing would allow. But waiving this, waiving all considerations of right and wrong, I ask, Is it common-sense to use force toward the Americans? A letter now before me, which I received yesterday, says, 'Four hundred of the regulars and forty of the militia were killed in the late skirmish.' What a disproportion is this! And this is the first essay of raw men against regular troops. You see, my lord, whatever has been affirmed, these men will not be frightened; and it seems they will not be conquered so easily as was at first imagined. They will probably dispute every inch of ground, and, if they die, die sword in hand. Indeed, some of our valiant officers say, 'Two thousand men will clear America of these rebels.' No, nor twenty thousand, be they rebels or not, nor perhaps treble that number. They are as strong men as you; they are valiant as you, if not abundantly more valiant for they are one and all enthusiasts —enthusiasts for liberty. They are calm deliberate enthusiasts; and we know how this principle breathes into softer souls stern love of war, and thirst of vengeance, and contempt of death. We know men, animated with this spirit, will leap into a fire, or rush into a cannon's mouth.

'But they have no experience of war.' And how much more have our troops? Very few of them ever saw a battle. 'But they have no discipline.' That is an entire mistake. Already they have near as much as our army, and they will learn more of it every day; so that in a short time, if the fatal occasion continue, they will understand it as well as their assailants. 'But they are divided among themselves.' So you are informed by various letters and memorials. So, doubt not, was poor Rehoboam informed concerning the ten tribes. So, nearer our own times, was Philip informed concerning the people of the Netherlands. No, my lord, they are terribly united. Not in the province of New England only, but down as low as the Jerseys and Pennsylvania. The bulk of the people are so united that to speak a word in favour of the present English measures would almost endanger a man's life. Those who informed me of this, one of whom was with me last week, lately come from Philadelphia, are no sycophants; they say nothing to curry favour; they have nothing to gain or lose by me. But they speak with sorrow of heart what they have seen with their own eyes, and heard with their own ears.

These men think, one and all, be it right or wrong, that they are contending *pro aris et focis;* for their wives, children, and liberty. What an advantage have they herein over many who fight only for pay! none of whom care a straw for the cause wherein they are

[1] John Wesley uses the term 'High Churchman' in the sense in which it was employed in his time. A High Churchman was a man who had a hearty zeal for the Church, who was strict in the observation of its rules and orders, who expressed concern for its safety, and supported all measures which were necessary for its security and preservation. See *John Wesley and the Religious Societies,* 50-51.

engaged; most of whom strongly disapprove of it. Have they not another considerable advantage? Is there occasion to recruit the troops? Their supplies are at hand, and all round about them. Ours are three thousand miles off! Are we then able to conquer the Americans, suppose they are left to themselves? Suppose all our neighbours should stand stock-still, and leave us and them to fight it out? But we are not sure of this. Nor are we sure that all our neighbours will stand stock-still. I doubt they have not promised it; and, if they had, could we rely upon those promises? Yet it is not probable they will send ships or men to America. Is there not a shorter way? Do they not know where England and Ireland lie? And have they not troops, as well as ships, in readiness? All Europe is well apprised of this; only the English know nothing of the matter! What if they find means to land but ten thousand men? Where are the troops in England or Ireland to oppose them? Why, cutting the throats of their brethren in America! Poor England, in the meantime! 'But we have our militia—our valiant, disciplined militia. These will effectually oppose them.' Give me leave, my lord, to relate a little circumstance, of which I was informed by a clergyman who knew the fact. In 1716 a large body of militia were marching towards Preston against the rebels. In a wood which they were passing by, a boy happened to discharge his fowling-piece. The soldiers gave in all for lost, and, by common consent threw down their arms and ran for life. So much dependence is to be placed on our valorous militia.

But, my lord, this is not all. We have thousands of enemies, perhaps more dangerous than French or Spaniards. As I travel four or five thousand miles every year, I have an opportunity of conversing freely with more persons of every denomination than any one else in the three Kingdoms. I cannot but know the general disposition of the people— English, Scots and Irish; and I know a large majority of them are exasperated almost to madness. Exactly so they were throughout England and Scotland about the year 1640, and in a great measure by the same means; by inflammatory papers which were spread, as they are now, with the utmost diligence, in every corner of the land. Hereby the bulk of the population were effectually cured of all love and reverence for the King. So that, first despising, then hating him, they were just ripe for open rebellion. And I assure your lordship, so they are now. They want nothing but a leader. Two circumstances more are deserving to be considered: the one, that there was at that time a decay of general trade almost throughout the Kingdom; the other, there was a common dearness of provisions. The case is the same in both respects at this day. So that even now there are multitudes of people, that, having nothing to do, and nothing to eat, are ready for the first bidder; and that, without inquiring into the merits of the cause, would flock to any who would give them bread. Upon the whole, I am really sometimes afraid that this evil is from the Lord. When I consider the astonishing luxury of the rich, and the shocking impiety of rich and poor, I doubt whether general dissoluteness of manners does not demand a general visitation. Perhaps the decree is already gone forth from the Governor of the world. Perhaps even now,

> As he that buys surveys a ground,
> So the destroying angel measures it around.
> Calm he surveys the perishing nation;
> Ruin behind him stalks, and empty desolation.[1]
>
> J. WESLEY.

It is impossible to read John Wesley's letter to Lord North without admiring its great knowledge of the actual condition of England and America at the time when it was written. Its foresight was remarkable. But while we read it we remember that the advice tendered came too late. On June 17, the day when Wesley yielded to the advice of his friends and consulted Dr. Laws at Lurgan, far away in Boston, in America, a battle was raging. The British troops on Bunker Hill were attacked, and had to fight hard to hold their position. After that strong assault the thought of peace vanished, and England and America knew that the hour of war had come.

---

[1] See Dr. George Smith's *History of Wesleyan Methodism*, Vol. i., 700-702; Wesley's *Journal*, viii., 325-28.

IV

THE NEED FOR AN ORDAINED MINISTRY

JOHN WESLEY prolonged his visit to Ireland and gradually recruited his strength. Then, on July 25, 1775, he landed at Parkgate; two days later he arrived at Cross Hall, the home of Miss Bosanquet, and prepared for the Conference which was to be held in Leeds. Subjects of special importance awaited discussion and settlement. Some time before the Conference assembled John Fletcher had been in correspondence with Joseph Benson on the question of a more careful inquiry into the character of the preachers and their fitness for the work of the ministry. In addition, Benson had raised a subject that demanded most serious consideration. It concerned the ordination of the preachers. He suggested that those preachers who were judged to be qualified for the work of the ministry should be set apart for that work by fasting, prayer, and the imposition of the hands of John Wesley, Charles Wesley, John Fletcher, and other presbyters of the Established Church. In his letter to Fletcher he said that such ordination would secure the following results: ' The preachers would be more solemnly devoted to the work; would consider themselves more seriously entrusted with it; would more heartily and confidently engage in it; and would be more united to each other and more connected together, whence they might expect more of the divine blessing, and, of consequence, greater success in their labours. Thus would we be furnished with an answer to those who allege we have no authority to preach for want of ordination; the minds of many, both preachers and people, who have been distressed with doubts and reasonings on that head would be satisfied, and one main plea for seeking episcopal ordination, or that of other Churches, would be quite laid aside.'

In considering Benson's proposals concerning the ordination of suitable preachers it must be remembered that he was appointed to the Edinburgh circuit by the Conference of 1773, and was its superintendent at the time of his correspondence with Fletcher. Constant contact with ministers who possessed Presbyterian orders influenced him. It suggested a way of escape from the difficulty caused by the conviction of many people, south of the Border, who maintained, with vehemence, that only bishops have the right to ordain preachers to the work of the Christian ministry.

Benson's suggestion concerning the ordination of 'suitable preachers' raised the question of the action that the Conference should take in the case of those who were deemed 'unsuitable.' Benson, with great courage, faced that problem. He recommended greater stringency in the annual examination into character which took place at the Conference. He suggested that preachers who were most blameable in their character and conduct, who had never possessed, or had lost 'converting grace,' and were remarkably deficient in common sense, or 'natural parts,' or capacity for improvement, should be laid 'quite aside.' We are especially interested in his suggestion concerning those who, though not thought fit to be admitted into 'full connexion,' yet were unexceptional in their conduct, appeared to be truly serious, and had a capacity for improvement. His opinion was that part of them should be admitted 'on trial,' and the rest should be sent to Kingswood School. He says: 'There let them stay a year, or longer if thought necessary, under the tuition of some of the ablest and most respected preachers, to study, not Latin and Greek, but their own mother-tongue, the Scriptures, the best English writers in Divinity, Church history, and the history of their own country.' Room at the School was to be provided by making it a school only for preachers' sons and the preachers sent there by the Conference. Whatever we may think of Benson's suggestions they certainly shed light on problems that were faced and solved in the next century. It is only necessary to say that Fletcher informed Wesley of these suggestions, and received a promise that Benson should have full leave to explain and enforce them at the Conference.

Wesley had much to occupy his time during his stay at Cross Hall. When we remember his severe illness in Ireland our sympathies are excited when we think of the strain that would test his newly-recovered strength at the Conference.

Our anxiety is lessened when we find that Samuel Bardsley, who took tea with him at Miss Bosanquet's, was surprised at his recovery. He says: 'He appeared with his usual cheerfulness, and as well as we had seen him for some years.' This good report was confirmed by Wesley himself in a letter he wrote to Miss Lewis, of Bristol. In it he says: 'By the blessing of God, I am at least as well as I was before my late illness, and I have now recovered my strength by slow degrees from the time I got into the open air.' The completeness of his recovery is shown by the facts that on Sunday, July 30, he preached 'under Birstall Hill,' and that the greater part of the huge audience could hear him while he enforced the text, 'When the breath of man goeth forth, he returneth again to his dust, and then all his thoughts perish.' In the evening he preached at Leeds, and 'found strength' in proportion to his work. We may, therefore, dismiss our fears when we think of the burden that rested on him at the Conference.

On Tuesday, August 1, the thirty-second Conference met in Leeds. In the opinion of Thomas Hanby, one of the preachers present, it was the largest Conference held for many years, and was unexampled for its free discussion. Consulting the report of its proceedings in the *Minutes* for the year it seems as if the business transacted ran along the usual lines; but turning to other sources of information we alter our opinion. Let us hear what Wesley says: 'Having received several letters, intimating that many of the preachers were utterly unqualified for the work, having neither grace nor gifts sufficient for it, I determined to examine this weighty charge with all possible exactness. In order to this, I read those letters to all the Conference, and begged that everyone would freely propose and enforce whatever objection he had to any one. The objections proposed were considered at large: in two or three difficult cases, committees were appointed for that purpose. In consequence of this, we were all fully convinced that the charge advanced was without foundation; that God has really sent those labourers into His vineyard, and has qualified them for the work. And we were all more closely united together than we have been for many years.'[1] Joseph Benson expressed his satisfaction with the result of the investigation; but the question of the closer annual examina-

[1] *Journal*, vi., 72-3.

tion of the character and capacity of the preachers was not settled. It was soon raised again, and the action of Wesley at the Conference of 1775 indicates the direction that was afterwards taken to secure for the Methodist people preachers not only of ability but of character beyond reproach.

The discussion on character gives the Conference of 1775 special distinction; but we cannot put the *Minutes* of its proceedings aside without noting a few entries that deserve attention. We may be pardoned for lingering over a name that occurs in the answer to the question—' Who are admitted on Trial?' It brings before us once more the scene of the 'huge audience' that assembled 'under Birstall Hill' when Wesley's sermon was preached there on the Sunday preceding the Conference. Standing in that crowd we see a family group. The father and mother were originally Dissenters; but, in 1748, they joined the Methodist Society in Birstall. Their descendants have been Methodists to the present day. By their side in the crowd stand their two sons; they had been well trained at home from their childhood. Their mother, before her marriage, lived for several years in the house of Philip Doddridge at Northampton. For him she had a great respect. She watched his method of training his students and learned many a lesson that was useful to her in her future life. Her two sons may be said to have been brought up in Dr. Doddridge's way. Both of them became Wesley's preachers. It was at the Conference of 1775 that Joseph Saunderson was received 'on trial.' His brother William was received 'on trial' in 1789. They were related to Professor Nicholas Saunderson, who succeeded Whiston, the successor of Sir Isaac Newton in the Lucasian Professorship at Cambridge. Nicholas Saunderson was blind almost from his birth. His eulogium has been pronounced by Edmund Burke in his essay on *The Sublime and Beautiful*. He died on April 19, 1739. As a great-grandson of William Saunderson, the present writer may be excused for recording his ancestor's entry on the work of a Methodist preacher.[1]

In examining 'the stations' of the preachers, recorded in the *Minutes* of the Conference of 1775, we find that the number of preachers appointed to America was increased from

[1] The sons of Mrs. George G. Findlay, who are Wesleyan ministers, possess the same ancestry.

seven to eleven, but we look in vain for the name of Francis Asbury. From other sources we know that Wesley desired his return to England; but, fortunately, he persisted in remaining in America. After 1775 the appointments for America disappear from the *Minutes,* and are not resumed until 1784. In the list of members in the Society we note that, notwithstanding the outbreak of war, the number of members in America had been increased from 2,204 to 3,148. The latter figures are quoted in 1776; then, the return of membership ceases. Seeking for further light on this important question we find it in the 'Introduction' of the *Appendix* to Charles Atmore's *Methodist Memorial,* published in 1802. Writing of America, he says: 'In the year 1777, the preachers were increased to forty, and the members to about seven thousand! So mightily grew the word of the Lord and prevailed!' We do not wonder at the notes of exclamation, but must reserve our comments on the extraordinary increase of Methodist preachers and members which took place during the American war.[1]

Returning to the *Minutes* of the Conference of 1775 we notice that the classes in some places were considered to be 'too large,' and the order was given that 'every class which contained above thirty members was to be divided.' Then, it is clear that the Conference was trying to stop the rapidity of the increase of preaching-houses. It was resolved that only three new houses were to be built during the coming year. The privileged towns were Oldham, Taunton and Halifax. The Conference closed with the signing of the 'Agreement' 'to adhere to each other, and to the old Methodist Doctrine and Discipline.' More than eighty preachers signed. After this Conference the practice of signing this 'Agreement' ceased. We think that John Wesley must have reached the conclusion that the 'Agreement' had answered its purpose.

At this Conference John Wesley received a letter from Fletcher which was of great importance. He does not seem to have made any public use of it; but he placed it among his papers which were found in the Wesleyan Methodist Book Room towards the end of the year 1897. It was published in *The Methodist Recorder* on January 6, 1898, and a leading article, written by Dr. Rigg, appeared in the same number of

---

[1] Atmore's *Appendix to the Methodist Memorial,* 539-40.

the *Recorder,* under the title ' A remarkable letter to Wesley from his Designated Successor.' Wesley's serious illness in Ireland made a deep impression on John Fletcher. He had to face the fact that Wesley expected him to fill his place as the leader of the Methodists when he died. He came to the conclusion that he ought to inform Wesley of his opinions concerning the possibility of a closer union of the Methodists with the Church of England. He sketches a plan of approach, and urges Wesley to adopt it. He agrees with Wesley that in several respects the Established Church needed reformation, but he thought that such reformation might be hastened if the following plan were adopted.

1. That the growing body of the Methodists in Great Britain, Ireland and America be formed into a general Society—a daughter Church of our holy mother.

2. That this Society shall recede from the Church of England in nothing but in some palpable defects, about doctrine, discipline, and unevangelical hierarchy.

3. That this Society shall be the *Methodist* Church of England, ready to defend the as yet *unmethodized* Church against all the unjust attacks of the dissenters—willing to submit to her in all things that are not unscriptural—approving of her ordination, partaking of her sacraments, and attending her service at every convenient opportunity.

4. That a pamphlet be published containing the 39 Articles of the Church of England rectified according to the purity of the gospel, together with some needful alterations in the liturgy and homilies—such as the expunging the damnatory clauses of the Athanasian creed, &c.

5. That Messrs. Wesley, the preachers, and the most substantial Methodists in London, in the name of the Societies scattered thro' the Kingdom, would draw up a petition and present it to the Archbishop of Canterbury informing his Grace, and by him the bench of the Bishops, of this design; proposing the reformed articles of religion, asking the protection of the Church of England, begging that this step might not be considered as a schism, but only as an attempt to avail ourselves of the liberty of English men, and Protestants, to serve God according to the purity of the gospel, the strictness of primitive discipline, and the original design of the Church of England, which was to reform, so far as time and circumstances would allow, *whatever* needed reformation.

6. That this petition contain a request to the Bishops to ordain the Methodist preachers which can pass their examination according to what is *indispensably* required in the canons of the Church. That instead of the ordinary testimonials the Bishops would allow of testimonials signed by Messrs. Wesley and some more clergymen, who would make it their business to inquire into the morals and principles of the candidates for orders, and that instead of a title, their lordships would accept of

a bond signed by twelve stewards of the Methodist Societies, certifying that the candidate for holy orders shall have a proper maintenance. That if his Grace, &c., does not condescend to grant this request, Messrs. Wesley will be obliged to take an irregular (not unevangelical) step, and to ordain upon a Church of England independent plan such lay preachers as appear to them qualified for holy orders.

7. That the preachers so ordained be the assistants in their respective circuits. That the helpers who are thought worthy, be ordained Deacons, and that doubtful candidates be kept upon trial as they now are.

8. That the Methodist preachers assembled in Conference shall have the liberty to suspend and degrade any Methodist preacher ordained or unordained, who shall act the part of a Balaam or a Demas.

9. That when Messrs. Wesley are dead, the power of Methodist ordination be lodged, in three or five of the most steady Methodist ministers under the title of *Moderators,* who shall overlook the flocks, and the other preachers, as Mr. Wesley does now.

10. That the most spiritual part of the common prayer shall be extracted and published with the 39 rectified Articles and the Minutes of the Conferences (or the Methodist canons) which (together with such regulations as may be made at the time of this establishment) shall be, next to the Bible, the *vade mecum* of the Methodist preachers.

12. That the important office of confirmation shall be performed with the utmost solemnity by Mr. Wesley or by the Moderators, and that none shall be admitted to the Sacrament of the Lord's Supper but such as have been confirmed or are ready to be confirmed.

13. That the grand plan upon which the Methodist preachers shall go, shall be to preach the doctrine of *grace* against the Socinians—the doctrine of *justice* against the Calvinists—and the doctrine of *holiness* against all the world : and that of consequence 3 such questions as these be put to the candidates for orders at the time of ordination :—

I.—Wilt thou maintain with all thy might the scripture doctrines of *grace,* especially the doctrine of a SINNER's *free* justification merely by a living faith in the blood and merits of Christ?

II.—Wilt thou maintain with all thy might the scripture doctrines of *justice,* especially the doctrine of a BELIEVER's *remunerative* justification by the good works which ought to spring from justifying faith?

III.—Wilt thou preach up Christian perfection, or the fulfilling of the law of Christ, against all the antinomians of the age; and wilt thou ardently press after it thyself, never resting till thou art perfected in humble love?

Perhaps to keep the work in the Church it might be proper to add :

IV.—Wilt thou consider thyself as a son of the Church of England, receding from her as little as possible; never railing against her clergy, and being ready to submit to her ordination, if any of the Bishops will confer it upon thee?

14. And lastly, that Kingswood School be entirely appropriated (1) To the reception and improvement of the candidates for Methodist orders:

(2) To the education of the children of the preachers: and (3) To the keeping of the worn-out Methodist preachers, whose employment shall be to preserve the spirit of faith and primitive Christianity in the place; by which means alone the curse of a little *unsanctified* learning may be kept out.[1]

John Wesley did not receive Fletcher's letter until the second day of the Conference. In it Fletcher expressed a hope that he would get it in time to consult the preachers if he found anything in it worth his attention. But the pressure of business was great, and the questions raised in the letter were too important to be discussed by a harassed Conference. So Wesley took the letter with him to London, where he arrived on the Tuesday of the next week.

As we watch the growth of the constitution of the Methodist Church we think we can perceive the influence of Fletcher's long lost letter. We pass by the suggestions concerning the relation of the Methodist Societies to the Church of England. Time has given its answer to Fletcher's suggestions. But when we reach the proposals concerning the ordination of the preachers by Methodist Presbyters we seem to pass into the light of coming day. It must be remembered that Wesley was firmly convinced that ordination by presbyters was valid. He had studied the question closely; for nearly thirty years before 1775 he had held the conviction without it wavering. It is probable that he had discussed the matter with Fletcher. We seem to hear echoes of intimate conversations in the Madeley study in several parts of Fletcher's letter. In addition, he was well acquainted with the methods of ordination that existed in Scotland. The practice of ordination by presbyters was the rule in the Church that had been established by law. It must be remembered that the English Episcopal Church was what we might call a dissenting church. It was protected by an Act passed in the reign of Queen Anne. The Act was entitled 'An Act to Prevent the Disturbing those of the Episcopal Communion in that Part of Great Britain called Scotland, in the exercise of their Religious Worship, and in the Use of the Liturgy of the Church of England.' As we read the Act in Bishop Gibson's

---

[1] The eleventh proposal is left out. It is probable that Fletcher did not notice the mistake in numbering of his paragraphs. See Letter *in extenso* in Wesley's *Journal*, Standard edition, Vol. viii. (Appendix xxix), 331-4.

Codex we find that, to a considerable extent, it resembles the Toleration Act of William and Mary. But the persons 'tolerated' have changed places. When John Wesley was in Scotland he was befriended by many of the ministers of the Presbyterian Church; we do not know of a single instance in which he questioned the validity of their 'orders.' His own convictions were the more strongly confirmed by his association with them, and with the members of the Presbyterian Churches in Scotland. He put aside Fletcher's letter for some years; but he remembered its suggestion concerning ordination by Presbyters when the time came to adopt it.

John Wesley remained in London until August 14, when he set out for Wales. On August 16 he received a pressing invitation to preach at Trevecca. Turning aside from his proposed route he went to a place that was full of memories of pleasant days. Howell Harris was much in his mind. It was a joy to him to find that the work of his old friend was still being continued. The 'family' at Trevecca consisted of six score persons. When he looked at them, and at the beautiful surroundings in which they lived, he said: 'What a lovely place! And what a lovely family!' The next morning he preached at eleven o'clock, to a large congregation. He seems to have thought only of the bright side of his former visits to the place. He says nothing of his disappointments. The treatment of Fletcher and Benson by Lady Huntingdon may have come into his mind; but there is not a note of sorrow in his description of his visit. Leaving Trevecca he went to Carmarthen. There he received another inspiration. This is the record of his *Journal*: 'How is this wilderness become a fruitful field! A year ago I knew no one in this town who had any desire of fleeing from the wrath to come, and now we have eighty persons in the Society.' Enheartened by these experiences, he set out on a little tour through Carmarthenshire, Pembrokeshire, and Glamorganshire. On Monday, August 28, he left Cardiff early in the morning and reached Newport about eight o'clock. Soon after that hour he preached to a large and serious congregation. Once more he praised God for the triumphs of the gospel. He says: 'I believe it is five-and-thirty years since I preached here before, to a people who were then wild as bears. How

NEED FOR ORDAINED MINISTRY 69

amazingly is the scene changed! Oh, what is too hard for God?'

After a short visit to Bristol, Wesley, on August 30, set out for Taunton, where he preached in 'the great Presbyterian meeting-house.' He found himself in the presence of 'a brilliant congregation.' He confesses his surprise that he was able to preach to such a congregation 'with such freedom and openness of spirit.' Leaving Taunton he went to Devon and Cornwall. We pause for a moment at an entry in his *Journal* which concerns Plymouth Dock. He held a Society meeting there. His description of its proceedings causes us to forget the sunshine of his Welsh journeys, and makes us once more face difficulties which were beginning to becloud his path. Remembering that we are dealing with the events of 1775, we read much in his *Journal* entry: 'Understanding some of our friends here were deeply prejudiced against the King and all his ministers, I spoke freely and largely on the subject at the meeting of the Society. God applied it to their hearts, and I think there is not one of them now who does not see things in another light.' The significance of this entry in the *Journal* is great. Events which we shall soon record will throw light on its importance. On September 12 he returned to Bristol, a city in which there was strong opposition to the war with America. At this point, however, we are concerned with an incident which occurred during this visit. On September 21 he received a message from a man in the prison who had been found guilty of house-breaking and had been condemned to death. The execution was to take place on the following day. The condemned man had earnestly desired that Wesley should be asked to preach to him at the solemn service that was to be held in the prison the day before the execution. He was willing to die. After deep agony of soul he had found peace with God. It was impossible that Wesley could resist such an appeal; so on September 21 he preached in the prison to the condemned man and a crowded audience. He must have been reminded of the old days when he often preached in that place during the early morning of the Methodist Reformation.

On Friday, October 6, Wesley returned to London. He soon began his usual visitation of the towns in the neighbourhood. On October 18 he was at Newbury. Hearing that there were many 'red-hot patriots' there, he gave the congregation a strong exhortation ' to fear God and honour the King.' The next day, when he was staying at Ramsbury Park, he wrote a letter to Charles Wesley which contains a sentence claiming our attention. He expresses a hope that he will soon be in London, and will then talk with the committee ' about building a new Foundery.' That is an arresting statement. The term of the lease of the Foundery was running out; in a short time the Methodists of London would have to decide the question of its renewal. The old Foundery was, in many respects, unsuitable for the needs of the ever-growing congregation. Was it worth while to remain on the site? Would it not be better to obtain a piece of ground on which a large chapel might be erected with dwelling-houses for the preachers, and offices that would be useful for a Book Room and other purposes? Was there not such a site fronting the narrow lane that led to the City? Many questions would be asked at the meeting of the committee that was to be held when Wesley returned to London. He arrived there on Saturday, October 28, and found that much important business demanded his attention.

On November 11 this entry appears in Wesley's *Journal*: ' I made some additions to the *Calm Address to our American Colonies*. Need any one ask from what motive this was wrote? Let him look round. England is in a flame!—a flame of malice and rage against the King, and almost all that are in authority under him. I labour to put out this flame. Ought not every true patriot to do the same? If hireling writers on either side judge of me by themselves, that I cannot help.' This entry is suggestive. Some months before he had written a little tract well known as the *Calm Address*. It was published at one penny, and many thousand copies were sold. When Dr. Samuel Johnson issued his well-known pamphlet, *Taxation no Tyranny*, a copy came into Wesley's hands. He was so much impressed by its arguments that he changed his views concerning the war in America. Fixing his attention on the one question of the right of the British Parliament to tax the colonies, though in it there were no members elected by the Americans, he used in his *Calm Address* the argument contained in Dr. Johnson's pamphlet. In the first edition of his tract he did not mention the source from which he had derived his arguments. That fact was soon seized by keen opponents. They denounced his conduct. In our copy of the edition, which was published towards the close of 1775, we see in the address ' To the Reader,' that he remedies this serious defect. Referring to his former views, which were strongly in favour of the actions of the Americans, he says : ' I was of a different judgement on this head, till I read a tract entitled *Taxation no Tyranny*. But as soon as I received more light myself, I judged it my duty to impart it to others. I therefore extracted the chief arguments from that treatise, and added an application to those whom it most concerns. I was well aware of the treatment this would bring upon myself; but let it be, so I may in any degree serve my King and country.' It is satisfactory to know that Dr. Johnson, on February 6, 1776, wrote a letter to him in which he said : ' I have thanks to return for the addition of your important suffrage to my argument on the American question. To have gained such a mind as yours may justly confirm me in my own opinion. What effect my paper has had upon the public I know not; but I have no reason to be discouraged. The lecturer was surely in the right who, though he saw his audience slinking away, refused to quit the chair while Plato stayed.'[1]

Wesley's *Calm Address* roused the partisans of America in England to fierce attacks on the writer. His principal antagonist was the Rev. Caleb Evans, the Baptist minister of the well-known Broadmead Chapel in Bristol. Tyerman describes him as ' a man of good sense, a diligent student, a faithful pastor, and extensively useful, but a rampant advocate of what was called liberty, and therefore a well-wisher to the republican rebellion across the Atlantic.' Early in November he published a ' Letter to the Rev. Mr. Wesley, occasioned by his *Calm Address to the American Colonies*.' Wesley did not reply to it; but it received an answer from John Fletcher on November 15, 1775. Once more Fletcher came to Wesley's defence. The literary contest between him and Evans lasted for some time. There lies before us a pamphlet which contains Fletcher's three letters. It was published early in the year 1776, and consists of seventy-one pages. We have read the letters carefully. In them several quotations from the letters of Evans are inserted. They prove that Tyerman was right when he indicated the ' rampancy ' of the

[1] Tyerman's *Life and Times of Wesley*, iii., 186.

writer. Answering one of Fletcher's letters, Evans thus describes it: 'Instead of argument, I met with nothing but declamation; instead of precision, artful colouring; instead of proof, presumption; instead of consistency, contradiction; instead of reasoning, a string of sophistries. Your letters abound, sir, as every intelligent reader will easily discover, with the *petitio principii*, the *fallacia accidentis*, the *non causa pro causa*, and those many other petty inventions by which, as the schoolmen very well know, a question may be embarrassed when it cannot be answered.' A controversy carried on in this spirit fails to attract us. There is one incident connected with this correspondence that is worth recording. We will state it in Tyerman's words. He says: 'Notwithstanding the depreciatory opinions of Mr. Evans, Dr. Price, and the Monthly Reviewers, the government of King George III desired to reward Fletcher for the service he had rendered them. His old friend, Mr. Vaughan, informed Wesley that he took one of Fletcher's political pamphlets to the Earl of Dartmouth, at that time Secretary of State for the Colonies. Lord Dartmouth carried it to the Lord Chancellor, who handed it to King George. The result was, an official was immediately commissioned to ask Fletcher whether any preferment in the Church would be acceptable to him? or whether the Lord Chancellor could do him any service? Fletcher replied, no doubt to the amazement of all concerned, "I want nothing, but more grace."'[1]

Turning aside from the war of pamphleteers we note that, on Saturday, November 11, Wesley was preparing to preach a charity sermon in Bethnal Green Church on the following day. At the service a collection was to be made for the widows and orphans of soldiers killed in the American War. Knowing the state of opinion in the congregation, and 'how many would seek occasion of offence,' he had written out the sermon. We have said that there was a strong division of opinion in England on the subject of the war. Preachers had to recognize that fact. But Wesley seems to have escaped hostile criticism on this occasion. After the service, he dined with Sir John Hawkins and three magistrates, and was 'agreeably surprised at a very serious conversation' which was kept up during the whole time he stayed in the house.

[1] Tyerman's *Wesley's Designated Successor*, 353.

V

MRS. JOHN WESLEY

JOHN WESLEY'S life during the year 1775 was crowded with important events. No one can read the records in his *Journal* without wondering at his extraordinary capacity for work and envying the brightness of spirit with which he faced and conquered formidable difficulties. He seems to be free from all personal troubles. But those who are acquainted with the incidents of his life are aware that, in 1775 and 1776, he was bearing a burden that would have wearied an ordinary man. We have reached a stage of his history that compels us to face a subject which cannot be ignored.

In a previous volume of this series of books on John Wesley we have mentioned the first flight of Mrs. Wesley from her husband. It occurred on January 23, 1771.[1] She went to Newcastle-on-Tyne, where she bought a house in which she lived for a time. Yielding to the persuasions of her son-in-law, William Smith, and her daughter, whom he had married, she returned to her husband. In *John Wesley the Master Builder* we have seen them together at Pateley Bridge, in Yorkshire, on June 29, 1772, and have followed them over the moors on the next day to Otley.[2] Another flight followed, from which she returned to London. In May, 1774, we know that she was residing at the Foundery. The fact is shown by a letter which John Wesley wrote to her from Edinburgh; it was written on May 18, 1774. That letter shows that a reconciliation and renewal of confidence had taken place between husband and wife. It concerns matters of business, but its style and contents reveal much to the eye that brings with it 'the power to see.' We submit it to the judgement of our readers.

[1] See *John Wesley the Master Builder*, 286.
[2] *Ibid*, p. 312.

MY DEAR LOVE,

    I am just now come hither from Glasgow, and take this opportunity of writing two or three lines. I desire you wou'd let Mr. Pine have a hundred pounds of that Money wch is in your hands, provided he gives you his full account first: wch I must beg of you to send to London to John Atlay, together with fifty pounds for Mr. Nind, the Papermaker, and fifty pounds for Robert Hawes. There is no use in letting the money lie dead. If I do not administer, I can but pay this again. I am just going to preach, and am in great haste,

My dear Molly,
Your affectionate Husband,
JOHN WESLEY.[1]

We reproduce this letter verbatim. It may refer to Mrs. Wesley's own money, which her husband wished to borrow, and which he promised to repay; but, if so, there can be no doubt it sheds light on the problem of the confidence which had been restored between Wesley and his wife. It is well known that she was a good business-woman, and that during Wesley's absence from London, she took some part in the management of the Book Room.

Having noticed this return of confidence in each other, it is disconcerting to find, in a letter written to Charles Wesley by his brother on June 2, 1775, the following questions: 'Has my friend taken a house in Bristol? Is Noah with her? What are they doing?'[2] John Wesley's letter was written from Londonderry shortly before he was laid aside in Ireland by sickness that threatened his life. He did not return to England until nearly the end of July; and, during his absence, he does not seem to have a certain knowledge of the place of his wife's residence. We know she had left the Foundery, and was still in London. Another fact is clear. In her possession were a number of letters written to Wesley by several Methodist women, which she had taken from the bureau in his study.

In 1775 and the following year there was a revival of the controversy between the Calvinists and the Methodists. It was carried on with regrettable sharpness, and it is not necessary to dwell upon it. There were incidents in its course, however, that demand attention as they throw light on the experiences of John Wesley at a critical stage of his history.

---

[1] See *Proceedings of the Wesley Historical Society*, ix., 181.
[2] Wesley's *Works*, xii., 131-32. Jackson's edition.

We have said that when his wife left the Foundery she took with her certain letters which had been written to him by women. What became of them? The problem has been studied; but we must look at it again.

It is undoubted that after she left her husband Mrs. Wesley came into close contact with the Calvinists of London. Tyerman says that on one occasion she read the letters taken from her husband's bureau to 'an elect party of Calvinists.' It was agreed that they should be sent to the *Morning Post* for publication. He declares that 'two masked assassins, who assumed the not inappropriate names of *Scorpion* and *Snapdragon*,' furiously assailed Wesley in the London newspaper, 'professing to ground their charges against him upon his own private papers, which the woman, who was legally his wife, had put into their hands.' As might be expected, Tyerman vigorously denounces Mrs. Wesley's action. After delivering his denunciation he adds these words: 'This is strong language, but the writer, knowing more than he chooses to make public, uses it with deliberate design.'[1]

In considering Tyerman's statement it is necessary to produce a footnote in Wesley's *Journal* which appears under the date December 11, 1775. Wesley then began a little journey into Kent. The editor of the *Journal*, in this note, says: 'On the eve of this journey into Kent an incident occurred which, not improbably, has been exaggerated. At all events, in the form it assumes in Tyerman's *Life of Wesley*, Vol. III. 233, it seems almost incredible. Briefly, it is alleged that Mrs. John Wesley stole some of her husband's letters, interpolated them, and handed them over to be published in the *Morning Post*. The persons directly responsible for the publication wore a mask named "Scorpion" and "Snapdragon." Needless to say, the use made of this discreditable proceeding was connected with the bitter theological controversy then raging between the Calvinists and Arminians.'[2] It will be seen that the competent editor of the latest edition of John Wesley's *Journal* thought that Tyerman's description of the incident was probably exaggerated, but he does not deny that some such incidents occurred at the time under consideration.

[1] See Tyerman's *Life of Wesley*, iii., 233.
[2] Wesley's *Journal*, vi., 89, note.

This difference of opinion concerning an important fact compels us to consult earlier records of the event. Comparing the statements of Tyerman and the note-writer in Wesley's *Journal*, we are in danger of rushing to the conclusion that the charge brought against Mrs. Wesley and her Calvinist companions was almost, if not quite, incredible. If we could get a correct estimate of the 'spirit of the times' in those distant days, we might get clear light on the subject we are considering. We will take up Thomas Jackson's *Life of Charles Wesley*, and try to increase our knowledge of the temper of some of the opponents of John Wesley. It must be remembered that Rowland Hill knew Mrs. Wesley and was aware of the existence of the letters she had purloined. It amazes us to know that he and Toplady described John Wesley 'as an object of abhorrence and detestation; as a man that was corrupt in mind and heart.' This absurd opinion suggests that they must have listened to some report concerning Wesley's conduct with women. Can we get light from Thomas Jackson? This is his explanation: 'Wesley's jealous wife was their oracle, and while she was attempting to persuade all who would listen to her that her husband was a bad man, Mr. Hill held her up to the public confidence as a person whose testimony was entitled to implicit credit. Whether she was always of a sound mind may be justly questioned. Repeatedly was she detected in the utterance of deliberate untruths, of her own invention, and in the distribution of forged and interpolated documents against her husband. Yet she found a patron in Mr. Hill. In one of the bitterest pamphlets that ever emanated from the press, he says, "I fear, by Mr. John's conduct, that he has been a stranger to true religion all his life-time: and while he behaves as he does to *the wife of his bosom*, with whom I have the honour of a personal acquaintance, I cannot be persuaded to alter my opinion."' As for Toplady, Jackson records an amazing incident. He tells us that when Toplady was on his death-bed he was informed that a report was being circulated that he had requested an interview with Wesley, and expressed regret for something he had written against him. When the report reached him he was indignant that any one should suppose he would make a concession to John Wesley. He managed to write a document which he called his *Dying Avowal,* in which he protested that he had nothing to retract with regard to the Arminian leader. He says: 'I most sincerely hope my last hours will be much better employed than in conversing with *such* a man.'[1]

There can be no doubt that the eighteenth century contained some 'good haters.' It is a relief to turn from them. Let us note a fact, recorded by Thomas Jackson, which will relieve the sombreness of our investigation. It is a mistake to suppose that the opinions of Hill and Toplady about Wesley were held by all the Calvinists in London. Lady Huntingdon knew him too well to join in the attacks of his assailants. She strongly opposed the Arminian articles of his creed, but she never lost her admiration for his Christian character. We are specially interested in Jackson's statement concerning Dr. Thomas Haweis, who was one of her chaplains. He was a strict Predestinarian. After Wesley's death he took the opportunity of avowing his prolonged friendship with him. He entered his protest against the reports which had been industriously propagated to his disadvantage. In his *History of the Church* he says: 'I hope never to be ashamed of the friendship of John Wesley. I need not speak of the exemplariness of his life. Too many eyes were upon him to admit of his halting: nor could his weight have been maintained a moment longer than the fullest conviction impressed his people, that he was an eminently favoured saint of God, and as distinguished for his holy walk as for his vast abilities, indefatigable labour, and singular usefulness.'[2]

Jackson's *Life of Charles Wesley* was published in 1841—over ninety years ago. We are not aware that his statements concerning the matter we are considering have been successfully challenged. But, in order to complete our investigation of a much disputed occurrence, we will produce the testimony of a witness who had exceptional opportunities of knowing the facts of the case at the time it occurred.

In Richard Watson's *Life of the Rev. John Wesley* there is a letter which Miss Sarah Wesley, the daughter of Charles Wesley, wrote to a friend a short time before her death. From this letter we quote the following paragraphs:

[1] Jackson's *Life of Charles Wesley,* ii., 279-80.
[2] *ibid,* ii., 281, for this quotation from Dr. Haweis's *History of the Church,* iii., 274-75.

MRS. JOHN WESLEY

I think it was in the year 1775 my uncle promised to take me with him to Canterbury and Dover. About this time Mrs. Wesley had obtained some letters which she used to the most injurious purposes, misinterpreting spiritual expressions and interpolating words. These she read to some Calvinists, and they were sent to *The Morning Post*. A Calvinist gentleman, who esteemed my father and uncle, came to the former, and told him that, for the sake of religion, the publication should be stopped, and Mr. John Wesley be allowed to answer for himself. As Mrs. Wesley had read, but did not show, the letters to him, he had some doubts of their authenticity; and though they were addressed to Mr. John Wesley, they might be forgeries; at any rate, he ought not to leave town at such a juncture, but clear the matter satisfactorily.

My dear father, to whom the reputation of my uncle was far dearer than his own, immediately saw the importance of refutation; and set off to the Foundery, to induce him to postpone his journey; while I, in my own mind, was lamenting such a disappointment, having anticipated it with all the impatience natural to my years. Never shall I forget the manner in which my father accosted my mother on his return home. 'My brother,' said he, 'is indeed an extraordinary man. I placed before him the importance of the character of a Minister; the evil consequences which might result from his indifference to it; the cause of religion; stumbling-blocks cast in the way of the weak; and urged him, by every relative and public motive, to answer for himself, and stop the publication.' His reply was, 'Brother, when I devoted to God my ease, my time, my life, did I except my reputation? No. Tell Sallie I will take her to Canterbury to-morrow.'

I ought to add that the letters in question were satisfactorily proved to be mutilated, and no scandal resulted from his trust in God.[1]

It will be seen that Miss Wesley thought that the events she records happened in 1775. It was evidently at the beginning of the serious attacks on John Wesley's character. From his *Journal* we know that he set out on a visit to Kent on December 11, 1775. The next day he preached at Canterbury, and the day after at Dover. On Saturday, December 16, he returned to London. *Journal*, v. 89.

It is clear that the controversy was continued in 1776. We have produced evidence of that fact. We were hoping to refer more fully to its appearance in newspapers, and especially in *The Morning Post*. Dr. Archibald W. Harrison, the author of that most interesting book *The Beginnings of Arminianism to the Synod of Dort*, has given us much assistance by searching the volumes in the British Museum which contain the English newspapers published in 1775 and 1776. Dr. Harrison could find nothing in *The Morning Post* that bears on our inquiry. He discovered another paper, however, entitled *The London Packet or New Lloyd's Evening Post*, in which he found letters relating to Wesley's conduct and character. He says: 'This paper seemed to come out about once a month, and was evidently well-disposed to Wesley.' In the number published in January, 1776, there was an article defending Wesley against Toplady's attack. In the next month's issue there was a letter 'To the Person who calls himself a Despiser of Hypocrites.' The 'Despiser' had published letters to Wesley written by 'a young lady who had been betrayed by a man.' In the February number of *The London Packet* Wesley's conduct is defended. His advocate denies that there was any-

[1] See *The Works of the Rev. Richard Watson*, v., 203-204.

thing improper in the correspondence. He regards it as 'a natural thing that the lady who had been wronged should confide in her spiritual adviser under such circumstances. We are much indebted to Dr. Harrison for his research work. He has spent much time in examining the newspapers issued in the critical years we have mentioned. We are especially interested in the fact that he has found nothing in *The Morning Post*, in 1775 and 1776, that shows that the paper joined in the attack on Wesley's moral character. That is an honour that rests on our oldest surviving English newspaper.

The attacks on John Wesley by a coterie of Calvinists continued for some months. But he went on with his work without wasting his time in self-defence. The wisdom of his course is evident. It will not be denied that he was 'the best-known man in England.' By this we mean that he was personally known to a larger number of people than any other man in the country. In towns and villages, in the huts of miners and shepherds, in 'lone houses' in the wilderness, his name was mentioned not only with respect but with strong affection. Crowds in the open air had seen him; congregations in not a few churches had seen him; he was a familiar figure in the ever increasing number of preaching houses; in his own Societies he was welcomed as a messenger sent by God to help them. There was no need for him to go about the country vindicating himself against attacks on his moral character. The people who knew him best were his strongest advocates. They held the charges against him in contempt. But as the years have gone by it has been necessary from time to time to speak some word in his defence. That must be our apology for once more stating the facts contained in this chapter.

VI
CITY ROAD CHAPEL

THE attacks on Wesley's character continued through the year 1776, but he ignored them altogether. The year was filled with important and successful work. On its closing day he made this entry in his *Journal*: 'We concluded the year with solemn praise to God for continuing His great work in our land. It has never been intermitted one year or one month since the year 1738, in which my brother and I began to preach that strange doctrine of salvation by faith.'[1] Briefly as possible we will record some of the events of that memorable year.

The American War finds a place among the first entries in the *Journal*. We have noted the fact that in several cities and important towns of England there was strong opposition to the attempt to coerce the Americans by force of arms. In Bristol the protest against the war was strong. Edmund Burke's views were shared by members of the Methodist Society in the city, and Wesley determined to leave London and bring his influence to bear on those who had been 'a little unsettled by the patriots.' On Tuesday, January 2, at night, he arrived in Bristol. He found that other work awaited him. In other volumes of this series we have mentioned some of the incidents in the tragic life of Westley Hall, who married and deserted one of John Wesley's sisters. The miserable story is relieved by the fact that Dr. Samuel Johnson proved himself Martha Hall's friend, and received her, for a time, into his home. When John Wesley arrived in Bristol he was told that Hall, who was then living in the city, was ill. He made up his mind to visit him in the morning, but he then found that he was dead. Wesley buried him. He expresses his trust that he died in peace, 'for God had given him deep repentance.' He adds: 'Such another

[1] *Journal*, vi., 135.

monument of divine mercy, considering how low he had fallen, and from what height of holiness, I have not seen, no, not in seventy years!'

John Wesley returned to London on Saturday, January 6. He was just in time to escape being detained in Bristol. On Sunday a severe frost set in, 'accompanied by so deep a snow as made every high road impassable.' It continued for several weeks.[1] On February 14, however, Wesley was able to make his way to Shoreham, where he was astonished at the progress of the Methodist Society. He says: 'Now is the last become first! No Society in the county grows so fast as this, either in grace or number. The chief instrument of this glorious work is Miss Perronet, a burning and a shining light.'

The time was approaching when Wesley was accustomed to visit the Societies in the West and North of England and in Scotland; but he was detained in London until the beginning of March. His delay in London is easily explained. The time had come when it was necessary to determine what should be done with the Foundery. The lease was running out. There was a rumour that it was the intention of the owners of the buildings to pull them down and to prepare the ground for the improvements that were required in the neighbourhood. It is clear Wesley, and the leading men at the Foundery, felt that it was expedient to secure another site. After much consultation a petition was sent to the City authorities asking for the lease of a piece of ground on which 'a new chapel' might be built. Knowing Wesley's preference for the use of the term 'preaching house,' we are somewhat surprised at the calmness with which he employs the word 'chapel' in his references to these proceedings. It is true that he constantly calls the building in West Street, London, 'The Chapel,' but he rarely applies the name to any other Methodist building, either in London or the country. There can be no doubt that, gradually, he was beginning to see that 'preaching house' was an insufficient description of the buildings that were being erected in several of the towns in the kingdom. They were being used not only for 'preaching,'

---

[1] In John Wesley's *Journal* there is a footnote which describes the effect of this memorable frost in the neighbourhood of London. See *Journal,* vi., 95.

but for the other parts of the worship of a Christian congregation. A new age was dawning and Wesley rather reluctantly faced that fact. We think we see evidence of the arrival of a new spirit in the record in his *Journal* on March 1, 1776. He says: 'As we cannot depend on having the Foundery long, we met to consult about building a new chapel. Our petition to the City for a piece of ground lies before their committee; but when we shall get any farther I know not, so I determined to begin my circuit as usual, but promised to return whenever I should receive notice that our petition was granted.' He did not return to London until Friday, July 19, then he received a full account of what had happened during his long absence.

After visiting his mother's grave in Bunhill Fields, John Wesley must have often looked across the narrow lane that led to the City. He would see fields that spread for a considerable distance, one of them well known as 'the Tenter Ground.'[1] It required courage to approach the City Council with the request that such a large piece of land should be granted to the Methodists for the erection of a chapel. But more than a chapel was contemplated. Dwelling-houses for Wesley and his preachers were required, as well as other buildings; and a part of the site was to be reserved as a burial ground. When we think of the petition to the Council we admire not only the daring but the wisdom of the men who made the attempt to secure for coming generations a site which is now known and honoured by a vast host of Methodists throughout the world. We think of the men who, during Wesley's long absence, bore the burden of a great responsibility, and completed the negotiations with the City authorities. When he returned he met them and found that affairs were so advanced as to warrant the opening of a subscription list. On August 2 he says in his *Journal*: 'We made our first subscription towards building a new chapel, and at this and the two following meetings above a thousand pounds were cheerfully subscribed.'[2]

Wesley's tour in the spring and summer of 1776 was full of interesting incidents. On March 6 he went from Bristol to Taunton. An octagon 'preaching house' had been built

[1] See 1777 map in G. J. Stevenson's *History of City Road Chapel*, p. 63.
[2] *Journal*, vi., 117-18.

in the town; in it at three o'clock, he conducted the opening service.[1] Returning to Bristol he stayed there until March 11, when he commenced his northern journey. We pause for a few moments at the entry in his *Journal* on March 27. It causes the past to shine out vividly. He had reached Wednesbury, that battle-field of the early days of his own and his brother's ministry. He preached once more to his 'old flock,' and was delighted to find that the ancient spirit was still among them. He must have thought of Francis Asbury, and may have got some news about him and the perils of his work in America. The next Sunday he was in Congleton, a town in which the Methodists had been strongly opposed by the clergyman. As we read the entry in his *Journal* we think of the past and recognize the change of spirit that was beginning to affect a large number of the laity of the Church of England. He says : 'The minister here, having much disobliged his parishioners, most of the gentry in the town came to the preaching, both in the afternoon and in the evening, and it was an acceptable time. I believe very few, rich or poor, came in vain.' On April 2 he was in Macclesfield. During his stay there he preached on 'The Green,' near Mr. Ryle's house. Mr. Ryle was his friend and host. He was an alderman and magistrate of the town. We find from a note in Wesley's *Journal* that he was the grandfather of the first Bishop of Liverpool.

Leaving Macclesfield Wesley climbed the mountains that rise between Cheshire and Derbyshire. He was on his way to New Mills. At that time it was a secluded little town hidden from the crowded highways of the world. Wesley's description of his visit to New Mills arrests us. We escape for a few moments from the noise, confusion, and antagonism of jarring sects. This is what he says : 'The people here are quite earnest and artless, there being no public worship in the town but at our chapel; so that they go straight forward, knowing nothing of various opinions and minding nothing but to be Bible Christians.' The influence of the quietude was so soothing that he forgets to call 'the chapel' 'a preaching house.' He also unconsciously coins a name that was afterwards adopted by a section of the Methodist people. The

[1] The old building still stands; but it has passed out of the possession of the Methodists.

note-writer in his *Journal* records a fact that brings the real Wesley into clear view. It appears that his host, Mr. Beard, had a daughter who was given to 'finery in dress.' Wesley listened to the charge, and then quietly said: 'For my part, I do not wish to see young people dress like their grandmothers.' In the absence of particulars it is impossible to express an opinion concerning Miss Beard's finery, but the skill and soundness of Wesley's remark is indisputable.

On Easter Sunday, April 7, Wesley preached to great congregations in Manchester. The 'preaching house,' at seven o'clock in the morning, contained the congregation 'pretty well,' but in the afternoon he was obliged to go into the open air. Thousands of people had flocked together. He took his stand in a convenient place, almost over against the infirmary, 'and exhorted a listening multitude to live unto Him who died for them and rose again.' Leaving Manchester he visited Chester, Liverpool, Wigan and Bolton. Then, on Tuesday, April 16, he went to Chowbent, 'once the roughest place in all the neighbourhood.' When he got there he tells us that there was not the least trace of the roughness remaining, 'such being the fruit of the genuine gospel.' In the afternoon it was raining heavily. Some one went to the vicar and asked him for the use of the church. He at once consented to the request. Wesley began reading prayers at half-past five o'clock. The church was crowded, 'pews, alleys, and galleries.' The great congregation listened attentively to the sermon, and 'God bore witness to His word.' On April 18 he was in Yorkshire, where he preached in several churches. Among them was the church at Haworth. He crossed the border into Lancashire and stood in the pulpit of the church at Colne. He must have been amazed at the change that had taken place in the town. The old days when George White, the vicar, stirred up and led the mob against him and his people had passed. A new spirit had been created in the churchmen of Colne.[1] He must have looked with wonder at the congregation that had assembled. He says: 'The church at Colne is, I think, at least twice as large as that at Haworth, but it would not in anywise contain the congregation. I preached on "I saw a great white throne

---

[1] For George White, see *John Wesley and the Advance of Methodism*, 100, 102-6, 116-21, 131. White died in 1751.

coming down from heaven." Deep attention sat on every face, and I trust God gave us His blessing.'

Making his way steadily towards the north, on May 18, Wesley arrived in Edinburgh. He stayed in Scotland nearly a month, and met with the usual hearty reception from the Presbyterian ministers and people. At Banff, on Saturday, May 21, he had a new experience. Arrangements had been made for his preaching in the morning in the Assembly Room, but he received a message from the Episcopal clergyman offering him the use of his chapel. He gladly accepted the offer. The news spread, and the chapel was quickly filled. After reading prayers he preached. The entry in his *Journal* possesses a tone of satisfaction that gives it exceptional value. So far as we know this was the first time he had preached in an Episcopal church in Scotland. He often attended the services in those churches during his visits to the north, but this was a new departure. The next day we see him, in the afternoon, in the English chapel in Aberdeen. His record in the *Journal* emphasizes a fact which much impressed him. He says: 'I was again delighted with the exquisite decency both of the minister and the whole congregation. The Methodist congregations come the nearest to this; but even these do not come up to it.' The following Sunday he was in Dundee, and preached to a great congregation. He was delighted with the devoutness of his hearers. This is his record: 'The people of Dundee, in general, behave better at public worship than any in the kingdom, except the Methodists and those at the Episcopal chapels. In all other kirks the bulk of the people are bustling to and fro before the minister has ended his prayer. In Dundee all are quiet, and none stir at all till he has pronounced the blessing.'

Wesley's expressions of satisfaction with the conduct of quiet and reverent congregations seem strange when we think of him as one of the greatest preachers to restless and dangerous mobs that this country has known. From the outset to the close of his career he was an open-air preacher. As the Methodist chapels increased in size and number he often had to exhort his preachers to go out to the crowd. His most powerful appeal to them was his own example. There can be no doubt, however, that his field-preaching was done under the compulsion of conscience. He was driven out to it by a voice he was compelled to obey. We have often paused over a statement he made in 1746. It enables us to look into the deeps of his heart. He says: 'To this day I have abundantly more temptation to luke-warmness than to impetuosity; to be a saunterer *inter sylvas Academicas,* a philosophical sluggard, than an itinerant preacher. And, in fact, what I now do is so exceeding little, compared with what I am convinced I ought to do, that I am often ashamed before God and know not how to lift up mine eyes to the height of heaven.' This was not the sigh of a tired man; it was a revelation of character. Thirteen years after, in 1759, this was the statement he made in his *Journal* : ' What marvel the devil does not love field-preaching! Neither do I. I love a commodious room, a soft cushion, a handsome pulpit. But where is my zeal, if I do not trample all these underfoot in order to save one more soul.'[1] The convictions of Wesley are revealed in these extracts. He delighted in reverent services conducted in chapels; but the stern voice of conscience compelled him to seek and to save the restless crowds of people who were outside all the churches.

John Wesley remained in Scotland until nearly the end of May. On June 1 he arrived in Newcastle. From that centre he visited the Societies in neighbouring towns. Then he began to make his way slowly towards London. Events were happening there which demanded his presence, but it was imperative that he should visit several of the northern towns. In his *Journal* we have brief descriptions of these visits. They brought inspiration not only to preachers and people but also to himself. He saw the wonderful progress that Methodism was making in the country; they deepened his conviction that the Societies would remain after he had passed away. As we follow him we often pause in the presence of events which reveal the onward march of Methodism; but we must, at this stage, content ourselves by describing two incidents that cast light on his earlier days and the years that were yet to come.

On June 19 Wesley preached at Osmotherley. In *John Wesley and the Advance of Methodism,*[2] we have described his first visit to the town. He went there in April, 1745, at the invitation of a man who was then known as Thomas Adams. There has been much discussion concerning him,

[1] *Journal,* iv., 325.   [2] See pp. 18-20.

especially on the question of his relation to the Roman Catholic Church. The experts of the Wesley Historical Society have considered this question. We think that Mr. Brigden's opinion may be safely accepted. He says: 'Probably our conclusion will be that Thomas Adams was at one time a priest, that he renounced Romanism; that he married; that he was *not* a priest when Wesley made his acquaintance; that Wesley never called him a priest; that a few nineteenth-century writers did so, and followed a local opinion.'[1] It must be remembered that even if Adams was a priest at the time he invited Wesley to visit Osmotherley that would not have caused him to decline the invitation. The town was known as 'the centre of the Papists in Yorkshire.' That fact would have quickened his desire to go there. He was a strong Protestant, but the strength of his convictions did not blind him to the excellence of people who differed from him in creed and opinion. He was aware of his popularity among large numbers of the Romanists in Ireland, and he would have gladly accepted the invitation to accompany Adams to Osmotherley.

When Wesley visited Osmotherley on June 19, 1776, he made this entry in his *Journal*: 'I preached to my old, loving congregation, and visited once more poor Mr. Watson, just quivering over the grave.' At first we are inclined to ask, 'Who was Mr. Watson?' But, turning to the entry in the *Journal* on May 8, 1777, we find this record: 'About eleven I preached at Osmotherley. I found my old friend Mr. Watson, who first brought me into this country, was just dead, after living a recluse life near fifty years. From one that attended him I learned that the sting of death was gone, and he calmly delivered up his soul to God.' We do not know why Thomas Adams changed his surname, but the words 'who first brought me into this country' enable us to identify him.

If the mention of Thomas Adams casts light on the past another name in Wesley's *Journal* brightens the future. On Tuesday, July 9, he was in Lincolnshire. He preached at Brigg in the morning, and then went to Horncastle and Spilsby with Robert Carr Brackenbury. So far as we know this was the time of their first meeting. Brackenbury's name

[1] *Wesley Historical Society Proceedings*, vii. 28-31; xi., 164-5.

shines in the annals of early Methodism. He was the eldest son of Mr. Carr Brackenbury of Panton House, Lincolnshire. Those who know his history are aware that Robert Carr Brackenbury was a county magistrate and a large landowner. Wesley's description of him, on the occasion of their first meeting, is exceptionally interesting. He says, 'While he was at Cambridge he was convinced of sin, though not by any outward means, and soon after justified. Coming to Hull, he met with one of our preachers. By long and close conversation with him, he was clearly convinced it was his duty to join with the people called Methodists. At first, indeed, he staggered at lay preachers, but after weighing the matter deeply, he began preaching himself, and found a very remarkable blessing, both on his own soul and on his labours.' We shall meet him again, and shall then understand why his name is reverenced, not only in Lincolnshire but in the Channel Islands, in Dorset, and in all places where he worked as a Methodist evangelist.

On July 18 Wesley, after preaching at Nottingham, set out in his chaise for London. The next evening he met the committee that was charged with the business of erecting the new chapel in London. The committee had borne a heavy burden of responsibility during Wesley's long absence in the country, which had lasted for nearly five months. He had promised to come back whenever he received notice that the petition to the City for a piece of ground had been granted. The members of the committee had not interrupted his work. When he returned they were able to report the satisfactory progress that had been made.

On Tuesday, August 6, the Conference met in London. At that time, according to Myles, there were one hundred and fifty-five travelling preachers in Great Britain and Ireland, and the responsibility of their oversight by the Conference was constantly increasing. In answer to the question 'Are there any objections to any of our preachers?' the following entry appears in the *Minutes*: 'Yes. It is objected that some are utterly unqualified for the work; and that others do it negligently, as if they imagined they had nothing to do, but to preach once or twice a day. In order to silence this objection for ever, which has been repeated ten times over, the preachers were examined at large, especially those concerning whom there was the least doubt. The result was, that one was excluded for insufficiency, two for misbehaviour. And we were thoroughly satisfied that all the rest had both grace and gifts for the work wherein they were engaged.' In making this record Wesley expresses a hope that he would hear 'this objection no more.' It is difficult to determine the exact meaning of his words. It must be remembered that the custom of examining objections to preachers became part of the business of the Conference in 1768. Since then it has been continued to the present day.

The list of 'stations,' and of 'the numbers of members in the Society' attract the special attention of those who are acquainted with the condition of national affairs in 1776. We look in vain for the appointment of the preachers in America. We shall not meet with them again until we reach the Conference of 1784. The number of members in Society is stated to be 39,826. America appears in this list; the number of members being 3,148. Turning to the *Minutes* of 1775, we find that the same number was then returned. Those who are acquainted with the extraordinary progress of Methodism in America during the period 1775-6, will see that the communication between the two countries had been interrupted by the fierce outbreak of the long-continued war. Later we shall have to show the effect of that struggle on the Methodism of America. It will be sufficient, at this point, to say that on July 4, 1776, at a Congress held in America, allegiance to George III had been renounced, loyalty to the Crown had been made a crime, and praying for the King in the congregation had been forbidden under penalty.[1]

In glancing over the further proceedings of the Conference of 1776 we see that Ireland was becoming one of Wesley's difficulties. An objection was raised there to the raising of contributions to the Yearly Expenses Fund. Bandon had raised thirty-five shillings and that was the whole of the money received for the Fund from Ireland. It was one symptom of an approaching disturbance which was soon to arrive. We find a suggestion of it in the following question and answer:

Q. 'Is there anything else in Ireland which we complain of?'

---

[1] See valuable note in Wesley's *Journal*. vi., 118-19.

A. There is. Part of the Leaders meet together on Sunday evening, without any connexion with, or dependence on, the Assistant. We have no such custom in the three kingdoms. It is overturning our discipline from the foundations. Either let them act under the direction of the Assistant, or let them meet no more. It is true, they can contribute money for the poor, but we dare not sell our discipline for money.

It will be seen that the difficulty arose from the action of 'a part of the Leaders.' Care must be taken to avoid a rash judgement on the men who took no part in these irregular meetings. Reading the *Minutes* of the Conference held in 1776 we note a significant omission. We have grown accustomed to the signing of the agreement by which the Preachers 'promised to adhere to each other, and to the old Methodist Doctrine and Discipline.' That 'Agreement' is not contained in the *Minutes* of 1776, nor does it appear again during the life-time of John Wesley. We would suggest that the contemplated erection of the City Road Chapel, and the consciousness of the need of stricter discipline, may have influenced Wesley and made him see that a stronger method of dealing with men who caused divisions, and declined 'to adhere to the old Methodist Doctrine and Discipline,' was needed. The plan, that was abandoned in 1776, did not touch the men who did not sign the 'Agreement.' He seems to have had trouble with some of them. So he waited patiently for the discovery of a more excellent way of dealing with them.

Leaving London Wesley arrived in Bristol on August 12. He met Fletcher there, who was worn down with heavy work. He had spent much time and strength in defending Wesley against the men who upheld the extreme form of Calvinist doctrine. His intervention in the fierce controversy had been of great service to Wesley. It had set him free to carry on his evangelizing work. Thereby Fletcher rendered a great service to the cause of Methodism at that time and in the future. Wesley was commencing his journey to Cornwall. Seeing that Fletcher was 'a little better' he suggested that his friend should accompany him; but Fletcher's physician would 'in no wise consent,' so he set out alone. It was a time when Wesley was losing some of his old friends. Charles Perronet, who had been with him in Georgia, died during this month.

We do not know the exact date of his death, but Wesley had visited him when he was in the north of England, and would not be surprised when the news reached him. He had great self-command, but he must have felt conscious of the fact that his little group of old friends was diminishing and would soon disappear. On Tuesday, August 13, he preached in Taunton. He found that he was to be the guest of the Rev. James Brown, the vicar of Kingston, a village which lies about four miles from Taunton. He speaks of 'the large old parsonage-house' as being 'pleasantly situated close to the churchyard,' and just 'fit for a contemplative man.' There is a wistfulness in the description that those who know him best will detect. Entering the house he found that Mr. Brown was not alone. Another clergyman was with him. He was the curate of the church at South Petherton. He had come from that distant place to see Wesley. They had not met before. We are attracted by this entry in Wesley's *Journal*: 'Here I found a clergyman, Dr. Coke, late Gentleman Commoner of Jesus College in Oxford, who came twenty miles on purpose. I had much conversation with him, and a union then began which I trust shall never end.'

Dr. Thomas Coke occupies such a prominent position in the history of Methodism that we must try to see him as he was at the time when Wesley met him at Kingston. The most reliable accounts of his early history are to be found in Henry Moore's *Life of John Wesley*, and in Dr. Etheridge's *Life of the Rev. Thomas Coke, LL.D*. We will take the latter book as our guide. It not only uses facts contained in Moore's second volume, but it adds much to our knowledge of the history of Coke during the years before Wesley met him in the Kingston parsonage.

Thomas Coke was born on October 9, 1747, at Brecon, in Wales. He was the son of Bartholomew Coke, an apothecary. His father's epitaph in the Priory Church at Brecon records the fact that 'he filled the office of chief magistrate of the borough several times, with universal approbation.' He was highly respected in the town, and was so successful in business that he retired with a fortune. When Thomas Coke was sixteen years of age his father took him to Oxford, where he was entered as a gentleman-commoner of Jesus College. Those who are aware of the moral condition of Oxford at that time will not wonder at the fact that Coke was not able to resist some of the temptations that assailed him. It is also certain that his religious faith was shaken; but it is clear that it was not destroyed. He took his Bachelor's degree on February 4, 1768, and then returned to Brecon. He was popular in the town and became a magistrate. But he had made up his mind to enter into holy orders, and during the three years he remained in Brecon he retained his purpose.

On June 10, 1770, Coke was ordained a deacon at Oxford; on August 23, 1772, he was ordained priest in the chapel of St. John within the palace of Abergwilly in the diocese of St. David's. It would seem that it was at this time of ordination, as priest, that there came upon him a strong conviction of his unfitness for the work of the ministry. That conviction deepened. After serving as a curate at Road in Somerset he went to South Petherton, and it was there that light came to him that led him into the experience of conscious salvation. The account of his 'conversion' is intensely interesting. The readers of *John Wesley and the Methodist Societies* will be familiar with the name of Thomas Maxfield, the first Methodist lay-preacher. In *John Wesley the Master Builder* an account of his separation from the Methodist Society is given. He had been ordained by the Bishop of Londonderry, but after leaving the Methodists he became the minister of a Dissenting congregation. At the point we have reached in the life-history of Dr. Coke, Thomas Maxfield comes into view. He was spending some time in the neighbourhood of South Petherton. Hearing that a great change had taken place in the character of Dr. Coke's preaching, Maxfield sought an interview with him. Conversations between the two men became frequent, and it became evident to Maxfield that Coke needed to be led into the experience of conversion. The light grew. He began to preach about 'salvation by faith.' He preached the doctrine not only in the church but in cottage-services which, with great zeal, he conducted among the villages in his parish. Then came the breaking of the day. One evening, while proceeding to a cottage-service, he was brooding over the great subject which Maxfield had explained to him. He paused in his walk. In the quiet country road he earnestly prayed that he might be assured of the pardon of his sins. Then he went to the cottage, held his service, proclaimed the doctrine of salvation by faith, and that very evening his wayside prayer was answered. The story is touched with unfading light. It is the story of an experience that has been repeated in innumerable instances. It possesses special beauty in the eyes of those who have been village preachers. It makes us think of the two men who, in the long years ago, walked sadly along a country road. Their sadness was turned into joy when the Stranger who had joined them in their journey and whom they had not clearly recognized, was made known to them in a quiet village room.

The great change which Coke experienced altered the whole character of his preaching. Not only so, his conversion led him to associate himself with men who knew John Wesley. Among them was Mr. Brown, of Kingston, who lent him books which cleared his mind concerning theological difficulties which had perplexed him. Among them were Wesley's *Journal* and *Sermons* and Fletcher's *Checks to Antinomianism*. He welcomed Mr. Brown's offer to introduce him to Wesley when he visited Taunton. As we have seen, they met on August 13, 1776. On the next morning Wesley walked in the garden with Dr. Coke. Etheridge says that Coke recounted to him the exercises of mind through which he had passed, and told him of his strong conviction that he ought to enter on a wider sphere of labour. Wesley seems to have thought, at the moment, that his resolves would be all the stronger and purer for a little longer trial in the ordinary duties of his parish. He advised him to go on as usual in his parochial services, ' doing all the good he could, visiting from house to house, omitting no part of his clerical duty, and avoiding every reasonable ground of offence.' Dr. Etheridge, in reporting Wesley's counsel says: ' In all which we listen to the dictates of the sober-minded wisdom, the Christian sagacity, by which, through the grace given to him, he was enabled, in such multitudes of cases, to suggest the right counsel at the right time.' In the following year circumstances had changed, and other advice was given. Coke was driven out of South Petherton. Under the date Tuesday, August 19, 1777, we find this entry in Wesley's *Journal*: 'I went forward to Taunton with Dr. Coke, who, being dismissed from his curacy, has bid adieu to his honourable name and determined to cast in his lot with us.'[1]

Leaving Somerset Wesley made his way to Cornwall. From the entries in his *Journal* it is clear that the former opposition to the Methodist preachers in Cornwall had ceased. On August 20 he preached at Helston. He says that prejudice there was at an end, and that all the town, except a few gentry ' willingly hear the word of salvation.' The next day he was in Penzance. He took his stand in a gentleman's balcony which commanded the market place. There was ' a huge congregation.' He preached from the text, ' Without holiness no man shall see the Lord.' The effect of his sermon was profound. He says : ' The word fell heavy upon high and low, rich and poor. Such an opportunity I never had at Penzance before.' The following day he preached in the market-place at St. Just. He tells us that two or three well-dressed people walked by, stopped a little, and then went on. Then they returned two or three times. But they were ashamed to be seen standing in the crowd, so withdrew. But the rest remained. From these incidents it is clear that the old days of persecution in Cornwall had ended.

Leaving Cornwall Wesley slowly made his way to London. His *Journal* fails us during the latter part of September, and through the whole of October, but we know that it was towards the end of the latter month that he returned to London with John Fletcher. On November 13 the two friends set out for Norwich. They returned to London on November 23, and Wesley was soon busy with the important business connected with the erection of the New Chapel. In his *Journal* there is an important *note* that throws light on the difficulties that confronted him and those who were associated with him in the great enterprise.[2] It is no wonder that they came to the conclusion that some of the members and friends of the Methodist Societies, outside London, should be asked to join in the attempt to meet the expense of building the chapel.[3] We note the emergence of the ' connexional principle ' that has so

---

[1] Dr. Etheridge's *Life of Dr. Thomas Coke* should be consulted for a fuller account of his experiences up to the time of his close association with John Wesley. See Chapters i.-vi.
[2] *Journal*, vi., 133.
[3] The 1776 *Minutes* (Ques. xx) give *two* Chapels ' to be built this year '— London and Colne, and sanctions connexional appeal for London. See Stevenson's *History*, 64.

often proved its value in the history of Methodism. We will close our account of this crowded year by reproducing the letter that was written by Wesley on October 18, and afterwards sent to people who were supposed to be able to assist in a courageous enterprise.

To the Members and Friends of the Methodist Societies.
(*Circular.*)

My Dear Brother,

The Society at London have given assistance to their brethren in various parts of England. They have done this for upwards of thirty years; they have done it cheerfully and liberally. The first year of the subscription for the general debt they subscribed above nine hundred pounds; the next, above three hundred; and not much less, every one of the ensuing years.

They now stand in need of assistance themselves. They are under a necessity of building; as the Foundery, with all the adjoining houses, is shortly to be pulled down: And the City of London has granted ground to build on; but on condition of covering it, and with large houses in front; which together with the New Chapel, will, at a very moderate computation. cost upwards of six thousand pounds. I must therefore beg the assistance of all the brethren. Now help the parent Society, which has helped others for so many years, so willingly and so largely. Now help me, who account this as a kindness done to myself; perhaps the last of this sort which I shall ask of you. Subscribe what you conveniently can, to be paid either now, or at Christmas, or at Lady-day, next.

I am,
Your affectionate brother.

The Trustees are—John Duplex, Charles Greenwood, Richard Kemp, Samuel Chancellor, Charles Wheeler, William Cowland, John Folgham.[1]

---

[1] See Wesley's *Works*, xii., 450, 1830 edition.

VII
BRISTOL AND THE WAR WITH AMERICA

THE winter of 1776-7 was severe in London. The Thames, in some places, was frozen; in many parts of London there was great suffering among the poor. Staying in London during the whole of January, 1777, Wesley devoted much of his time to the visitation of the members of his Society. We find him, again and again, in the presence of poverty-stricken and starving people. In his *Journal*, on January 15, he says: 'I began visiting those of our Society who lived in Bethnal Green hamlet. Many of them I found in such poverty as few can conceive without seeing it. Oh, why do not all the rich that fear God constantly visit the poor? Can they spend part of their spare time better? Certainly not. So they will find in that day when " every man shall receive his own reward according to his own labour." Such a scene I saw the next day in visiting another part of the Society. I have not found any such distress, no, not in the prison of Newgate. One poor man was just creeping out of his sick-bed to his ragged wife and three little children, who were more than half-naked, and the very picture of famine; when, one bringing in a loaf of bread, they all ran, seized upon it, and tore it in pieces in an instant. Who would not rejoice that there is another world?' From the days of the 'Holy Club' in Oxford to the end of his life Wesley was the compassionate friend of the poor.

Glancing over the entries in Wesley's *Journal* in January, 1777, we are reminded of another fact. We have had to record many instances of the fierce opposition of clergymen and members of the Church of England to him and his work. That opposition had been gradually lessening in town and country, but, at the period we have reached the movement in the right direction was quickened. Confining our attention at this point to London, we are arrested by this entry in Wesley's *Journal* on Sunday, January 26: 'I preached again at Allhallows Church, morning and afternoon. I found great liberty of spirit; and the congregation seemed to be much affected. How is this? Do I yet please men? Is the offence of the Cross ceased? It seems, after being scandalous near fifty years, I am at length growing into an honourable man!'

Wesley appreciated this interval of pastoral work in London. In addition to preaching and visiting the members of his Society he spent an hour every morning with the preachers. He says: 'We endeavoured not only to increase each other's knowledge, but to provoke one another to love and to good works.' These meetings reminded him of early days at Oxford. They revived his recollection of the hours spent with his pupils in his room in Lincoln College, hours which retained their brightness to the end of his life. But he soon had to awake to 'the living present.' Letters arrived from America. The writers informed him that all the Methodists there were 'firm for the Government,' and, on that account, were 'persecuted by the rebels, only not to the death.' As for the preachers, 'they were still threatened but not stopped.' Then came a gleam of light. He was assured that 'the work of God was increasing much in Maryland and Virginia.' These letters arrived at a time when America was giving him grave concern. He had received news from Bristol which revealed the fact that there was a sharp division of opinion in the city on the question of the war, and that the discussions that were taking place were affecting some of the members of the Methodist Society. So, on Monday, February 3, he left London and went to Bristol 'in the diligence.'

When Wesley arrived in Bristol he found that the city was in a state bordering on panic. Latimer in his *Annals of Bristol in the Eighteenth Century*, has described the events which had recently occurred.[1] Some weeks before Wesley's visit a number of incendiary fires had broken out in the city. Their origin perplexed the authorities. Wesley says that they caused 'general consternation.' Unfortunately, they aroused suspicion that they had a political origin. Failing to detect the criminal, the supporters and opponents of the war in America exchanged a fire of accusations. As a matter of fact, the culprit was a young man who also carried on his destructive

[1] See pp. 426-29.

work in other towns. At last he was detected in Portsmouth. He was tried at the Hampshire Assizes, found guilty, and condemned to death. In his confession he stated that the Bristol fires were devised solely by himself, and that he had made several other attempts in the city, but had been thwarted by the vigilance of the patrols. He was hanged at Portsmouth, as Latimer informs us, on a gallows sixty-seven feet high.

When Wesley reached Bristol he found that the news he had received about the controversy concerning the war in America was correct. The day after his arrival he preached in the New Room in the Horsefair, and strongly enforced the words: 'Put them in mind to be subject to principalities and powers, to speak evil of no man.' He thought that his exhortation convinced many 'that they had been out of their way.' The next evening he preached again to a crowded audience. Then, on Thursday, February 6, he spent the day in his study, and wrote a pamphlet entitled, *A Calm Address to the Inhabitants of England*. The attitude of Wesley towards the American War has been often discussed. There can be no doubt that it gradually changed. Its first stage is shown in a letter we have reproduced in a previous chapter. It was a duplicate letter, sent to Lord North and also to Lord Dartmouth on June 15, 1775.[1] In it Wesley's first position is clearly stated. He says: 'I do not intend to enter upon the question whether the Americans are in the right or in the wrong. Here all my prejudices are against the Americans, for I am a High Churchman, the son of a High Churchman, bred up from my childhood in the highest notions of passive obedience and non-resistance; and yet, in spite of my long-rooted prejudices, I cannot avoid thinking, if I think at all, these, an oppressed people, asked for nothing more than their legal rights, and that in the most modest and inoffensive manner that the nature of the thing would allow. But waving this, waving all considerations of right and wrong, I ask, Is it common sense to use force towards the Americans?' Wesley's description of his position at the first stage of the war must be remembered as we advance along the road he travelled.

It is not necessary to give a full description of the contents

[1] See pp. 56-9.

THE WAR WITH AMERICA

of Wesley's *Calm Address to the Inhabitants of England*. We are concerned only with the question of his change of attitude towards the war. It is well known that, as it went on, events occurred that caused him to stand out as one of the most powerful supporters of the policy of the King and the Government. One stage of his advance is indicated in the document we are considering. In it he says: 'About a year and a half ago, being exceedingly pained at what I saw or heard continually, I wrote a little tract entitled *A Calm Address to our American Colonies;* but the ports being then just shut up by the Americans, I could not send it abroad, as I designed. However, it was not lost; within a few months fifty, or perhaps an hundred thousand copies, in newspapers and otherwise, were dispersed throughout Great Britain and Ireland. The effect exceeded my most sanguine hopes. The eyes of many people were opened; they saw things in a quite different light. They perceived, and that with the utmost clearness, how they had been hoodwinked before. They found they had been led unawares into all the wilds of political enthusiasm, as far distant from truth and common sense as from the real love of their country.'[1]

Much had happened since Wesley wrote the 'Address' to the American Colonies. In the interval between 1775 and 1777, the course of the war had been marked by incidents that had made a deep impression on him and had caused his hesitation to cease. They had led him to take his stand on the side of his own country. He was well aware of the danger threatening some of his preachers who had declined to take the oaths which would have broken their allegiance to the King of England. The letters he had received in January strengthened his convictions concerning their peril. He must have noted the sentence in which it was said that the preachers were 'still threatened but not stopped.' The preachers who had been sent out by him from England were in exceptional danger. It is no wonder he determined that his own countrymen should know the facts concerning the condition of affairs in America. But there was another motive that urged him to action. He was in Bristol, a city in which some of the principal opponents of the war resided. Among them were Dissenting ministers, who, with great ability, attacked the

[1] Wesley's *Works*. xi., 129.

Government and denounced the war. Their influence was not confined to Bristol. It affected many people in the country. Remembering these facts we more clearly understand the reasons why he wrote his *Address to the Inhabitants of England.*

Wesley's 'Address' is a plain-spoken document; it answers to his own description of its contents. He aims at making known the real state of those affairs which had occasioned misunderstandings in England. He claims to have had means of information which many others did not possess. That claim he supports by saying: 'Over and above those accounts which have been published, I have had abundance of letters from persons in America, on whose judgement, veracity, and impartiality, I would safely depend; especially from the provinces of New York, Virginia, Maryland and Pennsylvania. I have likewise had the opportunity of conversing freely and largely with many that came from those provinces, and of comparing together the accounts of those who were attached to one or the other party. And I shall endeavour to deliver the plain facts, without speculations concerning them.' Wesley's 'Address' is still worth reading. It is a strong defence of the action of England. But we need not go over the old battle-field. It strongly impressed the Government. Soon after its publication we find Wesley in communication with Lord North, the Prime Minister of that day.

There is one section of the 'Address' which enables us to avoid a popular misconception. It is generally thought the desire for 'Independence' in America was created by the action of England, which followed the raid on the tea ships in Boston Harbour in December, 1773. Long before that time the longing for 'Independence' was in the hearts of the people of New England. That fact comes out clearly in John Wesley's 'Address.' He says: 'In the year 1737 my brother took ship, in order to return from Georgia to England. But a violent storm drove him up to New England, and he was for some time detained at Boston. Even then he was surprised to hear the most serious people, and men of consequence, almost continuously crying out, "We must be independent; we shall never be well till we shake off the English yoke." This sounded exceeding strange to him; as he could not form any imagination that they could be happier under any

Government than the mild one which they then enjoyed. A gentleman, who spent some time at Boston in the year 1739, informed me that he had frequently heard the very same conversation there, although at that time the people only spake what they had long and eagerly desired; but it seems, without any formed design, or having concerted any measures upon the head.'[1] Those who remember that New England was the home of the Pilgrim Fathers will be in no danger of supposing that the desire for 'independence' was created by the events that accompanied the attack on the tea ships. For many years before that event it was a 'fixed idea' in the minds of a great number of the American people. For several years before the outbreak of the Revolution events had occurred which brought the possibility of 'independence' into clearer view. One of them—the taking of Quebec in 1759—stands out with special prominence. It deserves John Richard Green's description of its importance. 'With the triumph of Wolfe on the heights of Abraham began the history of the United States. By removing an enemy whose dread had knit the colonists to the mother-country, and by breaking through the line with which France had barred them from the basin of the Mississippi, Pitt laid the foundation of the great republic of the west.'[2]

---

[1] Wesley's *Works*, xi., 130-31.
[2] *History of the English People*, iv., 193-4. Standard edition.

VIII
JOURNEYINGS OF 1777

ON Saturday, February 8, 1777, John Wesley left Bristol and returned to London, where an unpleasant task awaited him. He received a message from a clergyman, Dr. William Dodd, who had been arrested and was confined in the Wood Street Compter, who also strongly wished to see him. Thinking that the prisoner only wanted him 'to intercede for him with great men,' he judged that it would be lost labour if he went to see him, so he did not go to Wood Street. In 1767 he had been attacked by Dr. Dodd, who was then the editor of *The Christian Magazine*, and had replied to him in a letter which appeared in *Lloyds Evening Post*. This was not the first attack. In the opening paragraph of his letter he says: 'Many times the publisher of *The Christian Magazine* has attacked me without fear or wit, and hereby he has convinced his impartial readers of one thing at least—that (as the vulgar say) his fingers itch to be at me, that he has a passionate desire to measure swords with me. But I have other work upon my hands: I can employ the short remainder of my life to better purpose.'[1] The first message from Dr. Dodd having failed, he sent a second messenger, but Wesley still hesitated. Then a gentleman came to him and told him plainly that he would not leave the house without him. So he went to the Compter. On entering, the Keeper, who is described by Wesley as 'an extremely well-behaved man,' said to him: 'Sir, of all the prisoners that have been in this place I have not seen such a one as Dr. Dodd. I could trust him in any part of the house. Nay, he has gained the affection of even these wretches, my turnkeys.' Wesley's account of his interview with the prisoner moves our compassion. He says: 'When I came into his room, and sat down by his bedside (for he had then a fever) we were both of us silent for

[1] Wesley's *Journal*, v., 197-98.

some time, till he began, " Sir, I have long desired to see you, but I little thought our first interview would be in such a place as this." I replied, " Sir, I am persuaded God saw this was the best, if not the only, way of bringing you to Himself, and I trust it will have that happy effect." He said earnestly, " God grant it may! God grant it may! " We conversed about an hour, but I was agreeably disappointed. He spoke of nothing but his own soul, and appeared to regard nothing in comparison of it, so that I went away far better satisfied than I came. A few days after I saw him again, the day before he was removed to Newgate, in order to his trial, which was to be the day following. I then stayed but about half an hour. I found him in the same temper as before, affected as one in such circumstances ought to be, but withal, calm and composed. I asked, " Sir, do you not find it difficult to preserve your recollection amidst all these lawyers and witnesses? " He answered, " It is difficult, but I have one sure hold—' Lord, not as I will, but as Thou wilt.' " '

In Thomas Jackson's *Life of the Rev. Charles Wesley* particulars are given of the public life of Dr. Dodd which show the valuable work he had done and the high position he occupied in the esteem of many religious people. Jackson answers a question which will occur to those who watch him in the prison. ' He took a very active part in the erection of the Magdalen Hospital, for which he acquired a just popularity, and his ministry attracted many hearers. Vanity, accompanied by a lavish expenditure, was his ruin. Being pressed with pecuniary difficulties, he committed an act of forgery upon the Earl of Chesterfield, who had formerly been his pupil, for which he was condemned to be hanged, and all attempts to obtain for him even a commutation of punishment were unavailing.'[1] In these attempts Charles Wesley and other Methodists joined, and the execution was delayed. But on Friday, June 27, it was carried out, to the sorrow of many people.

Sunday, March 2, was a warm, sunshiny day in London. It called John Wesley into the open air. In the evening he preached to an immense crowd in Moorfields. A great silence rested on the multitude. He says : ' All were as still as night.' He thought of the disorder of other days, and in

[1] *Life of Charles Wesley,* ii., 309.

his *Journal* he expressed an opinion that the times of violence and rioting and scoffing at field-preachers were ended. So far as he was personally concerned there was ground for this opinion, but it must have surprised his lay preachers who, for many succeeding years, had to endure the assaults of rabbling mobs.

At this period Wesley found it was necessary to give special attention to London. The ground was being prepared for the building of the new chapel; the day for laying the foundation-stone was drawing near. But he judged that the condition of affairs in Bristol demanded his presence in that city. So we find him making his way there in the middle of March. We note that on Sunday, March 16, he preached in St. Werburgh's Church. The old church had been repaired and considerably altered. Latimer says that the most important alteration was the removal of the last end of the chancel, which projected so far into Small Street as to render carriage traffic dangerous. The church had been re-opened in February, 1761. From Wesley's entry in his *Journal* we judge that the accommodation in it for the congregation had been diminished. In reading that entry we have sometimes paused and tried to understand its meaning. He says: 'I preached at St. Werburgh's, the first church I ever preached in at Bristol. I had desired my friends not to come thither, but to leave room for strangers. By this means the church was well filled, but not over-much crowded, which gives occasion to them that seek occasion, as it is a real inconvenience to the parishioners.' It is so unusual for present-day preachers to ask people not to come to church that this incident excites our wonder. We think, however, that Latimer has once more come to our help and shed light on Wesley's request.[1]

During this visit to Bristol Wesley went to Bath and preached in the chapel in Avon Street. He says: 'I often wonder at this: our chapel stands in the midst of all the sinners, and yet, going or coming to it, I never heard an immodest word, but prayers and blessings in abundance.'[2] On Sunday, March 23, he preached at St. Ewen's Church in

[1] As to Wesley's statement concerning 'the first time' he preached in St. Werburgh's, see the note in his *Journal*, vi., 141.
[2] We note the fact that he calls the preaching-house a chapel. The change of description was becoming marked about this period.

Bristol. Again we have an interesting entry in his *Journal*. He tells us that he avoided the subject of Justification by Faith, as he had found that it was 'an unprofitable subject to an unawakened congregation.' He explained and applied this text: 'It is appointed unto men once to die,' a subject which has often preceded the cry, 'What must I do to be saved.'

Wesley's visit to Bristol was brief. He felt it necessary for him to return to London. The building of the new chapel demanded his presence. He arrived there on March 27. The next day he received 'an affectionate message from a great man.' Much mystery conceals the name of the sender of this message, but the guess of the note-writer in Wesley's *Journal* is probably correct. He attributes the message either to Lord Dartmouth or to Lord North. We know nothing about Wesley's reply to the 'affectionate message.' His comment in the *Journal* is capable of two meanings. He says: 'But I shall not wonder if the wind changes.' Some may think that he was referring to a change in the 'affectionate' tone; but we are inclined to accept another explanation. Up to that time the wind of public opinion had blown steadily, and often furiously, against Wesley and the Methodists. But there were signs that a change was coming. The progress of Methodism among the masses and the middle-classes was evident, and the message from the 'great man' showed that in the 'upper circles' of society some were beginning to understand the value of its mission. That discovery had been made by the King who, to the end of his reign, was an ardent admirer of the work of the Wesleys and Whitefield. It is no wonder that some of the members of the Government were beginning to perceive that it was a regenerating force in the nation.

Instead of watching for 'a change of wind' Wesley went on with his work. His mind was full of the business relating to the erection of the new chapel in London. He was aware of the serious financial difficulties that threatened the scheme. His thoughts often turned to the subject of their removal. We have noted the fact that he had sent out circulars in which he and the trustees of the new chapel had asked the Methodists in other parts of the country to come to the aid of 'the mother church' in London, but the time for laying the foundation-stone of the building was quickly approaching. On April 21 the ceremony was to take place. Thinking over the matter he determined to leave London and to visit the Societies in the north in order to evoke their practical sympathy with the scheme. On April 6 he set out on a journey that lasted for nearly a fortnight. In his *Journal* we find constant entries concerning his preaching during this tour, but he does not give us any information about the result of his appeals for money. His silence on the subject enables us to fix our attention on some events that give distinction to his journeys.

We are especially interested in Wesley's description of his visit to Macclesfield. In a former chapter we have seen him there, walking in the Mayor's procession on its way to the ' Old Church,' which was then the only church in Macclesfield. That was on Easter Day in 1774. His companions were two curates. In a book recently published, written by the Rev. Alfred Leedes Hunt, a clergyman of the Church of England, we get light on an interesting incident of that far-off day. One of the curates had conceived a strong prejudice against Wesley, but, as they walked along, they began to talk to each other. A conversation with Wesley was often fatal to prejudice. In this case the inevitable result happened. The curate listened, looked up brightly at his companion, and from that hour became his life-long friend. The curate's name was David Simpson. The name is familiar to many of us, but it shines out still more clearly by reason of the publication of Mr. Hunt's volume.[1] After 1774 the years went on their way and brought great changes in the religious life of Macclesfield. Simpson became a powerful and attractive evangelical preacher. He was no longer a Calvinist. He rejoiced in the freedom that comes to a man who knows that God wills all men to be saved. We can judge the temper of the times in which he lived when we say that his preaching excited intense hostility in some of the members of the congregation worshipping in the ' Old Church.' They complained to the Bishop of Chester, who proceeded to make inquiry into the facts of the case. In a letter he wrote to the Bishop, Simpson frankly acknowledged

---

[1] *David Simpson and the Evangelical Revival*, by A. Leedes Hunt, M.A. Published by Thynne and Jarvis, Ltd.

the truth of the charge of 'Methodism' which had been brought against him. He briefly explained the method of his preaching and its results.[1] The dispute continued. Mr. Hunt traces its course, and shows that it endangered the continuance of Simpson's ministry in St. Michael's Church. But, at this crisis, an event happened which is fully described in Mr. Hunt's volume. Mr. Roe built a church in the town, and Simpson was transferred to it. Set free from the assaults of the critics of the 'Old Church,' he continued his evangelical ministry in Christchurch, to the deep content of the congregation.

We have no wish to describe the bitterness of the controversy that led to the erection of Christchurch by Mr. Roe. Those who wish to trace its course and consequences should refer to Mr. Hunt's volume. It will be enough to quote Wesley's entry in his *Journal* on Wednesday, April 9, 1777. He tells us that, on that day, he left Congleton and went on to Macclesfield. Then he says: 'The new church here is far the most elegant that I have seen in the kingdom. Mr. Simpson read prayers, and I preached on the first verse of the second lesson, Heb. xi. And I believe many felt their want of the faith there spoken of. The next evening I preached on Heb. xii. 14: "Without holiness no man shall see the Lord." I was enabled to make a close application, chiefly to those that expected to be saved by faith. I hope none of them will hereafter dream of going to heaven by any faith which does not produce holiness.'

Leaving Macclesfield Wesley made his way to Liverpool, where he preached in the evening of Monday, April 14. In that city, as in Bristol, he found clear evidence of the American War. It is certain that there was no man in England who had a greater abhorrence of slavery than John Wesley. Root and branch he would have removed it from the face of the earth. He looked upon the harbour in Liverpool and found that many large ships were laid up; their occupation was gone. With withering scorn he says that they had been employed for many years 'in buying or stealing poor Africans, and selling them in America for slaves.' Then he continues: 'The men-butchers have now nothing to do at this laudable occupation. Since the American War broke

[1] See note in Wesley's *Journal*, vi., 142.

out there is no demand for human cattle. So the men of Africa, as well as Europe, may enjoy their native liberty.' John Wesley was in the front of the little band of men who at that time protested against English participation in the slave trade. His anger was stirred by the traffic in slaves that was carried on in Bristol and Liverpool. The evidences of that traffic were glaring. On the banks of the Bristol Avon there were rows of 'barracoons,' that is depôts for slaves, where negroes were confined until they were sold either in England or sent to America. Wesley often saw them.[1] At a later stage we shall see that he retained his abhorrence of the trade to the end of his life.

Wesley got back to London in time for the laying of the foundation-stone of the new chapel. Monday, April 21, was a day of heavy rain. In his *Journal* he says: 'The rain befriended us much by keeping away thousands who purposed to be there.' However, there were such multitudes present that when he had to lay the first stone he found it difficult to make his way through the crowd. He gives us light on a subject that has been much discussed—the date on which the stone was placed. When, after many years, it was uncovered, a plate of brass was found with an inscription giving the date of the stone-laying as April 1. It is indisputable that the correct date should have been April 21. It is possible that Wesley's original intention was to have the stone-laying ceremony on April 1. Then came the conviction that he ought to go north, and the ceremony was postponed.[2] Wesley, in his reference to the inscription on the stone, says: 'Probably this will be seen no more by any human eye, but will remain there till the earth and the works thereof are burned up.' He little thought of the work he would provide for the critics.

A few days after the stone-laying ceremony Wesley paid a short visit to the north of England. He returned to London on May 17, and three days later he met the committee for building the new chapel. That was the principal business which had induced him to return from the north. He was greatly encouraged by the progress that had been made. As

---

[1] The writer, who has known Bristol for more than seventy years, remembers those 'barracoons.' They still stood by the riverside in the days of his boyhood. Their old occupation was gone, but, in Wesley's time, the traffic flourished.
[2] See *Journal*, vi., 144, note.

the result of their consultation he and the committee were 'confidently persuaded that He who had incited us to begin would enable us to finish.' The committee being left once more to carry on the work, he returned to the north.

Wesley's visit to the north of England was marked by shadow and sunshine. He was much distressed by the serious illness of his friend, Miss Elizabeth Ritchie. He went to see her at Otley several times during his journeys. The last time it seemed that the final 'farewell' must be spoken. He turned away sorrowful. He little knew that the time would come when his faithful friend, Elizabeth Ritchie, would watch by his side when he answered the call of the angel to cross the river.

It is easy to see the sunshine that greeted Wesley during this visit to the north. At the end of May he reached Whitehaven, a town bright with the memories of former days. On May 30 he preached there in the evening. After the service he went on board a little vessel that was waiting for him. The next morning he landed at Douglas, in the Isle of Man. It was his first visit to the island, but it had been often in his thoughts. He found there the cheering results of the work that was commenced by John Crook, a man whose name we have previously mentioned. In a note in Wesley's *Journal*,[1] he comes out into the clear light. The writer says: 'In the year 1775 Mr. John Crook was sent as a "Gospel Missionary" to the Isle of Man from the Society in Liverpool. The son of a physician who was sole heir to Shaw Hall estate in Lancashire, he received a good education. His mother also was a lady of family and fortune. Extravagance wasted the family resources. The son, put to a laborious trade, enlisted in the army. In Limerick, the young soldier was drawn to the Methodist preaching, and was "arrested for Christ." A relative, accidentally finding him in Ireland, purchased his discharge. In Cork he had married an excellent wife. In Liverpool he was appointed class-leader, and so became the "Apostle of Methodism in the Isle of Man." As one of Wesley's preachers he travelled in Irish and English circuits, and was sent repeatedly to the Isle of Man.'[2] We

---

[1] vi., 150.
[2] See also *Proceedings of the Wesley Historical Society*, v., 80-4 and 255-6.

are indebted to a note-writer in Wesley's *Journal* for the information that Crook was not the first Methodist preacher to visit the Isle of Man. It appears that John Marlin, one of Wesley's well-known preachers, and a friend, embarked at Whitehaven for Liverpool in July, 1758. But the captain deceived them and carried them to the island. They stayed there a week. Marlin preached in a large barn on the second evening of his detention. When Sunday came the barn would not contain the people who flocked to hear him. He went into the open air and preached to the crowd. His sermons produced a great impression. The people sent to Whitehaven asking that another Methodist preacher should be sent to the island, but they had to wait until 1775 before their request was granted.[1]

During his visit Wesley ' entered into other men's labours.' He rejoiced in their success. He went in a chaise from Douglas to Castletown; at six o'clock he preached near the castle, as he believed, ' to all the inhabitants of the town.' On Sunday, June 1, he began the day by preaching in the Methodist ' room.' The people entreated him to stay ' if it were but an hour or two,' but he was forced to hasten away in order to be at Peel before the Church service began. Mr. Henry Corlett, the vicar of German, told him that he would gladly have asked him to preach, but the Bishop had forbidden him, and had also forbidden all his clergy to admit any Methodist preacher to the Lord's Supper. Wesley's comment on this prohibition is worth recording. He says : ' But is any clergyman obliged, either in law or conscience, to obey such a prohibition? By no means. The will even of the King does not bind any English subject, unless it be seconded by an express law. How much less the will of a bishop? " But did you not take an oath to obey him? " No, nor any clergyman in the three kingdoms. This is a mere vulgar error. Shame that it should prevail almost universally.' The Church service being over Wesley, as it rained, retired to a large malthouse. Most of the congregation followed, and listened eagerly to his sermon. As it was fair weather in the afternoon he preached in the churchyard to a large congregation. The next morning, at five o'clock, he held a service attended by the greater part of his churchyard congregation. He was

[1] Wesley's *Journal*, vi., 152.

much impressed by the reception he received at Peel. He says: 'A more loving, simple-hearted people than this I never saw. And no wonder, for they have but six Papists, and no Dissenters, in the island. It is supposed to contain near thirty thousand people, remarkably courteous and humane. Ever since smuggling was suppressed, they diligently cultivate their land; and they have a large herring fishery, so that the country improves daily.'

On Monday, June 2, Wesley preached at Douglas, and then went on board the vessel which carried him to Whitehaven. After spending more than a fortnight in Yorkshire and the Midlands, he got back to London on Saturday, June 21. Much work awaited him there. On Wednesday, June 25, he saw Dr. Dodd for the last time. He says: 'He was in exactly such a temper as I wished. He never at any time expressed the least murmuring or resentment at any one, but entirely and calmly gave himself up to the will of God. Such a prisoner I scarce ever saw before, much less such a condemned malefactor. I should think none could converse with him without acknowledging that God is with him.' The next day Wesley had a change of occupation. He read what he calls the truly wonderful performance of Mr. Rowland Hill. This was Hill's *Imposture Detected*. Following the example of the note-writer in Wesley's *Journal*, we may say that 'it is not necessary to repeat any of the scurrilities' contained in this pamphlet. We do not wonder that Wesley, after reading it, says in his *Journal*: 'I stood amazed! Compared to him, Mr. Toplady himself is a very civil, fair-spoken gentleman.' However, he took the trouble to answer Hill's attack, 'not rendering railing for railing, but speaking the truth in love.' It is a relief to find that this assault did not seem to affect his health. On Saturday, June 28, we find this re-assuring entry in his *Journal*: 'I have now completed my seventy-fourth year, and by the peculiar favour of God I find my health and strength, and all my faculties of body and mind, just the same as they were at four-and-twenty.'

Wesley's stay in London was short. He was soon at work again in the Midlands and in Wales. As we read his record for this month sentences shine out that are full of meaning. On July 2 he was at Oxford. He preached to 'a very serious congregation.' His comment on the service makes us linger:

'So all the seed sown here has not fallen either on stony or thorny ground.' On Tuesday evening, July 8, he was in Worcester. He preached there, and the rector of the parish was at the service. Wesley calls him 'a candid, sensible man.' His further comment is charming. It appears that the rector was much surprised at the character of the service, 'never having dreamed before that there was such a thing as common sense among the Methodists!' We read the rest of his entry in the *Journal* with the hope that it will speak again to the Methodists throughout this country. He says: 'The Society here, by patient continuance in well-doing, has quite overcome evil with good; even the beasts of the people are now tame, and open not their mouths against them. They profited much when the waves and storms went over them; may they profit as much by the calm!'

Wesley spent the rest of the month in Wales, he had a great reception and preached to large congregations. His visit to Pembroke attracts our special attention. He says that, in the evening of Saturday, July 19, he preached there to the most elegant congregation he had seen since he came into Wales. But some of them came in dancing and laughing, as into a theatre. Their mood was quickly changed. 'In a few minutes they were as serious as my subject—Death. I believe, if they do not take care, they will remember it—for a week.' The next day the congregation flocking to Daniel's was larger than the church could contain. After reading prayers he preached for an hour, an uncommon thing for him. His text was: 'Not everyone that saith unto Me Lord! Lord!' The sermon had an immediate effect. Many were cut to the heart, and at the Lord's Supper many were wounded and many healed. The next day, having been much pressed to preach at Jeffreston, a colliery village seven miles from Pembroke, he went there and began his service soon after seven o'clock. The preaching-house was soon filled, and all the space about the doors and windows. The people 'drank in every word.' He had finished his sermon when a 'gentleman,' violently pressing in, bade the people get home and mind their business. Wesley says: 'As he used some bad words, my driver spake to him. He fiercely said, "Do you think I need to be taught by a chaise-boy?" The lad replying, "Really, sir, I do think so," the conversation ended.'

On Monday, July 28, Wesley, after preaching at Newport, left Wales and went to Bristol, where the Conference was to be held on Tuesday, August 5. When we watched him, on June 27, writing his reply to Rowland Hill's attack we wondered why he was defending himself instead of handing over that work to John Fletcher. The explanation is soon given. For six years the controversy with the extreme Calvinists had continued. In it Fletcher had won great distinction. But, at the time we have reached there came for him a long period of rest from strife. Signs of threatened consumption revealed themselves; it seemed that he had only a short time to live. He had to leave his work at Madeley in other hands, and seek for rest and strength in the homes of loving friends. During the Conference of 1777 he was staying in the hospitable home of Mr. Ireland at Brislington, near Bristol. Wesley immediately went out to see him. He says : ' I spent an hour or two with Mr. Fletcher, restored to life in answer to many prayers. How many providential ends have been answered by his illness. And perhaps still greater will be answered by his recovery.' Wesley's possession of exuberant hopefulness is revealed by these sentences. If he could have looked into the future he would have seen that some years must pass before his strong defender could stand at his side.

In reading the *Minutes* of the Bristol Conference they seem to be a record of routine work. But in examining them more closely we find a few facts that give them special interest. For the first time the question is asked : ' What preachers have died this year ? ' Four names are mentioned, and in each case, a few words descriptive of character are added. This was the beginning of a method that continues to the present day. We are interested, also, in the return of the number of members in the various circuits. In 1776 the list contained an estimate of the number of members in America. Taking the figures of 1775, the return for America was 3,148. The total number of members in the Methodist Societies was then stated to be 39,826. Looking at the total number reported to the Conference of 1777 we find that it was 38,274, but examining the list again we find that America is not included in it. Therefore there had been a considerable increase in the membership in this country.

Putting aside the *Minutes* it is necessary to say that, in 1777, the depressing cry, 'The Methodists are a fallen people' had been heard in this country. The wail was heard in the Conference. Nothing is said about it in the *Minutes*, but we get our information from Wesley's *Journal*. In it he says:

> Tuesday 5. Our yearly Conference began. I now particularly inquired (as that report had been spread far and wide) of every Assistant, 'Have you reason to believe, from your own observation, that the Methodists are a fallen people? Is there a decay or an increase in the work of God where you have been? Are the Societies in general more dead or more alive to God than they were some years ago?' The almost universal answer was, 'If we must know them by their fruits, there is no decay in the work of God among the people in general. The Societies are not dead to God; they are as much alive as they have been for many years. And we look on this report as a mere device of Satan to make our hands hang down.'
>
> 'But how can this question be decided?' You, and you, can judge no farther than you see. You cannot judge of one part by another; of the people of London, suppose, by those of Bristol. And none but myself has an opportunity of seeing them throughout the three Kingdoms.
>
> But to come to a short issue. In most places the Methodists are still a poor, despised people, labouring under reproach, and many inconveniences; therefore, wherever the power of God is not, they decrease. By this, then, you may form a sure judgement. Do the Methodists in general decrease in number? Then they decrease in grace; they are a fallen, or, at least, a falling people. But they do not decrease in number; they continually increase; therefore, they are not a fallen people.

The mention of Bristol in these paragraphs causes us to examine returns of membership in that circuit. In 1775 the number was 1,427. In 1776 there was a slight decrease, the number returned being 1,414. At the Conference of that year John Hilton was appointed as Superintendent of Bristol. In 1777 the membership was 1,339. Hilton then resigned his connexion with the Methodists. The reason for resigning which he gave to the Conference was that 'he saw the Methodists were a fallen people.' Wesley says in his notice of the Bristol Conference: 'Some would have reasoned with him, but it was lost labour, so we let him go in peace.' He became a Quaker. It is possible that we have traced the rumour concerning the fall of the Methodists to its source.[1]

[1] See Wesley's *Journal*, vi., 168, note.

There is another entry in the *Minutes* which calls for notice. It is as follows:

Q. 6. Are there any objections to any of our preachers?

A. Yes. It is objected that 'most of them are not called of God to preach.' This deserves our serious consideration. In the Large Minutes we ask, 'How shall we try those who think they are moved by the Holy Ghost, and called of God to preach?' Pages 30, 31.

Q. 7. Is this method of trial sufficient? Can we find any better? Weigh this matter calmly and impartially.

A. We cannot find any better method, any more scriptural, or more rational.

Q. 8. But suppose they were called once, have not many of them forfeited their calling?

A. Examine them one by one, and whoever has any objection or doubt, concerning any one, let him now speak without any disguise or reserve, or for ever hold his peace.

This entry in the *Minutes* shows that the inquiry into ministerial character, which is one of the most important features of the proceedings of the Conference in the present day, has a long foreground. It is impossible to over-estimate its influence. The methods of conducting the inquiry have been changed, but it is still made to the great advantage of the Methodist Church.

There is one event in connexion with the sessions of the Conference of 1777 that makes us forget for a time its business transactions. We will describe it in the words of a man who, in his younger days, was present at the Bristol Conference for the purpose of offering himself as a candidate for the work of a Methodist preacher. On grounds of delicate health his offer was not accepted. After some years he was ordained by Bishop Horsley, who gave him the living of Llanbister, in Wales. His name was David Lloyd. Many years after the Bristol Conference he wrote a letter to Dr. Adam Clarke in which he described an incident which causes light to linger on a far distant year. Writing of the Conference of 1777, he says:

On the forenoon of a day, when the sitting of the Conference was drawing to a close, tidings announced the approach of Mr. Fletcher. As he entered the vestibule of the New Room, supported by Mr. Ireland, I can never forget the visible impulse of esteem which his venerable presence excited in the house. The whole assembly stood up, as if moved by an electric shock. Mr. Wesley rose, *ex cathedra,* and advanced a few paces to receive his highly respected friend and reverend brother, whose visage seemed strongly to bode that he stood on the verge of the grave; while his eyes, sparkling with seraphic love, indicated that he dwelt in the suburbs of heaven. In this, his languid but happy state, he addressed the Conference on their work and his own views, in a strain of holy and pathetic eloquence, which no language of mine can adequately express. The influence of his spirit and pathos seemed to bear down all before it. I never saw such an instantaneous effect produced in a religious assembly, either before or since. He had scarcely pronounced a dozen sentences before a hundred preachers, to speak in round numbers, were immersed in tears. Time can never efface from my mind the recollection and image of what I then felt and saw. Such a scene I never expect to witness again on this side eternity. Mr. Wesley, in order to relieve his languid friend from the fatigue and injury which might arise from a too long and arduous exertion of the lungs through much speaking, abruptly kneeled down at his side, the whole congress of preachers doing the same, while, in a concise and energetic manner, he prayed for Mr. Fletcher's restoration to health and a longer exercise of his ministerial labours. Mr. Wesley closed his prayer with the following prophetic promise, pronounced in his peculiar manner, and with a confidence and emphasis which seemed to thrill through every heart, 'He shall not die, but live, and declare the works of the Lord.'[1]

On August 11 Wesley returned to London. He spent a busy week there. The discussions in the Conference on the alleged decline in the number of the members in the Methodist Societies, and on the Hilton case, had convinced him that it was necessary to spread accurate information concerning the doctrines and the work of Methodism throughout the nation. On August 14 he drew up his proposals for publishing a monthly periodical under the title *The Arminian Magazine.* The first number was issued on January 1, 1778, and, under the title *The Methodist Magazine,* it continues to this day. In addition much of his time was occupied in consultations concerning the new chapel, which was making great progress and had reached the stage of being 'ready for the roof.' On Sunday, August 17, in a calm, fair evening, he took the opportunity to preach once more in Moorfields. The congregation was as large as he had ever seen there. It led him to conclude that as yet he did not see 'any sign of the decay of the work of God in England.' Concerning this service the

[1] *Life of Adam Clarke,* by Rev. Samuel Dunn, 127; Tyerman's *Wesley's Designated Successor,* 396-7.

note-writer in his *Journal* says: 'This, so far as present records go, was his last sermon in Moorfields. It must be remembered that this famous open-air resort was rapidly changing its character. The city was covering the ground with streets and houses.' The next day he left London and went to Bristol.

At the Bristol Conference Dr. Coke had been present, and seems to have waited for Wesley's return to the city. He had been dismissed from his position as curate of South Petherton, and had made up his mind, as Wesley says, 'to bid adieu to his honourable name,' and to cast in his lot with the Methodists. The note-writer in Wesley's *Journal* expresses our feeling when he says: 'It is a significant fact that exactly at the moment when Fletcher was failing and the Methodist movement needed the courage and vitality of a born optimist, Dr. Coke appeared on the scene.' We draw a veil over the extraordinary conduct of some of the influential persons in South Petherton who effected Dr. Coke's dismissal. Our gratitude to them for the gift they thrust on the Methodist Church by their action secures our silence.[1] In company with Dr. Coke Wesley went on to Taunton. There they separated for a time. Wesley went on to Cornwall, and visited the Societies until the end of the month.

In Wesley's *Journal* there is an interval during which no events are recorded until September 27. Then Wesley says: 'Having abundance of letters from Dublin informing me that the Society there was in the utmost confusion by reason of some of the chief members, whom the preachers had thought it needful to exclude from the Society, and finding all I could write was not sufficient to stop the growing evil, I saw but one way remaining, to go myself, and that as soon as possible.' He was hoping to borrow a sloop belonging to a friend who lived on the Welsh coast, but was disappointed. However, the captain of a sloop that sailed from Fishguard sent him word that he was going to Dublin. But there was delay. He, however, went on board on October 2, and after a stormy voyage, landed in Dublin on Saturday, October 4. In Crookshank's *History of Methodism in Ireland*, there is a full account of this visit, and a description of circumstances that compelled Wesley's presence in the disturbed Society. It

[1] See Dr. Etheridge's *Life of Dr. Coke*, 50-52.

will be enough to say that he met the excluded members and heard them at length. It is clear that he sympathized with them, considering that they had a grievance. We can read much between the lines of Crookshank's description of the interview. He says that the excluded members 'pleaded their case with earnestness and calmness, but refused to be satisfied. They were civil, even affectionate to him, but could never forgive the preachers who had expelled them, so he could not desire them to return to the Society. They remained, however, friends at a distance, meeting in class by themselves, but regularly attending the preaching services in Whitefriar Street Chapel.'[1]

John Wesley returned to London on October 18, and spent most of his time there until the end of a year that had been crowded with work. It is only necessary to mention a few incidents of his busy life that happened during the last two months of 1777. On November 16 he preached a charity sermon in St. Margaret's Church, Rood Lane. Once more he desired his friends not to come to the morning service; in the afternoon the church was crowded. The next Sunday he preached in Lewisham Church for the benefit of the Humane Society. Then on Monday, November 24, he spent the afternoon at Ebenezer Blackwell's house with Dr. Lowth, the Bishop of London.[2] It was during this visit that an incident occurred that finds a record in Thomas Jackson's *Centenary of Methodism*, and in Tyerman's *Life and Times of Wesley*. Wesley, speaking of the Bishop, says: 'His whole behaviour was worthy of a Christian bishop—easy, affable, courteous; and yet all his conversation spoke the dignity which was suitable to his character.'

Speaking of Wesley's description of the Bishop, Tyerman says: 'There is one incident, however, which Wesley, in his modesty, has not related. On proceeding to dinner, the Bishop refused to sit above Wesley at the table, saying with considerable emotion, "Mr. Wesley, may I be found at your feet in another world." Wesley objected to take the seat of precedence, when the learned prelate obviated the difficulty by requesting, as a favour, that Wesley would

---

[1] *History of Methodism in Ireland*, i., 312-14.
[2] Blackwell's second wife was Mary Eden, a niece of Mrs. Lowth. See note in Wesley's *Journal*, vi., 176.

sit above him, because his hearing was defective, and he desired not to lose a sentence of Wesley's conversation.'[1]

On Wednesday, December 3, Wesley spent the evening at Mr. Charles Greenwood's house at Newington with John Fletcher. Speaking of Fletcher's health, he says that 'he was almost miraculously recovering from consumption.' The next day, in company with Mr. Ireland, Fletcher set out for the South of France.[2]

On Tuesday, December 16, Wesley paid a short visit to Bristol, where he preached in the evening and the following morning. Then he went to Bath. At one o'clock he laid the foundation of the chapel in New King Street. He preached at 'the room' in the evening, and then 'took chaise' and drove through the night and next afternoon to London. We get light on the perils of a night-journey in those days from an entry in his *Journal*. He says: 'Just at this time there was a combination among many of the post-chaise drivers on the Bath road, especially those that drove in the night, to deliver their passengers into each others' hands. One driver stopped at the spot they had appointed, where another waited to attack the chaise. In consequence of this many were robbed; but I had a good Protector still. I have travelled all roads, by day and by night, for these forty years, and never was interrupted yet.' On Saturday, December 27, he had to sorrow over the death of his assistant, Mr. Baynes, whom he highly prized. He was an ex-master of Kingswood School, and had been ordained by the friendly Bishop of Bath and Wells. Wesley had invited him to assist him as curate in his London chapels. But, on Saturday morning, he passed away. Wesley's comment on his death sounds a note of deep regret: 'I had no desire to part with him, but God knew what was best, both for him and me.' The old year closed, and the opening moments of the new year commenced with the usual watch-night. It was marked by a fact that commands attention. Wesley, during this service, was assisted by four or five 'local preachers.' His comment on the fact opens the

---

[1] *Life and Times of John Wesley*, iii. 252.
[2] It was not until April, 1781, that Fletcher returned to England (Tyerman's *Wesley's Designated Successor*, 447). On Sunday, April 27, he preached in City Road Chapel, and the next day went to the home of his friend Mr. Ireland, at Brislington. During this long absence his place, as Wesley's special assistant, was taken by Dr. Coke.

gates of the future. He says: 'I was agreeably surprised; their manner of praying being so artless and unlaboured, and yet rational and scriptural, both as to sense and expression.' So far as we know this is one of the earliest examples of Wesley's association with 'local preachers' in an important London Methodist service.

IX

THE EFFECTS OF THE WAR IN ENGLAND AND IRELAND

STUDENTS of English history are aware of the fact that the year 1778 was crowded with events which threatened the safety of England. The war with America continued. On February 6 a war with France began. It lasted until the Peace of Paris was signed on January 20, 1783. It intensified the danger of the American Revolution; it did much to secure the independence of the United States. In the previous year La Fayette and other French officers had left France and gone to the assistance of the American troops. In 1778 the whole strength of France was thrown into the contest against this country. One effect of the French intervention was soon seen. We have heard the cry of Englishmen who were engaged in the Slave Trade; we have seen Wesley looking at their ships laid up in the harbour of Liverpool. The sorrows of the slave-traders failed to evoke our sympathy, but, when we think of the events of 1778, and the following years, it is quickened into intense activity. During that season of national anxiety, French ships appeared off our coasts. They made their way into the Atlantic. They captured English merchant-ships. They hindered, and in some cases, destroyed our trade with America. The ships of our merchants had to join those of the slave-dealers in our harbours. The blow dealt at British commerce had an effect which must be emphasized. It led to a considerable increase of 'the peace party' in this country. The determination of the Government to continue the war with America became a subject of fierce controversy, and those who defended the decision of the King and his ministers were bitterly denounced. We emphasize this fact because John Wesley, who supported the policy of the Government, was made the object of incessant literary abuse. Some of his biographers say that 1778 was the year when printed attacks on him reached their greatest height. That verdict may be questioned, but there can be no doubt of the severity of the assault. He was one of the best known men in England. Trusted by the King and Government he had to bear the consequences of conspicuous position. Without flinching, without losing temper, he endured and survived the fierce attacks.

It is necessary, at this point, to turn our attention from England and fix it, for a time, on America. Events were happening there which had a decisive effect on the future of the Methodist Church in that country. On July 4, 1776, a notable Congress was held in Philadelphia at which allegiance to George III was renounced, and loyalty to the English Crown was made a crime. In addition, praying for the King in congregations assembled for worship was forbidden, and ministers who defied the prohibition were made liable to severe penalties. At the stage we have reached it will be enough to say that clergymen, ministers, and preachers were under obligation to declare, on oath, that they accepted the form of national government that had been adopted by Congress. These regulations placed clergymen, ministers and preachers who were loyal to the King of England in a difficult and dangerous position. Some of them were Americans by birth, others considered themselves Americans because of their long residence in the country; a few had only recently arrived there from England. What would be the result if any of them refused to take the oaths we have mentioned? To that question it is necessary to find an answer. We will take the case of a Methodist preacher who had resided in America for a considerable time, and who may be looked upon as 'a native.' In Joseph Benson's *Apology for the People called Methodists* there is a brief account of the proceedings taken against him. Benson says:

> A remarkable occurrence happened in a county in Maryland. Mr. Chew, one of the preachers, was brought before Mr. Downs, then Sheriff of the county, and afterwards a member of the General Assembly of the State. The Sheriff demanded whether he was a minister of the gospel. On receiving from Mr. Chew an answer in the affirmative, he required him to take the oath of allegiance. Mr. Chew answered him, that he had scruples on his mind, and therefore could not consent at present. Mr. Downs informed him that he was bound on oath to execute

the laws and must in such case commit him to prison. Mr. Chew calmly replied that he by no means wished to be the cause of perjury, and therefore was perfectly resigned to suffer the penalty incurred. 'You are a strange man,' cried the Sheriff, 'and I cannot bear to punish you. I will therefore make my own house your prison.' He accordingly committed him under his hand and seal, and kept him in his own house for three months, during which time the Sheriff was awakened and his lady converted. They soon afterwards joined the Society; and Mr. Downs, with the assistance of some neighbouring gentlemen, built a preaching-house for the Society at Tuckaho, the place where he lived.[1]

We have selected this example because of the light which is 'in the dark cloud.' Urged by the same motive, we will make another selection from Joseph Benson's book. He says:

Many of the preachers that were dubious concerning the merit of the war, and therefore scrupled to take the oaths of allegiance to the States in which they respectively laboured, were fined or imprisoned. But in every instance, those who were confined soon found some powerful friend, yea, often one who had no connexion with the Society, who used his influence with the Governor and Council of the State, and obtained their liberty. The assembly of Maryland, partly perhaps to deliver the Judges from the trouble which was given them, and partly out of a spirit of candour, passed an Act expressly to allow the Methodist Preachers, so called, to exercise their function without taking the oath of allegiance.[2]

If we confined our attention to the State of Maryland we might be led to undervalue the severity of the laws which were enforced on preachers in other parts of America. It must be remembered that in Maryland the work of Robert Strawbridge, Lieutenant Webb, and other Methodists, had been exceptionally successful. That success had been appreciated by many of the leading people in the State. It is no wonder that some of the magistrates tempered judgement with mercy. But beyond the boundaries of Maryland the Methodist preachers felt the full force of oppressive laws. It is well known that, with one exception, the men who had been sent out to America by John Wesley, from 1769 to the time we have reached, had all returned to England. The principal exodus took place in 1778. Francis Asbury alone remained to bear the heat and burden of the day. Benson says of him that though he had preserved a perfect neutrality and had spoken nothing in public or private on the merits of the war, yet he was obliged, from the suspicions already

[1] Benson's *Apology*, 343-4. [2] *ibid*, 343.

raised against the Societies, to conceal himself for two years in the county of Kent, in Delaware, at the house of Mr. White, a Justice of the Peace, and a member of the Methodist Society.[1] With these descriptions of some of the effects of the war on the work of the Methodists in America, we must content ourselves for the present. In recording them we have often thought of the saying, 'the darkness of night is always greatest just before the dawn.'

We must now return to England, and note some of the principal events in the experience of John Wesley which occurred during the year 1778. On January 19, he went to Tunbridge Wells and preached in 'the large dissenting meeting-house' to a great congregation. The people listened to him with deep attention. Then a few days later he journeyed to Shoreham and rested in the house of his old friend Vincent Perronet. He stayed over the Sunday. The fact that Mr. Perronet, though in his eighty-fifth year, was able to go through the whole of the service, made him rejoice greatly. On Monday, February 2, he returned to London, and he had an interview with a highly placed member of the Government. The note-writer in his *Journal* says: 'It has been assumed, with considerable show of reason, that the reference is to the Earl of Dartmouth. From 1772 to 1775 he was Secretary of State for the Colonies, and afterwards Lord Privy Seal. He was one of the lay leaders of the Evangelical Revival in the Church of England. Cowper describes him as "one who wears a coronet and prays." He seems to have been the chief medium of communication between Wesley and the Prime Minister, and possibly, the King himself.' There can be little doubt that the 'assumption' is correct. We can imagine that the conversation between the two men was not confined to political questions, but it seems clear that, at one period of the confidential talk, they were discussed. The Earl of Dartmouth knew that England was on the eve of a war with France. Four days after this interview that war commenced. We can understand that he said nothing to Wesley about that subject. But we think he must have mentioned the condition of affairs in America; and he may have suggested that Wesley might support the King and his Government by correcting rumours

[1] See Benson's *Apology for the Methodists*, 342-3.

that were wide-spread among the people of England. Those rumours concerned the disastrous effects of the American War on the mercantile and labouring classes in this country. It is well known that the opponents of the war were constantly asserting that such effects were being produced, and, as Wesley was undoubtedly one of the best men to advise on 'the condition of England question,' a statement by him would be invaluable to the Government at this crisis.

We have no direct evidence to prove that the Earl of Dartmouth made any suggestion on the subject, but it is clear that, after the interview, Wesley's mind was full of the question concerning the effect of the war on the fortunes of commercial and labouring classes in this country. Immediately following the interview we have mentioned we find this entry in his *Journal*: 'This week I visited the Society and found a surprising difference in their worldly circumstances. Five or six years ago, one in three among the lower ranks of the people was out of employment, and the case was supposed to be nearly the same through all London and Westminster. I did not now, after all the tragical outcries of want of trade that fill the nation, find one in ten out of business; nay, scarce one in twenty, even in Spitalfields.' Not content with this brief exploration, he extended his inquiries. In his *Journal* on February 17, he says: 'I wrote *A Serious Address to the Inhabitants of England* with regard to the present state of the nation—so strangely misrepresented, both by ignorant and designing men—to remove, if possible, the apprehensions which have been so diligently spread, as if it were on the brink of ruin.' In writing this pamphlet of twenty-eight pages he did not wholly rely on the result of his own inquiries and observations. The important subject engaging his attention had been examined by the Dean of Gloucester, who had written a paper containing statistics that had been carefully compiled. He had shown that the panic reports of the condition of the country must be dismissed. With due acknowledgement, Wesley, in his pamphlet, reproduced the results of the Dean's careful inquiries, adding, now and then, a few facts suggested by his own experiences. The two men agreed in their opinions concerning the state of the nation. Wesley's pamphlet is worth reading in the present day. Adopting the plan laid down by the Dean, the following subjects are considered. Population, agriculture, manufactures, the land and fresh-water carriage of goods, salt-water carriage of goods, the state of our fisheries at home and abroad, the tendency of our taxes, the clear amount of the revenue, and the national debt. For the purposes of comparison the Dean had chosen the year 1759. He describes it as 'that period of glory and of conquest when everything was supposed to go right, as we are now told that everything now goes wrong.' The two writers produce evidence that should have silenced the doleful cries that were discouraging the nation. But their work was in vain. It is easy to account for Wesley's failure. His pamphlet is dated February 20, 1778, a fortnight after the beginning of the war with France. The principal effect of Wesley's intervention seems to have been a considerable increase in the virulence of the attacks of his enemies.[1]

On March 4 Wesley went to Bristol. He found the city in a state of panic. The outbreak of the war with France increased the depression in trade which had been the result of the contest with America. He used his influence to calm the agitation. From an entry in his *Journal* it would seem that he was not satisfied with some of the preachers who had been appointed to the Bristol circuit. It had been his practice to allow the Conference to choose the men who should be stationed in circuits, but he determined that, at the approaching Conference he would make the selection himself so far as Bristol was concerned. He left Bristol on March 16, and commenced his journey towards Ireland. He visited a number of towns on his way to Liverpool, where he arrived on March 21. On April 1 he landed in Ireland. Three weeks later, when he was at Rathcormack, he met Thomas Rankin, who had just arrived from America.

Before describing Wesley's visit to Ireland, we must deal with certain matters that call for immediate attention. In Joseph Benson's *Apology for the People called Methodists* there is an interesting description of the work carried on by William Black, a Yorkshireman, and 'a very zealous and useful preacher of the gospel.' Benson says that, during the war with America, Black repeatedly importuned Wesley to send preachers to Nova Scotia and New Brunswick. But

[1] For Wesley's *Serious Address*, see his *Works*, xi., 140-9.

Wesley had made up his mind not to send any missionaries across the Atlantic during the continuance of the war, and he declined the requests. Black was disappointed, but he was a strong man, and he determined that, so far as possible, he would do the work himself. He gave himself up to accomplish a big task. He found that it was impossible to introduce and to maintain the Methodist discipline in his extensive ' round.' He needed the help that comes from loyal colleagues like-minded with himself. He had to wait for their coming. At last they arrived, and work was done that makes the name of William Black conspicuous.

When we think of William Black's disappointment and John Wesley's determination, we are reminded of an event which occurred at this crisis. It illustrates the fact that there is a Providence which sometimes intervenes when men halt in the presence of a seemingly impossible enterprise. We can understand Wesley's determination concerning sending missionaries across the Atlantic during the American war. But, as we watch the ships sailing from England in the early months of 1778, we see on one of them a man who has been sent out to Antigua, not by Wesley, but by the English Government. There was a great need of shipwrights in that island. The naval actions that were taking place during the war in American waters increased the number of English ships that were damaged and had to be repaired. In Antigua, an island at a safe distance from the Continent, there was a shipyard insufficiently supplied with skilled men. On board the ship we are watching we note a group of them. They had been sent out from the Royal Dock at Chatham to meet the emergency. Among them we see a Methodist local preacher. His name was John Baxter. The shipwrights landed in Antigua, and on April 2 we see Baxter writing a letter to John Wesley.

In our book on *John Wesley the Master Builder* we have told the story of the introduction of Methodism into Antigua by Nathaniel Gilbert, a planter who was for some time the Speaker of the House of Assembly in the island.[1] We have described his work and shown its success. He returned to Antigua in 1759. Through his influence as a class-leader and preacher Methodism was introduced into the island. In 1774

---

[1] See pp. 43-5.

he died suddenly. He left in St. John's, a Society of sixty members. His death imperilled the existence of Methodism in Antigua, but that catastrophe was avoided. For a few months Francis Gilbert, his brother, visited the island. In a letter he says : ' The ground seems to be prepared for the seed, for many are ready to hear, and I trust from a better principle than mere curiosity. We have taken a house for preaching. But it is not half large enough, though it will contain two hundred persons. It has been crowded every night, while a number of attentive hearers stood without.'[1] Francis Gilbert returned to England, but there were a few workers left in Antigua who kept the Society in existence. We are especially interested by a fact that deserves prominent record. Some of the members of the Society were African slaves. Two of them, Mary Alley and Sophia Campbell, took charge of the negro Methodists. Moister, in his *History of Methodist Missions,* informs us that he had made inquiries concerning these two women, but had not been able to ascertain whether they were the two servants of Nathaniel Gilbert who were baptized in Wandsworth on November 29, 1758, by John Wesley.[2] Leaving that an open question, it is a pleasure to record the names of these women, who were unwearied in their efforts to do good, ' by holding prayer-meetings and other religious services among their fellow negroes almost every evening, till the Lord of the harvest provided more efficient help.'

In Baxter's letter to John Wesley, written on April 2, 1778, we get a glimpse of the position of Methodism at the time of his landing in Antigua. He says : ' The black people have been kept together by two black women, who have continued praying and meeting with those who attended every night.' Then he describes his own work. He says : ' I preached to about thirty on Saturday night. On Sunday morning to the same number, and in the afternoon to about four or five hundred. The old standers desire I would let you know that you have had many children in Antigua who you never saw. I hope, sir, we shall have an interest in your prayers.' In his letter to Wesley, Baxter gives us a glimpse of the condition of his own affairs. He says : ' Give me your advice.

---

[1] Benson's *Apology for the People called Methodists,* 346.
[2] See *John Wesley the Master Builder,* 43.

Provisions are very scarce, but I have all things richly to enjoy, as I have four shillings a day, besides the King's provisions. I am going to have a house built for me, with as much ground as is needful. I think God has sent me here for good to the poor souls, who are glad to hear, but unable to maintain a preacher.'[1]

We must now leave John Baxter to carry on his work in Antigua. We shall meet him again, and shall rejoice over his remarkable success as an evangelist. John Wesley claims our attention. We have said that, on April 1, he landed in Ireland. In Crookshank's *History of Methodism in Ireland* there is an interesting description of this visit.[2] As we read it we note the effect of the war at many stages of Wesley's journeys. It was during this visit that he wrote his *Compassionate Address to the Inhabitants of Ireland*. It was written in Limerick on May 10, 1778. The first and second paragraphs reveal the condition of public opinion, not only in Ireland but also in England. Wesley says :

1.—Before I left London (two or three months ago) a general panic prevailed there. Some vehemently affirmed, and others potently believed, that the nation was in a most desperate state; that it was upon the very brink of ruin, past all hopes of recovery. Soon after, I found that the same panic had spread throughout the city of Bristol. I traced it likewise wherever I went, in Gloucestershire, Worcestershire, Staffordshire, Cheshire, and Lancashire. When I crossed the Channel, I was surprised to find it had got before me to Ireland; and that it was not only spread through Dublin first, and thence to every part of Leinster, but had found its way into Munster too, into Cork, Bandon, and Limerick. In all which places people were terrifying themselves and their neighbours, just as they did in London. 2.—' How is it possible,' say they, that we should contend with so many enemies together?' If General Washington has (as Mr. Franklin of Limerick computes) sixty-five thousand men; if the powerful fleet and numerous armies of France are added to these; if Spain, in consequence of the family compact, declares war at the same time; if Portugal join in Confederacy with them, what will become of us? Add to these the enemies of our own household, ready to start up on every side; and when France invades us from without, and these from within, what can follow but ruin and destruction?[3]

There can be no doubt that Wesley, in these paragraphs, correctly represented the state of public opinion in many parts

---

[1] Tyerman's *Life and Times of Wesley*, iii., 273-4.
[2] See i. 316-28.
[3] Wesley's *Works*, xi., 149-50.

of this country. In his *Compassionate Address* he proves himself, as always, a persistent optimist. We are aware of the irritating power possessed by such a person. His address produced some impression, but it failed to soothe the fluttering nerves of people who were convinced that the day of the doom of the British Kingdom had arrived.

Wesley spent more than fifteen weeks in Ireland. Sunshine and shadow seem to alternate in his descriptions of his experiences in the places he visited. It will answer our purpose if we confine our attention to the proceedings of the Conference which was held in Dublin. It began on Tuesday, July 7. The *Minutes* of this Conference were printed in Ireland. That fact marks a new departure. A copy lies before us. With its help and with the assistance of William Myles, it will be possible to note some of its proceedings. About twenty preachers were present. The increase in the membership during the year amounted to one hundred and twenty-five. There were then five thousand three hundred and forty members of the Methodist Society in Ireland. It must be remembered that many Methodist families had emigrated to America. That fact had left a deep impression on the numerical condition of Irish Methodism. In the list of men admitted on trial at this Conference we notice the name of William Myles, a name that always excites our gratitude. We get an insight into the administration of the discipline of the Conference when we note that the preachers were examined one by one. The result is stated in words which suggest the thoroughness of the inquiry. 'The objections made to all of them, but one, were clearly and plainly answered.' According to the *Minutes* there were then thirty preachers in Ireland. The ordinary business followed the course taken by the English Conference. At one point of the proceedings a question was raised that demands our special attention. Myles, in the last edition of his *Chronological History of the People called Methodists,* throws light on an interesting discussion that took place in the Dublin Conference of 1778. He says: 'The Rev. Edward Smyth, who some time before had been expelled from a church in the North of Ireland for preaching the truth, was now in connexion with the Methodists. He revived the controversy respecting the Church of England, and laboured with all his might and with manifest uprightness of mind, to persuade Mr. Wesley and the brethren to separate from it. The debate ended by the Conference agreeing to the following propositions, which were afterwards adopted by the English Conference and published in the Minutes.' In the printed copy of the *Minutes* of the English Conference no notice appears of this discussion. Myles may mean that the 'propositions' are contained in the *Minutes* of the Dublin Conference, which would be a correct statement. The quotation of the resolutions in his *Chronological History,* differs slightly from the record in the *Minutes* of the Dublin Conference. It will, therefore, be better to reproduce from the latter the result of the discussion.

Q. 23. Is it not our duty to separate from the Church, considering the wickedness both of the Clergy and of the People?

A. We conceive not. 1—Because both the Priests and the People were full as wicked in the Jewish Church, and yet God never commanded the Holy Israelites to separate from them. 2—Neither did our Lord command His Disciples to separate from them; if He did not command just the contrary. 3—Because from hence it is clear, that this would not be the meaning of those Words asked by St. Paul, come out from among them, and be ye separate.[1]

John Wesley's record of this episode is enlightening. In his *Journal* on July 8, he says: ' We heard one of our friends at large upon the duty of leaving the Church, but, after a full discussion of the point, we all remained firm in our judgement—that it is our duty not to leave the Church, wherein God has blessed us, and does bless us still.'

On July 19 John Wesley left Ireland. After a tedious voyage, he landed in Liverpool. He visited the towns in that neighbourhood, and then made his way to Leeds, where the Conference was to be held. On Sunday, August 2, at one o'clock, he preached at the foot of Birstall Hill to a great congregation. He says that it was supposed there were twelve or fourteen thousand people present. Later in the day he preached in the open air in Leeds. Again there was an immense crowd. In his opinion it was the largest congregation he had seen for many years, except that at Gwennap in Cornwall. On Tuesday, August 4, the Conference began in Leeds. His entry in his *Journal* concerning this Conference tantalizes us by its brevity. All that he says about it is: ' So large a number of preachers never met at a Conference before.

[1] *Minutes of the Conference* held in Dublin in 1778, 4-5.

I preached morning and evening till Thursday night. Then my voice began to fail, so I desired two of our preachers to supply my place the next day. On Saturday the Conference ended.' When we turn to the published *Minutes* we find brief records of the business transacted. Most of them run along the usual lines, but some of them claim our attention.

In the stations of the preachers we find an important new departure in the appointments for London. John Pawson, Thomas Rankin and Thomas Tennant head the list. Then comes the name of Peter Jaco, a supernumerary. Then there is a new departure. John Wesley, Thomas Coke, and John Abraham are appointed to the London circuit. Looking at the appointments in the years following we find an alteration in the order of the names. In 1779 the initials of John Wesley and the name of 'T. Coke' head the list; the circuit preachers follow. The next year the name of Charles Wesley is added to those of John Wesley and Thomas Coke, who again precede the circuit preachers. It is not difficult to understand these changes. The City Road Chapel was soon to be opened, and it was necessary to improve arrangements which had sufficed when the services were held in the Foundery in Windmill Street.

Continuing our examination of the stations we note that a new circuit has been added to the list. For the first time the Isle of Man makes its appearance, the preachers appointed being John Crook and Robert Dall. Towards the close of the stations we note appointments in Scotland that arrest attention. The name of Joseph Saunderson appears as the superintendent of the Aberdeen circuit. He has two colleagues, J. Watson, Sen., and Duncan McAllum. In 1777 he was the junior colleague of Francis Wrigley in the Aberdeen circuit. He was then in the third year of his probation. In 1778, while still a probationer, the Conference made him the superintendent of the circuit. He had two colleagues under him. In 1779 he was admitted into 'full connexion' with the Conference. He was again appointed as the superintendent of Aberdeen, and remained there in that position until the Conference of 1781, when he completed his fourth year in the circuit. He was a great preacher. His name is still mentioned with affection in Dundee, where he resided for many years as a supernumerary minister.

In order that we may get a view of some other proceedings of the Leeds Conference we put the *Minutes* aside. The note-writer in Wesley's *Journal* once more befriends us. By way of contrast we will reproduce the impressions of two men concerning the character of this Conference. Joseph Benson's report is the more favourable. He speaks of Wesley's 'sweet spirit,' his 'excellent sermons,' his 'extraordinary congregations.' He then says that he dealt closely and plainly with the preachers, 'setting two aside for misdemeanours.' Thomas Taylor's entries in his *Diary* help us to see the Conference from another point of view. Under the date, August 5, he says: 'To-day we permitted all sorts to come into the Conference, so that we had a large company. The forenoon was occupied in speaking upon preaching-houses. In the afternoon the sending of missionaries to Africa was considered. The call seems doubtful. Afterwards the committee met, and we were an hour and a half in speaking what might have been done in five minutes. We are vastly tedious, and have many long speeches to little purpose.' In Taylor's jottings in his *Diary* there is a statement that demands special attention. He speaks of the proposal to send missionaries to Africa. The note-writer reproduces an interesting description of an incident in the discussion of this proposal. It seems that during its consideration a young man, far gone in consumption, promptly offered himself as a missionary for Africa or any other country. There is some uncertainty as to the identity of this volunteer. Duncan McAllum and John Prickard have been mentioned. But we think that Crookshank, in his *History of Methodism in Ireland,* has indicated the young speaker. Describing the debate he says that it arose in connexion with a proposal to send missionaries to Africa, that it continued for several hours, and was marked by deep piety, sound sense, and powerful eloquence. Then he continues: 'The deepest impression, however, was made on the minds of all present by the short speech of a young man, far gone in consumption, who promptly offered himself as a missionary, and in unaffected language, declared his readiness to go to Africa, or to any other part of the world to which it might please God and his brethren to send him. That young man was an Irishman of great promise, James Gaffney, who had travelled only two years, and was then received into full connexion; but his desire was not gratified, the way not being then open for such an undertaking, and in about eight months subsequently his pure and fervent spirit entered into everlasting light and glory.'[1]

The Leeds Conference having ended, John Wesley returned to London. On August 17, in company with his brother Charles and Dr. Coke, he set out for Bristol. In a letter that Charles Wesley wrote to his wife he calls him 'my youthful brother,' and declares that he seemed 'as active and zealous as ever.' On Thursday, August 20, he set out for Cornwall and did not return to London until Friday, October 9. He stayed in London for a short time and then began a visitation of some of the Societies in the Midlands. One entry in his *Journal* rivets our attention. On October 14 he says: 'I went on to Oxford, and having an hour to spare, walked to Christ Church, for which I cannot but still retain a peculiar affection. What lovely mansions are these! What is wanting to make the inhabitants of them happy? That without which no rational creature can be happy—the experimental knowledge of God. . . . How gladly could I spend a few weeks in this delightful solitude! But I must not rest yet. As long as God gives me strength to labour, I am to use it.' That is a sigh from the deep!

On Friday, October 30, Wesley got back to London. On Sunday, November 1 there is an entry in his *Journal* which indicates a new departure in Methodism. It will suffice, for the present, if we reproduce his *Journal* record of a great event, as it will be necessary to return to the subject at a later period. He says: 'Sunday, November 1, was the day appointed for opening the new chapel in the City Road. It is perfectly neat, but not fine, and contains far more people than the Foundery. I believe, together with the morning chapel, as many as the Tabernacle. Many were afraid that the multitudes crowding from all parts, would have occasioned much disturbance. But they were happily disappointed; there was none at all. All was quietness, decency, and order. I preached on part of Solomon's prayer at the dedication of the Temple, and both in the morning and the afternoon, when I preached on the hundred forty and four thousand standing

---

[1] See Crookshank's *History*, i., 325; *Methodist Magazine*, 1814, 508; *City Road Magazine*, 1875, 563.

with the Lamb on Mount Zion, God was eminently present in the midst of the congregation.'

The remainder of the year 1778 was filled with work. We note that on Sunday, November 29, John Wesley preached a charity sermon in St. Luke's Church in the morning, in the afternoon he conducted the service in the New Chapel; in the evening he preached in St. Margaret's Church in Rood Lane. That these churches were open to him evoked this comment in his *Journal*: ' Is then the scandal of the Cross ceased?' During the month of December there are several entries in his *Journal* that arrest our attention. On December 4 he was in Shoreham. He rejoiced to find Vincent Perronet ' once more brought back from the gates of death.' Then, on Friday, December 18, he called on Colonel Gallatin, his firm friend of other days. In his *Journal* he sounds a note of compassion : ' What a change is here. The fine gentleman, the soldier is clean gone, sunk into a feeble, decrepit old man, not able to rise off his seat, and hardly able to speak.' Wesley was in the habit of repressing his sadness when he looked upon the sorrows of his friends, but those who knew him best were aware of the depth of his sympathy. On the following Sunday he stood by the grave of another old friend. He was a man who is well known to those who are acquainted with the early history of Methodism. Wesley calls him ' Honest Silas Told.' Wesley buried him. In a few words he describes his remarkable work. He says : ' For many years he attended the malefactors in Newgate, without fee or reward, and I suppose no man for this hundred years has been so successful in that melancholy office. God had given him peculiar talents for it, and he had amazing success therein. The greatest part of those whom he attended died in peace, and many of them in the triumph of faith.'

On Christmas Day, Wesley held a service in the new chapel at four o'clock in the morning. He then went to the West Street Chapel and read prayers, preached, and administered the sacrament to several hundred people. In the afternoon he preached in the new chapel, ' which was thoroughly filled in every corner.' In the evening he preached at St. Sepulchre's, one of the largest parish churches in London. He declares that he was stronger after he had preached his fourth sermon than he was after the first. He ended this crowded year by holding a lovefeast. Then, after midnight, he retired to rest. A violent storm was raging. The roaring of the wind was like loud thunder. It kept him awake for half an hour. Then he slept in the New Year in peace.

X

A YEAR OF DIFFICULTIES

JOHN WESLEY began the year 1779 by holding a Covenant Service in the new chapel in City Road. He rejoiced in the fact that, at last, the Methodists had a house in London capable of containing the whole Society. He placed a high value on these meetings. He says: 'We never met on that solemn occasion without a peculiar blessing.' On Tuesday, January 12, he had an experience which must have reminded him of his earlier years. He dined and drank tea with four German ministers. In the previous year he had spent 'an agreeable and profitable hour' with three German gentlemen, two of them Lutheran ministers, and the third a Professor of Divinity at Leipzig. He had been charmed by their 'good sense, seriousness, and good breeding.' Describing those whom he met on January 12, he says: 'I could not but admire the wisdom of those that appointed them. They seem to consider not only the essential points, their sense and piety, but even those smaller things, the good breeding, the address, yea, the persons of those they send into foriegn countries.'

Wesley was soon busy with the work of the year. From letters he wrote in January we find that, at Tiverton and Exeter, difficulties had arisen in connexion with the licensing of Methodist preaching-houses. He had learned much since the time when that practice had begun. Much had happened since Charles Wesley poured scorn on 'the needless, useless, and senseless licence' that had been obtained for the New Room in Bristol.[1] The question of the validity of a licence granted to a Methodist preaching-house had come before the Court of King's Bench, and a decision had been given in its favour.[2] In some parts of the country, however, Justices continued to refuse applications for licences made to them by the representatives of trustees, and appeals were made to

---
[1] *John Wesley and the Advance of Methodism*, 56-9.
[2] *John Wesley the Master Builder*, 78.

Wesley for guidance in such cases. In January, 1779, two letters reached him. The first was sent by one of his preachers, Samuel Wells, who was stationed at Tiverton, in Devon. On January 28, he replied as follows:

> According to the Act of Toleration, 1—You are required to certify to the Registrar of the Bishops' Court, or the Justices, the place of your meeting for divine worship. This is all you have to do. You ask nothing at all of the Bishop or Justices. 2—The Registrar, or Clerk of the Court, is required to register the same, and to give a certificate thereof to such persons as shall demand the same; for which there shall be no greater fee or reward taken than sixpence.
> I advise you to go once more to the Sessions. and say, 'Gentlemen, we have had advice from London. We desire nothing at all of you; but we demand of your Clerk to register this place, and give a certificate thereof; or to answer the refusal at his peril.'
> Answer no questions to Justices, or Lawyers, but with a bow, and with repeating the words, 'Our business is only with your Clerk. We demand of him what the Act requires him to do.'
> If you judge proper, you may show this to any of the Justices. What I have written I am ready to defend.
> PS.—You led the Justices into the mistake by your manner of addressing them. Beware of this for the time to come: You have nothing to ask of them.[1]

In Exeter, in the same month, a similar difficulty arose, and Wesley gave his advice to Mr. Gidley, an officer of Excise, who was a Methodist. The difficulty had arisen in Exeter in the case of a recently-erected preaching-house. Wesley informs his correspondent that in case the Sessions give trouble, the Lord Chief Justice will protect Methodists. He adds: 'You should mildly and respectfully tell them so.'

Before commencing his usual tour through the northern English counties and Scotland, John Wesley, on March 11, went to Bath and opened the new chapel there. He read prayers, preached a sermon, and concluded the service by administering the sacrament of the Lord's Supper. It is interesting to note that soon after the chapel was opened an organ was erected in it. Mr. James T. Lightwood, who has done so much to give us information on many questions concerning the character of the Methodist services in early days, tells us that at least three organs were placed in preaching-houses during Wesley's life-time, the most important being the instrument erected in the New King Street Chapel, Bath,

[1] See Wesley's *Works*, xii., 496-8. Jackson's edition.

soon after its opening in 1779. In his description of the organ he says: 'Although it has, of course, undergone several alterations since that time, a good deal of the original work remains, and thus it forms a most interesting Wesley relic.'[1] The introduction of the organ seems to have led to some conversation in the Conference. An edition of the *Large Minutes*, published in 1780, contains this direction, 'Let no organs be placed anywhere till proposed in Conference.'

On March 15 Wesley began his northern journey. He arrived in Madeley on March 24. On the next day he preached in the new 'house,' which Fletcher had built in Madeley Wood. Fletcher was on the Continent. His absence explains a part of Wesley's comment on the condition of Methodism in the neighbourhood. He says: 'The people here exactly resemble those at Kingswood; only they are more simple and teachable. But, for want of discipline, the immense pains he has taken with them has not done the good which might have been expected.'

Making his way to Yorkshire we note that on Sunday, April 18, Wesley preached in the morning in Haworth Church. In the afternoon a great crowd assembled, and he was obliged to go into the churchyard because of the multitude of people. The next day he preached in Bingley Church to a numerous congregation; then went to Otley. It was during this visit to Otley that he read the description of Methodism that appears in Smollett's *History of England*. He was not the only reader of the *History* who has been lost in astonishment while reading that caricature. Smollett knew nothing about Methodism, so he described it with reckless courage. We can picture Wesley as he sat reading the following passage.

> Imposture and fanaticism still hang upon the skirts of religion. Weak minds were seduced by the delusions of a superstition, styled Methodism, raised upon the affectation of a superior sanctity, and pretensions to divine illumination. Many thousands were infected with this enthusiasm by the endeavour of a few obscure preachers, such as Whitefield, and the two Wesleys, who found means to lay the whole Kingdom under contribution.

The readers of Smollett's *History* will be aware that now and then he made statements that were singularly opposed to

[1] See Mr. Lightwood's article in *The Methodist Magazine* for August, 1926.

truth. In later editions he had to apologize to men whom he had misrepresented. We are not aware that he took the trouble to apologize to Wesley, so we must insert his reply to this attack. He says:

Poor Dr. Smollett! Thus to transmit to all succeeding generations a whole heap of notorious falsehoods!

'Imposture and fanaticism!' Neither one nor the other had any share in the late revival of scriptural religion, which is no other than the love of God and man, gratitude to our Creator, and good-will to our fellow creatures. Is this delusion and superstition? No, it is real wisdom; it is solid virtue. Does this fanaticism 'hang upon the skirts of religion'? Nay, it is the very essence of it. Does the Doctor call this enthusiasm? Why? Because he knows nothing about it. Who told him that these 'obscure preachers' made pretensions to divine illumination? How often has that silly calumny been refuted to the satisfaction of all candid men? However, they 'found means to lay the whole Kingdom under contribution.' So does this frontless man, blind and bold, stumble on without the least shadow of truth!

Meanwhile what faith can be given to his history? What credit can any man of reason give to any fact upon *his* authority?[1]

It is pleasant to turn from Smollett's blunder, and to follow Wesley as he continues his journey towards the north. On Sunday, May 2, he was in Leeds. Dr. Kershaw, the vicar, asked him to assist him at the Sacrament. It was a solemn season. Ten clergymen assisted in the administration of the sacrament to between seven and eight hundred communicants. Myles Atkinson, the vicar of Kippax, who was also the lecturer at the parish church in Leeds, desired Wesley to preach in the church in the afternoon. There was a very large congregation. In the evening he preached to a greater crowd in the Methodist chapel. On Sunday, May 9, he was in Darlington, and found there 'some of the liveliest people in the north of England.' He preached in the market-place, 'and all the congregation behaved well but a party of the Queen's Dragoons.' The conduct of the soldiers disappointed him. But he met with a different reception the next day at Barnard Castle. He preached there, and was delighted with the conduct of the Durham Militia. He declares that they were the handsomest body of soldiers he had ever seen, except in Ireland. The next evening they all came to the service, both officers and soldiers, and were 'a pattern to the whole congregation.' As he went on his way to Scotland he preached

[1] *Journal*, vi., 230.

A YEAR OF DIFFICULTIES 141

several times to large numbers of soldiers; the entries in his *Journal* reveal his delight at the conduct of officers and men.

John Wesley crossed the Border, and after preaching at Dunbar, went on to Edinburgh, arriving in the city on May 27. This visit to Scotland is especially interesting. One of his travelling companions was Robert Carr Brackenbury, his special friend in Lincolnshire. In addition, Mrs. Smith, of Newcastle, perhaps better known to our readers by her maiden name of ' Jenny Vazeille,' and her little girl, were with him. He draws a little picture of a family gathering which lingers in the memory. On Monday, June 7, his host was Sir Lodovick Grant, who lived at Grange Green, near Forres. When Wesley arrived he was received with cordial affection. Finding that Mrs. Smith and her little daughter had been left at Forres, Sir Lodovick insisted on their coming to the Grange. They came, and Wesley says : ' We were all here as at home, in one of the most healthy and most pleasant situations in the kingdom; and I had the satisfaction to observe my daughter sensibly recovering her strength almost every hour. In the evening all the family were called in to prayers; to whom I first expounded a portion of Scripture. Thus ended this comfortable day. So has God provided for us in a strange land.'[1] This little picture enables us to see ' the real Wesley.' Surrounded by those whom he loved, and who loved him, he seems to smile at us from the distant past.

Wesley remained in Scotland until the middle of June. As we follow him we miss the jubilant note he so often sounded during his visits to the far north. We think that the secret is revealed in the entry in his *Journal* on Thursday, June 17. He had reached Edinburgh on the previous day and had preached there. On June 17 he had examined the Society. This is his record : ' In five years I found five members had been gained !—ninety-nine being increased to a hundred and four. What, then, have our preachers been doing all this time? (1) They have preached four evenings in the week, and on Sunday morning, the other mornings they have fairly given up. (2) They have taken great care not to speak too plain, lest they should give offence. (3) When Mr. Brackenbury preached the old Methodist doctrine one of them said, " You must not preach such doctrine here. The doctrine

[1] *Journal*, vi., 237.

of Perfection is not calculated for the meridian of Edinburgh." Waiving, then, all other hindrances, is it any wonder that the work of God has not prospered here?' We can imagine the effect which was produced on Wesley's mind by the condition of things in Edinburgh. On Friday and Saturday he preached with all possible plainness, and 'some appeared to be stirred up.' On Sunday he preached twice. He said that God gave a parting blessing, but it is clear that the condition of Methodism in Edinburgh filled him with deep concern. However, he crossed the border; on June 22 he reached Newcastle.

We watch John Wesley at this time with sympathy and some anxiety. We do not know when he received a letter written to him by his brother on Wednesday, June 16. It contained news concerning the condition of affairs at the City Road Chapel. The inevitable had arrived. When we recorded the alteration of the order of the names of the preachers appointed to the London circuit we knew what would happen. In John Wesley's *Journal* there is a footnote in which the beginning of a contest that lasted for some time is stated with great restraint. Dealing with Charles Wesley's letter, the writer says: ' Charles Wesley wrote from London to his brother. The letter reveals a curious dispute in which are involved the preachers at City Road Chapel (John Dawson, Thomas Rankin, and Thomas Tennant) and the " clergy," including John Richardson, Dr. Coke, and Charles Wesley himself. The complaint made by the former was that Charles Wesley served the chapel on Sunday afternoons as well as in the morning. He (Charles) adds the following: " My reasons for preaching there (at the new chapel) twice every Sunday are : (1) because after you I have the best right; (2) because I have so short a time to preach anywhere; (3) because I am fully persuaded I can do more good there than in any other place. They, I know, are of a different judgement, and make no secret of it, declaring everywhere that the work is stopping, the Society scattering, the congregation at the new chapel dwindled away and quite dead."' This letter must have caused John Wesley to ponder as he moved about among the northern Societies. He did not get back to London until nearly the end of July. After preaching in Coventry in the evening of July 22, he took coach for London. He had

A YEAR OF DIFFICULTIES

a strange experience during this journey. It must have prevented close brooding over coming difficulties. He says: 'I was nobly attended; behind the coach were ten convicted felons, loudly blaspheming and rattling their chains; by my side sat a man with a loaded blunderbuss, and another upon the coach.' He must have been thankful when he arrived in London. On Sunday, July 25, he preached in 'both the chapels,' and says that they were 'full enough.'

On Tuesday, August 3, the Conference assembled in London. It is difficult to find any helpful description of its proceedings. In Wesley's *Journal* the only reference to it is in these words: 'Our Conference began, which continued and ended in peace and love.' Turning to the printed *Minutes* we get a little more light. Our attention is quickened by the question concerning the decrease in the number of members in many of the Societies throughout the country. Twenty circuits, including London, Liverpool, Leeds, York, Aberdeen, Cork, Athlone and Belfast, had suffered during the year. It is true that there was an increase in the total number of members, but that fact was obscured by the omission of the American membership which, in 1778, had been returned at 6,968. The significant fact, however, was that the decreases had occurred in some of the strongest circuits in this country. It is no wonder that the question was asked: 'How can we account for the decrease in so many circuits this year?' The answer was: 'It may be owing partly to want of preaching abroad, and of trying new places; partly to prejudice against the King, and speaking evil of dignities, but chiefly to the increase of worldly-mindedness, and conformity to the world.' There can be no doubt that there were divisions of opinion among the Methodists concerning the war in America. That fact was recognized by the Conference, as is shown by a supplementary question and answer: 'How can we stop this evil-speaking? Suffer none that speak evil of those in authority, or that prophesy evil to the nation to preach with us. Let every assistant take care of this.' According to the *Minutes*, the last question discussed by the Conference had reference to the condition of Methodism in Scotland. It was asked: 'What can be done to revive the work in Scotland.' The following answers were given: 'Preach abroad as much as possible.

Try every town and village; visit every member of Society at home. Let the preacher at Dundee and Arbroath never stay at one place more than a week at a time. Let each of them once a quarter visit Perth and Dunkeld, and the intermediate villages.'

In trying to get light from the records of the proceedings of this Conference we are conscious of the fact that too little time was allowed for the transaction of important business. One sign of haste is shown by the omission of the usual question: 'When and where may the next Conference begin?' At the next Conference, which was held in Bristol, the subject of the pressure of business was considered. The result is shown in Wesley's *Journal*. Under the date August 1, 1780, he says: 'Our Conference began. We have been always hitherto straitened for time. It was now resolved, " For the future we allow nine or ten days for each Conference, that everything relative to the carrying on the work of God may be maturely considered."' When we watch Wesley dispatching the business of the Conference in 1779 we think we can understand one reason for his haste. His thoughts were much occupied with a personal question which made strong demands on his time and temper. Among the men present at the Conference was Mr. William Smith, of Newcastle, who had married the daughter of Mrs. Vazeille. He had come to London to interview Wesley on an unpleasant subject. In the MS. *Life of Benson* we get light on this matter. It is there said: ' Mr. William Smith, of Newcastle, attended this Conference, the chief object of his long journey being to propose terms of reconciliation between Mr. and Mrs. Wesley. In a letter written by him to Benson he says: " I talked freely to both parties, and did all in my power to lay a foundation for future union; but alas! all my attempts proved unsuccessful. I had to leave matters no better than I found them. It is indeed a melancholy affair, and I am afraid productive of bad consequences."' We can understand William Smith's motive in attempting this useless task, but to busy himself with the interview he mentions at a time when Wesley needed to rest after guiding the affairs of the Conference, was an error of judgement. It is no wonder that Wesley hastened the business of the Conference and escaped from London.

On Sunday, August 8, John Wesley preached at West Street in the morning and at the new chapel in the evening. At the latter place he took 'a solemn leave of the affectionate congregation.' The next day he set out for Wales with Charles Wesley and his family. They seem to have travelled together for a short time; then he went on to Oxford, where he preached in the evening. On Thursday he made his way to Wales, and remained there until August 27. In his *Journal* he gives a bright account of this visit. The services he held were full of encouragement. Returning to Bristol, he stayed there for two days, then set out for the west. On September 1 he was in Exeter. During this visit he met a gentleman who had just come from Plymouth. He listened to a story which is worth repeating, as it casts a flash-light on the conditions of the country at the time we have reached. This gentleman told him that the combined fleets of France and Spain lay at the mouth of Plymouth Harbour for two days.[1] They might have entered it with perfect ease. The wind was fair, there was no fleet to oppose them, and the island, which is the great security of the place, was incapable of giving them any hindrance, for there was scarce any garrison on it, and the few men that were there had no wadding at all, and but two rounds of powder. Listening to this story Wesley asked: 'But had they not cannon?' The answer was: 'Yes, in abundance, but only two of them mounted!' Recording this conversation in his *Journal*, Wesley asks himself the question: 'Why, then, did not the fleet go in and destroy the dock, and burn, or at least plunder, the town?' He says: 'I believe they could hardly tell themselves.' Then he gives the solution that all who knew him would have expected: 'The plain reason was, the bridle of God was in their teeth, and He had said, "Hitherto shall ye come, and no farther."'

The closing months of the year 1779 were marked by circumstances that gave Wesley considerable trouble. We have mentioned the name of the Rev. Edward Smyth in our description of the Irish Conference held in Dublin in July, 1778.[2] In 1779, owing to the illness of his wife he had

---

[1] The war with Spain began on April 17, 1780, and closed on January 20, 1783.
[2] See p. 130.

brought her to Bath, where a new Methodist chapel had been opened in March. John Wesley, recognizing the work he had done as a clergyman in Ireland, desired him to preach every Sunday evening in the chapel during the time he remained in Bath. Alexander McNab had been appointed as the superintendent of the Bristol circuit at the recent Conference. Bath at that time was a place in that circuit. His colleagues were John Valton and John Bristol. We have seen that Wesley took a special interest in the appointments to Bristol, and there can be no doubt of the wisdom of the choice of Alexander McNab as the superintendent of the circuit. Wesley's action in appointing Edward Smyth to preach in the Bath chapel every Sunday evening while he remained in the city caused a dispute. McNab thought that the right of appointing preachers to the chapels of a circuit of which he was the superintendent belonged to him. John Wesley, relying on the twelfth 'Rule of a Helper,' considered that he alone possessed that power. In the edition of the *Minutes of the Conference*, published in 1862, the six editions of the 'Rules of a Helper' issued during Wesley's life-time are contained. In the 1772 edition the twelfth rule stands as follows: ' 12. Act in all things, not according to your own will, but as a son in the Gospel. As such it is your part to employ your time in the manner which we direct: partly in preaching and visiting from house to house, partly in reading, meditation and prayer. Above all, if you labour with us in our Lord's vineyard it is needful that you should do that part of the work which we advise, at those times and places which we judge most for His glory.'[1] At this distance of time we find it difficult to see how this rule takes the right of appointing preachers altogether out of the hands of the superintendent of a circuit. Instead of quoting the rule as it appears in the 'Rules of a Helper,' Wesley gives it as follows: ' Above all, you are to preach when and where I appoint.'

There can be no doubt that the rule referred to appointments to circuits, not to the preaching-houses and chapels in circuits. It is no wonder that McNab was surprised. When Wesley had left the neighbourhood McNab opposed the arrangement made with Edward Smyth. A dispute arose.

[1] See *Minutes* i. 497.

It became so severe that 'the Society was torn in pieces, and thrown into the utmost confusion.' It will be enough to say that, on November 22, John and Charles Wesley set out from London to settle the disturbance. Some will think that it would have been better if John Wesley had gone alone. The Bath Society was assembled. John Wesley read a paper he had written 'nearly twenty years before on a like occasion.' It included the version of the quotation from the 'Twelve Rules of a Helper' to which we have referred. Alexander McNab seems to have challenged the application of that rule to the case then being considered. The next morning, at a meeting of preachers, Wesley informed him that 'as he did not agree to our fundamental rule he could not receive him as one of his preachers till he was of another mind.' Those who are interested in this dispute should read Tyerman's account of it in his *Life and Times of John Wesley*.[1] It will be enough to say that, at the Conference of 1780, McNab was restored to his place in the Methodist ministry. In recording the fact, John Dawson says that the preachers in general thought he had been cruelly used.

Before closing our records of the year 1779 it is necessary to return, for a few moments, to the condition of the Society in London. The state of affairs in the Society may be judged from two entries in John Wesley's *Journal*. Towards the close of November, when in London, he says: 'I examined the rest of our Society, but did not find such an increase as I expected. Nay, there was a considerable decrease, plainly owing to a senseless jealousy that had crept in between our preachers, which had grieved the Holy Spirit of God, and greatly hindered His work.' On December 13 he went to Lewisham and 'settled' the London Society Book. He found that a hundred and seventy members had left the Society, and he records his opinion that the cause of their leaving was 'senseless prejudice.' Many years ago we had reason to consult an 'Assignment and Declaration of Trust of the New Chapel and Premises in the City Road, London.' It was dated May 21, 1804. In it were recitals of some of the provisions contained in the deed bearing the date on or about the sixth day of August, 1779. The original deed

[1] Vol. iii., 303-13.

vested the right of appointing preachers to the City Road Chapel in John Wesley during his life. Then followed a clause worth reproducing. The recital is as follows :

From and after the decease of the said John Wesley, it should and might be lawful to and for such person or persons as the said John Wesley, in and by his last Will and Testament in writing, or in aim by any other Deed or Writing duly signed and sealed by him in the presence of and attested by two or more credible witnesses, should nominate, during the natural life or lives of such person or persons respectively, or during the time or times to be limited by the said John Wesley in and by his last Will and Testament, or other Deed or Writing as aforesaid, and subject to the proviso and power of removal thereinafter mentioned, to have the like free liberty of ingress, (&c.) . . . and also the free use and benefit and enjoyment of the said Chapel, Morning Chapel, and Vestries for the purpose of Public Worship and preaching as aforesaid, and to and for no other use, intent or purpose whatsoever : And that, from and after the decease of such person or persons respectively, or from and after the expiration of such time or times as should or might be limited by the said John Wesley in and by his last Will and Testament, or otherwise as aforesaid, or in case of no such nomination, appointment, or limitation should be made by the said John Wesley, then, from and after the decease of the said John Wesley and from thenceforth for and during all the residue of the said term of fifty-nine years which should be then to come and unexpired, it should and might be lawful to and for such person or persons as should or might from time to time be nominated at the yearly meetings or conferences of the people called Methodists, held at London, Bristol or Leeds, and approved by the Trustees of the said Chapel for the time being, or the major part of them, for and during the term of such appointment, and subject to the said proviso and powers of removal next thereinafter mentioned, to have the like free liberty of ingress (&c.) . . . and also the free use and benefit and enjoyment of the said Chapel, Morning Chapel, and Vestries, for the purpose of Public Worship and Preaching as aforesaid, and to and for no other use, intent and purpose whatsoever. . . .[1]

When we read the foregoing recitals from the Deed dated August 6, 1779, we see that no power of appointing himself to preach in the new chapel was conferred on Charles Wesley. It will be enough to say that shortly after the period we have reached, at the request of the trustees, he was released from what seems to have been his self-imposed task. We will close our review of this subject by quoting an extract from John Wesley's Will, dated February 20, 1789. He says : ' Whereas I am empowered by a late Deed to name the persons who are

[1] We have reproduced the actual words contained in the recitals of the deed dated May 21, 1804, rather than attempting a paraphrase.

A YEAR OF DIFFICULTIES

to preach in the new chapel in London (the Clergymen for continuance), and by another Deed to name a Committee for appointing preachers in the new chapel at Bath, I do hereby appoint John Richardson, Thomas Coke, James Creighton, Peard Dickinson, Clerks; Alexander Mather, William Thompson, Henry Moore, Andrew Blair, John Valton, Joseph Bradford, James Rogers, and William Myles to preach in the New Chapel at London, and to be the Committee for appointing preachers in the New Chapel at Bath.'[1] Four clergymen and eight Methodist preachers were in this way appointed by John Wesley to preach in the City Road Chapel, and that fact causes us to forget a somewhat painful episode. The appointment of the Committee in the Bath case is interesting in the light of the circumstances we have recorded, but it does not give us a clearer view of the action taken by John Wesley when he removed Alexander McNab from the superintendency of the Bristol circuit.

---

[1] Charles Wesley died on March 29, 1788.

XI

WESLEY'S ATTITUDE TO THE CHURCH OF ENGLAND AND THE ROMAN CATHOLICS IN 1780

JOHN WESLEY'S records of the events of 1780 commence with a cheerful note. On Sunday, January 2, he says: 'We had the largest congregation at the renewal of our covenant with God which ever met upon the occasion; and we were thoroughly convinced that God was not departed from us. He never will, unless we depart from Him.' This service was held in the City Road Chapel. It was fortunate that he received this inspiration for he was soon face to face with difficulties. Some came to him in the ordinary course of his work, but we have now to deal with one which was caused by his own action. The reign of George III was marked by the passing of several Acts of Parliament that softened the stringency of certain regulations that had been passed in the case of Roman Catholics and Protestant Dissenting ministers and schoolmasters. 'The Catholic Relief Act' of 1778, and 'The Act for the further relief of Protestant Dissenting Ministers and Schoolmasters,' passed in 1779, are well known to students of the legislation of the period. At this point we are only concerned with the former. When that Act was passed it created much discontent among certain classes in England. The feeling increased, and in 1780, it produced a panic. We will deal with the Gordon Riots at the close of this chapter. John Wesley's attitude towards the Roman Catholics in Ireland has been described in former volumes of this series. It will be enough to say that in his open-air services many Roman Catholic listeners were present. In some parts of the country they came to hear him in defiance of the commands of their priests. So far as we can remember he made no attacks on their system of belief and Church government. He proclaimed the evangelical doctrines of the Christian religion, and pointed, with steady hand, to the cross of Christ. As one result of the absence of attack he gained the attention of Roman Catholics, some of whom became members of the Methodist Societies in Ireland.

On January 18, 1780, we find this paragraph in Wesley's *Journal*: 'Receiving more and more accounts of the increase of Popery I believed it my duty to write a letter concerning it, which was afterwards inserted in the public papers. Many were grievously offended, but I cannot help it. I must follow my own conscience.' The letter appeared in *The Public Advertiser*, and attracted much attention. It is printed in his *Works*.[1] If read with care it will be seen that in it there is no attack on the chief doctrines of the Roman Catholic Church. Wesley says in his letter : 'With persecution I have nothing to do. I persecute no man for his religious principles. Let there be as " boundless a freedom in religion " as any man can conceive. . . . I will set religion, true or false, utterly out of the question. . . . I consider not, whether the Romish religion be true or false; I build nothing on one or the other supposition.' He confined himself to one question, which he states in a few words : ' I insist upon it, that no government, not Roman Catholic, ought to tolerate men of the Roman Catholic persuasion.'

It is essential that we should understand the reason of Wesley's intervention in the controversy that was raging at this time. He had received a pamphlet entitled *An Appeal from the Protestant Association to the People of Great Britain*. A few days before writing his letter 'a kind of answer' to this pamphlet was put into his hand. In it the 'Appeal' was denounced, its style was called contemptible, its reasoning futile, its object malicious. Wesley was of a different opinion. He considered that its style was 'clear, easy and natural; the reasoning, in general, strong and conclusive; the object or design, kind and benevolent.' He determined to answer the attack. He says : 'In pursuance of the same kind and benevolent design, namely to preserve our happy constitution, I shall endeavour to confirm the substance of that tract by a few plain arguments.'

When reading Wesley's letter it is necessary to remember

[1] Wesley's *Works*, x., 159-61, third ed.

that it was written in the eighteenth century, and that it deals with a question which was then of great importance. It concerns the value of the oath of a Roman Catholic. Wesley says: 'That no Roman Catholic does, or can, give security for his allegiance or peaceable behaviour, I prove thus: It is a Roman Catholic maxim, established, not by private men, but by a public Council, that "no faith is to be kept with heretics." This has been openly avowed by the Council of Constance, but it never was openly disclaimed. Whether private persons avow or disavow it, it is a fixed maxim of the Church of Rome. But as long as it is so, nothing can be more plain than that the members of that Church can give no reasonable security to any Government of their allegiance or peaceable behaviour. Therefore they ought not to be tolerated by any Government, Protestant, Mahometan, or Pagan.' He then dwells on the important fact of the 'dispensing' power possessed by the Pope and priests, and concludes with these words: 'Setting then religion aside, it is plain that, upon principles of reason, no Government ought to tolerate men who cannot give any security to that Government for their allegiance and peaceable behaviour.' Having dealt with the main question, he relates a fact that carries us back to the dim light of the eighteenth century. He says: 'Some time since, a Romish priest came to one I knew, and, after talking with her largely, broke out, "You are no heretic, you have the experience of a real Christian!" "And would you," she asked, "burn me alive?" He said, "God forbid!—unless it were for the good of the Church!"'

Wesley's letter in *The Public Advertiser* was followed by two others sent to the editors of *The Freeman's Journal*, published in Dublin. Its publication brought into the arena a formidable antagonist, Father O'Leary, a Capuchin Friar. He wrote voluminously and Wesley replied briefly. It will be enough to quote Southey's estimate of this controversy. He says: 'Wesley had exposed the errors of the Romanists in some controversial writings, perspicuously and forcibly. One of those writings gave the Catholics an advantage because it defended the Protestant Association of 1780, and the events which speedily followed were turned against him. But upon the great points in dispute he was clear and cogent, and the temper of this, as of his other controversial tracts, was such that some years afterwards, when a common friend invited him to meet his antagonist, Father O'Leary, it was gratifying to both parties to meet on terms of courtesy and mutual goodwill.'[1] This meeting took place on May 12, 1787. Wesley, describing his old antagonist, says : ' I was not at all displeased at being disappointed. He is not the stiff, queer man that I expected, but of an easy, genteel carriage, and seems not to be wanting either in sense or learning.'[2]

On April 13 John Wesley set out from Bristol on his northern journey. He had intended to go to Ireland, but his controversy with Father O'Leary had created a difficulty. Several of the preachers in Ireland, and some of the people, had sent letters to him telling him that it would not be safe for him to come to the country. Threats of danger did not disconcert him; but, thinking over the matter, he came to the conclusion that it would not be prudent to visit Ireland at that time. As we follow him on his northern journey we are impressed by the fact that as he went on his way many clergymen opened their churches to him and welcomed him to their pulpits. He preached in the churches at Pitchcombe, Bengeworth, Pebworth, Warrington, Leeds, Otley, Bingley, Heptonstall, Todmorden, and Pateley Bridge. Haworth was not included in this list. In his *Journal* Wesley explains the reason. He says that Mr. Richardson was unwilling that he should preach any more in Haworth Church; but, in a footnote in the *Journal,* it is suggested that it was not his own desire that he should be excluded. Against this disappointment we must place the opening of the church at Pateley Bridge, a former scene of fierce persecution. As time went on the number of the churches where Wesley was welcomed rapidly increased. Towards the close of his life he found it difficult to accept all the invitations he received from friendly clergymen. That stage, however, was not reached during the year under consideration.

Wesley's preaching in the church at Otley has a pathetic interest. We always connect the name of Miss Elizabeth Ritchie with Otley. She had recovered from her serious illness, but when Wesley reached the town on April 18, he found her mourning the loss of her father. Dr. Ritchie

[1] Southey's *Life of Wesley,* ii., 322. Fitzgerald's edition.
[2] John Wesley's *Journal,* vii., 274.

was a native of Edinburgh. He had served for many years as a surgeon in the Navy. Leaving the sea, he settled in Wharfedale, where he continued his practice as a doctor. He married Miss Beatrice Robinson. Their second child, who was born in Otley in 1754, was named Elizabeth. She became the friend of Wesley, and was one of the noblest women in the large group that adorned the early Methodist Society.[1] Wesley entered the house of mourning, and heard the story of the 'passing' of Dr. Ritchie. He had 'witnessed a good confession.' When someone said to him, 'You will be better soon,' he replied: 'I cannot be better, for I have God in my heart. I am happy, happy, happy in His love.' It was thought well that a funeral sermon should be preached in the church and that John Wesley should be the preacher. The vicar, Mr. Wilson, was approached; after a little hesitation he consented to the arrangement. He preached from a text that had been chosen by Dr. Ritchie—'To you that believe He is precious.' Wesley, in describing the service says: 'Perhaps such a congregation had hardly been in Otley Church before. Surely the right hand of the Lord bringeth mighty things to pass.'

Those who have rambled through the Yorkshire dales in the month of May, will pause at several entries in Wesley's *Journal*. The beauty of the country in spring, summer, and the early autumn makes an ineffaceable impression on the memory of those who are worthy to see it. They will linger over Wesley's description of his visit to Grassington. He reached that restful town on May 1 at ten o'clock in the morning. The news of his coming had been spread abroad. He had intended to hold a service in the small Methodist preaching-house, but 'a multitude' had assembled. Clouds were in the sky, but they sailed along, and the morning was fair. Wesley went into the open air and preached to the great crowd. We seem to forget the present as we picture the scene. We listen to the singing and to the sound of the preacher's voice, and Grassington, on that May Day shines out before us. Then dark clouds cover the sky and heavy rain descends. But Wesley has to preach at Pateley Bridge. The road there goes over high hills and then descends into the valley in which the little town lies. We pause for a few

[1] See Wesley's *Journal*, vi., 274, note.

moments at the bridge. We think of Thomas Lee, who was flung into the river by the mob, which was usually led by a paid captain, or in his absence, by the parson of the parish. That was about the year 1752. As we follow Wesley in the afternoon of May 1, 1780, what do we see? The vicar of the parish approaches him and offers him the use of his church! A crowd had assembled to hear Wesley. It could not get into the Methodist preaching-house, and the vicar places his church, which was twice as large, at Wesley's disposal. Even then many had to stand outside. As we look at the record in Wesley's *Journal* we read into it a deep meaning. He says: 'How vast is the increase of the work of God! Particularly in the most rugged and uncultivated places! How does He "send the springs of grace" also "into the valleys, that run among the hills."'[1]

On May 6, making his way farther north, Wesley reached Whitehaven. He was hoping to sail from that port to the Isle of Man. A little vessel was waiting for him; but the wind turned against him, and he had to abandon his intention. On May 9 he went to Cockermouth. After visiting Newcastle, he set out for Scotland on May 15. His visit to Scotland did not invigorate him. His comment after preaching in Edinburgh on Sunday, May 21, is suggestive. He says: 'In the evening the house was well filled, and I was enabled to speak strong words. But I am not a preacher for the people of Edinburgh. Hugh Saunderson and Michael Fenwick are more to their taste.' He was glad to get back ' to the loving colliers at Plessey, and to the Orphan House at Newcastle.' In a letter to Joseph Benson, written by William Smith on June 6, he says: ' Mr. Wesley left us last week. I never was better pleased with him in my life, nor do I remember ever to have been more profited by his preaching. . . . His congregations were very large.' During his journey to the south we note repetitions of a fact we have already emphasized. On Sunday, June 4, at Staveley, near Boroughbridge, the rector, Mr. Hartley, invited him to preach in his church. A great crowd assembled. It was so large that, after the rector had read prayers, Wesley went out into the grave-yard, and preached, standing on a tombstone. In the afternoon he preached again in the same place. But a

---

[1] For Thomas Lee, see *John Wesley the Master Builder*, 115-16.

more remarkable event is connected with the date, Sunday, June 25. The rector of Epworth Church was Sir William Anderson, his curate in residence was Joshua Gibson. The latter was strongly opposed to Wesley and the Methodists. But, to his disgust, he received a letter from the rector containing an 'express order' that Wesley was to preach in the church. He dare not defy that order. So Wesley held a memorable service in the church of his father. At ten o'clock he began reading prayers to a large congregation. Then he preached from the text: 'Take heed therefore how ye hear: for whosoever hath to him shall be given; and whosoever hath not, from him shall be taken even that which he seemeth to have.' His comment on the service is: 'Not a breath was heard; all was still "as summer's noontide air," and I believe our Lord then sowed seed in many hearts, which will bring forth fruit to perfection.'[1] On Monday, June 26, he preached in Finningley Church; and on Sunday, July 2, he preached twice in 'the old church' at Sheffield. On Wednesday, July 5, after leaving Derby, he preached in a church at a place not named, but is supposed to be Risley. At the close of the week he arrived in London.

Wesley returned to London at a critical time in the history of the country. On June 2 the Gordon riots had commenced. They lasted for several days. London was terror-stricken. The riots began as a protest against 'The Catholic Relief Act' of 1778, to which we have already referred.[2] That Act was entitled 'An Act for relieving His Majesty's subjects professing the Popish religion from certain penalties and disabilities imposed on them by an Act made in the eleventh and twelfth years of the reign of King William the Third entitled *An Act for farther preventing the growth of Popery.*' It is easy to see that an Act bearing such a title would raise the suspicion of many Protestants. Those who examined it closely would see that it contained no allusion to the Pope's spiritual authority in England, and that it required no renunciation of any Catholic doctrine.[3] We have shown that Wesley had not based his attack on Romanism on these subjects. It is no wonder that other people were alarmed at

[1] See article by the Rev. H. J. Foster in the *Wesley Historical Society Proceedings*, v., 204-5.
[2] See p. 150.
[3] See Dr. Bennett's *Laws against Nonconformity*, 220.

the action of the Government. On June 2 a great crowd of protesters, led by Lord George Gordon, marched to the House of Commons bearing an immense petition, signed by a multitude of people who demanded the repeal of the Act. That procession might be considered as consisting of 'Protestants.' But, as the days went on, a change took place. The ruffians of London saw their opportunity. They joined the assemblies of the protesters and, for several days, London became the scene of outrageous riots. The houses where the principal representatives of the Government resided were attacked. We may judge the mixed character of the mob when we note that Newgate Prison was an object of special hatred. A mob broke into it, liberated some of the prisoners, and set the place on fire. We are especially interested in the proceedings of one section of the rioters. The incident carries us back to long vanished years. We think of Charles Wesley when he was a boy at Westminster School. When there he was distinguished by his skill in 'the art of self-defence.' Better than that he was known as the defender of small boys when they were attacked by bullies. One day he interfered with prompt effect when some of the lads were ill-treating a newcomer into the school. The boys had found out that his people had taken the side of the 'Pretender' when he arrived in Scotland. That discovery kindled their rage. They furiously attacked him. But Charles Wesley protected him. He fought the bullies and ended the persecution. The Scotch boy never forgot his defender. His name was James Murray, but in later life he was known as Lord Mansfield.

Thinking of Lord Mansfield and his friendship for Charles Wesley, for a few moments we have forgotten the roar of the mob in 1780. But again it fills the air. In Sydney's *England and the English in the Eighteenth Century*, the 'Gordon riots' are fully described. It will be enough to quote his description of an incident in which Charles Wesley must have been profoundly interested. Sydney says:

A fifth desperate gang proceeded to Earl Mansfield's town house in Bloomsbury Square, where they broke down the door, smashed the windows, entered the apartments and flung all the costly furniture out of windows to the howling rioters who stood below, and by whom it was promptly committed to the flames of a fire which they had kindled amid shouts of fiendish delight. A most valuable collection of pictures, and some of the scarcest manuscripts supposed to be in the possession of any private person in the world, together with all his lordship's notes on important legal cases and the constitution of England, fell a sacrifice to the flames. Lord and Lady Mansfield fortunately contrived to escape through a back door a few minutes before the rioters broke in and took possession of the house. The military were sent for, and of course arrived too late, but the menacing attitude which the mob adopted compelled them to fire in their own defence, with the result that six men and a woman lost their lives, and several were sorely wounded. From Bloomsbury it had been the intention of the rioters to march to Lord Mansfield's country seat at Caen Wood, Hampstead, which intention they would most certainly have carried out, had not a troop of soldiers been sent thither for the protection of the house.[1]

John Wesley must have listened to the story of the riots with disgust. He and his people knew what mob-violence meant. He was a sturdy Protestant, but his strong convictions did not make him blind to the excellence of some of the books, written by Roman Catholics, which he had read in former years, and from which he often made extracts which he printed for the instruction of his people. He was gifted with the fine power possessed by those who are able to see the good side of people who differ from them in opinion. As to the persecution of the Romanists his view was stated in a sermon he preached on that ominous date, November 5, in City Road Chapel. This is his entry in the *Journal*: ' I preached at the new chapel on Luke ix. 55 : " Ye know not what manner of spirit ye are of," and showed that, supposing the Papists to be heretics, schismatics, wicked men, enemies to us, and to our Church and nation, yet we ought not to persecute, to kill, hurt, or grieve them, but barely to prevent their doing hurt.' That opinion was expressed at a time when the country was seething with excitement caused by the Gordon Riots.

On Sunday, July 9, after his return to London, John Wesley preached at the new chapel. After recording the fact he says: ' In the following days I read over, with a few of our preachers, the *Large Minutes* of the Conference, and considered all the articles, one by one, to see whether any should be omitted or altered.' We are sometimes disappointed

---

[1] Sydney's *England and the English in the Eighteenth Century*, ii., 208-9. The name Caen Wood afterwards became corrupted to Kenwood. *The Times* has done good service by printing it Ken Wood.

with the brevity of the records contained in what were then known as *The Penny Minutes,* and are apt to forget the existence of *The Large Minutes.* Those who possess the volume of *The Minutes of the Methodist Conferences,* which was published in 1862, will see that in the Appendix the six successive editions of *The Large Minutes* published during the life of John Wesley appear. The first was published in 1753 or 1757. The others in 1763, 1770, 1772, 1780, and 1789. The earlier editions were prepared by John Wesley, but the 1780 edition possesses special value because it was issued after being considered by a committee of the preachers. The six editions, printed in parallel columns, fill more than two hundred large pages of the 1862 edition. Students who are determined to understand the Methodism of Wesley's day, will examine them closely. In a clear fashion they reveal the steady growth of the constitution of the Methodist Church during Wesley's life-time. At present we are only concerned with the light they cast on a question that came into special prominence about the year 1770, and which is dealt with in *The Large Minutes* in that year, and in 1780 and 1789. It was the question of the relation of the Methodists to the Church of England. There can be no doubt that as the dignitaries of the Church of England never carried out their threat to excommunicate John Wesley, he considered himself as a clergyman of that Church to the end of his life. At certain crises, when he was in special danger of excommunication, he declared that he was prepared to accept that punishment rather than abandon his work, which certainly was not carried on in accordance with eighteenth-century ideas of clerical employment. Many Dissenters crowded into his Societies, and a host of men and women, who could only be properly described as belonging to 'no church,' came under his influence and that of his lay-preachers. A rapidly increasing number of the members of the Church of England became members of his Societies in many parts of England, and an extraordinary problem presented itself which demanded patient consideration. At first he told the Dissenters that they must attend the services at their own chapels, the rest of the members were supposed to come to short services on Sundays held in their own preaching-houses out of church hours, and afterwards to attend the services in the Church of England.

160 ATTITUDE TO CHURCH OF ENGLAND

But in 1780 the problem had become complicated by the erection of many Methodist preaching-houses in different parts of England, Scotland, Wales, and Ireland. As in many places the Methodists were unwelcome visitors to the churches, it will be useful if we attempt to discover the number of Methodist preaching-houses that existed in this country at the period we have reached.

In Myles's *Chronological History of the People called Methodists,* we get light on the subject we are considering. He gives us a list of the Methodist 'Chapels' in England, Wales, Scotland, the Isle of Man, the Norman Isles, the Isle of Wight, the Isle of Scilly, and Ireland. We have carefully examined his lists. In the first instance we have tried to ascertain the number of Methodist preaching-houses that were in existence in 1780. Confining ourselves for the moment to double figures, we see that in Yorkshire there were fifty-four preaching-houses; in Ireland thirty-seven; in Cornwall twenty-six; in Durham fifteen; in Lancashire fourteen, and in Lincolnshire eleven. Only Herefordshire, Rutlandshire and Monmouthshire were without a preaching-house. Passing away from the counties that we have mentioned, we find that the total number of Methodist preaching-houses in these islands, in 1780, was three hundred and three.[1] It must be remembered that Wesley and the Conference had for several years put a strong constraint on the desire to build preaching-houses in the circuits, but in spite of that fact, they were rising, here and there, in these islands. It is easy to understand that, among other reasons, the attitude of the clergy, and the unfriendliness of the mass of the church people, had kindled an irresistible desire to have places in which Methodists could worship in peace.

In examining the *Large Minutes* of 1780, we see some sign of Wesley's clearer view of the subject. Among the 'warnings' contained in them, we see that the preachers are directed to warn the people 'against calling our Society the Church; against calling our preachers ministers, our houses meeting-houses, call them plain preaching-houses or chapels.' That last clause arrests us. In 1772 the direction, in the case

---

[1] Myles gives us the number in 1812. In England there were 1,255; in Wales 85; in Scotland 25; in the islands 30; in Ireland 145; the total number being 1,540. See his *Chronological History,* 445. Fourth edition.

of the chapels, was: 'Call them plain preaching-houses.' But in 1780 the rigour of the rule was relaxed. Since 1772 the City Road Chapel had been built. Its erection, and the order of its services, had made it difficult to describe it as a mere 'preaching-house.' Wesley had been careful to call West Street Chapel by its old name, but he seems to have hesitated before he allowed the name of chapel to be used in the case of his 'preaching-houses' in the country. We think that one of his reasons for restraining the Methodists from calling their chapels 'meeting-houses' was that, with all his might, he strove to prevent them from running the risk of being considered Dissenters. In his early years he had formed strong prejudices against the Nonconformists. It is true that his views had changed; he had become friendly with some of them, and had preached in their places of worship. Still, although he had become a wiser man, he could not suffer himself to be called a 'dissenter.' When we see his definition of the word Dissenter, in 1772, and compare it with that which he gives in 1780, we can understand that his prejudices were waning. In the former year he says: 'We are not Dissenters in the only sense which our law acknowledges, namely, persons who believe it is sinful to attend the service of the Church, for we do attend it at all opportunities.' In 1780 he says: 'We are not Dissenters in the only sense which our law acknowledges, namely, those who renounce the service of the Church.' It is not needful to say that, in the present day, both definitions are inaccurate, but every student of the history of this country is aware that, at one time, Wesley's definition fairly described a militant section of the Dissenters of England.

On Tuesday, August 1, the Conference began in Bristol. Both John and Charles Wesley were there. They had been engaged in trying to settle the disputes we have described, which still continued to agitate the Society in Bath. On the previous Sunday John Wesley had preached in Bristol, and, in his *Journal*, he notes that forty or fifty of the preachers had arrived. Acting on the suggestion of the foregoing Conference, it was resolved that 'for the future we allow nine or ten days for each Conference; that everything relative to the carrying on the work of God may be maturely considered.' The business proceeded on the usual lines. We note that an important paragraph was added to the answer to the question, 'Who desist from travelling?' 'N.B.—As we admit no one as a travelling preacher, unless we judge him to have grace, gifts, and fruit, so we cannot receive any one as such any longer than he retains those qualifications.' But Wesley says that the main business for which this Conference met was: 'To revise and enforce the *Large Minutes.*' In his *Journal* he gives no information concerning the character of the 'conversation' which arose on this important subject. On Wednesday, August 9, he says: 'We concluded the Conference in much peace and love.' We should have valued any light on the course of the discussion of the contents of the *Large Minutes,* but putting aside the *Journal,* we must look in another direction for valuable information.

We have said that Charles Wesley was present at the Conference. We turn to Thomas Jackson's illuminating *Life of the Rev. Charles Wesley.* Describing Charles Wesley's experiences at this Conference, Jackson says: 'He saw, or thought he saw, in that annual assembly, the working of principles unfavourable to that strict Churchmanship which he believed to be essential to the continuance of that revival of religion which had long been in progress.' It is certain that some things were said in the course of discussion that caused him to despair of the future of Methodism. We think it probable that statements concerning the relation of the Methodists to the Church of England were challenged, and that some of the sturdy lay preachers who were present refused to consider themselves as subordinate to that Church. Certainly the *Large Minutes* contained statements that would excite the surprise of men who were at that time constantly hindered in their work by hostile clergy. Charles Wesley saw the trend of affairs more clearly than his brother. After the Conference Jackson says 'he poured forth the feelings of his mind' in a hymn. Its character can be judged from these verses:

> Why should I longer, Lord. contend,
> My last important moments spend
>   In buffeting the air?
> In warning those who will not see,
> But rest in blind security,
>   And rush into the snare?

> Prophet of ills, why should I live,
> Or by my sad forebodings grieve
>   Whom I can serve no more?
> I only can their loss bewail,
> Till life's exhausted sorrows fail,
>   And the last pang is o'er.

John Wesley's influence with the preachers was so great that he was able to secure the acceptance of the *Large Minutes* of 1780 and 1789 by the Conference. Jackson reminds us of his 'cheerful buoyancy,' and contrasts it with his brother's 'sadness and despondency,' but buoyancy does not always create clear sight.[1]

On Thursday, August 10, the day after the Bristol Conference closed, we see John Wesley writing a letter. We have reserved our references to the American War, but it is necessary, at this point, to mention facts that cast light on the question we have just considered. It is well known that the war dealt a heavy blow at the position of the Church of England in America. The number of churches and clergymen was diminished. In many instances there was no church or clergyman in the neighbourhoods where Methodist Societies had been formed. The Methodists were quickly increasing in number. Tyerman states the case clearly. He says that there were thousands of American Methodists who were left without the sacraments. Their need was urgent. Facing a difficult problem Tyerman asks these questions: '1. Were unordained Methodist preachers to administer sacraments? Or was an effort to be made to send a clergyman of the Church of England to supply this lack of sacred service? Or was Wesley himself to assume episcopal functions, and by ordination, turn his preachers into priests? It is well known that, for many years, John Wesley had held strong views concerning the right of presbyters to ordain.'[2] So late as June 8, 1780, he had written a letter to his brother in which these sentences occur: 'Read Bishop Stillingfleet's "Irenicon," or any impartial history of the ancient Church, and I believe you will think as I do. I verily believe I have as good a right to ordain, as to administer the Lord's Supper. But I see abundance of reasons why I should not use that right unless

---

[1] See Jackson's *Life of Charles Wesley*, ii., 327.
[2] See Wesley's *Works*, xiii., 179. *John Wesley the Master Builder*, 303.

I was turned out of the Church. At present we are just in our place.'¹

Wesley, being much impressed by the urgency of the case, thought the matter over and decided that he would attempt to secure for America an ordained clergyman of the Church of England who might go out there and minister to the religious necessities of the Methodist people in that country. He had applied to an English bishop, who had previously shown him great courtesy, for a clerical helper to assist him in London, but had met with a refusal. Undaunted, he laid the case of America before the same bishop, but again failed. These failures induced him to write the plain-spoken letter which he sent to the bishop after the Bristol Conference. In Tyerman's *Life and Times of Wesley*, the letter can be read. It was addressed to Dr. Lowth, the Bishop of London. Having failed with him, is it any wonder that, in after years, he considered another alternative?

Wesley's letter to Dr. Lowth reveals his disappointment, but, keeping an eye on the future, we cannot share his regret. We have no hesitation in giving the incidents we have just recorded a place among his fortunate failures. He soon recovered his high spirits. Leaving Bristol he set out for Cornwall on Monday, August 14, and did not return to the city until nearly the end of the month. On September 24 he preached in Temple Church, which he describes as 'the most beautiful and most ancient church in Bristol.' The correctness of his description has been challenged, but there can be no doubt that no other church in Bristol can be compared with it in its wealth of Wesley memories. In *John Wesley and the Methodist Societies* we have recorded the fact that in this church there is a beautiful window which was placed there in 1872, to his memory.² It is in that part of the church which is known as the Weavers' Chapel, a place often visited by the Methodist pilgrim.

Wesley left Bristol on Monday, October 2, and preached at Devizes. He was visiting an old battlefield, a place full of memories of a hard-won victory. Then he went further south and west. We pause for a few moments to record the fact that, at Sarum, he found 'the fruit of Captain Webb's preaching.' That sentence opens to us the pages of the past.

¹ Tyerman's *Life and Times of Wesley*, iii., 331-2.   ² See p. 33.

It brings Captain Webb once more before us. We think of the fine work he was then doing as a fervent evangelist, not only in Bristol and Bath, but also in other places in which his influence still lingers. On October 7 Wesley returned from Portsmouth to London, where he stayed for a little more than a week. He seemed to be unable to rest. We are especially interested in his description of his visit to Oxford on October 31. He says: 'We had such a congregation at noon in Oxford as I never saw there before, and what I regarded more than their number was their seriousness. Even the young gentlemen behaved well, nor could I observe one smiling countenance, although I closely applied these words, " I am not ashamed of the gospel of Christ." '

John Wesley spent the closing months of the year in London and its neighbourhood. We note that, on November 20, he visited Chatham and Sheerness, where the Societies were confronted by serious financial difficulties. He says: ' I went on to Chatham, and, finding the Society groaning under a large debt, advised them to open a weekly subscription. The same advice I gave to the Society at Sheerness. This advice they all cheerfully followed, and with good effect.' Returning to London he faced a greater financial problem. The debt on the new chapel was a much more serious matter. He gave the same advice to those who were struggling with a great difficulty. The advice was followed. In one year one thousand and four hundred pounds were raised, and the heavy burden was lightened. Leaving the field of finance we note that on Sunday, December 10, he held a Society meeting in London in which he read and explained the *Large Minutes* of the Conference. His action has not lost its significance. It is worth while to ponder the following words. He says: ' I desire to do all things openly and above board. I would have all the world, and especially all our Society, see not only all the steps we take, but the reasons why we take them.' Those who are acquainted with the history of the storm-periods that have occurred in Methodism since his time will pause for a while in the presence of his action, and will see the wisdom of his word.

In this chapter we have looked beyond the boundaries of the Methodist Societies, and have dealt with facts which have influenced the national life. We have referred to the condition of London in the days of the Gordon riots. Reading some of the closing words of Wesley's *Journal*, written in December, 1780, we are reminded of that dangerous outburst of fury. On Saturday, December 16, this is Wesley's entry in his *Journal* : ' Having a second message from Lord George Gordon, earnestly desiring to see me, I wrote a line to Lord Stormont, who, on Monday, the eighteenth, sent me a warrant to see him. On Tuesday, the nineteenth, I spent an hour with him at his apartment in the Tower. Our conversation turned upon Popery and religion. He seemed to be well acquainted with the Bible, and had abundance of other books, enough to furnish a study. I was agreeably surprised to find he did not complain of any person or thing, and cannot but hope his confinement will take a right turn and prove a lasting blessing to him.' Nine years later Lord George Gordon was confined in Newgate in the cell formerly occupied by Dr. Dodd. He wished to see Wesley again, but Wesley sent the Rev. Peard Dickinson in his place. In the course of their conversation Lord Gordon ' expressed much respect for Mr. Wesley's character and the good he had done in the nation.' [1]

---

[1] Wesley's *Journal*, vi., 301, note.

XII

A CROWDED YEAR

THE year 1781 was distinguished by the fact that it was devoted by Wesley to constant work among the Societies in England, Scotland and Wales. The erection of the City Road Chapel in London had brought a heavy burden of responsibility on him, but that burden had been lightened by the successful efforts that had been made to meet the heavy cost of the building. He rejoiced at the return of the opportunities of his itinerant life. Following him in his wanderings we will note some of his experiences. He spent the first month of the year in London. On Sunday, January 14, he preached in St. John's Church, Wapping. He says: 'Although the church was extremely crowded, yet there was not the least noise or disorder while I besought them, by the mercies of God, to present themselves a living sacrifice, holy, acceptable to God.' The quietness and reverence of the congregations in the churches in which he preached during the closing years of his life made a deep impression on him. It was a sign of the passing of the former days of storm and contempt. It showed that many people were beginning to welcome the neglected truths that he and the evangelical clergy had brought to light. Later in the month he went to Birling, in Kent, to see his old friend, the Rev. Edward Holme. He had heard that he was 'extremely weak.' The report was true. He found him 'very near worn out, just tottering over the grave.' Wesley took the evening service. The night was exceeding dark, but Mr. Holme 'crept with him to the church.' It was well filled. His text was: 'Repent, and believe the gospel.' The congregation was much affected by the sight of its afflicted pastor and by the sermon. Wesley says that it appeared 'quite stunned.' The two old friends returned to the parsonage, where Wesley spent the night. In the morning he went back to London.

This visit to Birling touches our sympathy. But Wesley's experiences a week later in London excite our envy. On Thursday, January 25, he tells us, in his *Journal*, that he spent an agreeable hour at a concert given by his nephews. It is true that he adds to his brief description a few words in a tone with which we are familiar. He says: 'But I was a little out of my element among lords and ladies. I love plain music and plain company best.' Those who are intimately acquainted with his *Journal* will be familiar with somewhat similar statements when he describes his visits to noblemen's estates, gazed on lovely landscapes or listened to imperishable music. When we read his descriptions of a nobleman's mansion, standing in the midst of spreading woods, we know what to expect. He will remind us of the brevity of human life, and the coming of a day when the owner of the estate will have to say 'farewell' to its splendours. He used that consideration as a shield against the attacks of envy. It did not always avail. To the end of his life he had to fight hard against everything that would allure him from the work his Master had given him to do.

The concert in Charles Wesley's house in Chesterfield Street, Marylebone, makes a strong appeal to us. In our volume of *John Wesley the Master Builder*[1] we have recorded the fact that Charles Wesley's occupation of the house was made possible by the kindness of his friend, Mrs. Gumley. It was a large, well-furnished house, which stood in a rural neighbourhood. Close to it were green fields that spread towards the far-off hills that seemed to lean against the sky. The only drawback to its position was its distance from the chapel in the City Road. It must be noted that in 1781 John Wesley was absent from London from March 4 to August 16, and that he left again on August 19 and did not return until October 12. In addition to the oversight of the Society at West Street, Charles Wesley was left in charge of the Society at the City Road Chapel, which stood three miles away from his home.

In the Chesterfield Street house there was a large room capable of containing about eighty persons. After certain alterations had been made it was used as a concert room. It was often filled with people who were attracted to the house

[1] See pp. 299-300.

by the fame of Charles Wesley's two sons, who held a high position in the musical world of London. In this room the concert was given which now claims our attention. Watching the assembly we note, first of all, the two musicians. Charles Wesley, Jun., was then a young man of about twenty-four years of age, his brother Samuel being ten years younger. Then we catch sight of their mother. There is a look of brightness on her face which reveals her confidence in her sons. In the Rev. John Telford's *Life of the Rev. Charles Wesley* there is an admirable account of the early musical training of the two boys by their mother. Those who know Charles Street in Bristol, which lies at the foot of the hill that reaches up to Kingsdown, will pause at the house. It is now marked by a tablet which records the fact that it was the home of Charles Wesley. It was in this house that the boys began their career as musicians. Their trainer was their mother. Samuel Wesley in after years, speaking of his early musical training, says that his father never played any instrument save a little German flute at Oxford. He also says that his father had not 'a vocal talent, but could join in a hymn or simple melody, tolerably well in tune.' We are inclined to agree with Mr. Telford when he says that Samuel Wesley somewhat under-rates his father's musical gifts. He thinks that he must have been a fairly good singer. His opinion rests on the fact that he was accustomed 'to break out in praise sometimes in his sermons.' But Charles Wesley himself declared that the boys had music 'on the mother's side.' It must be remembered that she was born in Wales—that land of song. Those who have listened to the music and the singing of Welsh choirs at their great festivals will not wonder at the training that Mrs. Wesley's sons received in the days of their youth.

In Thomas Jackson's edition of *The Journal of the Rev. Charles Wesley*, there is an account of the two sons which was contributed to *The Philosophical Transactions of the Year 1781*. It was written by the Hon. Daines Barrington, the fourth son of Viscount Barrington. He was the Recorder of Bristol in 1764, but there is no clear evidence that he knew the Wesley's at that time. But, in 1775, he made their acquaintance in London. He soon became an enthusiastic admirer of the young musicians. He does full justice to the elder brother. Then, in his article, he says: 'I had first an opportunity of being witness of Master Samuel Wesley's great musical talents at the latter end of 1775, when he was nearly ten years old.' He then proceeds to give a description of Samuel Wesley's 'musical talents.' It fully justifies his enthusiasm. We will content ourselves with producing one illustration which occupies a conspicuous position in that description. He tells us that the boy was desired to compose a march for one of the regiments of guards. He declares that it evoked 'the approbation of all who ever heard it.' One of them, a distinguished officer of the Royal Navy, said that 'it was a movement which would probably inspire steady and serene courage when the enemy was approaching.' Barrington's description of his visit to St. James's Park with Samuel Wesley must be quoted. He says:

> As I thought the boy would like to hear this march performed, I carried him to the parade at the proper time, when it had the honour of beginning the military concert. The piece being finished, I asked him whether it was executed to his satisfaction; to which he replied, 'By no means,' and I then immediately introduced him to the band (which consisted of very tall and stout musicians), that he might set them right. On this, Sam immediately told them that they had not done justice to his composition; to which they answered the urchin, with both astonishment and contempt, by, 'Your composition!' Sam, however, replied, with great serenity, 'Yes, my composition!'; which I confirmed. They then stared, and severally made their excuses, by protesting that they had copied accurately from the manuscript which had been put into their hands. This he most readily allowed to the hautboys and bassoons, but said it was the French horns that were in fault; who making the same defence, he insisted upon the original score being produced; and, showing them their mistake, ordered the march to be played again, which they submitted to with as much deference as they would have shown to Handel.[1]

Returning to the Concert Room in Chesterfield Street, we must again glance at the audience. It is difficult to name those who were present. We think it is probable that the Earl of Mornington, the father of the Duke of Wellington, was there. Mr. Telford says that for some years he breakfasted once a week at Chesterfield Street and practised with the young musicians on various instruments. He brought his violin under his coat, and often said that he should never be ashamed to be taken for a teacher of music. But in that

[1] See Jackson's edition of *The Journal of the Rev. C. Wesley*, 162-3.

crowded room one figure stands out distinctly. We see an old man grasping the hand of John Wesley. He raises it to his lips and kisses it. Why do our thoughts fly over the Atlantic to the woods of Georgia? Why do we recall the troubled days of Wesley's missionary life in America? The questions are soon answered. The old man who greeted John Wesley in the concert-room with such affection and reverence was General Oglethorpe.[1]

John Wesley left London on March 4. He spent two or three days at Bath, then went to Bristol. The city was slowly recovering from the effects of a memorable election to Parliament. One of the candidates, Mr. Cruger, was a native of New York. His sympathies, like those of many of the electors, were wholly with the Americans. The election began on January 31 and lasted until February 24. Many collisions occurred in the streets between the hired mobs of the two parties. At the close of the election a deadly affray occurred. In his *Annals of Bristol* Latimer says: 'A party of Crugerites, passing along the quays, took offence at some flags displayed by a Swansea vessel, and ordered the crew to lower them. The demand being accompanied by some stone-throwing, the sailors fired several swivel guns upon the crowd, killing two men instantly, and wounding many other persons, including three children. The verdict of the coroner's jury on the bodies of the victims was " justifiable homicide," but there is in Temple churchyard an inscription to their memory, alleging that they were " inhumanly murdered " by three men, whose names appear on the tombstone.'[2] This election reveals the growth of the opposition in Bristol to the war with America. That opposition was then spreading through the country. It assisted in the movement that brought the war to an end at the close of the next year.

On Sunday, March 18, Wesley preached morning and evening at the room in Broadmead. Then, in the afternoon, he went to Temple Church and preached there. He must have thought of the experiences of his brother at the outset of the Methodist Mission. On July 27, 1740, Charles Wesley and

---

[1] See Telford's *Life of Charles Wesley*, 191-2; Simon's *John Wesley and the Religious Societies*, 107-73, *passim*.
[2] *The Annals of Bristol in the Eighteenth Century*, 446-7.

his little band of Kingswood colliers were repelled from the sacrament in Temple Church.[1] Now all was changed. On August 21, 1779, Joseph Easterbrook became the vicar. It it pleasant to contrast some of the entries in Charles Wesley's *Journal* with John Wesley's note on March 18, 1781. He says: ' The congregation here is remarkably well behaved, indeed so are the parishioners in general.' He attributes the improvement not only to the presence of Joseph Easterbrook, but also to the character of his predecessor, Alexander Catcott, ' who was indeed as eminent for piety as most clergymen in England.'

John Wesley left Bristol on Monday, March 19, and began his long journey to the north of England. We must confine our attention to a few of the more important incidents which occurred during his travels. The careful reader of his *Journal* will note that, in 1781, his entries become shorter. He often confines himself to noting the name of the towns in which he preached, but gives us no information concerning the state of Methodism in them.

On Thursday, March 22, leaving Worcester, he went to Bengeworth, where his old friend, Mr. Beale, the clergyman, lived. He preached in the church. Then in the evening he preached in Pepworth Church. He had visited these places before and had been welcomed by their clergymen. On Saturday, March 24, he reached Birmingham. The next day he preached at Birmingham, Dudley, and Wednesbury, but he gives us no particulars concerning the services. On Tuesday, March 27, he went ' a little out of his way ' to open the new preaching-house at Shrewsbury. He expands his reference by giving a brief description of his impression of the service. He says that he did not so much wonder at the largeness as at the seriousness of the congregation. Then he continues: ' So still and deeply attentive a congregation I did not expect to see here. How apt are we to forget that important truth that " all things are possible with God! " ' Those who possess the art of ' reading between the lines ' will draw their own conclusions concerning his experiences during previous visits to the town.

On Friday, March 30, John Wesley was in Manchester. He had come to open a new chapel which had been built in

[1] See *John Wesley and the Methodist Societies*, 31-3.

Oldham Street. He says that the chapel was about the size of that in London. His reference is, without doubt, to the chapel in City Road. He was much impressed with the seriousness of the congregation, and expresses the hope that 'much good might be done in the place.' His hope has been fulfilled. It is true that the chapel has disappeared, but on its site stands its successor, the Central Hall. It would be difficult to define the limits of the influence of the work that has been done in that place. It has been felt throughout the Methodist world. On the following Sunday his *Journal* contains this record: 'I began reading prayers at ten o'clock. Our country friends flocked in from all sides. At the communion was such a sight as I am persuaded was never seen at Manchester before; eleven or twelve hundred communicants at once, and all of them fearing God.' On Tuesday he said 'farewell' to his 'affectionate friends,' and went on to Bolton. There he was again delighted with the condition of the Society. He declares that the members were 'true, original Methodists.' He says: 'They are not conformed to the world, either in its maxims, its spirit, or its fashions, but are simple followers of the Lamb; consequently they increase both in grace and number.'

The careful readers of his *Journal* will have noted that Wesley had not been in Ireland since 1778. He had accepted the warning against visiting Ireland during the height of the Father O'Leary controversy in 1780, but he had made up his mind to go there in the month we have now reached. On Monday, April 9, he went to Liverpool, and found a ship ready to sail. He shall describe his adventures.

Mon. 9.—Desiring to be in Ireland as soon as possible, I hastened to Liverpool, and found a ship ready to sail; but the wind was contrary, till on Thursday morning the captain came in haste, and told us the wind was come quite fair. So Mr. Floyd, Snowden, Joseph Bradford, and I, with two of our sisters, went on board. But scarce were we out at sea, when the wind turned quite foul, and rose higher and higher. In an hour I was so affected as I had not been for forty years before. For two days I could not swallow the quantity of a pea of anything solid, and very little of any liquid. I was bruised and sore from head to foot, and ill-able to turn me on the bed. All *Friday*, the storm increasing, the sea of consequence was rougher and rougher. Early on *Saturday* morning the hatches were closed, which, together with the violent motion, made our horses so turbulent that I was afraid we must have killed them, lest they should damage the ship. Mrs. S. ow crept to me, threw her arms over me, and said, 'Oh, sir, we will die together!' We had by this time three feet water in the hold, though it was an exceeding light vessel. Meantime we were furiously driving on a lee-shore; and when the captain cried, 'Helm a-lee,' she would not obey the helm. I called our brethren to prayers, and we found free access to the throne of grace. Soon after we got, I know not how, into Holyhead harbour, after being sufficiently buffeted by the winds and waves for two days and two nights.

The more I considered, the more I was convinced it was not the will of God I should go to Ireland at this time. So we went into the stage-coach without delay, and the next evening came to Chester.

John Wesley rested for a few days in Chester. Abandoning his hope of reaching Ireland, he considered the places where he could spend his time to the greatest advantage. He soon thought of the Isle of Man, and those parts of Wales which he had not been able to see in his ordinary course. The surrender of his plans for the visitation of Ireland had given him an unexpected opportunity of helping Societies which he had not been able to assist for some time. He made up his mind to go first to Wales. On his way he preached in several towns in England. Then on Monday, April 23, he preached at Brecknock to a large congregation. Two days afterwards he set out for Carmarthen. He was accompanied by Joseph Bradford, his 'travelling-companion,' who had been with him on board the Liverpool ship that had failed to reach Ireland. The voyage had told severely on Bradford. After going for six miles from Brecknock he could go no further. Wesley was obliged to leave him at a friend's house, where he was nursed for about three months.[1]

Wesley remained in Wales until the middle of May. In addition to preaching in the Methodist 'rooms,' we note that, on Sunday, April 29, he preached in St. Daniel's Church in Pembroke. On Friday, May 4, he preached in Newport Church in the morning and at four o'clock in the afternoon. The following Sunday he preached in St. Thomas's Church in Haverfordwest, and on Tuesday, May 8, in the church near Bridgend. It was at Haverfordwest that an incident occurred which delighted him. He had preached in the 'room' on Sunday, April 29, to the liveliest congregation he had seen in Wales, but the next day he had an experience that

[1] For Squire Walter Williams and his wife, Bradford's kindly hosts, see *Journal*, vi., 314, note.

must be recorded in his own words. He says: 'I met about fifty children; such a company as I have not seen for many years. Miss Warren loves them, and they love her. She has taken true pains with them, and her labour has not been in vain. Several of them are much awakened, and the behaviour of all is so composed that they are a pattern to the whole congregation.' Those who know Wesley best are aware of his love for little children; they will be able to picture this scene which shines out from the pages of his *Journal*. It is followed by a description that will interest those who wish to realize the condition of some parts of Wales during the days of his wanderings.

May 1, Tues.—I rode to St. David's, seventeen measured miles from Haverford. I was surprised to find all the land, for the last nine or ten miles, so fruitful and well-cultivated. What a difference is there between the westermost parts of England and the westermost parts of Wales! The former (the west of Cornwall) so barren and wild, the latter so fruitful and well improved. But the town itself is a melancholy spectacle. I saw but one tolerable good house in it; the rest were miserable huts indeed. I do not remember so mean a town even in Ireland. The cathedral has been a large and stately fabric, far superior to any other in Wales. But a great part of it is fallen down already, and the rest is hastening into ruin: one blessed fruit (among many) of bishops residing at a distance from their see. Here are the tombs and effigies of many ancient worthies, Owen Tudor in particular; but the zealous Cromwellians broke off their noses, hands and feet, and defaced them as much as possible. But what had the Tudors done to them? Why, they were progenitors of Kings.

Wesley returned to England, and on Wednesday, May 30, he embarked on board the packet-boat at Whitehaven for the Isle of Man. He must have compared his recent experiences of sea voyages. There was a dead calm for many hours, and he did not land at Douglas until Friday morning. Two of his preachers met him. One of them was John Crook. He was the superintendent of the circuit, and was then in his third year of office. His name will ever be remembered in the Isle of Man.[1] There is not a jarring note in the whole of Wesley's description of his wanderings in the Isle of Man. He preached in the open air and in the Methodist chapels to large congregations. We will fix our attention on two entries in his *Journal*. On June 2, being at Peel, he met what he calls

[1] At the 1781 Conference Crook was appointed to Ireland. He stayed there for two years. He was again appointed for two years to the Isle of Man in 1786.

'our little body of preachers.' They were two and twenty in all. Twenty of them were local preachers. His comment on them is worth recalling. He says: 'I never saw in England so many stout, well-looking preachers together. If their spirit be answerable to their look, I know not what can stand before them.' The result of the work of the preachers in the Isle of Man may be tested by comparing the number of members then in the Society in the island with those reported to the Conference of 1780. The year before Wesley's visit that number was 1,486; at the Conference of 1781 it was 1,597.[1] It is no wonder that Wesley, on June 8, makes the following comment in his *Journal*:

Having now visited the island round, east, south, north and west, I was thoroughly convinced that we have no such circuit as this, either in England, Scotland, or Ireland. It is shut up from the world; and, having little trade, is visited by scarce any strangers. There are no Papists, no Dissenters of any kind, no Calvinists, no disputers. Here is no opposition, either from the Governor (a mild, humane man), from the Bishop (a good man), or from the bulk of the clergy. One or two of them did oppose for a time; but they seem now to understand better. So that we have now rather too little than too much reproach; the scandal of the cross being, for the present, ceased. The natives are a plain, artless, simple people; unpolished, that is unpolluted: few of them are rich or genteel; the greater part moderately poor; and most of the strangers that settle among them are men that have seen affliction. The local preachers are men of faith and love, knit together in one mind and one judgement. They speak either Manx or English, and follow a regular plan, which the assistant gives them monthly.

John Wesley sailed from the Isle of Man on Monday, June 11, and was becalmed at sea. He did not reach Whitehaven until Wednesday morning. He spent the rest of the month, and the whole of July in the northern counties, constantly preaching and meeting the Societies. On Sunday, July 29, he was in Birstall, and attended the morning service in the church. After its close he was surprised to hear the clerk exclaiming with a loud voice: 'The Rev. Mr. Wesley is to preach here in the afternoon.' He had intended to preach at one o'clock, as usual, 'under the hill.' He asked John Pawson to take the open-air service, and in the afternoon he preached in the church to such a congregation as he

[1] In 1791, the year of Wesley's death, four Methodist circuits reported more than two thousand members. London stood at the head of the list with 2,950 members; the Isle of Man occupied the second place with a membership of 2,500. Manchester and Leeds followed with memberships of 2,090 and 2,080.

had never met there before. In the evening he preached at Bradford, in the open air, to a great multitude. It was above his powers of reckoning. He contents himself by saying that he preached 'to thousands upon thousands.' After that busy Sunday he visited York, Malton, Scarborough, Beverley, Hull, Pocklington, and then returned to York.

At the beginning of August the Conference met in Leeds. The Sunday before it assembled Wesley attended the morning service at 'the old church.' Speaking of the sacramental service, he says: 'We had eighteen clergymen and about eleven hundred communicants.' He and John Fletcher assisted the other clergymen at this service. In the afternoon Wesley preached in the church. It was thoroughly filled. He believed that most could hear, while he explained the new covenant 'which God had made with the Israel of God.'[1]

On Tuesday, August 7, the Conference began in Leeds. John Wesley's descriptions of its proceedings are brief. He tells us, in his *Journal*, that about seventy preachers were present whom he had severally invited to come and assist him with their advice in carrying on the work of God. This marks a new departure. In earlier times it would seem that the right to attend the Conference did not depend on Wesley's individual invitation. The fact that a man was a recognized Methodist preacher was sufficient. But, as the years went on their way it became necessary that some change should be made. The number of preachers had rapidly increased. At the Conference of 1781 the names of 178 preachers appear on the stations in the circuits of Great Britain and Ireland. With this fact we must place another. In the circuits there were 44,461 members. They formed a considerable part of the congregations who gathered together in the 303 chapels erected in England, Wales, Scotland and Ireland. We must weigh all these facts before we pronounce a hasty opinion on Wesley's new method of summoning the Conference. Those who are well acquainted with the present rules concerning attendance at Conference will see that Wesley's action was a kind of starting point to a position that still exists. Before describing this important Conference it is noteworthy that on the day before it

[1] Hebrews viii. 10-13.

assembled Wesley made an arrangement that pointed in the
direction of the limitation of his own power. He says: 'I
desired Mr. Fletcher, Dr. Coke and four more of our
brethren to meet every evening, that we might consult
together on any difficulty that occurred.'

Failing to receive much light from John Wesley's *Journal*,
we must look elsewhere for information concerning the
proceedings of this Conference. We will consult Myles and
Tyerman, and note a few incidents which cast some light on
the progress that was being made towards the position which
the Methodist Societies occupied during the closing years of
Wesley's life. We have touched the important question
of the reduction of the number of preachers who were
permitted to attend the Conference. Wesley's action
evidently had the approval of the Leeds Methodists.
Tyerman says that the burden of so many preachers being
present was found to be greater than the Leeds Society could
conveniently bear, and it was agreed that every preacher
should pay the expenses of his horse-keep during the
Conference sittings. This decision of the Conference throws
some light on the wisdom of Wesley's action. His reduction
of the number of the preachers having permission to attend
the Conference was not simply an arbitrary act. It was
founded, to some extent, on his knowledge of the
inconvenience that had been caused to the Societies in the Conference towns. There was another financial question which
had to be faced. The number of married men received into the
ranks of the travelling preachers was causing difficulties in
many circuits. Myles gives us the light we need on this
subject. After consideration the Conference asked and
answered the question: 'As we have neither money nor
houses for any more wives, what can we do?' The decision
was: 'We must admit no more married preachers, unless in
defect of single preachers.' The difficulty persisted for
several years. Even so late as the Conference of 1798 we
find the following entry in the *Minutes*: 'Q. Why cannot
more married preachers be taken out to travel, seeing we
have many unblemished characters in divers circuits? A. 1.
Because our temporal circumstances are exceedingly
straitened, so that we cannot provide for them. 2. We have
at present a sufficiency of single men to supply the circuits.'

A CROWDED YEAR

We are indebted to Tyerman for his record of two events which give this Leeds Conference special importance. He says:

> A number of Methodists at Baildon, in Yorkshire, had written to Wesley, stating that, in accordance with his instructions, they attended the services of their parish church; but their minister preached what they considered to be 'dangerously false doctrine,' inasmuch as he publicly declared, that men 'must not hope to be perfected in love, on this side eternity'; and this had made them doubt whether they ought to hear him. Wesley laid their letter before the Conference; and, as the difficulty applied to many others besides the Methodists at Baildon, he invited a friendly and free discussion. It was unanimously agreed: (1) That it was highly expedient that all the Methodists who had been bred therein, should attend the service of the church as often as possible. But that, (2) If the minister began either to preach the absolute decrees, or to rail at, and ridicule Christian perfection, they should quietly go out of the church; yet attend it again the next opportunity. . . .
>
> But this was not all that occurred, on the Church question, at the Conference of 1781. One of the principal Methodists, in Leeds, was William Hey, now in the forty-fifth year of his age, a medical man of great repute, an intimate friend and correspondent of Dr. Priestley, and who had been a Methodist for seven-and-twenty years. Mr. Hey intimated to Wesley his desire to address the Conference, and to offer some suggestions and advice; declaring, at the same time, that, if his proposals were rejected, he could no longer remain a member of the Methodist Society. By Wesley's permission he began to read a paper to the effect that Dissenting ideas had been, for many years, gradually growing among the Methodists. In proof of this, he held that the Methodists preached in places already supplied with pious ministers; that meetings in some instances were held in church hours; that the intervals of church service were so filled with public and private assemblies that there was no time for suitable refreshment nor opportunity for instructing families; that many of the largest Societies rarely went to church, and some never carried their children there; and that church ministers who formed Societies for private instruction were looked upon with an envious eye. Such were the complaints which Mr. Hey intended to lay before the Conference; but, as he proceeded, the marks of disapprobation were such that Wesley interposed, and said: 'As there is much other business before us, brother Hey must defer reading the remainder of his paper to another time.'
>
> Brother Hey forthwith left the Society; a few months later he was elected alderman; and, more than once, filled the office of chief magistrate in the town of Leeds. Of his ability and piety there can be no question; but Wesley was not prepared to allow him to be the dictator of the Methodists.[1]

[1] Tyerman's *Life and Times of Wesley*, Vol. iii., 362-4. For Dr. William Hey, see *John Wesley the Master Builder*, 180, 181.

On Tuesday, August 14, the remaining business of the Conference was finished. Wesley says that it ended 'with solemn prayer and thanksgiving.' He and Dr. Coke went to Sheffield. He preached there in the evening to a crowded audience. Then the two companions 'took chaise,' and 'travelling day and night,' they reached London. Wesley's stay in London was short. On August 19 he 'took coach' in the evening. He had a new 'travelling companion.' His name was George Whitfield, who is well known to all readers of the later *Journal*. The travellers made their way to the southern and western counties, and had reason to rejoice in the progress that was being made in the Societies. It is refreshing to read some of the entries in Wesley's *Journal* during this tour. We linger over such records as the following: 'Tuesday, August 28. In the evening I preached in the High Street at Helston. I scarce know a town in the whole county which is so totally changed; not a spark of that bitter enmity to the Methodists in which the people here for many years gloried above their fellows.' Then, on another evening, he preached in the market-place at Penzance. This is his comment: 'I designed afterwards to meet the Society, but the people were so eager to hear all they could that they quickly filled the house from end to end. This is another of the towns wherein the whole stream of the people is turned, as it were, from east to west.' On Sunday, September 2, he took his stand once more on the edge of Gwennap Pit. He says: 'About five in the evening I preached at Gwennap. I believe two or three and twenty thousand were present, and I believe God enabled me so to speak that even those who stood farthest off could hear distinctly. I think this is my *ne plus ultra*. I shall scarce see a larger congregation till we meet in the air.'[1]

John Wesley did not return to London until Friday, October 12. When he got there he was informed that his wife had died on the previous Monday. In the evening of the day of his return she was buried. He was not informed of the fact until a day or two after the funeral had taken place. She was interred in the churchyard of Camberwell. We have already described some of the incidents that

---

[1] For the Gwennap Pit of Wesley's time see *John Wesley the Master Builder*, 199-200.

occurred in the course of Wesley's unhappy married life; it is not necessary that we should return to the subject.

Making London his centre John Wesley completed his year's work. He made several excursions into places where his help was needed. We are interested in his visit to Fakenham, in the county of Norfolk. He was there on Monday, October 29, and preached in a room built by Miss Franklin, before she became Mrs. Parker. The next day he went to Wells, 'a considerable seaport twelve miles from Fakenham.' Wesley says that Miss Franklin had opened a door in Wells by preaching abroad, though at the peril of her life. He was aware that she had been an open-air preacher at Fakenham and had met with much success in that town. At Wells she was succeeded as a preacher by a young woman with whom he had a long talk. He found her 'very sensible, and much devoted to God.' It is well known to students of Methodist history that John Wesley differed from the majority of his people on the subject of women preachers. This visit to Fakenham must have confirmed him in his opinion. He never forgot that his mother, during the absence of her husband in London, had preached to growing congregations assembled in the Epworth Rectory.[1] In later years he had given carefully expressed encouragement to some of his women class-leaders who had given 'addresses' to their members. But the Fakenham and Wells incidents seem to have encouraged him to take a further step. In the *Proceedings of the Wesley Historical Society* for the year 1902 there is a valuable article by the late Rev. J. Conder Nattrass entitled 'Some Notes from the Oldest Register of the Great Yarmouth Circuit.' The entries begin in 1785, when Yarmouth formed part of the Norwich circuit, which then included Fakenham and Wells. On the second page of the 'Register' there is a list which reveals the progress made in the matter of the preaching of women in Norfolk. It seems to us probable that we may trace that progress to John Wesley's visit in 1781. In the short list of 'Local Preachers' Names' we find that of Mary Sewell, who was a class-leader at Thurlton. That is not all. In Mr. Nattrass's article a document is printed which had appeared in *The Methodist Recorder* some years before.

[1] See *John Wesley and the Religious Societies*, 61-2.

It was signed by Joseph Harper, the superintendent of the Norfolk circuit in 1787. It is so important that we reproduce it:

October 27, 1787.

We give the right hand of fellowship to Sally Mallett, and shall have no objection to her being a preacher in our connexion so long as she continues to preach the Methodist Doctrine and attends to our Discipline.

—JOSH. HARPER.

B.N. You receive this by order of Mr. Wesley and the Conference.

The note at the end of this document suggests that the subject of the preaching by women had received the careful attention of the Conference.

On November 2 Wesley returned to London. He began visiting the classes and found a considerable increase in the Society. He attributed it chiefly to the fact that for some time a small company of young people had held a prayer-meeting at five o'clock every morning. A few days afterwards he received the welcome news of the marriage of John Fletcher and Miss Bosanquet. The wedding took place in Batley Church, Yorkshire. On November 28 Wesley preached at Tunbridge Wells in the large Presbyterian meeting-house. Two days afterwards he went to Shoreham to see his old friend, Vincent Perronet, who was in his eighty-ninth year. He had nearly lost his sight. He says of him: 'But he has not lost his understanding, nor even his memory, and is full of faith and love.' On December 2 John Wesley preached in St. Swithin's Church, and on December 21 he joined in the service of fasting and prayer which was observed all over England. Those who know the critical condition of the country at that time will read a deep meaning in his words: 'Surely God will be entreated for a sinful nation.'

XIII

TOIL AND TROUBLE

In our attempts to describe the events of John Wesley's career we have been assisted by the fullness of the entries in his *Journal*. His custom was to make jottings in his *Diary* which were extended in his *Journal*. But, in 1782 and afterwards, we find that in his *Journal* there are many days without records. The latest editor has thrown light on this fact. He has shown that for some time the entries in the *Diary* had ceased to be made. Referring to the opening days of December, 1782, he says: 'At this point Wesley's *Diary* is resumed and continues day by day, and sometimes hour by hour, until within a few days of his death.' Those who are familiar with the closing volumes of the latest edition of Wesley's *Journal* will have noticed the abundance of the extracts from the *Diary*. They give us an understanding of events of which we should otherwise have been ignorant. With the help of the *Journal*, the *Diary*, the *Editorial Notes*, and other sources of information, we will try to make our way through years of exceptional importance.

We are indebted to Tyerman for rescuing from oblivion an event that occurred during January, 1782. In association with Dr. Coke, Wesley then formed a Tract Society in London. For many years he had been a writer and distributor of tracts, but in this year he took the important step which Tyerman describes. He says:

> The most notable occurrence, during this period, was the institution of a tract society—the first that ever was formed. The Religious Tract Society was originated in 1799; Wesley's seventeen years previous to this. We have before us an original document printed in 1783, entitled, 'A Plan of the Society, instituted in January, 1782, to distribute Religious Tracts among the Poor.' The rules are three: '1.—Every member must subscribe half-a-guinea, a guinea, or more, annually. 2.—A proportionable quota of tracts shall be delivered yearly to each subscriber, according to his subscription, and, as nearly as possible, at prime cost, and carriage paid. 3.—Every subscriber shall have a right to choose

his own tracts, if he please; otherwise, he will receive a proportionable variety of the whole.' After this follows a list of thirty tracts already printed, all of them either written or published by Wesley. Then there is subjoined the following: 'An Extract of the Original Proposals.'

'I cannot but earnestly recommend this to all those who desire to see true Scriptural Christianity spread throughout these nations. Men wholly unawakened will not take pains to read the Bible. They have no relish for it. But a small tract may engage their attention for half-an-hour; and may, by the blessing of God, prepare them for going forward.'[1]

JOHN WESLEY.

London, January 25, 1782.

John Wesley left London on March 3 and did not return until July 20. During that interval he visited the Societies in the west, the midlands, the north of England, and Scotland. We will note some of the most important incidents which occurred during this tour. When he was in Bristol, on March 9, he wrote a letter to Robert Carr Brackenbury, who was mourning the death of his first wife. In stepping into her carriage at Raithby she met with an accident which proved fatal. In a letter that Wesley wrote to Brackenbury in the August of 1781, we get light on her character. At that time the health of her husband was causing anxiety to her and his friends. In his letter he says: 'I shall not soon forget the agreeable conversation I had with dear Mrs. Brackenbury at Raithby. The sweetness of her temper, and the open, artless account she gave of her experience, increased my love for her. I trust you shall not die, but live to strengthen each other's hands in God, and provoke one another to love and to good works. Who is so great a God as our God? To His care I commit Mrs. Brackenbury and you.' Then, the next year, came the blow that fell so heavily on her husband. When the news of her death reached Wesley he wrote to Brackenbury a letter full of sympathy. He had a theory which, now and again, finds expression. He was convinced that the most strengthening occupation in times of trouble was steady work for God. We do not wonder that he proposed this remedy to his friend. He says: 'On April 4, I expect to be in Manchester, in order to visit the Societies in Lancashire, Cheshire, Yorkshire, and thence, if God permit, to Scotland. Perhaps it would be of use if

[1] Tyerman's *Life and Times of Wesley*, iii., 369.

you took part of the journey with me. Let me know your thoughts. It is exceedingly clear to me—First, that a dispensation of the gospel is committed to you, and secondly, that you are peculiarly called to publish it in connexion with us. It has pleased God to give so many and so strong evidences of this, that I see not how any reasonable person can doubt it. Therefore, what I have often said before I say again, and give it under my hand, that you are welcome to preach in any of our preaching-houses in Great Britain or Ireland, whenever it is convenient for you. . . . We have need to work while it is day.' It is well known to those who are acquainted with the early history of Methodism, that Brackenbury acted on Wesley's advice.[1]

On March 23 we see Wesley leaving Kidderminster, in his chaise, and toiling along roads blocked with snow, to Bridgnorth. He left that town in the afternoon and set out for Madeley. The roads were so rough and deep that he and his companion were 'in danger of leaving their wheels behind them.' He got over his difficulty by adding two horses to his own. At length he drew up at Fletcher's house, and was welcomed by him and his wife. It will be remembered that Fletcher married Miss Mary Bosanquet on November 12, 1781. They remained at Cross Hall, Batley, until January 2, 1782, and soon after settled in Madeley. We have recorded the fact of Fletcher's absence from his parish before his marriage, when he spent a considerable length of time on the continent seeking for the restoration of his health. It is no wonder that, under such circumstances, the advance of Methodism in Madeley was arrested. At the fireside, after Wesley's arrival, there was a serious conversation on this subject. We can judge its character from the following entry in Wesley's *Journal*:

'Both Mr. and Mrs. Fletcher complained that, after all the pains they had taken, they could not prevail on the people to join in Society, no, not even to meet in class. Resolving to try, I preached to a crowded audience on " I am not ashamed of the gospel of Christ." I followed the blow in the afternoon by strongly applying those words, " Awake, thou that sleepest," and then enforcing the necessity of Christian fellowship on all who desired either to awake or keep awake.

[1] Wesley's *Works,* xiii. 3, Jackson's edition.

I then desired those that were willing to join together for this purpose to call upon Mr. Fletcher and me after service. Ninety-four or ninety-five persons did so, about as many men as women. We explained to them the nature of a Christian Society, and they willingly joined therein.'

On Good Friday, March 29, Wesley reached Macclesfield. We must pause for a time to recall facts which give the town a distinguished position in the annals of the revival of religion in England in the eighteenth century. We have recorded the fact that on April 4, 1774, Wesley walked in a procession to 'the old church' in Macclesfield with the mayor and two clergymen. One of the clergymen was David Simpson who, although an evangelical preacher, had formed a prejudice against Wesley. That prejudice, during the walk to the church, vanished. From that time the two men understood each other and became firm friends. In 1774 there was only one church in the town. Simpson was one of its 'licensed curates.' His evangelical sermons were much disliked by his fellow clergymen and others. They stirred up an opposition against him. At that time William Markham, who afterwards became the Archbishop of York, was the Bishop of Chester. He yielded to the influences brought to bear on him, and withdrew Simpson's licence. The only reason that he seems to have given for this important step was that to Simpson the Methodists owed all their successes in Macclesfield. His reply to this charge was, 'My Lord, I cannot take this honour to myself.'

The silencing of Simpson led to remarkable results. Mr. Hunt has given us full particulars concerning the erection of a chapel in Macclesfield by Mr. Charles Roe, who also had built the first silk-mill in the town. He was a silk manufacturer who stood high in public opinion. Mr. Hunt traces the early history of this chapel. It was opened on Christmas Day, 1775. After many searchings of heart, and correspondence with other people on the question of the ecclesiastical status of himself and the building, Simpson became its minister. It will be enough to say that, in 1779, Christ Church was consecrated. It became an Anglican Church, and Simpson was appointed as its minister. Mr. Hunt tells us that the church stood in a waste piece of ground called 'the meadows,' and that it was surrounded by pastureland. He also says that in it was an organ that was said to have once belonged to Handel. This statement makes us forget the rough road that Simpson had travelled. It fixes our attention on Good Friday, March 29, 1782. In his *Journal* Wesley makes an entry that arrests us. He says: 'I came to Macclesfield just time enough to assist Mr. Simpson in the laborious service of the day. I preached for him morning and afternoon, and we administered the sacrament to about thirteen hundred persons. While we were administering I heard a low, soft, solemn sound, just like that of an Aeolian harp. It continued five or six minutes, and so affected many that they could not refrain from tears. It then gradually died away. Strange that no organist (that I know) should think of this.' The organist was Mr. Maclardie. After the service Wesley said to him: 'Mr. Maclardie, if I could ensure a similar performance to yours this afternoon I would have an organ introduced into every one of our chapels.'[1]

Leaving Cheshire Wesley made his way into Lancashire. On April 5 he was in Oldham. An incident occurred there which throws a pleasant light on his character. He preached in the town at one o'clock. Before the service he was surprised to see all the street lined with little children. Seeing him they broke their ranks and ran round about and before him.

After the service a whole troop of boys and girls surrounded him, and would not be content until he had shaken each of them by the hand. Those who have only a superficial knowledge of Wesley will wonder at this scene; those who have closely studied his character will understand it. He was, indeed, 'the friend of little children.' That fact received further proof the next month, when he was in Yeadon, in Yorkshire. At the morning service on Sunday, May 5, an army of little children was present at the service. He says that they were as numerous, and almost as loving as those who surrounded him at Oldham.

Intent on paying a visit to Scotland, Wesley gradually made his way through Yorkshire, Lincolnshire and Northumber-

[1] Maclardie's daughter married Dr. Jabez Bunting. In a note in the *Journal* it is said: 'It has been suggested that the soul of the Maclardie organ-music reappears in the hymns of William Maclardie Bunting.' See *Journal*, vi., 346.

land. He preached in several churches, and in Methodist chapels that were rapidly springing up in the northern counties of England. We are especially interested in his record concerning his visit to Epworth. He arrived there in the evening of May 10, and soon heard news that filled him with delight. During his journeys he had been told that a great revival of religion had taken place in the town. He found that the news was true. Listening to the descriptions given him on his arrival, he makes a special note in his *Journal*. He says: ' I found the accounts I had received of the work of God here were not at all exaggerated. Here is a little country town, containing a little more than eight or nine hundred grown people; and there has been such a work among them as we have not seen in so short a time, either at Leeds, Bristol, or London.' He was now in his element. The revival had influenced many young people. On Sunday, May 12, he preached at Upperthorpe. He tells us that many of the Epworth children were there, and that ' their spirit spread to all around them.' Then he continues the entry in his *Journal*: ' The huge congregation was in the market-place at Epworth, and the Lord in the midst of them. The love-feast which followed exceeded all. I never knew such a one there before. As soon as one had done speaking, another began. Several of them were children, but they spoke with the wisdom of the aged, though with the fire of youth. So out of the mouth of babes and sucklings did God perfect praise.'

John Wesley, in his *Journal*, lingers over his description of this revival in Epworth, his native town, in which he had received much opposition from a clergyman of the church. In his *Journal* we get further light on the change that had taken place in the population of the town. He says: ' Some years ago four factories for spinning and weaving were set up at Epworth. In these a large number of young women, and boys and girls were employed. The whole conversation of these was profane and loose to the last degree. But some of these, stumbling in at the prayer-meeting, were suddenly cut to the heart. They never rested till they had gained their companions. The whole scene was changed. In three of the factories no more lewdness or profaneness were found, for God had put a new song in their mouth, and blasphemies were turned to praise.' Wesley visited the three factories, and found that religion had taken deep root in them. He found it 'exceeding good to be there,' and rejoiced with others 'in the God of our salvation.'

We think that Wesley would have lingered in Epworth, but voices were calling him away. On May 16 he preached in 'the new house at Barrow.' That town, in Lincolnshire, is better known by the name of Barton-on-Humber.[1] It was during this visit that he met an old friend, who gave him an invitation to lodge at his house. His friend was Charles Delamotte, his companion in Georgia.[2] Wesley says that 'he seemed to be just the same as when they lodged together, five and forty years ago.' Delamotte complained of 'the infirmities of old age,' of which Wesley once more assures us he himself 'knew nothing.'

On Monday, May 27, Wesley set out for Scotland. Three days later he reached Edinburgh, and became the guest of Lady Maxwell at Saughton Hall, a house which stood about three miles from the city. He stayed in Scotland until the middle of June. Reading the entries in his *Journal* we judge that the condition of Methodism in some of the places he visited gave him considerable concern. Preaching in Edinburgh on June 2, he says: 'At six the house was well filled, and I did not shun to declare the whole counsel of God. I almost wonder at myself. I seldom speak anywhere so roughly as in Scotland. And yet most of the people hear and hear, and are just what they were before.' This doleful note was silenced when he reached Aberdeen. He preached to large congregations and was cheered by the accounts he received of the progress of the work of God in the north. It is a relief to read his entry in his *Journal* on June 9. He says: 'We had a lovely congregation in the morning, many of whom were athirst for full salvation. In the evening God sent forth His voice, yea, and that a mighty voice. I think few of the congregation were unmoved, and we never had a more solemn parting.' He was exhilarated by the visit to Aberdeen. He returned to Edinburgh on June 12 and preached there that evening. He had such congregations both then and the next evening as had not been seen on a weekday for many years. He comforted himself by thinking that

---

[1] Wesley's *Journal*, vi., 353, note.
[2] See *John Wesley and the Religious Societies*, 115, *et passim*.

he had gathered some fruit of his labours, and expresses a hope that a token had been given him of the coming of better days in Edinburgh.

Returning to England, Wesley preached at Alnwick on Sunday, June 16, and spent the remainder of the month in the northern counties. On June 28 he was in York. We are always interested in the record he usually makes on this day. He says: 'I entered my eightieth year, but, blessed be God, my time is not "labour and sorrow." I find no more pain or bodily infirmities than at five-and-twenty. This I impute (1) to the power of God fitting me for what He calls me to; (2) to my still travelling four or five thousand miles a year; (3) to my sleeping night and day, whenever I want it; (4) to my rising at a set hour; and (5) to my constant preaching, particularly in the morning.' Rejoicing in his strength he made his way to Birmingham. Reaching the town on Saturday, July 6, he preached once more in 'the old, dreary preaching-house.' It was a disused theatre which stood in a dark court of Moor Street. In it Methodist services had been held for twenty years. But the time of deliverance had come. The next morning, at eight o'clock, he opened a new chapel that had been erected in Cherry Street. It would seat quite a thousand people.[1] At the morning service it accommodated the congregation, but in the evening many had to go away as the chapel was crowded. At the evening service a startling incident occurred. While Wesley was preaching there was 'a huge noise.' It was caused by the crash of a bench on which some people were standing. A panic commenced, but the preacher's calmness had its usual effect. In a few minutes 'all was quiet,' and Wesley continued his sermon from the text: 'But we preach Christ crucified, unto the Jews a stumbling block, and unto the Greeks foolishness, but unto them which are called, both Jews and Greeks, Christ the power of God, and the wisdom of God.'

Wesley stayed in Birmingham for several days. He refreshed himself by visiting several places of interest in the town and its neighbourhood. He spent an hour in Hagley Park, the seat of the Lyttelton family. He would have lingered there longer but was pressed for time. Then

---

[1] The chapel was enlarged in 1823 to seat a thousand and four hundred persons. In 1886 it was demolished for street improvements.

he went to the Leasowes, a place that will always be connected with the name of William Shenstone, the poet. Wesley's enthusiasm was kindled. His description is such a revelation of his own character that it must be quoted. He says: ' I never was so surprised. I have seen nothing in all England to be compared with it. It is beautiful and elegant all over. There is nothing grand, nothing costly, no temples, so called, no statues (except two or three which had better have been spared), but such walks, such shades, such hills and dales, such lawns, such artless cascades, such waving woods, with water intermixed, as exceed all imagination! On the upper side, from the openings of a shady walk, is a most beautiful and extensive prospect. And all this is comprised in the compass of three miles! I doubt if it be exceeded by anything in Europe.' Refreshed by his Saturday rambles he went the next day to 'the old church' in Birmingham, and had an opportunity of listening to a sermon that was full of abuse directed against the Methodists. The preacher described them as 'hair-brained, itinerant enthusiasts.' Fortified by his visits to Hagley Park and the Leasowes, his comment on the sermon reveals his self-restraint. He contents himself by saying that the preacher, who had made his assault with great vehemence, had totally missed his mark, ' having not the least conception of the persons whom he undertook to describe.'

On Saturday, July 20, Wesley reached London. During his absence, on April 21, his old friend, Ebenezer Blackwell, the banker, had died. In company with Charles Wesley, he went to Lewisham, and spent a few pensive hours with the widow. It was his last visit. He took one more walk round the garden and meadow he knew so well. For upwards of forty years Blackwell's house had been his place of retirement when he could spare two or three days from London. It was with many a sobering thought that he said ' farewell.'

It had been Wesley's custom to hold a Conference in Ireland when he went there in the spring. On May 1, 1782, he wrote a letter to one of his preachers in which he said that ' if nothing unforeseen prevented ' he would be in Dublin at the beginning of July. But he did not go there. He made an arrangement which casts light on a path we must soon travel. In Crookshank's *History of Methodism in*

Ireland, the following significant paragraph appears: 'Mr. Wesley fully purposed up to May 1 to visit Ireland this year, but for some reason not given, changed his intention, and sent as his deputy the Rev. Dr. Coke, an honoured name, ever dear to Ireland. This was the commencement of a new era in the history of Irish Methodism. Dr. Coke was directed to convene the Irish preachers, and to hold for the first time a regularly constituted Conference, similar to those held in England. During the visits of Mr. Wesley he had in almost, if not every, instance, called together the preachers labouring in Ireland, and consulted with them as to the work in this country; but these occasional meetings did not control the affairs of the Society. No official record was published or apparently ever made of the proceedings, and at best nothing further was done than to receive reports and make suggestions to the British Conference. But now the preachers in Ireland had become so numerous, and the business had obtained an extent and gravity which rendered it expedient that the Irish ministers should receive a corporate status of their own, and hence the appointment of Dr. Coke.'[1]

On Tuesday, August 6, the Conference assembled in London. Being obliged to leave sooner than he had intended, Wesley concluded its sessions on the following Tuesday, and commenced his journeys to the West of England. In the *Journal* there is no record of the business which was transacted at the Conference. The *Minutes,* however, give us considerable help. It is clear that some important subjects were discussed. We will confine our attention to one of them. The following question was asked and answered: 'Q. What can be done with regard to the preaching-house at Birstall? A. If the trustees still refuse to settle it on the Methodist plan, 1, Let a plain state of the case be drawn up; 2, Let a collection be made throughout all England in order to purchase ground, and to build another preaching-house as near the present as may be.' The Birstall Chapel case occupied a prominent place in the history of Methodism in the eighteenth century; it is necessary to make an attempt to understand it.

[1] At the close of the meeting it was agreed 'that thenceforward a yearly Conference should be held in Dublin.' Crookshank's *History of Methodism in Ireland,* i., 360-61.

On August 29, 1750, when the Birstall preaching-house was in course of erection, John Nelson wrote a letter to John Wesley in which he asked his advice on the subject of the legal settlement of the building. In this letter he said:

> The stewards and trustees of the chapel we are building, and which is now slated, desire you to give them advice how the writings must be made, which are to convey the power into the hands of seven men to be as trustees, and for what use the house and ground are to be employed; and as it is intended for pious use, whether it must not be enrolled in Chancery. They desire you to send a copy of the deeds of some of the houses you have been concerned in, as soon as possible; for all is in the hands of one man, and, if he should die, it would cause great confusion before things could be properly settled.[1]

We judge that Wesley complied with Nelson's request and sent him information concerning the legal settlement of some of the preaching-houses that had been erected. The first Birstall chapel deed is dated December 3, 1751. It contains clauses similar to those which appear in the deeds of the preaching-houses at Bristol and Newcastle-on-Tyne. In those deeds John Wesley is given the right of nominating or appointing the men who should preach in the buildings. If he died before his brother that right was to be exercised by Charles Wesley. On the death of the survivor of the two Wesleys, the right passed to the trustees of the preaching-houses, the major part of them being empowered, ' from time to time, and at all times thereafter, monthly or oftener at their discretion, to nominate and appoint one or more fit person or persons to preach and expound God's holy word in the said house.'

During the years following the opening of the preaching-house at Birstall, there was a considerable advance in the erection of Methodist chapels throughout the country. The deeds on which they were settled varied. Their contents convinced the Conference that the use of the provision we have just quoted concerning the right of appointment to the preaching-houses in Bristol and Newcastle-on-Tyne contained an element of danger. The opinions of eminent lawyers were obtained. The danger was admitted. In the *Large Minutes,* published in 1763, a *Model Deed* appears. It was drawn up by skilful conveyancers who were well known at that time

[1] See *John Wesley and the Advance of Methodism,* 188.

in England. The new deed contained a clause which bears on the subject we are considering. After the death of the survivor of the two Wesleys the major part of the trustees of chapels settled on this 'model deed' are directed 'from time to time and at all times thereafter to permit such persons as shall be appointed at the Yearly Conference of the People called Methodists . . . and no others to have and enjoy the premises,' provided that they preach no other doctrine than is contained in Wesley's *Notes upon the New Testament* and his *Four Volumes of Sermons*.

The preaching-house in Birstall went through many experiences. It was enlarged. We might say that it was rebuilt. During the closing years of John Wesley's life it was determined by the trustees of 1782 to have a new deed. It contained some remarkable provisions. We are only concerned with the fact that the right of the trustees to appoint preachers to the chapel after the death of the survivor of the two Wesleys was retained. The arrangement of the new Model Deed concerning the right of the Conference to appoint preachers to chapels was not accepted. When John Wesley was at Alnwick, on May 28, 1782, he wrote to his brother an interesting letter. In it he says: ' When I was at Dawgreen, near Birstall, the trustees for Birstall house brought me a Deed, which they read over, and desired me to sign. We disputed upon it about an hour. I then gave them a positive answer that " I would not sign it," and, leaving them abruptly, went up into my room. About noon I preached at Horbury. In the evening I preached and met the Society at Wakefield. At night, a little before I went to bed, the trustees came again, got round and worried me down.' Wesley's objection to the new deed was that it placed in the hands of the trustees the right to choose preachers for themselves and to dismiss them at their pleasure. If they had consented to adopt the arrangement contained in the model deed of 1763 he would have immediately signed the new deed. However, being 'worried down,' he signed it.

Wesley's signature to the deed must have had an effect on the decision of the Conference respecting the building of a new chapel in Birstall. We cannot dismiss this interesting case without recording an important fact which belongs to later times. Towards the end of the year 1853 the Birstall

Chapel case was taken into Vice-Chancellor Wood's Court. Several deeds relating to the chapel had been executed during the interval, in which the clause concerning the right of the trustees to appoint preachers to the chapel had been repeated. It was fortunate that the Vice-Chancellor was a man who mastered the case submitted to him. As Myles's *Chronological History of the People called Methodists* was accepted by counsel on both sides, he read it carefully. Prolonged consideration was given to the Birstall case. It was argued by eminent counsel. On November 8, 1853, the Vice-Chancellor delivered his judgement. Confining ourselves to one of the questions then decided we will reproduce his decision on the subject of the appointment of preachers to the chapel. He decreed as follows:

> It further appearing to the Court that the said Circuit Preachers, and in particular of the Birstall Circuit, at and before the date of the said indenture (December 3, 1751) and at all times thereafter during the lifetime of the said John Wesley, were appointed either by the said John Wesley, with the advice of the said Conference, or by the said Conference presided over by the said John Wesley, and that since the death of the said John Wesley the appointment of all the Circuit Preachers, and in particular of the Preachers in the said Birstall Circuit, has been made and that according to the rules and regulations of the said people called Methodists, such appointment ought to be made by the said Conference only—Declare, that the trusts contained in the said Indenture, with reference to the appointment of a Preacher in the said Chapel after the decease of the survivor of John Wesley, Charles Wesley and William Grimshaw, therein-mentioned, by the major part of the Trustees for the time being of the said Indenture, cannot be carried into effect, consistently with the due appointment of such Preacher or Minister, as by the said indenture was intended to be provided for the said Chapel, and that the said trust premises ought at all times to be held by the Trustees for the time being, acting under the said indenture, upon trust to permit and suffer such persons respectively to be Preachers or Ministers of the said Birstall Circuit, as shall, from time to time, be duly appointed by the said Conference for that purpose, to have and enjoy the free use and benefit of the said trust premises.[1]

In the Vice-Chancellor's 'decree' our attention is arrested by the statement that since the death of John Wesley the appointment of all the preachers in the Birstall circuit had been made 'according to the rules and regulations of the people called Methodists.' We presume that though the

---

[1] See *The Birstall Chapel Case; Vice-Chancellor Wood's Court*, 57-8. We are much indebted to the Rev. John Hornabrook for the use of documents that have assisted us in our study of this case.

power of appointment to the Birstall Chapel was vested in the trustees they had not exercised it, but had accepted the preachers sent to the circuit by the Conference. It is well known to the students of Methodist history that the trustees of 'the room' in the Horsefair in Bristol did not follow this example. In 1794 they excluded Henry Moore from their pulpit. The result was that a site for a new chapel was secured, which was built in King Street. We have sometimes wondered at a sentence contained in the decision of the Conference of 1782 in the Birstall Chapel case. If it was necessary to erect a new chapel, then it was to be built 'as near the present as may be.' We do not know if the new trustees of the Bristol Chapel remembered this direction; but those who are familiar with the King Street class-rooms will be aware that close to the window of one of them, the roof of the 'room in the Horsefair' is a conspicuous object.[1]

It is pleasant to turn from these disputes and to follow Wesley as he sets out on his journey to the West of England. He left London in the afternoon of August 13, by coach, and reached Bristol early in the afternoon of the next day. He soon left the city. On Sunday, August 18, he was in Exeter. He worshipped in the cathedral in the morning, and was delighted with 'the decent behaviour of the whole congregation.' Once more we find him deeply impressed by 'the solemn music at the post-communion.' He thought it one of the finest compositions he had ever heard.[2] The Bishop, John Ross, invited him to dinner. The invitation was accepted. He must have thought of his old adversary, Bishop Lavington when he sat down at the table with the Bishop, five clergymen, and four aldermen. He tells us that he was treated by the Bishop with 'genuine, unaffected courtesy.' During this tour we have another evidence of the advance of John Wesley in the respect of the people of England. In the evening of August 21, he preached in the square of Plymouth Dock. A little before he concluded, an officer came into the square with his regiment. When he saw Wesley he immediately stopped the drums and drew up all his men in order on the high side

[1] In *The London Quarterly Review* for October, 1884, an article appeared in which there was a description of the events leading to the erection of the King Street Chapel. It was written by the writer of this volume.
[2] The organist was William Jackson, the composer of a well-known setting of the *Te Deum*.

of the square. He says: 'They were all as still as night; nor did any of them stir till I had pronounced the blessing.'

Among the incidents of this journey there is one that makes a strong appeal to those who are acquainted with the members of the inner circle of Wesley's friends. On September 3 he preached in the street at Camelford. After the service he was told that his old friend, Mr. Thompson, the vicar of St. Gennys, was near death, and had expressed a desire to see him. Borrowing the best horse he could find he set out, and rode quickly to St. Gennys. It is better to give his own account of the interview. He says: 'I found Mr. Thompson just alive, but quite sensible. It seemed to me as if none in the house but himself was very glad to see me. He had many doubts concerning his final state, and rather feared than desired to die, so that my whole business was to comfort him and to increase and confirm his confidence in God. He desired me to administer the Lord's Supper, which I willingly did; and I left him much happier than I found him, calmly waiting till his change should come.' Two months after this interview Wesley's old and faithful friend passed away.

On October 12 Wesley returned to London. Making it his centre he visited many of the midland and southern towns. It is interesting to note that, on December 1, he resumed the use of his *Diary*. It is crowded with jottings which show the extent and variety of his work. We search the *Journal* and the *Diary* in vain for a notice of an event in which he must have been deeply interested. The war with America began in 1775. We have shown that throughout its course he had supported the King and his ministers. But, to the relief of many Englishmen, the war came to an end towards the close of 1782. On September 27 England acknowledged American independence; on November 30, preliminaries of peace were signed by representatives of the two countries. The signing of 'the treaty' was postponed until France had been consulted. On September 3, 1783, the 'definitive treaty' was signed at Versailles. We have not dwelt on its incidents. In the next chapter we will try to show its influence on the work of the Methodists in America.[1]

---

[1] Dr. William Hunt's volume of *The Political History of England*, 241-3.

XIV

PASSING CLOUDS

ON January 4, 1783, John Wesley wrote a letter to Robert Carr Brackenbury that is full of interest. It shows that Brackenbury acted on the advice given him by Wesley in his letter of the previous year. He had become a preacher. In January he was not only a preacher but had found a sphere in which Methodism had been only recently introduced. He had gone to the Channel Islands at the time when two of the Newfoundland fishermen were gathering a few of the Jersey people into a class meeting. In Wesley's letter we catch a glimpse of the situation. He says: 'I rejoice to hear that you have had a safe passage, and that you have preached both in Guernsey and Jersey. We must not expect many conveniences at first. Hitherto it is the day of small things. I should imagine the sooner you begin to preach in French the better. Surely you need not be careful about accuracy. Trust God, and speak as well as you can. While those poor sheep were scattered abroad without a shepherd, and without any proper connexion with each other, it is no wonder they were cold and dead. It is good that everyone should know our whole plan. We do not want any man to go on blindfold. Peace be with your spirit.' We shall have to recur to the subject of Methodism in the Channel Islands at a later stage, and will leave Brackenbury there to commence his pioneer work.

In 1783 Wesley had to face one of the most difficult problems he had to encounter. The close of the war in America compelled him to consider the condition of Methodism in the United States. So far as possible he had kept in touch with his preachers in that distant land, but the peace brought letters that gave him a clearer insight into the actual condition of things in America during and at the end of the conflict. It is well known that the war dealt a disastrous blow to the

Church of England in America. Many clergymen were driven out of their churches and left the country. Those who remained saw that it was necessary to reconsider the constitution of their Church, and to bring it into more complete harmony with the spirit of the time. Its name was changed into 'The Protestant Episcopal Church,' and, after much discussion, important alterations were introduced into its constitution.[1]

Confining our attention to some of the effects of the war on the Methodist Societies in America, we may say that during its continuance considerable progress had been made. It was fortunate that Methodist preachers possessing great courage and zeal were in the country at this critical time. Foremost among them was Francis Asbury. He had to seek a place of hiding at the commencement of the struggle, but at last his way was opened. He used his freedom to travel through the country, and wherever he went he brought encouragement to the men who were working in the towns and the wilderness. The result of the toils of fearless men may be judged from this fact—in 1773, when the war began, there were about one thousand members in the Methodist Societies. Writing of the Methodist Episcopal Church, Stevens says: 'Its almost continual growth in such apparently adverse circumstances is one of the marvels of religious history. In 1776 it was equal, in the number of its preachers and congregations, to the Lutherans, the German Reformed, the Reformed Dutch, the Associate Church, the Moravians, or the Roman Catholics. At the close of the war it ranked fourth or fifth among the dozen recognized Christian denominations of the country. During the war it more than quadrupled both its ministry and its members.'

We rejoice in the results of the work of the pioneers in America. But its progress raises questions that made a deep impression on the mind of Wesley. In Henry Moore's *Life of the Rev. John Wesley* there are two paragraphs concerning Methodism in America which are of supreme importance. We will reproduce them. Moore says:

> During the Civil War, the Societies were destitute of the Sacraments, except in two or three of the cities. They could not obtain Baptism

[1] In Bishop Wilberforce's *History of the American Church* a full account of the discussions that then took place may be found.

for their children, or the Lord's Supper for themselves, from the Presbyterian, Independent, or Baptist Ministers, but on condition that they would leave the Society of which they were members and join those Churches respectively. And almost all the Clergy of the Church of England had left the country. The Societies in general were so grieved on this account, and so influenced the minds of the Preachers by their incessant complaints, that, in the year 1778, a considerable number of them earnestly importuned Mr. Asbury to take proper measures, that the people might enjoy the privileges of all other Churches, and no longer be deprived of the Christian Sacraments. Mr. Asbury's attachment to the Church of England was, at that time, exceedingly strong. He, therefore, refused them any redress. On this, the majority of the Preachers withdrew from him, and consequently from Mr. Wesley, and chose out of themselves three senior brethren, who ordained others by the imposition of their hands. The Preachers thus set apart administered the Sacraments to those whom they judged proper to receive it, in every place where they came. However, Mr. Asbury, by indefatigable labour and attention, and by all the address in his power, brought them back one after another; and, by a vote of one of the Conferences, the ordination was declared invalid, and a perfect reunion took place.

When peace was established between Great Britain and the States, the intercourse was opened betwixt the Socities in both countries. Mr. Wesley then received from Mr. Asbury a full account of the progress of the work during the war; and especially of the division which had taken place, and the difficulties he met with before it was healed. He also informed Mr. Wesley of the extreme uneasiness of the people's minds for want of the Sacraments; that thousands of their children were unbaptized, and the members of the Societies in general had not partaken of the Lord's Supper for many years. Mr. Wesley then considered the subject, and informed Dr. Coke of his design of drawing up a plan of Church-government, and of establishing an ordination for his American Societies. But, cautious of entering on so new a plan, he afterwards suspended the execution of his purpose, and weighed the whole for upwards of a year.[1]

The American problem was of pressing importance. We shall have to consider it in our next chapter, and must now mention other experiences of Wesley in the year 1783. In his *Journal* on Sunday, January 19, there is an entry that enables us to see the change that had taken place in the attitude of many of the London clergy of the Church of England towards Wesley. He says: 'I preached at St. Thomas's Church in the afternoon and at St. Swithin's in the evening. The tide is now turned, so that I have more invitations to preach in churches than I can accept.' He might have used

[1] Moore's *Life of John Wesley*, 325-6.

the same words when referring to some of the clergy in other parts of the country, but in many neighbourhoods the old prejudice survived. There is an entry on another subject in the *Journal* on February 21 that arrests attention. Being still in London, he says: ' At our yearly meeting for that purpose we examined our yearly accounts. Money received upwards of £3,000. What I receive of it yearly is neither more nor less than thirty pounds.'

During the month of March Wesley was laid aside with a fever, but the next month we find him so far recovered that he was able to pay his long-delayed visit to Ireland. He spent two or three weeks there ' with much satisfaction.' On April 29 he held ' a little Conference ' there which closed on May 2. On May 8 he returned to Holyhead and was soon busy among the Lancashire Societies. Once more we hear his cheerful note. On May 13 he preached in the evening at Liverpool. He says: ' Here the scandal of the cross seems to be ceased, and we are grown honourable men.' On Sunday, May 18, he was in Manchester. He preached in the new chapel. This is his record: ' Mr. Bayley came very opportunely to assist me in the morning service. Such a sight, I believe, was never seen in Manchester before. It was supposed there were thirteen or fourteen hundred communicants, among whom there was such a spirit as I have seldom found, and their whole behaviour was such as adorned the gospel.' Two days later he met the select Society in Manchester. It consisted of between forty and fifty members. He was delighted with its condition. He believed that among the Methodists there was no place but London where so many people ' so deeply devoted to God could be found.' He declared that in Manchester the work of God was rapidly increasing on every side.

On Saturday, May 24, Wesley did a day's work which must have wearied him. He ' took chaise ' at three o'clock in the morning and travelled from Derby to Buxton. He had been asked to marry two of his friends. When he arrived he found that notice had been given that he would preach in St. Anne's Church. After the wedding he did so. He had arranged to preach in Nottingham in the evening at six o'clock. Starting on his way at eleven o'clock, he made all haste, but did not reach Nottingham until seven o'clock. He found that the service had been held. He must have been surprised to see the preacher who had taken his place. He was his friend, Robert Carr Brackenbury. There can be little doubt that Wesley's continuous work since his attack of fever had left its mark on him, and must have excited Brackenbury's sympathy. It was clear that both of them needed rest. Wesley made up his mind to leave England for a time. He had a strong desire to visit Holland. On June 11 he and Mr. Brackenbury 'took coach' and rode to Harwich, where they embarked for Hellevoetsluis. They landed there on Friday, June 13. Their visit to Holland lasted until the first week in July when Wesley returned to London. He gives a full account of the visit in his *Journal*. It will be enough to quote his final paragraph. He says: 'I can by no means regret either the trouble or expense which attended this little journey. It opened me a way into, as it were, a new world, where the land, the buildings, the people, the customs, were all such as I had never seen before. But as those with whom I conversed were of the same spirit with my friends in England, I was as much at home in Utrecht and Amsterdam as in Bristol and London.'[1]

When Wesley was in Holland he celebrated his birthday. In his *Journal* we find the following record on June 28: 'I have this day lived four score years, and by the mercy of God my eyes are not waxed dim. And what little strength of body or mind I had thirty years since, just the same I have now. God grant I may never live to be useless! Rather may I

> My body with my charge lay down
> And cease at once to work and live.'

In this record there is a softening of the triumphant note to which we have become accustomed. We think he must have remembered his experience in March, when he was laid aside by sudden illness at Stroud, and had 'no strength at all, being scarce able to move, and much less to think.' He then had a warning which made him face the possibility of the coming of that great affliction—'the useless life.' When he returned from Holland he found that he was confronted by difficulties that demanded clear insight, foresight, and the power of a calm and resolute will. He had postponed the solution of the

---

[1] See *Journal*, vi., 416-30. On p. 415 there is a valuable note which explains the reason of his choice of Holland as the place of his holiday.

urgent American problem, but he knew that questions awaited him that demanded his immediate attention.

Wesley got back to London on July 4. The Conference was to assemble in Bristol on July 29. He soon found that questions would meet him there that would tax his strength. Writing to a correspondent, he says: 'I expect a good deal of difficulty at this Conference, and shall stand in need of the prayers of you and your friends.' His expectation was realized. On July 18 he arrived in Bristol and found the first of his troubles. He had asked Dr. Coke to see if it would be possible to persuade the trustees of the 'Room' in the Horsefair to consent to such an alteration of the terms of their deed as would place the appointment of preachers, after his own and his brother's death, in the power of the Conference. Dr. Coke made the attempt, with the result that might have been expected. On July 29, the day of the opening of the Conference, he received the following protest against the proposal. It was signed by six trustees:

> At a meeting held this day by the Trustees of the New Room in Bristol, to take into consideration the propriety of Dr. Coke's proposal respecting the alteration of the Deed enroll'd irrevocably in Chancery by the Rev. Mr. Wesley many years ago—They having maturely and seriously weighed the great Trust repos'd in them, namely for the use of the Methodist Church, in connexion with the Church of England, are of opinion that they cannot conscientiously, legally, or justly, give up, or transfer the same, to any persons whatever. They hold the Trust with which they are invested to be sacred, that they stand in it accountable to God, to the Society of Bristol, and to all the world. The Trustees have no desire or wish but to act in concurrence with ye Conference as long as they continue to support Mr. Wesley's Doctrines, and they hope the time will never come in which they shall be witnesses to the contrary.

This Bristol Conference occupies a conspicuous place among those that were held by John Wesley. His summary of its proceedings, in his *Journal*, is brief. He says: 'Tues. 29.—Our Conference began at which two important points were considered: first, the case of Birstall House, and secondly, the state of Kingswood School. With regard to the former, our brethren earnestly desired that I would go to Birstall myself, believing this would be the most effectual way of bringing the trustees to reason. With regard to the latter, we all agreed that either the school should cease or the rules of it be punctually observed, particularly that the children should never play, and that a master should be always present with them.' As to the visit to Birstall, Wesley was convinced that it would be useless. But after the Conference he went there, and his conviction was firmly established. As to Kingswood School, he knew that the playing of the children was only a small part of the danger that threatened the ruin of the school. In the previous year he had received much enlightenment from the experiences of Adam Clarke who, acting on his advice, had sailed from Ireland in August, 1782, and had gone to the school. He had expected to continue his education there, but was doomed to disappointment. The story of his first interview with the headmaster and his wife is found in his book entitled *An Account of the Life of Adam Clarke.* It pours a flood of light on the condition of Kingswood School in those days. Speaking of Wesley's censure, which we have quoted, he says: 'This censure is perfectly correct; it was the worst school I had ever seen; and though the teachers were men of adequate learning, yet as the school was perfectly *disorganized,* and in several respects each did what was right in his own eyes, and there was no efficient plan pursued, they mocked at religion and trampled underfoot all the laws. The little children of the preachers suffered great indignities, and, it is feared, their treatment there gave many of them a rooted enmity against piety and religion for life. The parlour boarders had every kind of respect paid to them, and the others were shamefully neglected. Had this most gross mismanagement been known to the Methodist preachers, they would have suffered their sons to die in ignorance rather than to have sent them to a place where there was scarcely any care taken either of their bodies or souls.'[1]

We will say nothing concerning the way in which Adam Clarke was treated. It still rouses keen indignation. His stay in the school was short. On September 6, 1782, John Wesley arrived in Bristol. The headmaster had an interview with him. Adam Clarke supposed that he told 'his own tale—that they had not room for him in the school, and that it was a pity that he had not been sent out into the general work.' Wesley listened, and then said that he wished to see Adam

[1] See *Account,* 162-9.

Clarke. The description of the interview soothes us. Adam Clarke says:

> I went into Bristol, saw Mr. Rankin, who carried me to Mr. Wesley's study, off the great lobby of the rooms over the chapel in Broadmead. He tapped at the door, which was opened by this truly apostolic man. Mr. R. retired: Mr. W. took me kindly by the hand, and asked me, 'How long since I had left Ireland?' Our conversation was short. He said, 'Well, brother Clarke, do you wish to devote yourself entirely to the work of God?' I answered, 'Sir, I wish to *do* and *be* what God pleases.' He then said, 'We want a preacher for Bradford (Wilts.); hold yourself in readiness to go thither; I am going into the country and will let you know when you shall go.' He then turned to me, laid his hands upon my head, and spent a few moments in praying to God to bless and preserve me, and to give me success in the work to which I was called.
>
> I departed, having now received, in addition to my appointment from God to preach His gospel, the only authority I could have from man in that line in which I was to exercise the Ministry of the Divine Word.[1]

On September 26, 1782, Clarke received orders to go to Bradford-on-Avon, and commenced a ministry that has left a deep mark on Methodism in the Channel Islands and many other places. At the Bristol Conference of 1783 he was admitted into 'full connexion.' We may close our account of his Kingswood experiences by saying that, in that year, Wesley effected great reforms in Kingswood School. The headmaster was dismissed, and changes were effected that altered the character of the school. It began a career that has raised it to a conspicuous position among the great schools of England.[2]

The *Minutes* of the Bristol Conference, published soon after it was held, show that the business transacted followed the usual course. Wesley's anticipation of coming difficulties was not realized in the form which he expected. During the first week he presided. If we had not information from another source we should have supposed that he did so in all the sessions of the Conference. But John Pawson gives us information that enlightens us. He says: 'In 1783 our Conference was in Bristol, during which Mr. Wesley was dangerously ill, and we were obliged to do a considerable part of our business without him. It was very agreeable to see

[1] See *Account*, 164.
[2] In 1851 the 'New Kingswood School' on the heights of Lansdown, Bath, was occupied, the old school at Kingswood, near Bristol, being vacated.

how deeply the minds of the preachers were affected, and with what unity and harmony everything was settled.'[1] Wesley's illness was severe. He was absent from the Conference during the second week of its sessions and was in the doctor's hands. From his *Journal* we see that he was unable to resume his work until Sunday, August 24. Then he preached twice in the 'New Room' at Bristol. Finding that his strength was 'in some measure restored,' the next day he set out for Gloucester, and preached in the town hall. These experiments encouraged him to re-commence his itinerant work.

It is necessary that we should record an event that occurred at the Bristol Conference of 1783 which is not mentioned in the *Minutes* of that year. It happened during the first week of the sessions when Wesley was present. In the *Minutes* of the Conference held in 1785, we find a copy of a document which arrests our attention. It is dated July 30, 1785, and is signed by thirty-nine preachers who were present at the Bristol Conference. It concerns a subject of the greatest importance which was soon to be discussed. We will reproduce its contents:

We, whose names are under written, do declare that Mr. Wesley was desired, at the last Bristol Conference, without a dissenting voice, to draw up a Deed which should give a legal specification of the phrase, 'The Conference of the People called Methodists,' and that the mode of doing it was entirely left to his judgement and direction.

We shall have to deal with this important subject in the next chapter. At this stage we only wish to show the origin of the attempt that was soon made to give a legal status to the Methodist Conference.

Watching John Wesley as he re-commences his itinerant work, we feel considerable concern. But we dismiss our fears when we see him, on September 3, in consultation with several preachers in Leeds. The Birstall Chapel case was the theme of their discussion. Wesley solicited their advice on the best method to adopt in an attempt to persuade the trustees of the chapel to settle it 'on the Methodist plan.' This consultation shows that Wesley's courage was rising with the increase of his health. On September 5, after preaching at Birstall in the morning, he met the trustees of

[1] *Early Methodist Preachers*, iv., 50.

the chapel. We will give the result of the interview in his own words:

> About nine I met the nineteen trustees, and, after exhorting them to peace and love, said: 'All that I desire is that this house may be settled on the Methodist plan: and the same clause may be inserted in your Deed which is inserted in the deed of the new chapel in London, viz., "In case the doctrine or practice of any preacher should, in the opinion of the major part of the trustees, be not conformable to Mr. Wesley's *Sermons* and *Notes on the New Testament*, on representing this another preacher shall be sent within three months."' Five of the trustees were willing to accept of our first proposals, the rest were not willing. Although I could not obtain the end proposed, and in that respect had only my labour for my pains, yet I do not at all repent of my journey. I have done my part; let others bear their own burden.[1]

Leaving Birstall, Wesley arrived in Bristol on Saturday, September 13. He says that he went back nearly the same way that he came. It is clear that his health was re-established. This is his comment on the effects of his journey: 'I had likewise good reward for my labour in the recovery of my health, by a journey of five or six hundred miles.' He did not return to London until October 11. Staying there for only a few days he began a visitation of the Societies in the eastern counties and those in the neighbourhood of London. In the latest edition of his *Journal*, footnotes containing extracts from his *Diary* abound. They show that his vigour was restored, and that he was ready to face the exacting work that awaited him in one of the most important years of his life.

---

[1] See *Journal*, vi., 444-6.

XV
THE LEGAL HUNDRED

THE year 1784 was marked by events which have made it conspicuous in the history of Methodism in England and in America. We have referred to the unanimous request of the preachers assembled at Bristol that John Wesley should consider the question of the constitution of the Conference. In addition we know that, about the same time, letters were arriving from America which revealed the fact that serious agitation was disturbing some of the Methodist Societies in that country on the subject of the administration of the sacrament of the Lord's Supper. During the war Methodism had made rapid advance, not only in some of the American towns, but also in villages that were scattered among woods and in thinly inhabited wildernesses. The war had caused many clergymen to abandon their churches and to leave the country. The Methodists found themselves deprived not only of the sacrament of the Lord's Supper but also of the baptism of their children. It is no wonder that, in one part of the country the Methodist preachers yielded to the request of their people and commenced to administer the Lord's Supper to the members of their Societies. Francis Asbury was much concerned by this departure from the Methodist usage. He wrote to John Wesley asking for his direction. Asbury's influence was so strong in the country that he managed to persuade the preachers who were administering the Sacraments, to await the decision of Wesley on their proceedings. He thereby arrested for a time the secession of many of the Methodist people who were determined to receive the sacrament from the hands of their own preachers. It is no wonder that, in England and America, 1784 was 'a year of suspense.' Fortunately for Methodism in both countries, it became 'a year of deliverance.'

Observing the order of time we will deal first with the question of the constitution of the English Conference. The

THE LEGAL HUNDRED

demands on Wesley's time and strength were incessant. It was fortunate that, in Dr. Coke, he found a helper who assisted him in the solution of several difficult questions. The result of their joint consideration of the constitution of the Conference was that they saw that the problem was beyond their powers of solution and that it ought to be submitted to a competent lawyer. Wesley was fortunate in having for his legal adviser Mr. Clulow, a solicitor who had his office in Chancery Lane. Dr. Coke interviewed him, and explained the case to him. The conclusion they reached was that the matters they had discussed were of such importance that they ought to be submitted to an eminent counsel for his opinion. Mr. Clulow was asked to draw up 'a case,' and to lay it before Mr. Maddox, who occupied a high position in the legal world of London.

We shall be able to understand the difficulties that confronted John Wesley and his advisers if we reproduce an extract from the deed for the settlement of preaching-houses which is printed in the *Large Minutes* of 1781. It is provided that 'the major part of the trustees of the premises shall from time to time and at all times for ever, permit such persons as shall be appointed at the Yearly Conference of the people called Methodists in London, Bristol, or Leeds, and no others, to have and enjoy the said premises for the purposes aforesaid. Provided always, that the said persons preach no other doctrine than is contained in Mr. Wesley's *Notes upon the New Testament* and four volumes of *Sermons.*' In the case laid before Mr. Maddox we see that his opinion was especially directed to this clause of the deed. These questions were asked: 'Will the general description of the Yearly Conference of the people called Methodists in London, Bristol or Leeds, together with constant usage, be sufficient marks of identity of the very persons who actually do compose the Conference, so as to carry the exercise of the trust fully into them, and safely through them into their appointees, so effectually as to enable such appointees to *maintain and enforce* their right to the benefit of the trusts, in case of the resistance on the part of the trustees, or any other persons?' If not, 'What means would you advise to be taken for the aforesaid purposes?' Those who are not acquainted with the actual condition of affairs at the time we have reached may

210   THE LEGAL HUNDRED

fail to perceive the significance of these questions. But there was a deep meaning in them. Henry Moore lifts the veil. After a reference to Wesley's right to appoint preachers to chapels during his lifetime, which right was secured to him by deeds, Moore says: 'The generality of those deeds specified also that, after his death, the Conference of the People called Methodists should appoint the preachers in like manner. Some of those deeds had no reference to any posthumous appointment, and so would have been completely in the power of the trustees at Mr. Wesley's decease. Several even of those trustees, where the chapels were settled according to the Methodist plan, did not scruple to say, " That the Conference was not an assembly that the law would recognize; and that, therefore, they would, after Mr. Wesley's death, appoint whom they should think proper." One of them said to me, " They might appoint a Popish Priest, if they should think it proper." ' [1]

The opinion of Mr. Maddox was soon given. It was as follows: ' As to the means of fixing the sense of the word Conference, and defining what persons are to be members of the Conference, and how the body is to be continued in succession, and to identify it, I think Mr. John Wesley should prepare and subscribe a declaration for that purpose, to be enrolled in the Court of Chancery for safe custody, naming the present members, and prescribing the mode of election to fill vacancies, and making the Minutes or Memorials of their proceedings, signed by their Secretary, evidence of such elections; to which declaration of Mr. Wesley, so enrolled, all the Trust Deeds should refer.' [2]

The opinion of Mr. Maddox is dated December 5, 1783. His advice was accepted. Mr. Clulow, in consultation with Dr. Coke, without any loss of time, proceeded to draw up the well-known deed entitled ' The Rev. John Wesley's Declaration and Establishment of the Conference of the People called Methodists.' It was well that he had the assistance of Dr. Coke, whose Oxford degree shows that he was a Doctor of Civil Law. We also know that, when Coke left the University and returned to Brecon, he became for some time the chief magistrate in that town. His biographer comments

[1] Henry Moore's *Life of the Rev. John Wesley*, ii., 294-5.
[2] Dr. Warren's *Digest of the Laws of Methodism*, second edition, p. 2.

on Dr. Coke's knowledge of the law by saying: 'I hesitate not to place this arrangement of circumstances as coming under the general head of his education for the life before him, inasmuch as the habits of attention to business which it formed, the contact into which it brought him with actual life, the forensic knowledge he would be bound to acquire, and the facility in public speaking to be attained in the practice of the court, were all of service to the future man, and entered, under the providence of God, into his preparation for the career for which he had been born.'[1]

We will avail ourselves of Tyerman's condensed statement concerning the contents of the Deed of Declaration. He says:

The document proceeds to state that the said Conference has always consisted of Methodist preachers whom Wesley had annually invited to meet him for the following purposes: namely, to advise with him for the promotion of the gospel of Christ; to appoint the said preachers, and other preachers, and exhorters in connexion with him, to the use and enjoyment of chapels conveyed upon trust as aforesaid; to expel unworthy preachers; and to admit others on probation.

The deed then gives the names and addresses of one hundred preachers, who are now declared to be the members of the said Conference; and proceeds to state—(1) That they and their successors, for the time being for ever, shall assemble once a year. (2) That the act of the majority shall be the act of the whole. (3) That their first business, when they assemble, shall be to fill up vacancies. (4) That no act of the Conference assembled shall be valid unless forty of its members are present. (5) That the duration of the yearly Conference shall not be less than five days, nor more than three weeks. (6) That immediately after filling up vacancies, they shall choose a president and secretary of their assembly out of themselves. (7) That any member of the Conference, absenting himself from the yearly assembly thereof for two years successively, without the consent or dispensation of the Conference, and who is not present on the first day of the third yearly assembly thereof, shall forthwith cease to be a member, as though he were naturally dead. (8) That the Conference shall and may expel any member thereof, or any person admitted into connexion therewith, for any cause which to the Conference may seem fit or necessary. (9) That they may admit into connexion with them any person, of whom they approve, to be preachers of God's holy word, under the care and direction of the Conference. (10) That no person shall be elected a member of the Conference, who has not been admitted into connexion with the Conference as a preacher, for twelve months. (11) That the Conference shall not appoint any person to the use of a chapel or chapels, who is not either a member of the Conference, or admitted into connexion with the same, or upon trial;

[1] Etheridge's *Life of the Rev. Thomas Coke, D.C.L.*, pp. 18-9.

and that no person shall be appointed for more than three years successively, except ordained ministers of the Church of England. (12) That the Conference may appoint the place of holding the yearly assembly thereof, at any other town, or city, than London, Bristol, or Leeds. (13) That the Conference may, when it shall seem expedient, send any of its members as delegates to Ireland, or other parts out of the Kingdom of Great Britain, to act on its behalf, and with all the powers of the Conference itself. (14) That all resolutions and acts whatsoever of the Conference shall be written in the journals of the Conference, and be signed by the president and secretary thereof for the time being. (15) That whenever the Conference shall be reduced under the number of forty members, and continue so reduced for three years successively, or whenever the members thereof shall decline or neglect to meet together annually during the space of three years, the Conference of the people called Methodists shall be extinguished, and all its powers, privileges, and advantages shall cease. (16) That nothing in this deed shall extinguish or lessen the life estate of the said John Wesley and Charles Wesley, or either of them, in any of the chapels in which they now have, or may have, any estate or interest, power or authority whatsoever.[1]

When Mr. Clulow and Dr. Coke had finished their part of the work of drafting the deed, they left a vacant space in which the names of the preachers who were to be the members of the first Legal Conference were to be inserted. John Wesley had undertaken that part of a difficult task. Dr. Coke was of opinion that the name of every preacher who was then in ' full connexion with the Conference,' should appear in the deed. At the Conference of 1783 there were nearly two hundred preachers who were appointed to the sixty-nine circuits in England, Wales, Scotland, and Ireland. The number included several probationers; but, if Dr. Coke's suggestion had been adopted by Wesley, several difficulties would have arisen. The Conference of 1784 was to be held in Leeds, a town which had found it difficult to entertain the comparatively small number of preachers who were accustomed to attend the Conference. In answer to the complaint of the Leeds people Wesley had reduced the number of preachers attending recent Conferences to about seventy, and had thereby met an acknowledged difficulty. If he had accepted Dr. Coke's suggestion, and had summoned nearly two hundred men to the Leeds Conference, we can

[1] Tyerman's *Life and Times of Wesley*, iii., 418-19. The Deed is set forth at full length in the *Summary of Methodist Law and Discipline*, 5th edition, 373-80.

imagine the effect their arrival would have produced in Yorkshire.[1]

John Wesley was soon at work. He had a clear view of the meaning of the Deed of Declaration. He knew that it was intended to create a Conference within a Conference, and that its purpose was to give legal efficacy to the decisions of the larger assembly. In thinking out his plan he at first thought that ten or twelve preachers might be formed into a committee that would, by its vote, approve of the decisions of the Conference, and thereby might give them legal effect. But on second thoughts he put that plan aside. He saw that if a case should arise which would involve an appeal to the Law Courts it would be wiser to have the decision of the Conference confirmed by a larger proportion of its members. So he adopted another plan. He proceeded to make out a list of one hundred preachers, taking care that it should represent not only some of the oldest of them, but those who were at all stages of the itinerancy. He was convinced that the Methodist Societies would not disappear at his death, but he was not ignorant of the fact that forces were at work which threatened the existence of Methodism and called for the protection of a Conference that represented all ranks of the Methodist preachers.

In the *Proceedings of the Wesley Historical Society* for December, 1919, an article on Wesley's Deed of Declaration appeared. Dealing with the selection of the members of the Legal Hundred, the writer said :

'In making his selection Wesley had to keep one thing steadily in mind. He had to arrange a method by which the Conference could be easily identified. It was necessary that its personnel should have a strong element of permanence. It is interesting to watch him as he compiles his list. He might have named all the senior preachers, but he knew that death, and retirement from " the work," would act most swiftly in that section. He might have gone to the other extreme and given an overwhelming preponderance of representation to the young men. But he guided his hand wittingly, and avoided the errors so often found in extremes. Let us consult the deed and discover the method adopted. In

---

[1] See Wesley's 'Thoughts upon some late Occurrences.' *Works,* xiii., 215-17. Jackson's edition.

the "Hundred" we find the names of four clergymen, John and Charles Wesley, Thomas Coke, and James Creighton, who was one of Wesley's "readers" at City Road Chapel. A little patient analysis shows that the ninety-six lay preachers chosen form separate groups. At the Conference of 1784 five of them would have "travelled" thirty years and upwards. They were the "veterans," Christopher Hopper, who had been in the work thirty-seven years, heading the list. The next group consists of those who had travelled for twenty up to twenty-seven years. They numbered sixteen, and amongst them was Thomas Rankin, a supernumerary. If we include the Wesleys in the list we find that the " seniors " numbered twenty-three, or nearly a quarter of the "Hundred." The next group consists of men who had itinerated ten, but less than twenty years. They were in the height of their strength. Among them were Joseph Benson, Joseph Bradford, James Wood and Samuel Bradburn, all of them, in their turn, Presidents of the Conference, three of them being twice elected to that position. This group numbered thirty-six preachers. There remained thirty-nine vacancies, and Wesley determined that they should be filled by the younger men. He selected five who would have travelled nine years at the approaching Conference; the same number from the eight years men, four from the seventh year, two from the sixth, and seven from the fifth year. The remainder he took from among the men who would be in their fourth year, and under, at the next Conference, judging that most of them would be then received into " full connexion." Two of them were not so received until 1786, and a third not until 1789. Our analysis reveals the fact that forty-seven per cent. of the first " Hundred " were young men who had travelled only ten or fewer years.'[1]

Looking at Wesley's list of the names of the members of the Legal Hundred, it is impossible to share the illusion of some people of his time that he intended to limit the attendance of his preachers at the Conference to the men whose names appeared in the deed.

On February 28, 1784, the deed was signed. It was endorsed as *The Revd. John Wesley's Declaration and Appointment of the Conference of the People called*

[1] See *Proceedings of the Wesley Historical Society*, xii., 86-7.

Methodists. On March 9 it was enrolled in His Majesty's High Court of Chancery, 'being first duly stamped according to the tenor of the Statutes made for that purpose.' For the first time in its history Methodism obtained the full recognition of the law. It is no wonder that Mr. Clulow and Dr. Coke rejoiced over the part they had taken in bringing about this result. Dr. Coke came to the conclusion that it was his duty to send copies of the deed to all assistants of circuits throughout Great Britain, and afterwards, to carry copies of it to Ireland. We have no evidence which proves that John Wesley was aware of this distribution at the time it was made. He may have consented to Dr. Coke's action, but he soon became aware of its serious consequences. Some of the preachers, whose names did not appear in the deed, began to show their opposition to the action that had been taken. They began to organize an attack on the whole scheme.

On Tuesday, July 27, 1784, the Conference assembled in Leeds. There was a large attendance. The business was conducted on new lines. Its proceedings were entered in a book bearing the title, *The Minutes or Journal of the Conference of the People called Methodists.* It has sometimes been asked if Wesley's 'Deed of Declaration' came into action before his death. The adoption of the *Journal* is part of the answer that may be given. But it is possible to complete the reply if we watch the order in which the business of the Conference was transacted. It was necessary to fill up two vacancies which had occurred in the Legal Hundred. The question was asked: 'Is any member of the Conference laid aside because he has desisted from travelling.' In the answer the names of Robert Lindsay and Joseph Saunderson appear. Robert Lindsay had been stationed in Ireland. He was absent from the ranks of the preachers for only a year, but he lost his position in the 'Hundred.' Joseph Saunderson returned to the active work of the ministry in 1786. His temporary retirement caused him to share Robert Lindsay's fate.[1]

Fixing our attention on the proceedings of this Conference, which cast light on the manner in which the creation of the

---

[1] Joseph Saunderson was the brother of William Saunderson, the great-grandfather of the present writer. William Saunderson was 'admitted on trial' at the Conference of 1789.

'Legal Hundred' was received, we will, in the first place, note the way in which the two vacancies were filled. In one section of the preachers who were present the feeling respecting the omission of their names from the Deed of Declaration was intense. They may have watched the proceedings with hope. If so, they were disappointed. In our next chapter we shall have to deal with the question of the change in the constitution and government of the Methodist Church in America. We are not surprised to find that by the vote of the members of the Legal Conference, Francis Asbury was elected to fill the place of Robert Lindsay. The election of the successor to Joseph Saunderson is full of interest. In the *Journal* we find that Robert Carr Brackenbury took his place. Referring to the 'Deed of Declaration,' we see that the tenth clause provides that 'no person shall be elected a member of the Conference who has not been admitted into connexion with the Conference, as a preacher, for twelve months.'[1] Our admiration for Brackenbury is great. But it is clear that his election was not in accordance with the provisions of the deed. In 1870 we contributed a series of five articles on 'The Establishment of Methodism in the Channel Islands,' to the *Wesleyan Methodist Magazine*. We mentioned the fact that, at the beginning of December, 1783, Brackenbury was staying with Wesley in the City Road house in London. While there letters were received by Wesley begging him to send a preacher to the Channel Islands. We have, in this volume, recorded Brackenbury's former visit to those pleasant places. Wesley handed to him the letters. He read them and weighed their contents for a few moments. Then he returned them to Wesley with the solemn words: 'Here am I, send me!' A little later there was held, in the City Road Chapel, a solemn meeting in which, 'amidst the earnest prayers of the people, he was commended to God, in view of the important work he had undertaken.'[2] The story of his work in the Islands stirs the heart. Its success was increased by the fact that Adam Clarke became his colleague, and gave him enthusiastic support. They have left a bright mark on the history of Methodism in the Channel Islands. It will be enough to say

---

[1] See p. 211.
[2] See *The Methodist Magazine*, 1870, 140-41.

that, in the following year, the Conference recognized the mistake that had been made in the case of Brackenbury's election to the Legal Hundred. In the *Journal* of 1785 the following entry occurs : ' The former election of Robert Carr Brackenbury, Esq., as a member of the Conference is confirmed.'

It is interesting to watch the first actions of the newly-created Legal Conference; but more serious matters demand our attention. In James Macdonald's *Memoirs of the Rev. Joseph Benson*, published in 1822, we get light on proceedings which have made this Conference conspicuous. The following quotation from Benson's account of those eventful days is given. He says : ' In the morning of July 27, the Declaration Deed, and the Appeal, which some of the brethren had published against it, were considered. Mr. Wesley traced his power from its first rise, and showed that the Conference, from its commencement, had consisted of persons whom he had desired to meet for the purpose of conferring with him. He insisted that he had a right to name the members of it and fix their number. This " Appeal," he said, represented him as unjust, oppressive and tyrannical, which he was not; and the authors of it had betrayed him, and, by doing so, had hurt the minds of many, and kindled a flame throughout the kingdom. Hence he required that they should acknowledge their fault, and be sorry for it, or he could have no further connexion with them.'[1]

It is easy to see the connexion between the distribution of the copies of the *Deed of Declaration* and the *Appeal*, in which the denunciation of Wesley's conduct appeared. When the *Deed* was read by people unaccustomed to examine legal documents, its purpose and provisions would not be understood. That fact must be remembered. It does not excuse the strong language employed by the writers of the *Appeal*, but it raises a question as to the wisdom of Wesley's threat. He had an enviable power of self-restraint; but the charges of injustice, oppression, and tyranny, seem to have roused his temper. In watching the proceedings of his opponents we find that his threat did not intimidate them. They continued their attacks in the Conference. It was fortunate that a man, whose

[1] Macdonald's *Memoirs of Benson*, 160.

name was not in the *Deed,* was present. The discussion broke out again and again. But at last he intervened as a peace-maker. He softened the indignation of Wesley by reminding him that he was 'the father' of the men who had attacked him and he ought to treat them as his 'children.' But the main service he rendered at this crisis was the appeal he made to the men who had assailed Wesley. He had a great influence with all who were present. Need we say that his name was John Fletcher? It was his last appearance in the Conference. On Sunday, August 14, 1785, he died.

The scene of Fletcher's appeal to Wesley and the Conference has been often described. It will be enough to reproduce Charles Atmore's record which is contained in his manuscript 'Memoir.' He says: 'Never while memory holds a seat in my breast shall I forget with what ardour and earnestness he expostulated, even on his knees, both with Mr. Wesley and the preachers. To the former he said: "My father, my father! They are your children!" To the latter: "My brethren! My brethren! He is our father!" And then, portraying the work in which they were unitedly engaged, he fell again on his knees, and prayed with such fervour and devotion that the whole Conference was bathed in tears, and many sobbed aloud. Thus were the preachers, except in the case of one or two individuals who left the Connexion, subdued and reconciled to the glory of God and of His Gospel.' It is necessary to say that Atmore slightly under-estimates the number of preachers who left the Connexion as a consequence of this discussion. Otherwise his description of the close of an unpleasant incident may be accepted.

As we have no wish to refer to this matter again we may say that when Wesley was in Chester, on April 7, 1785, he wrote the following letter to the Legal Hundred that would assemble after his death:

MY DEAR BRETHREN,

Some of our Travelling Preachers have expressed a fear that after my decease you would exclude them, either from preaching in connexion with you, or from some other privileges which they now enjoy. I know no other way to prevent any such inconvenience than to leave these my last words with you.

I beseech you, by the mercies of God that you never avail yourselves of the Deed of Declaration, to assume any superiority over your brethren: but let all things go on among those Itinerants who choose to remain together, exactly in the same manner as when I was with you, so far as circumstances will permit.

In particular, I beseech you, if you ever loved me, and if you now love God and your brethren, to have no respect of persons in stationing the Preachers, in choosing children for Kingswood School, in disposing of the yearly contribution, and the Preachers' Fund, or any other public money. But do all things with a single eye, as I have done from the beginning. Go on thus, doing all things without prejudice or partiality, and God will be with you even to the end.

JOHN WESLEY.

This letter was put into the custody of Joseph Bradford, Wesley's 'travelling companion.' After Wesley's death he handed it to the President of the Conference that met in Manchester on July 26, 1791. At that Conference more than two hundred preachers were present. The letter was read and entered in the *Journal*. The following N.B. was added to the entry: 'The Conference have unanimously resolved, that all the preachers who are in full connexion with them shall enjoy every privilege that the members of the Conference enjoy, agreeably to the above written letter of our venerable deceased Father in the Gospel, except in voting for the President and Secretary.'[1]

The exception in the original resolution relating to voting for the President and Secretary, was soon withdrawn. The rest of the resolution was observed for more than one hundred and forty years until the Legal Conference was dissolved by the Deed of Union of 1932.

---

[1] See *Minutes of the Methodist Conferences*, i., 242-3, 696.

XVI
THE AMERICAN PROBLEM

ON Tuesday, August 3, 1784, the eventful Leeds Conference was concluded. John Wesley left Leeds, and made his way through Wales to Bristol. He arrived there on August 28. Throughout this journey he was thinking of a subject that had caused him much perplexity. When we say that it concerned the condition of the Methodist Societies in America its importance will be recognized. During the war, and after the Peace, he had been in close communication with Francis Asbury, who had been struggling in America with serious difficulties. The other Methodist preachers who had been sent out from England had left America and Asbury had to bear burdens that would have broken the strength of an ordinary man. Wesley had been full of sympathy with him; but, for a long time, he was unable to send him relief. At last light had come, a perplexing problem had been solved. The problem concerned the administration of the sacraments of Baptism and the Lord's Supper in the Methodist Societies that were rapidly increasing in number in the United States.

It will help us to understand the difficulty of the problem if we emphasize the fact that the Methodists were not the only people in America who were confronted by serious ecclesiastical questions at the termination of the war. In Bishop Samuel Wilberforce's *History of the Protestant Episcopal Church in America,* we find a clear account of the difficulties that attended the establishment of the new Church in the United States that took the place of the Church of England.

What was the condition of the Church of England in America, in 1783, when the Peace was signed? That question shall be answered by Bishop Wilberforce. He says: 'The peace found the Church wasted and almost destroyed. The ministrations of the northern clergy had been suspended by their conscientious loyalty, and, with the recognition of

THE AMERICAN PROBLEM

American Independence, the connexion of the missionaries of the venerable Society with the land in which they had laboured hitherto was abruptly ended. In the South its condition was not greatly better. Virginia had entered on the war with one hundred and sixty-four churches and chapels, and ninety-one clergymen spread through her sixty-one counties. At the close of the contest, a large number of her churches were destroyed; ninety-five parishes were extinct or forsaken; of the remaining seventy-two, thirty-four were without ministerial services, while of her ninety-one clergymen, only twenty-eight remained. . . . At the time, the prospect was indeed depressing. The flocks were scattered and divided, the pastors few, poor and suspected, their enemies dominant and fierce. Nothing but that indestructible vitality with which God has endowed His Church could have kept it alive in that day of rebuke and blasphemy.'[1]

Accepting Bishop Wilberforce's description of the condition of the Church of England in America at the close of the war our sympathies are roused. We watch the progress of events with interest. It must be remembered that while many of the clergy failed in the day of adversity, a few refused to abandon their work. Acting in consort with many laymen, they faced the difficulties that had arisen and determined to conquer them. With courage and wisdom they looked facts in the face. It became clear to them that the 'Church of England' must give way to a Church that was more in harmony with the tone of the American mind. The result of prolonged discussions was the formation of the 'Protestant Episcopal Church of America.' In Bishop Wilberforce's book the steps taken are fully described. Conventions were held in which the views of all parties were considered. At last a scheme of government was accepted. We are not surprised that the Bishop of Oxford severely criticized some of its details. They were certainly opposed to his ecclesiastical convictions.

In watching the course of events we are especially interested in a convention of the clergy of Connecticut that was held at the earliest stages of the inquiry. Bishop Wilberforce describes the eastern clergy as men who were

---

[1] Wilberforce's *History of the Protestant Episcopal Church*, 182-4. The statement concerning Virginia is quoted from Dr. Hawks's *Virginia*, 154.

'wedded to the strongest and most clearly ascertained Church principles.' At the earliest stage of the discussions on the formation of the new Church their fears were aroused by the manner in which the question of the need of bishops, as the rulers of the Church, was treated. Their position is described by Dr. Wilberforce. He says: 'In their new circumstances they esteemed it their first duty to perfect their system by securing the presence and rule of a bishop. In this they were confirmed by the avowed temper of the South, from which they greatly feared the adoption of a spurious and nominal episcopacy. They began, therefore, at once to act for themselves, and refused to take any share in organizing their scattered communion until they had a bishop at their head.'[1] That decision was carried into effect.

As soon as the Peace made it possible the clergy of Connecticut met in 'voluntary convention,' and considered the subject of the election of a bishop of their diocese. Their choice seems to have been soon made. Among them there was a clergyman whom they held in exceptionally high esteem. He had been a missionary of the Gospel Propagation Society in Staten Island, and had been treated with great severity by the insurgents during the war. Though hunted from place to place, and more than once imprisoned, he had maintained his ministry till the last moment. His name was Samuel Seabury. It is no wonder that the choice fell on him. He was elected by the clergy of Connecticut as their future bishop. Before the British troops had evacuated New York he sailed for England. In addition to the certificate of his election, he carried with him testimonials from the leading clergy of New York, and letters in which the English bishops were earnestly requested to consecrate him.

When Dr. Seabury landed in England he found that serious difficulties confronted him. The see of Canterbury was vacant. He therefore made his application for consecration to Dr. William Markham, the Archbishop of York. He was informed that 'without a special Act of Parliament' the Archbishop could not consecrate a citizen of America, for no subject of a foreign State could take the oath of allegiance, to dispense with which the Archbishop had no power, and for such an act ministers would not apply, until they were assured

[1] Wilberforce's *History*, 197.

that the step would not offend America. He therefore felt that it was hopeless to expect to be ordained by an English Archbishop. Bishop Wilberforce casts light on his reflections. He says: 'Under these circumstances he looked anxiously around to see if he could properly obtain from any other quarter the episcopal succession. The Church in Scotland at once attracted his attention. There the true succession, derived of old time from ours, was carefully preserved, whilst the bishops, unlike those in England, were fettered by no connexion with the State. The Presbyterian Kirk had been long established in Scotland, and the Episcopalians were barely tolerated there. They consequently would be able, without any application to the State, so to vary, if need were, the form of consecration, as to make it suit a citizen of the American republic.'[1] Leaving England Dr. Seabury got into communication with the bishops of the English Church in Scotland. The result was that, on November 17, 1784, he was admitted to the episcopate at Aberdeen by Bishops Kilgour, Petre, and Skinner, who were the bishops of Aberdeen, Ross, and Moray. Rejoicing in his success, he returned to London. On March 1, 1785, he sailed for America. For two years he enjoyed the distinction of being the only bishop of the new Church in America. But, on Sunday, February 4, 1787, in the Archiepiscopal Chapel of Lambeth, two presbyters of the newly-formed American Episcopal Church, Dr. White and Dr. Provoost, were consecrated bishops by the Archbishops of the English Church, the Bishops of Bath and Wells, and the Bishop of Peterborough. In describing these ordinations Dr. Wilberforce says:

Thus, at last, did England grant to the daughter Church this great and necessary boon. For almost two whole centuries had she, by evil counsels, been persuaded to withhold it, until, as it would seem, the fierce struggle of the war of independence, and the loss of these great colonies, chastized her long neglect, and by a new and utterly unlooked-for issue, led her to discharge this claim of right. Awful, doubtless, was the hour to these two when the holy office was conferred upon them; when, at the hands of him, whom Bishop White, full of affectionate respect for his mother Church, calls this 'great and good archbishop,' they were set apart to bear into the western wilderness the likeness and the office of the first apostles. Solemn must have been their landing on the 7th of April, the afternoon of Easter Sunday, 1787, upon the shores of their own land, as the especial witnesses of that

[1] See Wilberforce's *History*, 198.

resurrection of which 'the holy Church throughout all the world' was on that day keeping glad remembrance—the especial stewards of those mysteries which she was on that day dispensing unto all her faithful children.[1]

Without pausing to criticize some of the statements contained in Bishop Wilberforce's record of the landing of the two bishops in America, it will be enough to say that, after the holding of Conventions in 1792, 1799, and 1801, the Protestant Episcopal Churches of America became fully organized. To some arrangements in its final form Bishop Wilberforce strongly objected. For instance, he considered that the episcopal character of the new Church was not distinctly marked in its organization. In his criticism he declared that the veto of the bishops was as essential to the completeness of the system as the possession of the power of 'the believing laity.' His concluding remarks throw light on his objection to the limitation of the power of the bishops. He says that the power of veto was withheld from them, and that 'the agreement of four-fifths of the lower house forced upon them any measures approved by the majority.' This is his conclusion: 'If episcopacy be indeed of Christ's appointment, such infractions on its principles must have weakened this infant Church, and that it did so, there is ample proof. To these various errors admitted into its constitution we may doubtless trace much of the slow and feeble progress of the body. Conventions never, even in America, have commanded the respect which has always waited on the personal rule of a holy and devoted bishop.' After describing the contentions that sometimes had arisen in diocesan meetings he gives one illustration. In a diocesan meeting it had actually been proposed that the canons should be so modified as to give rectors and vestries the power of admitting to the pulpits of the churches clergymen of other denominations. Recording this fact, he cries: 'Hence wanton alterations in the creeds and liturgy; hence a feeble and faltering tone, which soon infected thought and action, first among the clergy and then amongst the laity, and helped on the impression, at one time common in the South, that the Church was cold and lifeless, and indifferent to the religion of the heart.'

It is only fair to Dr. Wilberforce and the Protestant

[1] Wilberforce's *History of the Protestant Episcopal Church*, 222.

Episcopal Church to record the closing words of the chapter from which we have quoted. The bishop says: 'While therefore, we regret the compromise, and see too clearly the evils to which it has given birth, we must rejoice that still more of ancient truth was not lost in those perilous times, and we hail with peculiar pleasure many after-modifications of injurious practices, and many gradual returns to higher and more primitive principles. The Churchmen of America had amongst them the true principle of life, and the true law of its development, and year by year they have cast off some cause of weakness, and, through God's good guidance, carried on the mighty work to which His grace has called them.'[1]

We have followed the fortunes of the Church of England during and after the war because they form a prelude to a subject that must now engage our attention. With the aid of Dr. Abel Stevens we will try to see some of the experiences of the Methodist Societies in America in those years of severe testing. It will be remembered that, in the opinion of many Americans, the Societies were considered as belonging to the English Church, and therefore they should share the fate of that Church, and cease to exist in their country. Let us watch the progress of events. In Dr. Stevens' *History of American Methodism,* there is a figure that stands out with special distinction. We have recorded the departure of the English preachers from America at the outbreak of the war. Only one of them remained in the country. The name of Francis Asbury will live for ever in American Methodist history. He refused to return to England. He was aware that his decision might cost him his life. It was fortunate that he possessed that finest form of courage, courage free from recklessness. He, at first, accepted the protection of men such as Judge White, Judge Barrett, and Judge Bassett, who gave him the shield of their great influence. Judge White's house seems to have been his principal hiding-place. Then, at the end of two years and one month, he recommenced his regular journeys among the Methodist Societies in spite of the war.

Losing sight of Asbury for a time we think of the men who had to bear the outbreak of the tempest of persecution. Dr. Abel Stevens has reproduced in his *History* a valuable

[1] Wilberforce's *Protestant Episcopal Church,* 262.

quotation from an authority who possessed his confidence. This writer, describing these days of suffering, says:

> I shall principally confine myself to Maryland, my native State, where I was best acquainted, and where probably their sufferings were as great, perhaps greater, than in any other State. Some of the preachers were mulcted or fined, and others were imprisoned, for no other offence than travelling and preaching the gospel; and others were bound over in bonds and heavy penalties and sureties, not to preach in this or that county. Several were arrested and committed to the common county jail; others were personally insulted and badly abused; some were beaten with stripes and blows nigh unto death, and carried their scars down to the grave. Garrettson was, for preaching the gospel, committed to prison in one county, and severely beaten and wounded, even to the shedding of blood, in another. In the city of Annapolis, the capital of the State, Jonathan Forrest and William Wren, and I believe two or three others, were committed to jail.... In Prince George County a preacher was shamefully maltreated by a mob; 'honoured' according to the cant of the times, 'with tar and feathers.' In Queen Anne, Joseph Hartley was bound over in penal bonds of five hundred pounds not to preach in the county. In the same county, Freeborn Garrettson was beaten with a stick by one of the county judges, and pursued on horseback till he fell from his horse and was nearly killed. In Talbot County, Joseph Hartley was whipped by a young lawyer, and was imprisoned a considerable time. He used to preach, during his confinement, through the grates or window of the jail, to large concourses of people on Sabbath days. They frequently came from ten to fifteen miles to hear him, and even from other counties. His confinement produced a great excitement, and God overruled it for good to the souls of many. Christ was preached, and numbers embraced religion. Even his enemies at length were glad to have him discharged. In Dorchester, Caleb Pedicord was whipped and badly hurt on the public road; he carried his scars to the grave. We might perhaps with propriety notice some other cases in different counties and States, both north and south, of the sufferings both of preachers and members, but time would fail.[1]

We must now face another subject that demands close attention. We have described the effects of the war on the position of the Church of England in America. Before the conflict began it was the custom of the Methodists to attend the sacramental services held in the English churches that then existed in many of the towns in the country. But the war led to the destruction of a large number of these churches, and to the flight of a host of clergymen into places of safety. In spite of fierce persecution the Methodist preachers continued

[1] Stevens' *History of American Methodism*, 103-4. English edition.

their perilous work in the forsaken neighbourhoods. The result was that as the Societies increased in number[1] their members lost the opportunity to receive the sacrament of the Lord's Supper in the towns which had been abandoned by the clergy. In some neighbourhoods the Methodists made application to the Baptists for permission to attend their sacramental services, but they were told that such attendance could only be granted on the condition that those who applied would become members of the Baptist Church.

It was inevitable that the subject of the administration of the Sacrament of the Lord's Supper should be discussed in the American Conferences. It was mentioned in the first, which was held in 1773. But it was not until 1779 that it was fully considered at the Fluvanna Conference. At the outset of the discussion the position of affairs was described in these words: 'The Episcopal Establishment is now dissolved in this country, and therefore, in almost all our circuits the members are without the ordinances.' It was imperative that some action should be taken. Dr. Abel Stevens gives us light on the result of the deliberations of this Conference. He says:

> They appointed 'a committee'—Gatch, Foster, Cole, and Ellis—and constituted it 'a Presbytery': 'first, to administer the ordinances themselves; second, to authorize any other preacher or preachers, approved by them, by the form of laying-on of hands.' The committee, or presbytery, ordained one another, and afterward such of the preachers present 'as were desirous of receiving ordination.' Such were the proceedings of the Conference on this important question. The Fluvanna Conference not only included a majority of the preachers and circuits, but comprised, in the list of its appointments, a very preponderating majority of the membership of the Church. 'Most of our preachers,' says Lee 'in the South fell in with this new plan; and as the leaders were very zealous, and the greater part of them very pious men, the private members were influenced by them and pretty generally fell in with their measures; however, some of the old Methodists would not commune with them, but steadily adhered to their old customs. There was great cause to fear a division, and both parties trembled for the ark of God, and shuddered at the thought of dividing the Church of Christ. But, after all, they consented, for the sake of peace and the union of the body of Methodists, to drop the ordinances for a season, till Mr. Wesley could be consulted.'[2]

The years that followed the Fluvanna Conference tested the

---

[1] In 1776 there were 4,921 members in the Methodist Societies in America; in 1784 the number had risen to 14,988.
[2] *History of American Methodism*, 146-7. English edition.

loyalty of the American Methodists to their own Church. Appeals to John Wesley were made, but they brought little light on the sacramental problem. In some parts of America it seemed as if there would be a great loss of members if the Fluvanna plan was not adopted. Instead of lingering among those days of danger we will turn our attention to the brighter times when peace came to the agitated Societies in America.

In 1862 the first volume of a new edition of the *Minutes of the Methodist Conferences* was published. It contains records of the Conferences held in England from 1744 to 1798. Those who possess it will see that after 1775 until 1784 America is rarely mentioned. Now and then we get light on the number of members in the Societies there, but we look in vain for information concerning the advance of the work, and the number of preachers who were employed in it. We must look in other directions for information on these subjects. If we turn to the *Minutes* of the English Conference held in Leeds in 1784 we find that America appears once more in the list of stations. We see that the preachers then appointed to that country were Thomas Coke, Richard Whatcoat, and Thomas Vasey. These names arrest our attention. We remember that Dr Coke was a clergyman who had become Wesley's right-hand man in the management of the English Societies. We know that Richard Whatcoat, in 1783, had been the superintendent of the Norwich circuit, and was a member of the Legal Hundred. Thomas Vasey had been a clergyman of the Church of England until 1775, when he became a Methodist preacher. He also was a member of the Legal Hundred. Weighing these facts we come to the conclusion that the appointments to America in 1784 had a special purpose, and claim close attention.

We are aware that, in 1780, John Wesley made a strong attempt to persuade Bishop Lowth to examine and ordain a Methodist preacher in order that he might be sent to America to administer the Sacraments to the Methodist Societies in that country. The appeal to the bishop was in vain.[1] When the war ended and the United States secured their independence, the situation in America changed. Keeping our mind on the interesting history of the Churches in that country, we note that in 1784, the Church of England had

[1] See Wesley's *Works*, xiii. 116. 1830 edition.

lost its strong position. It had been displaced by the creation of the Protestant Episcopal Church. That fact cleared John Wesley's way. He had hesitated to send men to America to administer the Sacraments there who had not been ordained by an English bishop. The act, so long as the Church of England held its high position in the country, would have been strongly resented by the clergy in America. But, in 1784, that difficulty had disappeared.

In Dr. Etheridge's *Life of the Rev. Thomas Coke,* we get valuable information which enables us to understand the events which led to the Conference appointments to America. In February, 1784, Wesley had a serious conversation with Dr. Coke in the study of the house in City Road, London. It concerned the condition of the Methodist Societies in America. Wesley expressed the opinion that the Revolution had separated the United States from the Mother Country for ever. In addition he said that his correspondence convinced him that the Church of England would cease to be numbered among the Churches of America. When the conversation turned towards the position of the Methodist Societies in that country he said that they had been represented to him as being 'in a most deplorable condition.' He was aware of their increase in number and membership, but he was much concerned with their dangerous lack of organization. This is evident from the fact that, in this conversation, he informed Coke that an appeal had been made to him, through Francis Asbury, to provide for the Societies 'some mode of church-government suited to their exigencies.' He then proceeded to explain a plan he had determined to adopt. In his study of Early Church History he had much admired the mode of ordaining bishops which the Church of Alexandria had practised. In order to preserve its purity, that Church would never suffer the interference of a foreign bishop in any of its ordinations; the presbyters, on the death of a bishop, had exercised the right of ordaining a bishop chosen from their own number. This practice continued among them for two hundred years. At the close of the conversation he suggested that, being himself a presbyter, Dr. Coke should accept ordination at his hands, and then proceed to America and ordain other presbyters for the Societies in the United States.[1]

[1] Etheridge's *Life of the Rev. Thomas Coke,* 100.

The interview in Wesley's study came to an end without any conclusion being reached. Dr. Etheridge gives us light on a subject that has been much misrepresented. He says: 'To this great innovation upon Church of England order Dr. Coke certainly did not feel himself, at first, at liberty to accede. A writer in the *Quarterly Review* affirms that it was Coke who first requested Wesley to make him a bishop, and send him as such to America. The opposite is the truth, the request came from Wesley, and took Coke by surprise. He had not even given the clerical question involved in the project any serious consideration, and he first required of Mr. Wesley some time for investigation before he could express, with confidence, an opinion upon it. He now applied himself to those biblical and patristic studies which bear upon the subject, and after the lapse of two months, spent partly in Scotland, communicated to Mr. Wesley that the conclusions at which he had arrived enabled him, without any hesitation, to concur with himself as to the abstract lawfulness of the measure which had been propounded.'[1]

It was well that Dr. Coke visited Scotland. He had an opportunity of seeing a Presbyterian Church that was the Established Church of a nation. It is no wonder that he came to the position which Wesley had occupied for nearly forty years. During that long term of time he had held the doctrine of the right of presbyters to ordain men to the work of the ministry. He had not exercised that right, but an opportunity had come when he could act on his convictions, and secure the prosperity of a Church in America that now numbers its members by millions.

Although the *Minutes of Conference* contain no reference to any consideration of this important subject Dr. Etheridge informs us that the question of sending preachers to America was brought before the Leeds Conference, and that John Fletcher took part in the deliberation 'and fully concurred in the affirmative resolution then confirmed.' Dr. Etheridge included in his brief statement the fact that Dr. Coke was requested to meet Mr. Wesley shortly after in Bristol to make the final arrangements for carrying the decision of the Conference into effect.

John Wesley did not arrive in Bristol until August 28, but

[1] *Life of the Rev. Thomas Coke, D.C.L.*, 100-101.

THE AMERICAN PROBLEM

he soon received letters from Dr. Coke in which suggestions were made that demanded immediate consideration. It will be remembered that in their interview in the City Road house Wesley had startled Coke by suggesting that he should receive ordination from his hands. He was surprised at the suggestion, and seems to have looked upon it as a thing impossible. But, as the day of sailing from Bristol to America was approaching he thought it would be wise to write to Wesley and state the convictions that had come to him by much thinking on a difficult problem. It is only necessary to reproduce the following extracts from his letter. He says:

> The more maturely I consider the subject the more expedient it seems to me that the power of ordaining others should be received by me from you, by the imposition of your hands; and that you should lay hands on Brother Whatcoat and Brother Vasey, for the following reasons: 1. It seems to me the most scriptural way, and most agreeable to the practice of the primitive Churches. 2. I may want all the influence in America that you can throw into my scale. . . . As the journey is long, and you cannot spare me often, and it is well to provide against all events, and an authority *formally* received from you will be fully admitted by the people, and my exercising the office of ordination without that formal authority may be disputed, if there be any opposition on any other account; I could therefore earnestly wish you would exercise that power in this instance, which I have not the shadow of a doubt but God hath invested you with for the good of the Connexion. I think you have tried me too often to doubt whether I will in any degree use the power you are pleased to invest me with further than I believe absolutely necessary for the prosperity of the work. 3. In respect of my brethren, Whatcoat and Vasey . . . propriety and universal practice make it expedient that I should have two presbyters with me in this work. In short, it appears to me that everything should be prepared, and everything proper to be done, that can possibly be done, this side the water. You can do all this, and afterwards, according to Mr. Fletcher's advice, give us Letters Testimonial of the different offices with which you have been pleased to invest us. For the purpose of laying hands on brothers Whatcoat and Vasey, I can bring Mr. Creighton down with me, by which you will have two presbyters with you.[1]

Dr. Coke's suggestions remind us of the conversation he had with Wesley in the City Road house in London at the beginning of the year. They reveal a great advance in his ecclesiastical convictions. That advance had been quickened by his recent consultation with Fletcher, and led him to form a scheme that was immediately accepted by Wesley. Dr. Etheridge gives us the result of his advice. He says: 'Mr.

[1] Etheridge's *Life of the Rev. Thomas Coke*, 102-3.

Wesley at once desired Dr. Coke to repair to Bristol, bringing with him the Rev. Mr. Creighton, a presbyter also of the Church of England, at that time officiating at City Road Chapel. The two ministers who had been designated for America at the late Conference, Messrs. Whatcoat and Vasey, were also desired to join them, and thereupon were ordained by the three clergymen as presbyters for America, after which Dr. Coke was ordained superintendent.'[1]

Dr. Coke and his companions sailed for America on Saturday, September 18. They were 'accompanied to the ship' by a multitude of Bristol Methodists who were aware of the purpose of their voyage. Before we lose sight of them for a while we must give copies of two documents in John Wesley's handwriting that were in Dr. Coke's possession.

I

To all to whom these presents shall come, John Wesley, late Fellow of Lincoln College, in Oxford, Presbyter of the Church of England, sendeth greeting.

Whereas many of the people in the southern provinces in North America who desire to continue under my care, and still adhere to the doctrine and discipline of the Church of England, are greatly distressed for want of ministers to administer the sacraments of Baptism and the Lord's Supper, according to the usage of the same Church; and whereas there does not appear to be any other way of supplying them with ministers:

Know all men, that I, John Wesley, think myself to be providentially called at this time to set apart some persons for the work of the ministry in America. And therefore, under the protection of Almighty God, and with a single eye to His glory, I have this day set apart as a superintendent, by the imposition of my hands, and prayer (being assisted by other ordained ministers) Thomas Coke, doctor of civil law, a presbyter of the Church of England, and a man whom I judge to be well qualified for that great work. And I do hereby recommend him to all whom it may concern, as a fit person to

[1] The place where these preachers for America were ordained has been a subject of much discussion. The editor of Wesley's *Journal* is probably right when he says: 'The house in which this service was held was ascertained, with "approximate certainty," by the late H. J. Foster, as No. 6, Dighton Street.' See *Journal*, vii., 16.

preside over the flock of Christ. In testimony whereof I have hereunto set my hand and seal this second day of September, in the year of our Lord one thousand seven hundred and eighty-four.

JOHN WESLEY.

II

To Dr. Coke, Mr. Asbury, and our Brethren in North America.

By a very uncommon train of providences, many of the provinces of North America are totally disjoined from the mother country, and erected into independent States. The English Government has no authority over them, either civil or ecclesiastical any more than over the States of Holland. A civil authority is exercised over them partly by the Congress, partly by the Provincial Assemblies. But no one either exercises or claims any ecclesiastical authority at all. In this peculiar situation some thousands of the inhabitants of these States, desire my advice, and in compliance with their desire, I have drawn up a little sketch.

Lord King's account of the primitive Church convinced me, many years ago, that bishops and presbyters are the same order, and consequently have the same right to ordain. For many years I have been importuned from time to time to exercise this right, by ordaining part of our travelling preachers. But I have still refused, not only for peace sake, but because I was determined as little as possible to violate the established order of the national Church to which I belonged.

But the case is widely different between England and North America. Here there are bishops who have a legal jurisdiction. In America there are none, neither any parish minister. So that for some hundreds of miles together there is none either to baptize, or to administer the Lord's Supper. Here, therefore, my scruples are at an end, and I conceive myself at full liberty, as I violate no order, and invade no man's right, by appointing and sending labourers into the harvest.

I have accordingly appointed Dr. Coke and Mr. Francis Asbury to be joint superintendents over our brethren in North America, as also Richard Whatcoat and Thomas Vasey to act as elders among them by baptizing and administering the Lord's Supper. And I have prepared a Liturgy, little differing from that of the Church of England (I think the best constituted Church in the world), which I advise all the travelling preachers to use on the Lord's Day in all the congregations, reading the Litany only on Wednesdays and Fridays, and praying extempore all other days. I also advise the elders to administer the Supper of the Lord on every Lord's Day.

If any one will point out a more rational and scriptural way of feeding and guiding these poor sheep in the wilderness, I will gladly embrace it. At present I cannot see any better method than that I have taken.

It has indeed been proposed to desire the English bishops to ordain part of our preachers for America. But to this I object. 1. I desired the Bishop of London to ordain one, but I could not prevail. 2. If they consented, we know the slowness of their proceedings, but the matter admits of no delay. 3. If they would ordain them now, they would expect to govern them: and how grievously would this entangle us! 4. As our American brethren are now disentangled, both from the State and the English hierarchy, we dare not entangle them again, either with the one or the other. They are now at full liberty simply to follow the Scriptures and the primitive Church. And we judge it best that they should stand fast in that liberty wherewith God has so strangely set them free.

JOHN WESLEY.

Bristol.
September 10, 1784.

XVII

THE METHODIST EPISCOPAL CHURCH

DR. COKE and his companions, Richard Whatcoat and Thomas Vasey landed at New York on November 3, 1784. During his short stay in the city Coke preached three times in the chapel, then, in company with Whatcoat, he set out in quest of Francis Asbury. We note that on Sunday, November 7, he preached in St. Paul's Church at Philadelphia in the morning and in the Methodist Chapel in the evening. We think he must have got light on Asbury's movements, for we see him making his way through the State of Delaware and pausing at Dover. In that town there was a preacher who was well acquainted with Asbury, and could give him the directions he required. When we say that his name was Freeborn Garrettson our interest in the interview that took place in Dover is increased. In the 'Supplementary Notes' of Dr. Etheridge's *Life of Coke* we get a clear view of him. He says that Garrettson was a gentleman of good family and ample estate. In his early manhood he was converted to God by the instrumentality of one of the first Methodist preachers in America, and that he dedicated the entire remainder of his life to the work of the gospel. He describes him as ' a man who had the gentleness of a child combined with the zeal of an apostle and the heroic patience of a martyr.' In the preceding chapter we have mentioned some of Garrettson's sufferings during the war. But when the war was over, he wrote a letter to John Wesley in which he gave a description of some of his adventures when he was a young preacher. That description was intended for Wesley's eyes; but we cannot resist the temptation to reproduce it. He says : ' My lot has mostly been in new places to form circuits, which much exposed me to persecution. Once I was imprisoned, twice beaten, left on the highway speechless and senseless, and must have gone into the world of spirits, had not God in mercy sent a good Samaritan, that led and took me to a friend's house, once shot at, guns and pistols presented at my breast, once delivered from an armed mob in the dead-time of night, on the highway, by a surprising flash of lightning, surrounded frequently by mobs, stoned frequently. I have had to escape for my life at night. Oh! shall I ever forget the Divine Hand which has supported me?'[1] When Wesley read this description of the perils of an American preacher he must have thought of the days when he had to face furious mobs, and preached at the peril of his life.[2]

On Sunday, November 14, Dr. Coke preached in Barrett's Chapel, which stood in the midst of a forest. He had a large congregation. As the Sacrament was to be administered he lingered in the pulpit after preaching his sermon. Then an event occurred that he shall describe. He says: 'After the sermon, a plain, robust man came up to me in the pulpit and kissed me: I thought it could be no other than Mr. Asbury, and I was not deceived. I administered the Sacrament, after preaching, to five or six hundred communicants, and held a lovefeast. . . . After dinner Mr. Asbury and I had a private conversation on the future management of our affairs in America. He informed me that he had received some intimations of my arrival on the continent, and had collected a considerable number of the preachers to form a council, and if they were of opinion that it would be expedient immediately to call a Conference, it should be done. They were accordingly sent for, and after debate, were unanimously of that opinion. We therefore sent off F. Garrettson, like an arrow, from north to south, directing him to send messengers to the right and left, and to gather all the preachers together at Baltimore on Christmas Eve. Mr. Asbury has also drawn up for me a route of about a thousand miles in the meantime. . . . I exceedingly reverence Mr. Asbury; he has so much wisdom and consideration, so much meekness and love, and under all this, though hardly to be perceived, so much command and authority.'

[1] Etheridge's *Life of Dr. Coke*, 430.
[2] In John Wesley's *Works* several letters to Garrettson may be found. They are marked by that tone of confidence and affection which distinguishes his letters to intimate friends. See his *Works*, xiii.. 53-7. Jackson's edition.

Coke and Asbury parted for a time. It would be interesting to follow the former in his journeys through Delaware, Virginia, and Maryland. But there are several entries in Coke's *Journal* which must detain us. They reveal the effects of the war on the religious life of the country and justify the step which Wesley had taken to meet the difficulty which had arisen in America by the withdrawal of so many clergymen from the United States. Etheridge has made several extracts from Coke's *Journal,* which give us the light we need. After stating that at Barrett's Chapel he had baptized thirty or forty infants and seven adults, we note the following entries in his *Journal*:

Wednesday, December 1. Preached at a chapel of ours in a forest, called Lane's Chapel. Here I had a large, lively congregation, baptized a great many children, and administered the Sacraments to many communicants.

Sunday, 5th, Cambridge. In this town, which has been remarkable above any other on the continent for persecution, there arose a great dispute whether I should preach in the church or not. The ladies in general were for it, but the gentlemen against it; and the gentlemen prevailed. Accordingly, the church door was locked, though they have had no service in it, I think, for several years; and it has frequently been left open, I am informed. for cows, dogs, and pigs. However, read prayers and preached at the door of a cottage to one of the largest congregations I have had in America.

Dr. Allen's, Monday 6th. I preached at noon at a place called Bolingbroke. Our chapel is in a forest. Perhaps I have in this tour baptized more children and adults than I should in my whole life, if stationed in an English parish.[1]

We have noted the fact that the work of summoning the preachers to the approaching Conference had been entrusted to Freeborn Garrettson. With the aid of other helpers he spread the news that the Conference would assemble in Baltimore on Friday, December 24; the news was welcomed by the preachers who had heard of the arrival of Dr. Coke and his companions from England. It is probable that the purpose of their visit was well known. The preachers were scattered abroad in the United States, but the thoroughness of the work of Garrettson and his helpers may be judged from the fact that sixty, out of the eighty-three Methodist preachers then at work in the United States, made their way to Baltimore. They were convinced that a time had arrived

[1] Etheridge's *Life of Rev. Thomas Coke,* 111-12.

in the history of American Methodism when it was necessary to place it on foundations that could not be moved.

Leaving the preachers on their way to Baltimore, we fix our attention on Dr. Coke and Francis Asbury. They had become, with other preachers, the guests of Mr. Gough, of Perry Hall. It was a beautiful place. It had been a shelter for Asbury during the war. Dr. Coke was delighted with it. He describes it as 'the most elegant house in this State.' He adds: 'Here I have a noble room to myself, where Mr. Asbury and I may, in the course of a week, mature everything for the Conference.' Four days were spent in revising the 'Rules and Minutes,' and making provision for the approaching Conference. We are especially interested in one subject that was discussed. It concerned the position that Asbury was to occupy in the newly-organized Church. It must be remembered that, towards the close of 1772, Asbury received a letter from John Wesley appointing him to act as his 'assistant' in America. That arrangement was disturbed by the arrival of Thomas Rankin, who landed in America on June 1, 1773. Dr. Abel Stevens says that Wesley had appointed him as 'general assistant or superintendent of the American Societies, for he was not only Asbury's senior in the itinerancy, but was an experienced disciplinarian.' That arrangement led to difficulties and misunderstandings which we need not recount. When the war between England and America began in July, 1774, it led to the withdrawal of the English Methodist missionaries from the country with the exception of Asbury, who declined to depart. In 1782 the American Conference unanimously recognized him as a 'General Assistant' according to Wesley's former appointment. In addition, on December 24, 1783, he received a letter from Wesley in which he was directed to act again in that capacity. Bearing these facts in mind we cease to wonder that in his conversations with Dr. Coke he insisted on the necessity of submitting their appointment by Wesley as 'joint superintendents' over the Methodist preachers in America to the vote of the Conference that was to assemble in Baltimore.[1]

Friday, December 24, 1784, is a date that stands out with exceptional prominence in the history of American Methodism.

[1] See p. 236.

Early in the morning of that day we see a little company of horsemen setting out from Perry Hall. We recognize Dr. Coke, Francis Asbury, Richard Whatcoat, and Thomas Vasey. We follow them until they dismount at the Lovely Lane Chapel in Baltimore, where they were welcomed by a crowd of preachers and people. In Dr. Tipple's valuable volume entitled *The Heart of Asbury's Journal,* there is a picture of the 'preaching-house.' Looking at it we are inclined to agree with Dr. Stevens when he says that, in 1784, it was 'a rude structure.' But the Baltimore Methodists had done their best to prepare it for the meeting of the Conference, and we know that Dr. Coke commended them for their kindness in furnishing a large stove, and also backs to some of the seats ' for the comfort of the Conference.' We are inclined to linger over the picture of the little 'preaching-house,' but we must now enter the chapel and try to realize the events which have made the first 'General Conference' held in America conspicuous in the annals of the Methodist Church.

We are indebted to Dr. Abel Stevens for light on some of the proceedings of this memorable Conference. When Dr. Coke took the chair he presented the letter from Wesley which was addressed to 'Dr. Coke, Mr. Asbury, and our Brethren in North America.' It appears at the close of the preceding chapter. In that letter Wesley had said that he had appointed ' Dr. Coke and Mr. Francis Asbury to be joint superintendents over our brethren in North America; as also Richard Whatcoat and Thomas Vasey to act as elders among them, by baptizing and administering the Lord's Supper.' We have seen that Asbury considered that the appointment to the high office of 'superintendent' should be submitted to the Conference for its approval. He had argued the question with Dr. Coke, and seems to have made some impression on him. Dr. Etheridge's record of the action of the Christmas Conference on this critical question is concise. He says : ' The great feature of this Conference was the ordination of the " superintendent and elders." The Conference, by a unanimous vote, signified their concurrence in the appointment and designation of Dr. Coke and Mr. Asbury to the office of general superintendents. After this act Mr. Asbury was ordained, first a deacon, then an elder or presbyter, and then by Dr. Coke, assisted by two presbyters, one of whom, the Rev. Mr. Otterbine, was of the Lutheran Church, he was consecrated to the office of superintendent.'[1]

We get a clear view of the stages of Francis Asbury's ordinations when we consult his *Journal*. In it there is a copy of the certificate that was given to him by Dr. Coke when his consecration to his high office was completed. We will quote its contents:

Know all men by these presents, That I, Thomas Coke, Doctor of Civil Law; late of Jesus College, in the University of Oxford, Presbyter of the Church of England, and Superintendent of the Methodist Episcopal Church in America; under the protection of Almighty God, and with a single eye to His glory; by the imposition of my hands, and prayer (being assisted by two ordained elders), did on the twenty-fifth day of this month, December, set apart Francis Asbury for the office of a deacon in the aforesaid Methodist Episcopal Church. And also on the twenty-sixth day of the said month, did, by the imposition of my hands, and prayer (being assisted by the said elders), set apart the said Francis Asbury for the office of elder in the said Methodist Episcopal Church. And on this twenty-seventh day of the said month, being the day of the date hereof, have, by the imposition of my hands, and prayer (being assisted by the said elders), set apart the said Francis Asbury for the office of a superintendent in the said Methodist Episcopal Church, a man whom I judge to be well qualified for that great work. And I do hereby recommend him to all whom it may concern, as a fit person to preside over the flock of Christ. In testimony whereof I have hereunto set my hand and seal this twenty-seventh day of December, in the year of our Lord 1784.[2]

THOMAS COKE.

John Wesley's choice of Francis Asbury as a 'general superintendent' was fully justified. For more than thirty years he devoted himself to the work of visiting the circuits in his vast diocese. Dr. Tipple, in his Introduction to *The Heart of Asbury's Journal*, describes him in language which may be safely adopted. He says: 'He was a wise administrator; he had a genius for government almost as marked as Wesley's. He was a man of remarkable piety and devotion, and equally remarkable in his labours. Freeborn Garrettson said he prayed the best and prayed the most of all the men he knew. No man of his generation or since, was more abundant in labours. He attended and presided at

---

[1] *Life of Rev. Thomas Coke*, 114-15. There is a slight mistake in this description. Three presbyters, Richard Whatcoat, Thomas Vasey, and Philip Otterbein assisted Dr. Coke in this consecration.

[2] Tipple's *The Heart of Asbury's Journal*, 230-1.

almost every Annual Conference during his long and illustrious superintendency, stationed all the preachers; everywhere made careful inquiries into the state of the work; and had a wider and more accurate knowledge of the field and the workers than any man of his day.'

We have dwelt on the consecration of Francis Asbury because of its special significance. We must now, with the aid of Dr. Stevens, record the fact that, at this Conference, other men were ordained. He says: 'In compliance with the call from Nova Scotia, Garrettson and James O. Cromwell were ordained elders for that province. Jeremiah Lambert was ordained to the same office for Antigua, in the West Indies. For the United States the elders were John Tunnel, William Gill, Le Roy Cole, Nelson Reed, John Haggerty, Reuben Ellis, Richard Ivey, Henry Willis, James O'Kelly and Beverly Allen. Tunnel, Willis and Allen were not present, but received ordination after the session. John Dickins, Ignatius Pigman, and Caleb Boyer were chosen deacons. Boyer and Pigman were ordained in June following at the Conference in Baltimore.'[1] In this list there is a name that arrests our special attention. Jeremiah Lambert, who was ordained for work in Antigua, was sent there to assist John Baxter, who had given up his position at the shipyard, and had devoted himself to the work of an evangelist. He had met with remarkable success. In 1785 the number of the members in the Methodist Society in Antigua were returned as 'eight Whites and eleven hundred Blacks.' It is clear that Baxter needed help. It was given to him. In the *Minutes* of the British Conference of 1785 we see that he and Lambert were appointed as 'elders' to Antigua. At this point it will be enough to say that Dr. Coke, soon after his landing at Antigua on Christmas Day, 1786, set Baxter apart to the high office of the Christian ministry.

We cannot close our description of the proceedings of the Baltimore Conference without referring to a subject that was eagerly discussed by the assembled preachers. In 1780 the American Conference had considered the subject of slavery and had passed the following resolutions. 'Ques. Does this Conference acknowledge that slavery is contrary to the laws of God, man, and nature, and hurtful to society, contrary to

[1] *History of American Methodism*, 171; English edition.

the dictates of conscience and religion, and doing that which we would not that others should do to us and ours? Do we pass our disapprobation on all our friends who keep slaves, and advise their freedom? Ans. Yes.' In 1783 the subject was again discussed by the Conference. This question was asked: 'What shall be done with our local preachers who hold slaves contrary to the laws which authorize their freedom in any of the United States?' The answer was: 'We will try them another year. In the meantime, let every assistant deal faithfully and plainly with everyone, and report to the next Conference. It may then be necessary to suspend them.'

The report on the slave question was presented to the Baltimore Christmas Conference, at which the new Church was organized. It was closely considered. We reproduce the questions that were asked and the answers that were given. They throw a clear light on the opinions of the men who were present at this memorable Conference.

Ques. What shall we do with our local preachers who will not emancipate their slaves in the States where the laws permit it? Ans. Try those in Virginia another year; and suspend the preachers in Maryland, Delaware, Pennsylvania and New Jersey. Ques. What shall be done with our travelling preachers that now are, or hereafter shall be, possessed of slaves, and refuse to manumit them where the law permits? Ans. Employ them no more. Ques. What methods can we take to extirpate slavery? Ans. We are deeply conscious of the impropriety of making new terms of communion for a religious Society already established, excepting on the most pressing occasion: and such we esteem the practice of holding our fellow-creatures in slavery. We view it as contrary to the golden law of God, on which hang all the law and the prophets, and to the inalienable rights of mankind, as well as every principle of the Revolution, to hold in the deepest debasement, in a more abject slavery than is, perhaps, to be found in any part of the world except America, so many souls that are capable of the image of God. Whereupon it is enacted, (1) That every member emancipate his slaves between the ages of forty and forty-five within twelve months; and every other slave in a gradation of time corresponding. (2) A register of such manumissions shall be kept in each Circuit. (3) Recusants to be excluded from the Church. (4) No person henceforth to be admissable who is unwilling to comply with the condition. Buyers and sellers of slaves to be expelled.[1]

We have quoted the decisions of the Baltimore Conference in order that we might show the opinions of its members on the subject of slavery. It is clear that the preachers hated it

[1] Etheridge's *Life of the Rev. Thomas Coke*, 143-4.

vehemently. But it is impossible to ignore the fact that there were serious difficulties in the way of the Conference when it made an attempt to carry its decisions into effect. Dr. Etheridge recognizes that fact. He says: 'Now came a dilemma. The Church ordained one thing, and the State another. These Church rules clashed with the laws of the country, which prohibited the emancipation demanded by the Conference. So, in 1785, it was perforce "resolved to suspend the execution of the rule for the present." The Conference, however, still expressed the deepest abhorrence of the practice, and a determination to seek its destruction by all wise and prudent means. In the Discipline, 1796, 1, All office-bearers are required to give security for the emancipation of their slaves, either immediately or gradually, as the laws of the States and the circumstances of the case will admit; and 2, That no slave-holders shall be admitted to the Society, until the preacher has spoken to him freely and faithfully on the subject.'[1]

Dr. Coke remained in America until June 2, 1785. He visited the Methodist circuits in several States, and increased his knowledge of the condition of the Churches in many parts of the country. When he was about to leave America for England an incident occurred that calls for special recognition. Being in the State of Virginia in the company of Bishop Asbury, he paid a visit to General Washington. We will give his description of this interesting event. He says:

Thursday, May 26.—Mr. Asbury and I set off for General Washington's. We were engaged to dine there. The General's seat is very elegant, built upon the Potomac; for the improvement of the navigation of which he is carrying on some amazing plans. He received us very politely. He is quite the plain country-gentleman. After dinner we opened to him the grand business, presenting to him our petition (agreed upon by the late Conference) for the Negroes, and entreating his signature, if the eminence of his station did not render that inexpedient. He informed us that he was of our sentiments, and had signified his thoughts on the subject to most of the great men of the State; that he did not see it proper to sign the petition; but, if the Assembly took it into consideration, he would signify his sentiments to the Assembly by a letter. He asked us to spend the evening and lodge at his house; but our engagement at Annapolis the following day would not admit of it. We returned that evening to Alexandria; where, at eight o'clock, after the bell was rung, I had a considerable congregation.[2]

[1] *Life of Dr. Coke*, 144.
[2] Etheridge's *Life of Rev. Thomas Coke*, 148-9.

Watching the two travellers on their way from Washington's house, it has been impossible to banish from our memory the great crowd of the members of the Second Ecumenical Methodist Conference, held in Washington, that made its way to Mount Vernon on Saturday afternoon, October 10, 1891. We think of the men and women from many countries who stood silent in the presence of Washington's tomb; then walked through the gardens, or paused for a few moments to watch the play of the sunlight on the Potomac River. The whole of the visit was a beautiful tribute to the man who had received with courtesy the two Englishmen in the far-away days of the past.

There can be no doubt that the visit of Coke and Asbury made a deep impression on Washington. In evidence of our conviction we may say that, in September, 1920, we received a copy of the Boston edition of *Zion's Herald,* a well-known publication in America. It contained an article which stated that a large part of Washington's private library was still in existence, and that over three hundred and fifty of his nine hundred books could be seen in a special room on the fourth floor of the Athenaeum Library in Boston. The writer of the article says: 'With the possible exception of agriculture, military science, and politics, no subjects seemed quite so attractive to Washington, if we may judge him by his books, as philosophy and theology. . . . We were, of course, especially eager to discover whether Methodism was represented in this collection, and were glad to find a number of writings from the pens of our early pioneers. Of Wesley's sermons we found " The Great Assize," " Salvation by Faith," " The Almost Christian," " Original Sin," " The Important Question " (Matt. xvi. 26), and " Thoughts on Slavery."' In addition, a copy of the sermon preached by Thomas Coke at the ' Christmas Conference ' in Baltimore in 1784 was discovered. It had been carefully treasured by Washington. It is probable that he received it from Coke during the visit which we have described.

XVIII

A MEMORABLE YEAR

On March 24, 1785, John Wesley was in Worcester. He found rest in a quiet home. In his *Journal* he gives us the result of his musings on the position of Methodism in the world at that time. He says: 'I was now considering how strangely the grain of mustard-seed, planted about fifty years ago, had grown up. It has spread through all Great Britain and Ireland, the Isle of Wight, and the Isle of Man; then to America from the Leeward Islands, through the whole continent into Canada and Newfoundland. And the Societies in all these parts walk by one rule; knowing religion is holy tempers, and striving to worship God, not in form only, but likewise "in spirit and in truth."' As the pictures of the past moved before him we are impressed by the clearness of his view. We note that he obeys the law of progression. When he mentions the missions to America, for instance, he puts the Leeward Islands in their right place, and brings before us the pioneer work of Nathaniel Gilbert.[1]

On Good Friday, March 25, Wesley went by chaise to Birmingham, starting from Worcester at five o'clock in the morning. He tells us that he made this early journey in order to reach Birmingham before the church service began. He gives us no record of his attendance at that service. Later in the day we find that he was busy writing letters. We are especially interested in one of them. A note-writer in Wesley's *Journal* expresses his opinion that the letter was addressed to Barnabas Thomas, who had been an itinerant Methodist preacher from 1765 to 1781. In this letter he once more states his views on a presbyter's right to ordain. He says: 'I know myself to be as real a Christian bishop as the Archbishop of Canterbury. Yet I was always resolved, and am so still, never to act as such except in case of necessity.

[1] See *Journal*, vii. 59.

... In America it did exist. This I made known to the Bishop of London, and desired his help. But he peremptorily refused it. All the other bishops were of the same mind. This rather because they said they had nothing to do with America. Then I saw my way clear.'[1]

The reader of the last three volumes of the latest edition of John Wesley's *Journal* will be impressed by the abundance of their footnotes. The explanation is given by the editor. He says: 'On December 1, 1782, Wesley's *Diary*, of which for forty years we have lost sight, reappears, and with but a few slight breaks, due chiefly to sickness, continues until within a few days of the writer's death. In form and, more important still, in purpose, it differs little from the *Diary* of an earlier time. It records in briefest possible outline the outward life—the hours, the journeys, the means of travel, whether by chaise or coach, the persons interviewed, the meals and services, and, occasionally, the episodes of a romantic life. But essentially it is a record of the diarist's inner religious life and of his friendships. If the student of a very singular document regards it as the *Diary* of a member of the Holy Club, he will easily understand the significance of its peculiarities.'[2] There can be no doubt that the insertion of the extracts from the *Diary* has greatly increased the value of the *Journal*. Some of them throw much needed light on subjects which have been difficult to understand.

In making his way to Liverpool he was expecting to embark for Ireland. It is likely that the absence of Dr. Coke in America caused him to undertake this journey. Dr. Coke had supplied his place in recent years when the Irish Conference had assembled, and it was inconvenient for Wesley to attend. But there were other reasons that caused him to visit Ireland at this time. He must have heard the good news of a remarkable revival of religion that was in progress among the Irish Methodist Societies. That fact would appeal to him with irresistible force. On April 6 he preached in Liverpool. He had expected to find a ship there that would sail at once to Ireland, but he was disappointed. The next day he hastened to Chester. Making inquiries he found that there was no ship at Parkgate, so he was again disappointed. At Chester, however, he used the unexpected leisure to write

---

[1] Wesley's *Journal*, vii., 59, note. [2] John Wesley's *Journal*, vi., 370.

the important letter to the Legal Hundred which was given in full in Chap. XV.¹

On Friday, April 8, 1785, he 'took coach' with his travelling companion, George Whitfield, who afterwards became his Book Steward in London, and rode on to Holyhead. The next day they went on board the *Clermont*, a packet well known to Irish travellers of that day. She was delayed by 'a dead calm.' On Sunday, Wesley was asked to preach to the passengers. After preaching he prayed that God would give him and his hearers 'a full and speedy passage.' He says: 'While I was speaking the wind sprung up, and in twelve hours brought us to Dublin Bay.' Landing he made his way to 'the preachers' house.' His description of his stay there reveals the fact that, after writing his letter to the Conference when he was in Chester, the cloud that had hung over him for many months had vanished. It is pleasant to read his description of the welcome he received from his hosts in Dublin. He says: 'I found such a resting-place at our own house as I never found in Ireland before; and two such preachers, with two such wives, I know not where to find again!' When we see that the preachers were James Rogers and Andrew Blair, and that the former had married Hester Ann Roe, of Macclesfield, we understand his joy at meeting old friends again.²

Wesley immediately set to work in Dublin. He found that the news of the great revival which he had received when in England, was correct. He devoted four days to the examination of the Society. In his *Journal* he says that he had never found the Society in such a state before. It numbered seven hundred and forty-seven members, above three hundred of them having been added in a few months. He rejoiced in the great success, but his experience of sudden revivals of religion led him to take a sober view of the increase. In the *Journal* he gives us the result of his own observations of revivals in other places. He says: 'In various places, indeed, we have frequently felt "the o'erwhelming power of saving grace," which acted almost irresistibly. But such a shower of grace never continued long, and afterwards men might

¹ See p. 218.
² In the well-known picture of John Wesley's death-bed, James Rogers and his wife may be seen quietly watching his passing away. See Wesley's *Journal*, viii. 141.

resist the Holy Ghost as before. When the general ferment subsides, everyone that partook of it has his trial for life, and the higher the flood, the lower will be the ebb; yea, the more swiftly it rose, the more swiftly it falls. So that, if we see this here, we should not be discouraged. We should only use all diligence to encourage as many as possible to press forward, in spite of all the refluent tide. Now, especially, we should warn one another not to grow weary or faint in our mind; if haply we may see such another prodigy as the late one at Paulton, near Bath, where there was a very swift work of God; and yet, a year after, out of a hundred converted, there was not one backslider!'[1]

On Monday, April 18, John Wesley left Dublin; he did not return to that city until Saturday, June 18. It is pleasant to read the records of his visits to places where the Methodists had formerly met with fierce opposition. He found that the old spirit of hatred had vanished. As he passed from town to town he was received with enthusiasm. He frequently preached to large crowds, and the records in his *Journal* show his thankfulness for the coming of a great revival in Ireland. He had no doubt concerning the future of Methodism in that country. The depression caused by the discussions in the English Conference on the 'Deed of Declaration' passed away. When he left Ireland he had renewed his strength. Once more he dared to believe in the coming of a time when the influence of the Methodist Church would be felt throughout the world.

There is an entry in Wesley's *Journal* during this visit to Ireland that possesses exceptional power of arrest. On Saturday, May 7, 1785, one of his most loved friends in England was touched by the hand of death. We do not know when the news reached Ireland, but under that date there is this entry in his *Journal*:

On this day that venerable saint Mr. Perronet desired his granddaughter, Miss Briggs, who attended him day and night, to go out into the garden and take a little air. He was reading and hearing her read the three last chapters of Isaiah. When she returned he was in a kind of ecstasy; the tears running down his cheeks, from a deep sense of the glorious things which were shortly to come to pass. He continued unspeakably happy that day, and on Sunday was, if possible, happier still. And, indeed, heaven seemed to be opened to all that were round about him. When

[1] *Journal*, vii., 67-8.

he was in bed, she went into his room to see if anything was wanting; and as she stood at the feet of the bed, he smiled and broke out, 'God bless thee, my dear child, and all that belong to thee! Yea, He *will* bless thee!' Which he earnestly repeated many times till she left the room. When she went in the next morning, Monday the 9th, his spirit was returned to God.

So ended the holy and happy life of Mr. Vincent Perronet, in the ninety-second year of his age. I follow hard after him in years, being now in the eighty-second year of my age. Oh that I may follow him in holiness, and that my last end may be like his![1]

On board the *Prince of Wales,* which he describes as one of the neatest ships he was ever in, Wesley came into Holyhead Bay before one o'clock in the afternoon of Monday, July 11. He spent a few days in the north of England. He then made his way to London, where he arrived toward the end of the week. At this point his entries in the *Journal* give us little help on a subject of exceptional interest. Fortunately, the editorial footnote extracts from his *Diary* are numerous. There is one topic on which they cast a few rays of much-needed light. It is true that we are only informed that on Saturday, July 16, he was visited by his brother, and that on Tuesday, July 19, he had an interview with Dr. Coke. Nothing is said about the subject of their conversations. We think there can be little doubt that the sermon Coke had preached in America at the ordination of Francis Asbury came under review. It had been printed and published in London, early in 1785, by John Paramore, at the Foundery, Moorfields. It was read by Charles Wesley, and several of its statements roused his anger. He had rushed into print and had attacked Dr. Coke in an anonymous pamphlet. We think we are right in suggesting that the conversations between John Wesley and his brother, and afterwards with Dr. Coke, on the dates we have mentioned, must have included some reference to the Baltimore sermon.

Those who are acquainted with the leading events recorded in Methodist histories are aware that Charles Wesley disapproved of the action of John Wesley which led to the creation of a new Methodist Church in America. He seems to have waited for an opportunity to express his opinion. He found it when Dr. Coke's sermon, preached in Baltimore, was published in London. We are indebted to the Rev. John

[1] *Journal,* vii., 75-6.

Telford for the opportunity of seeing that sermon in its first edition. We have read it with care, and can understand the cause of Charles Wesley's attack on some of its contents. We will confine our attention to one subject.

The sermon was founded on Revelation iii. 7-11, a text full of comfort to the members of a Church that had been sorely persecuted. Instead of 'opening the words of his text,' Dr. Coke spent a considerable amount of time in vindicating the conduct of the American Methodists in forming themselves into an independent Church. By so doing he gave Charles Wesley his opportunity. We reproduce this section of Dr. Coke's discourse.

> The Church of *England,* of which the Society of Methodists, in general, have till lately professed themselves a part, did for many years groan in *America* under grievances of the heaviest kind. Subjected to a Hierarchy, which weighs everything in the scales of politics, its most important interests were repeatedly sacrificed to the supposed advantages of *England.* The Churches were, in general, filled with the parasites and bottle-companions of the rich and the great. The humble and most importunate entreaties of the oppressed flocks, yea, the representations of a General Assembly itself, were contemned and despised; everything sacred must lie down at the feet of a party, the holiness and happiness of mankind be sacrificed to their views; and the drunkard, the fornicator, and the extortioner, triumphed over bleeding *Zion,* because they were faithful abettors of the ruling powers. But these intolerable fetters are now struck off, and the anti-Christian union which before subsisted between Church and State, is broken asunder. One happy consequence of which has been the expulsion of most of those hirelings 'who ate the fat and clothed themselves with the wool, but strengthened not the diseased, neither healed that which was sick, neither bound up that which was broken, neither brought again that which was driven away, neither sought that which was lost.'
>
> The Parochial Churches in general being hereby vacant, our People were deprived of the Sacraments through the greatest part of these States, and continue so still. What method can we take at this critical juncture? God has given us sufficient resources in ourselves; and after mature deliberation, we believe that we are called to draw them forth.[1]

When Coke's *Sermon* was published in London we see that an important footnote was added to his description of the hireling clergymen who had occupied the churches in America before the war. Fearing that he might be mis-

[1] Coke's *Sermon preached at Baltimore before the General Conference of the Methodist Episcopal Church at the Ordination of the Rev. Francis Asbury to the office of a Superintendent.* Published at the desire of the Conference, 6-7.

understood, he guarded himself by inserting this disclaimer of any intention to bring 'a railing accusation' against the whole of the clergy of the English Church in America. He says: 'I am deeply conscious that the observation by no means reaches to the *whole* body of the Clergy of the Church of *England*. There are many of them whose characters I greatly esteem, and at whose feet I should think it an honour to sit.'[1]

It is not necessary to record the progress of the controversy between Charles Wesley and Dr. Coke. It soon came to an end. Coke's place was taken by John Wesley. For many months the discussion was continued. At last it died out. It had been carried on with good temper. At its close, so far as the main question was concerned, each of the brothers occupied the position where he had stood at the beginning of the friendly debate. Charles Wesley yielded a few points of minor importance, but, seeing that it was useless to continue the controversy, he wisely brought it to a close.

As we have watched the discussions between John and Charles Wesley, we have been impressed by the fact that John Wesley seems to have renewed his youth while his brother bears the marks of advanced old age. We will dismiss the subject of their controversy from our mind, we will try to find out the reason of the weary look that often arrests us during the closing years of Charles Wesley's life.

In Thomas Jackson's *Life of the Rev. Charles Wesley* there is a brief account of an event which brought a cloud that darkened the closing years of Charles Wesley's life. Unknown to his father, his son Samuel had become a member of the Roman Catholic Church. The secret was kept for a considerable time. At last some of the members of the Church he attended consulted together and came to the conclusion that Charles Wesley ought to be informed of his son's reception into the Church of Rome. Thomas Jackson shall be our guide to the proceedings that were taken in consequence of this decision. He says:

It was deemed requisite that his connexion with the Church of Rome should be disclosed to his unsuspecting father; and a consultation was held among his new friends as to the manner in which this should be done. It was suggested that Samuel himself was the most suitable

[1] Coke's *Sermon*, 7.

person to inform his parent of the change which had taken place in his views. But he declined the task, and declared that he could not bear to witness the distress into which he knew the discovery would plunge his susceptible and aged father, whose tenderest affection he had shared from his infancy. . . . At last it was agreed to request the Duchess of Norfolk, as the highest Roman Catholic Peeress in the realm, to wait upon Mr. Charles Wesley at his house in Chesterfield-street, and inform him that his son had renounced the Protestant faith, and become a member of the Church to which she herself belonged. There was a propriety in this arrangement, because her own son had subjected her to a similar trial, by renouncing the Church of Rome and embracing the Protestant religion. She assented to this proposal, and communicated to the venerable man, trembling with age and infirmity, the intelligence which embittered the residue of his life. Being aware of her intended visit, he received her in his robes, as a Priest of the Church of England. She soon perceived the deep distress of mind into which he was thrown by the disclosures which she made to him respecting his unhappy son, and attempted to soothe him by suggesting that the young convert might be acting under the influence of divine grace, and be swayed by the love of God. The father, who too well knew the character of his son, and the nature of the errors which he had embraced, pacing his large drawing-room in great agitation, exclaimed. ' Say the loaves and fishes, Madam ! Say, the loaves and fishes ! '[1]

The visit of the Duchess of Norfolk left a deep impression on Charles Wesley. It must be remembered that, in 1785, Samuel Wesley was still under age.[2] The news that he had joined the Roman Catholic Church without saying a word to his father produced a shock from which Charles Wesley never recovered. We will not linger on this domestic tragedy. In Thomas Jackson's *Life of Charles Wesley,* we have a selection from the hymns which the sorrowful father composed in this time of keen disappointment. It will be enough to say that, in after years, Samuel Wesley returned to the Church of England. Those who are best acquainted with his history may be left to express their opinion concerning the reason of the exchange.

We must now fix our attention on John Wesley. We are especially interested in him when we watch him making his preparations for the holding of the Yearly Conference in London. It was to begin on July 26, and much was to be done by him before that date. The first question he had to decide concerned the summoning of the Conference. With few exceptions that duty had been discharged by himself, as

[1] Jackson's *Life of the Rev. Charles Wesley,* ii.. 359-60.
[2] He was born in Bristol on February 24, 1766.

is plainly set forth in the 'Deed of Declaration.' In defining the term Conference in the deed he makes the following declaration:

John Wesley doth hereby declare that the Conference of the people called Methodists in London, Bristol, Leeds, ever since there hath been any yearly Conference of the said people called Methodists in any of the said places, hath always heretofore consisted of the Preachers and Expounders of God's Holy Word, commonly called Methodist Preachers, in connexion with and under the care of the said John Wesley, whom he hath thought expedient year after year to summons to meet him in one or other of the said places of London, Bristol or Leeds, to advise with them for the promotion of the Gospel of Christ, to appoint the said persons so summoned, and the other Preachers and Expounders of God's Holy Word, also in connexion with and under the care of the said John Wesley, not summoned to the said Yearly Conference, to the use and enjoyment of the said Chapels and premises so given and conveyed upon trust for the said John Wesley, and such other person and persons as he should appoint during his life as aforesaid, and for the expulsion of unworthy and admission of new persons under his care and into his Connexion to be Preachers and Expounders as aforesaid, and also of other persons upon Trial for the like purposes, the names of all which persons so summoned by the said John Wesley, the persons appointed, with the Chapels and Premises to which they were so appointed, together with the duration of such appointments, and of those expelled or admitted into Connexion or upon Trial, with all other matters transacted and done at the said Yearly Conference, have year by year been printed and published under the title of *Minutes of Conference*.[1]

Directing our attention to the subject of the summoning of preachers to the Conference, it is clear that for many years the power to summon them had been exercised by John Wesley. Those who wish to understand the constitutional arrangements of early Methodism will ask if he retained that power after signing the Deed. There can be no doubt that he was convinced that he did. If he had been inclined to part with it the disorder that had disturbed the Leeds Conference of 1784 must have shown him that the time had not come to surrender his right. He was much depressed by the attack then made on him. His visit to Ireland came at an opportune time. It gave him back his physical strength and his courage in the presence of great difficulties. When the time arrived to issue invitations to the Conference of 1785 he sat down and wrote letters to the preachers whom he summoned to

[1] See *A Summary of Methodist Law and Discipline*, 375. Fifth edition.

London. He seems to have kept his eye on that clause in the *Deed of Declaration* which affirms 'that no act of the Conference, as aforesaid, shall be taken, or be the act of the Conference until forty of the members thereof are assembled, and during the assembly of the Conference there shall always be forty members present at the doing of any act, or otherwise such act shall be void.'[1] When he sent out his notices concerning the holding of the Conference in London, he took care to invite a large number of the members of the 'Legal Hundred.' In addition, the records show that ten men were present whose names were not in the *Deed of Declaration*. Taken together there were about seventy preachers present at the London Conference. The next year, at Bristol, the number was eighty. In 1789 the attendance at Leeds amounted to nearly one hundred. These figures cast light on the question of the attendance of preachers at the Conferences held by John Wesley in the last years of his life.

We must now fix our attention on the London Conference held in July, 1785. Wesley's references in his *Journal* to its proceedings are brief. On Tuesday, July 26, we find this entry: 'Our Conference began, at which about seventy preachers were present, whom I had invited by name. One consequence of which was that we had no contention or altercation at all, but everything proposed was calmly considered and determined as we judged would be most for the glory of God.' Then, on Wednesday, August 3, we find the following cheering words in his *Journal*: 'Our peaceful Conference ended, the God of power having presided over all our consultations.'[2] These entries in his *Journal* are encouraging, but we must look elsewhere for the record of the business that was transacted at this eventful Conference. It will be remembered that a small pamphlet, called the *Minutes of Conference,* had recently been published. We turn to it, and our disappointment at the brevity of the *Journal* record begins to disappear. It vanishes when we open the latest edition of his *Journal*. We find that it is full of extracts from his long-lost *Diary*. Using these sources of information we shall be able to understand the exceptional importance of the London Conference of 1785. We will confine our attention

---

[1] *Summary*, 376. Fifth edition.
[2] *Journal*, vii., 100, 102.

to three subjects that were then considered by Wesley and his preachers.

It was inevitable that the subject of the *Deed of Declaration* should spring up in a Conference summoned in the manner we have described. At some period of discussion John Wesley made the following statement: ' No power which I ever enjoyed is given up by the Declaration Deed. No such thing could have been supposed, had it not been for that improper and ambiguous word *Life-Estate*. This also has given the grand occasion of offence to them that sought occasion.'[1] Instead of lingering over this statement we will content ourselves by saying that, on July 30, 1785, the members of the Conference signed the following declarations:

' We whose names are underwritten do declare that Mr. Wesley was desired at the last Bristol Conference, without a dissentient voice, to draw up a Deed which should give a legal specification of the phrase " The Conference of the People called Methodists," and that the mode of doing it was entirely left to his judgement and discretion. And we do also declare that we do approve of the *substance* and *design* of the Deed which Mr. Wesley has accordingly executed and enrolled.'

Thirty-nine preachers who were present at the London Conference signed this declaration. Among them we note the names of men who still occupy the highest places in the esteem of those who are best acquainted with the early history of Methodism. Their statement was followed by another that was signed by thirty preachers who were not present at the Bristol Conference. It was as follows:

' We whose names are underwritten, but who were not present at the last Bristol Conference, do declare our approbation of the substance and design of the Deed which Mr. Wesley has lately executed and enrolled, for the purpose of giving a legal specification of the phrase, " The Conference of the People called Methodists." ' In this Declaration we again note the names of men who rendered conspicuous service in the early Methodist Church. We have seen that John Wesley considered that ' about seventy preachers were present ' at this Conference, so we may safely say that these documents express the unanimous opinion of the preachers who then assembled in London.

[1] *Minutes of Conference*, i., 180.

On Monday, August 1, there is an entry in Wesley's *Journal* which demands our attention. It is a record of an exceptionally important event. It marks a new departure which soon had its effect on English Methodism. This is the entry: 'Having, with a few select friends, weighed the matter thoroughly, I yielded to their judgement, and set apart three of our well-tried preachers, John Pawson, Thomas Hanby, and Joseph Taylor, to minister in Scotland, and I trust God will bless their ministrations and show that He has sent them.'[1] In the stations we find that John Pawson was appointed to Edinburgh, Thomas Hanby to Dundee, and Joseph Taylor to Aberdeen, each being the superintendent of the circuit named. Thomas Jackson's record of this event, in his *Life of the Rev. Charles Wesley*, throws a clear light on the meaning of this event. He says: 'For several years Mr. Wesley's preachers had been stationed in some of the principal towns in Scotland, and Societies were formed under their care, but the members, in many instances, were in circumstances scarcely better than those of their brethren in America immediately after the war. There were indeed clergymen in Scotland, but several of them absolutely refused to admit the Methodists to the Lord's Table, except on the condition that they would renounce all future connexion with the Methodist ministry and discipline. During the Conference . . . therefore, which was held in London, Mr. Wesley ordained three of his preachers to administer the sacraments in North Britain.'[2]

The third subject of special importance that was considered at the Conference of 1785 still possesses exceptional interest. For several years America had disappeared from the list of stations printed in the English *Minutes of Conference*. The great war had arrested communication between the two countries. When it came to an end the veil was lifted, and facts came to light that must have astonished many of the English Methodists. They found that in spite of bitter persecution the American Methodists had held on their way and had increased in number. It will be enough to say that, in 1784, America re-appears in the English *Minutes of Conference*. In the return of the number of members in the

[1] *Journal*, vii., 101.
[2] Jackson's *Life of Charles Wesley*, ii., 382.

A MEMORABLE YEAR

Societies America was included. In spite of furious persecution it was found that the number in America was 14,988. That fact will ever remain to the honour of the men who carried on their work in defiance of brutal attacks, and of the people who were faithful in days of sore distress.

When we consult the *Minutes of Conference*, published in 1785, we find that a remarkable change has taken place in its contents. In it America occupies a considerable amount of space. We are especially interested in the long list of the numbers of members in the American Methodist Societies. It had been carefully compiled. The circuits are named, and the number of members in each is stated. There had been a considerable advance during the year. In the Societies there were sixteen thousand, six hundred and twenty-seven members. As to the preachers, we find that sixteen men occupied the office of Elder, a position that gave them special responsibility. Eighty-six other preachers were stationed in the circuits. We can imagine the joy of the men who had faced the persecution of the war-time, when they greeted the arrival of the days of prosperity. But we are sure that not one of them saw, in the far distance of time, the coming of a day when the Methodist Episcopal Church of America would number its members by millions.[1]

John Wesley must have looked back on the London Conference of 1785 with satisfaction. But a shadow soon fell on his path. We have recorded the fact that in the month of May he lost one of his principal friends. Vincent Perronet quietly passed away. He was a man who had often helped him not only with sound advice, but with strengthening sympathy. The days went on their way and Wesley was looking forward to meeting another of his principal friends at the London Conference. Perronet having gone, that friend may easily be named. We know that Fletcher was looking forward with great expectation to their meeting. But they never saw each other again in this world. On August 14, 1785, Fletcher died in Madeley in the fifty-sixth year of his age. We can understand the keenness of Wesley's sorrow at the loss of two such friends in one year. It must

---

[1] In our statement of the number of members in the American Societies we have not included those in Antigua. In 1787 a section headed 'The British Dominions' was introduced into the *Minutes of Conference* and Antigua finds its place in that section.

have been some relief to him when he began to write his book entitled *A Short Account of the Life and Death of the Reverend John Fletcher*. The old days of companionship lived again. But in the closing paragraph of his book there seems to linger a note of sadness. Describing Fletcher he says: ' I was intimately acquainted with him for thirty years. I conversed with him morning, noon, and night, without the least reserve, during a journey of many hundred miles, and in all that time I never heard him speak an improper word, or saw him do an improper action. To conclude: Within fourscore years I have known many excellent men, holy in heart and life. But one equal to him I have not known; one so uniformly and deeply devoted to God. So unblamable a man, in every respect, I have not found either in Europe or America. Nor do I expect to find another such on this side eternity. Yet it is possible we may be such as he was. Let us then endeavour to follow him as he followed Christ.' [1]

The news of John Fletcher's death came to John Wesley when he was preaching to the Methodist Societies in Somerset. It was fortunate that he was so employed. He extended his visits to the neighbouring counties and did not return to London until October 2. We note that on Sunday, November 6 he preached a funeral sermon ' for that great and good man, Mr. Fletcher.' It was not until December arrived that he secured opportunities for rest. But all the time John Fletcher was on his mind. He was gathering together the materials for the book, which was published the next year, in which he paid high tribute to the character and influence of his beloved friend.

---

[1] John Wesley's *Works*, xi., 365.

XIX

A WORLD EVANGELIST

We have now reached a period in John Wesley's history that calls for special carefulness of treatment. The first half of the records of his work in the year 1786 were included in the volume of his *Journal* which was published at the beginning of the year 1789. The next volume, which contained the records of his work from June 29, 1786, to October 24, 1790, was not published until after his death. When it was issued the following cautionary note appeared in it: 'There are unavoidable chasms in this *Journal* owing to some parts being mislaid; and it is probable that many of the proper names of persons and places are not properly spelt, as the whole of the manuscript was so ill-written as to be scarcely legible.' It is fortunate that we now possess an edition of the *Journal* which can be used with confidence. In it difficulties that troubled the men who published the volume of his *Journal* that appeared soon after Wesley's death have been faced. Extracts from his long-lost *Diary* abound. Helpful notes appear that throw light on difficult questions, and a successful attempt has been made to enlarge our knowledge of events which occurred during the closing years of his life. It is clear that the year 1786 was crowded with work. When we read John Wesley's comment on the arrival of his birthday we do so without any desire to criticize it. On June 28, 1786, this is the record in his *Journal*: 'I entered into the eighty-third year of my age. I am a wonder to myself. It is now twelve years since I have felt any such sensation as weariness. I am never tired (such is the goodness of God!), either with writing, preaching, or travelling. One natural cause undoubtedly is my continual exercise and change of air. How the latter contributes to health I know not, but certainly it does.'[1]

[1] *Journal*, vii., 174-5.

We must deny ourselves the pleasure of following Wesley during his wanderings over this country in 1786, and will fix our attention on certain events which must be recorded, as they have left a strong influence on the Methodist Church of the present day. It will be remembered that John Wesley had relieved Dr. Coke of the task of answering the attacks which Charles Wesley had made on him. One result of John Wesley's intervention in the controversy was that it gave Dr. Coke an opportunity to consider a question that weighed on his mind. He mentioned it to John Wesley, and found in him not only a strong sympathizer, but also a powerful helper. Light on the subject that was discussed comes to us from a footnote contained in the latest edition of John Wesley's *Journal*. On Sunday, March 12, 1786, Wesley was in Bristol. He then wrote a letter to Coke in which he answered his appeal 'for missions to the Highlands of Scotland, the Islands of Guernsey and Jersey, the Leeward Islands, Quebec, Nova Scotia, and Newfoundland.' It must be understood that missions in the places named had been commenced. Coke's letter urged the adoption of a well-organized attempt to support the Societies already formed and of such other Missionary Societies as might be afterwards added to their number.[1]

It must be remembered that Wesley's father and his mother came under influences which made them passionate admirers of men who had given themselves up to the work of Foreign Missions. We have often paused to consider his mother's reply when John Wesley told her that he was thinking of going to Georgia. She said to him: 'Had I twenty sons, I should rejoice that they were all so employed, though I should never see them more.'[2] His motive in undertaking his work there was 'the salvation of his own soul.' He was convinced that 'the end was not to be achieved by musing and contemplation merely, but through the influence of austere and dangerous work.' When he landed in Georgia he was convinced that he ought to forsake the beaten paths of ordinary clerical life in an English colony, and to strike and follow the trail which led through forests to the Indian

[1] Wesley's letter to Coke came to light in 1840. It was published in the *Wesleyan Methodist Magazine* of that year. See John Wesley's *Journal*, vii., 145.
[2] *John Wesley and the Religious Societies*, 111.

A WORLD EVANGELIST

hunting-camps and towns. He believed that the way of righteousness could be best found apart from the white man's settlement, and he welcomed the prospect of work that would make him endure hardness, and might even imperil his life. At the early stage of his work in Georgia such were his convictions. But the influence of General Oglethorpe kept him away from the jungles and caused him to spend his time among the British settlers in Savannah, Frederica, and other parts of the State. We have given a description of his experiences as a colonist in *John Wesley and the Religious Societies*. It is only necessary to mention one event that throws light on the principal reason of his visit to Georgia.

On Tuesday, November 23, 1736, we find the following entry in Wesley's *Journal*:

Mr. Oglethorpe sailed for England, leaving Mr. Ingham, Mr. Delamotte, and me at Savannah, but with less prospect of preaching to the Indians than we had the first day we set foot in America. Whenever I mentioned it, it was immediately replied, 'You cannot leave Savannah without a minister.' To this indeed my plain answer was, 'I know not that I am under any obligation to the contrary. I never promised to stay here one month. I openly declared both before, at, and ever since my coming hither that I neither would nor could take charge of the English any longer than till I could go among the Indians.' If it was said, 'But did not the Trustees of Georgia appoint you to be minister of Savannah?' I replied, 'They did; but it was not done by my solicitation: it was done without either my desire or knowledge. Therefore I cannot conceive that appointment to lay me under any obligation of continuing there any longer than till a door is opened to the heathen; and this I expressly declared at the time I consented to accept of that appointment.' But though I had no other obligation not to leave Savannah now, yet that of love I could not break through; I could not resist the importunate request of the more serious parishioners 'to watch over their souls yet a little longer till someone came, who might supply my place.' And this I the more willingly did because the time was not come to preach the gospel of peace to the heathen; all their nations being in a ferment; Paustoobee and Mingo Mattaw having told me, in terms, in my own house, 'Now our enemies are all about us, and we can do nothing but fight; but if the beloved ones should ever give us to be at peace, then we would hear the great Word.'[1]

We think that no one can read these extracts from John Wesley's *Journal* without asking the questions: 'What made Wesley a world evangelist?' It is clear that he did not

[1] *The Journal of John Wesley*, i., 297-8. Standard edition.

possess the spirit of that great calling when he was in Georgia. The right answer to the question will not be found in America. We must watch him as, after his return to England, he sits in a room in Nettleton Court, Aldersgate Street, London, on May 24, 1738. He is listening to a man who is reading Luther's preface to the Epistle to the Romans. Suddenly light shines in his heart. He trusts in Christ, in Him alone, for salvation. An assurance is given him that the Saviour has taken away his sins, ' and saved him from the law of sin and death.' He enters on a new experience. He sees at last that it is possible for all who sorrow for their sins, and simply trust in Christ for pardon, to pass out of darkness into marvellous light. Having learned that lesson he determined to teach it, not only to members of a particular church or nation, but to the whole world. It is well-known that his change of view influenced him to the close of his life. For some years it caused him to be attacked by clergymen, but he held his ground. He was soon surrounded by preachers and people who had passed through the experience that came to him in the Aldersgate Street room, and the controversy that had made a considerable impression in London and elsewhere, died out in the presence of incontestable facts.

We must now fix our attention on the proceedings of the Conference that commenced its business in Bristol on Tuesday, July 25, 1786. Wesley's *Journal* entries on this Conference are brief, but the footnotes in the latest edition are abundant. As we glance at them we come to the conclusion that Wesley was expecting that difficulties would arise at this Conference which might cause him considerable trouble. John Fletcher, his firm defender, had passed away, and he was still mourning over his loss. It is with considerable relief that we read the note he made at the close of this Conference. He says: 'Great had been the expectations of many that we should have had warm debates; but by the mercy of God, we had none at all. Everything was transacted with great calmness, and we parted as we met, in peace and love.'[1] It is noteworthy that after Wesley re-introduced his old method of summoning the members of the Conference by name, disturbances such as we have described in a previous chapter

[1] *Journal*, vii., 193.

of this book ceased to hinder the transaction of business in the Conferences over which he presided.

At the end of the list of preachers who were in the American circuits in 1785, we find evidence of the fact that the missionary spirit had declared itself in the Western world. In connexion with Nova Scotia and Newfoundland we see the names of F. Garrettson and James Cromwell, who are appointed as Elders and missionaries to those places. It is surprising to find that in the *Minutes of Conference* for the year 1785, Antigua is placed in a position that suggests that it was one of the American circuits. At this point it will be enough to say that an American preacher had been appointed to assist John Baxter in the great work he was conducting in Antigua. His name was Jeremiah Lambert. He was well known and highly esteemed by the American preachers. He stands out among them as a man who was successful in leading his hearers to the Cross of Christ. We can imagine how Baxter would have received him. He had given up his position in the dockyard, and had faced a life of poverty in order to dedicate himself to the service of a Society that numbered more than a thousand members. But, in this year, his burden was lightened not only by the prospect of the coming of a helper, but by the good news that he had been admitted to the ranks of the Methodist ministers by the English Conference.[1] We have sought for evidence of a meeting of Baxter and Lambert in Antigua, and have failed to find it. But in *A History of the Methodist Episcopal Church* by Dr. Nathan Bangs, there is this entry in the record of the deaths of preachers in 1786 : ' Jeremiah Lambert, who had been six years in the work, of whom it is said that he was " a man of sound judgement, good gifts, of genuine piety, and very useful " as a preacher, much esteemed in life and lamented in his death.'[2] We think it is clear that Baxter had to carry the burden of responsibility for the oversight of the Methodist Society in Antigua for another year. We know that he was recognized as ' a minister ' by the members of the Society in the island, and that he had not long to wait for the coming of a helper.

[1] See *Hill's Arrangement of the Wesleyan Methodist Ministers and Preachers on Trial*. Baxter commenced his ministry in 1785 and died in 1806.
[2] Vol. i., 254.

We must now return to the Bristol Conference of 1786, and note some of its principal events. The *Journal* states: 'We met every day at six and nine in the morning, and at two in the afternoon. On Tuesday and on Wednesday morning the characters of the preachers were considered whether already admitted or not. On Thursday, in the afternoon, we permitted any of the Society to be present, and weighed what was said about separation from the Church. But we all determined to continue therein, without one dissenting voice; and I doubt not but this determination will stand, at least till I am removed into a better world. On Friday and Saturday most of our temporal business was settled. . . . On Monday the Conference met again and concluded on Tuesday morning.'[1]

The mention of the 'conversation' concerning separating from the Church of England, which took place in the presence of members of the Society attracts our attention. It is clear that Wesley did not consider that a final decision on the subject had been reached; he thought that such a decision might stand 'until he was removed into a better world.' Can we learn more about this important conversation? We are chiefly interested in trying to ascertain John Wesley's position on that question. We close the *Journal* and take up the *Minutes of Conference* for 1786. We find in that book the report of the arguments used by Wesley when he explained the difference between ordaining men for England, and for the work in America and Scotland. It is better that he should state his own case.

After describing the creation of the first Conference in London, Wesley's contribution to the *Minutes* of 1786 proceeds as follows:

Some years after, we were strongly importuned by our brethren in America to 'come over and help them.' Several preachers willingly offered themselves for the service, and several went from time to time. God blessed their labours in an uncommon manner. Many sinners were converted to God; and many Societies formed, under the same rules as were observed in England: insomuch that at present the American Societies contain more than eighteen thousand members.

But since the late Revolution in North America, these have been in great distress. The clergy, having no sustenance, either from England, or from the American States, have been obliged almost universally to leave the country, and seek their food elsewhere. Hence those who had been members of the Church had none either to administer the Lord's

[1] *Journal*, vii., 192-3. Standard edition.

Supper, or to baptize their children. They applied to England over and over: but it was to no purpose. Judging this to be a case of real necessity, I took a step which, for peace and quietness, I had refrained from taking for many years. I exercised that power which I am fully persuaded the great Shepherd and Bishop of the Church has given me. I appointed three of our labourers to go and help them, by not only preaching the word of God, but likewise administering the Lord's Supper, and baptizing their children, throughout that vast tract of land, a thousand miles long, and some hundred broad.

These are the steps which, not of choice, but necessity, I have slowly and deliberately taken. If any one is pleased to call this *separating from the Church,* he may. But the law of England does not call it so; nor can any one properly be said so to do, unless out of conscience he refuses to join in the service, and partake of the Sacraments administered therein.

After Dr. Coke's return from America, many of our friends begged I would consider the case of Scotland, where we had been labouring so many years, and had seen so little fruit of our labours. Multitudes, indeed, have set out well, but they were soon turned out of the way, chiefly by their ministers either disputing against the truth, or refusing to admit them to the Lord's Supper, yea, or to baptize their children, unless they would promise to have no fellowship with the Methodists. Many who did so, soon lost all they had gained, and became more the children of hell than before. To prevent this, I at length consented to take the same step with regard to Scotland which I had done with regard to America. But this is not a separation from the Church at all. Not from the Church of Scotland, for we were never connected therewith, any further than we are now: not from the Church of England; for this is not concerned in the steps which are taken in Scotland. Whatever then is done either in America or Scotland is no separation from the Church of England. I have no thought of this. I have many objections against it. It is a totally different case.

But, for all this, is it not possible there may be such a separation after you are dead? Undoubtedly it is. But what I said at our first Conference above forty years ago, I say still, 'I dare not omit doing what good I can while I live for fear of evils that may follow when I am dead.'[1]

These extracts from the *Minutes of Conference* are of the utmost value. They prove that John Wesley was satisfied that his action in the case of America and Scotland was right. But they also show that he had an open mind concerning the course he ought to take if it became necessary to ordain preachers for England. It was not long before he had to decide that question.

We must now fix our attention on one more incident which has given this Bristol Conference its special distinction. In

[1] *Minutes of Conference,* i., 192-3.

John Wesley's *Diary*, on July 28, 1786, we find the following entries: 'Prayed, Ordained J.K., W.War, Wa.' The next day the entry is shorter. It is: '4. Prayed, ordained.' We may say that these somewhat mysterious entries refer to the ordination services which took place at four o'clock in the morning, and that the capital letters indicate Joshua Keighley, William Warrener, and William Hammet. The stations for 1786 show that Keighley was appointed to Inverness. He had only a short ministry. He was received by Wesley in 1780, and died in 1788. Consulting the stations for 1786 we see that Warrener was appointed to Antigua and Hammet to Newfoundland. The news was conveyed to them by Dr. Coke, who was to accompany them in their voyage. It must be remembered that Warrener, in 1785, had spoken to Wesley and had told him that 'he was at his, and the Lord's, disposal, to go to America or wherever he might be wanted.' After his interview with Dr. Coke he hastened to Wesley. His account of the interview is interesting. He said to Wesley: 'Sir, is it your desire that I should go to Antigua?' The answer was: 'It is.' That was enough. The interview closed when Warrener said: 'I have nothing more to say. I go in the name of the Lord.'

On September 24, 1786, Dr. Coke and his companions sailed from Gravesend in a ship that met with great adventures. Dr. Coke had laid out a scheme which would have enabled him to land the missionaries who were with him in their stations in Newfoundland and Antigua. But he had not made allowance for the weather. For ten weeks the ship battled with heavy storms. On one occasion it seemed as if she would be lost. She was blown right out of her course. The captain decided that the only way to save her was to give up the attempt to reach the American coast and make for the West Indian islands. Warrener must have been relieved when he heard this decision. In his account of the voyage he says: 'When, instead of persisting in our course, our vessel bore away for the West Indies. . . . We seemed "to ride on the wings of the wind." We were borne rapidly along our new line of voyage, and soon made the Island of Antigua, where we all joyfully landed on the morning of Christmas Day. A scene like that which we witnessed on reaching the shore was scarcely ever beheld. The negroes in the streets of St. John's were shouting, clapping their hands, and with greatest enthusiasm praising God that their new "massas," as they were pleased to call us, had come.'

Coke's first action on landing was to find out John Baxter. The record in his *Journal* is brief, but suggestive. It is as follows: 'December 25. This day we landed in Antigua, and in going up the town we met brother Baxter in his band going to perform Divine service. After a little refreshment I went to our chapel, and read prayers, preached, and administered the sacraments. I had one of the cleanest audiences I ever saw. All the negro women were dressed in white linen gowns, petticoats, handkerchiefs, and caps; and the men as neatly. In the afternoon and evening I had very large congregations.'[1] We can understand his delight. A little later we meet with the following entry in his *Journal*: 'Our Society in this island is near two thousand.' When we consider these paragraphs we are more than ever disinclined to adopt the opinion that Dr. Coke's landing on that Christmas morning in Antigua marks 'the beginning of Methodist Foreign Missions.' If we look at the returns of membership in the American Societies, contained in the *Minutes of Conference* for 1786, we find that out of the fifty-two circuits in America thirty-one make returns of negroes who were members of the Methodist Society. It is true that Antigua stands at the head of the list, so far as numbers are concerned. In that Society there were ten Whites, and 1,559 Blacks.

Dr. Coke's statement quoted in the foregoing paragraph concerning Baxter's 'band' may be misunderstood. It refers to the clerical white 'band' that the clergy were accustomed to wear. After the ordinations in America, which we have described, the 'band' came into common use by the 'elders,' who were set apart to their high office. Baxter was not present at the American Conference, but he was then chosen as an elder and his name and office appear in the English *Minutes*. When Dr. Coke arrived in the island he, and the 'elders' with him, set Baxter apart for his high office. He continued to fill it with conspicuous ability.

---

[1] Etheridge's *Life of Coke*, 166-7.

XX
ADVANCE

ON January 6, 1787, we see a ship that is making her way slowly out of the harbour of Antigua. We note a group of passengers she is carrying away from the island. We catch sight of Dr. Coke. Near him stand two preachers who had been appointed by the Bristol Conference to Newfoundland. We have seen how the ship that had carried them from England was blown out of her course. Looking at the little group we are arrested by the sight of John Baxter. It is clear that Dr. Coke and his companions are on an expedition to places not far from Antigua. Our curiosity is aroused, and we feel that we must follow them in their voyage.

In Dr. Etheridge's *Life of Dr. Coke*, we find the information concerning this expedition which we need. He tells us that while Dr. Coke and his companions were in Antigua 'openings began to appear in the other islands. An invitation came from St. Vincent's, another from St. Eustatius, and a third from St. Christopher's. The missionaries held a little Conference, and decided 'that Messrs. Hammet and Clarke should accompany the Doctor to St. Vincent's, while Mr. Warrener continued in Antigua.'[1] In addition it was agreed that John Baxter should join the group of travellers. Furnished with introductory letters, Coke and his companions set out on their eventful voyage.

It would be interesting to follow Dr. Coke on his voyages to the islands. But it is only necessary to show the results of his visits to three of them. Once more we are indebted to Dr. Etheridge for his guidance. When Dr. Coke and his companions landed at St. Vincent's they met with a hearty welcome at the house of a gentleman named Claxton. Our attention is aroused by that name. It is quickened when we are told that Mr. Claxton had been 'awakened under Mr.

[1] *Life of Dr. Coke*, 167.

Gilbert, and had met in class with him.' Mr. Claxton left Antigua, but there can be no doubt that, when he came to reside in St. Vincent's, the influence of Nathaniel Gilbert still rested on him.

In the evening of the day that Dr. Coke arrived in St. Vincent's, he preached to a large congregation in Mr. Claxton's house. The next day he made a tour of the island. The result was most encouraging. Dr. Etheridge says: 'On a tour in the country he met with equal welcome from other planters, one of whom showed him a large room which he was willing at once to appropriate for religious services. Mr. Claxton also, on their return, had fitted up a spacious warehouse as a chapel, and learning that the Doctor had decided on leaving Mr. Clarke in the island, he assigned him a study and bedroom in his own house. Among the chief people, several promised them their concurrence and support. Six of them already offered themselves as members of the Society. The poor negroes, understanding what was going on, gave characteristic expression to their joy. "These men," said they, "have been imported for us." Under these circumstances, Dr. Coke considered that the will of God in the appointment of a missionary to St. Vincent's had a revelation as clear as if it had been written with a sunbeam.' [1]

Sailing to St. Christopher's, Dr. Coke and his companions found that preparations had been already made to receive them, and crowds of all ranks assembled to hear the opening of their commission. They left the island, but soon returned. They preached in the court-house to crowded audiences. Dr. Etheridge says that with the friendly concurrence of the principal inhabitants and the clergyman of the parish, Mr. Hammet was designated as the stationed missionary.[2]

Leaving St. Christopher's, Dr. Coke and his companions sailed for St. Eustatius, an island in the possession of the Dutch. It is somewhat difficult to understand why this island was included in their programme. They had been joyfully received in the English possessions, but they must have been uncertain about the attitude of the Dutch authorities. We must place ourselves again under the guidance of Dr. Etheridge. We have, in a former chapter, recorded Dr.

[1] *Life of Dr. Coke*, 168.
[2] *ibid*, 169.

Coke's detestation of slavery. From a sentence in Dr. Etheridge's description of his landing at St. Eustatius, it is plain that some of the negro slaves had been in communication with him. 'Dr. Coke,' we are told, ' on landing, found some of these negroes waiting for their arrival. They had fitted up a cottage for them, and contributed from their humble means toward the defrayment of their expenses.' Etheridge goes on to tell the pathetic story of a Christian slave named Harry who, when imported from America, began to preach to his companions in St. Eustatius. He met with much success. A small building was constructed in which the negroes began to worship. In it some of the negroes assembled. Harry's preaching often stirred them into almost uncontrollable excitement. The news reached the ears of the Governor of the island, and Harry was forbidden to preach, under penalty of a flogging. Dr. Etheridge tells us that Harry, constrained by his desire to do good, broke through the prohibition by praying with the people, and he submitted, like a martyr, to the lash. Proving incorrigible, he was at length transported from the island.[1]

When Dr. Coke landed on the island he was eagerly requested to hold a public service. But he was aware of the situation and, having been himself a magistrate in Wales, he declined to preach until he had waited on the Dutch governor. He did so, and was informed ' that he must be silent till his credentials had been examined by the court.' The investigation was so far favourable, that on the following Sunday he was permitted to preach. Dr. Etheridge sums up the situation by saying : ' But no decisive steps could be taken for the establishment of a mission till a time more propitious should arrive.' He heard the voice of America calling him away. The time for holding a Conference there was approaching. On February 10 he embarked on board a Dutch vessel at St. Eustatius. She was bound for Charleston. After a passage of eighteen days Dr. Coke was landed in that port. It is a pleasure to record his opinion of the captain and his crew. He says : ' The passage of eighteen days was rendered the more pleasant by the quiet and orderly habits of the crew, with whom, it appeared, it was a rule of the worthy captain to read a portion of the Scriptures night and morning,

[1] *Life of Dr. Coke*, 170.

a practice not uncommon in those days among the maritime people of Holland.'

Dr. Coke stayed in America until May 7, 1787. He spent much time with Bishop Asbury in long journeys into the far places of the country where the Methodist preachers were working often at the peril of their lives. He held two Conferences, one at Charleston, and the other in Mecklenburg County. Then, on April 2, he presided over a Conference held at Baltimore. Dr. Etheridge says that in the two former Conferences held in Baltimore Dr. Coke had perceived ' some coldness and jealousy towards himself among the preachers.' At this Conference his suspicion was confirmed. It is necessary to allude to the subject, as it had an influence on the future of Methodism in America.

At the preceding Conference held in Baltimore the date of the next meeting there had been fixed. But, on September 6, 1786, Wesley had written a letter to Coke in which he had said : ' I desire that you would appoint a General Conference of all our preachers in the United States to meet at Baltimore on May the first, 1787, and that Mr. Richard Whatcoat may be appointed superintendent with Mr. Francis Asbury.' It is clear that John Wesley had not a correct understanding of the number of Methodist preachers in America at the period we have reached. Dr. Coke was better acquainted with the men who were scattered over a wide expanse of country. He knew that many of them could not abandon their work to attend a meeting in Baltimore. He seems to have used his judgement in sending out his notices to this ' General Conference of all our preachers in the United States.' We have no record of the names of the men who attended; from all that happened we judge that the preachers in the neighbourhood of Baltimore were strongly represented, and that, from several parts of the country, excuses were sent for non-attendance.

We will pass by much that might detain us, and will fix our attention on two incidents only. We have mentioned John Wesley's request that Richard Whatcoat might be appointed a superintendent with Francis Asbury. Dr. Etheridge gives us the reason why the Conference did not obey a request that had in it the strength of a command. He says : ' This order, unlooked for by the American preachers, gave many of them great inconvenience and prevented others from attending the Conference at all. They began to feel that, however great their reverence for Mr. Wesley might be, his unavoidable ignorance of their local affairs, at a distance of three thousand miles, would render his absolute dictatorship over their movements a not infrequent cause of inconveniences, and would make it necessary for them to claim the right of an untrammelled action in their own affairs. At the Conference of 1784 they had recorded a declaration that " during the life of Mr. Wesley they were ready to obey his commands in matters belonging to church-government." But, to indicate that such a pledge must not be considered as applying to all the minute details of their connexional movements, the sentence was henceforth omitted from their printed Minutes.'[1]

It is a relief to know that, some years afterwards, Richard Whatcoat was elected to the episcopal office, but many things had happened in the interval following the action of the American Conference in 1787. Coke learned that the impression had been created that he was disposed to exceed his legitimate powers. His opponents alleged that while in England he had altered, on his own authority, the time for holding the Baltimore Conference after that point had been fixed by the Conference itself in its last year's session. As a matter of fact, John Wesley had fixed the date of this *special* Conference, but Dr. Coke had to alter it because of difficulties which had arisen. His opponents brought the matter before the Conference, and Dr. Etheridge informs us that Dr. Coke listened to his accusers with ' respectful attention.' When the Conference closed he drew up a pledge which was to be recorded in the register.

'I do solemnly engage by this instrument, that I never will, by virtue of my office as superintendent of the Methodist Church, during my absence from the United States of America, exercise any government whatever in said Methodist Church. And I do also engage that I will exercise no privilege in the said Church when present, except that of ordaining according to the regulations and laws already existing or hereafter to be made in said Church, and that of presiding when present in Conference, and, lastly, that of

[1] *Life of Dr. Coke*, 173-4.

travelling at large. Given under my hand the second day of May in the year 1787.'

THOMAS COKE.

It must be remembered that in 1787 the following 'manifesto' appears in the American *Minutes*: 'We have constituted ourselves an Episcopal Church, under the direction of bishops, elders, deacons, and preachers, according to the form of ordination annexed to our Prayer-Book, and the regulations laid down in the Form of Discipline.' We may be surprised at Dr. Coke's pledge, but we must remember that he knew of the great 'forward movement' that was then deciding the future of the Methodist Episcopal Church. He records the fact that during this Conference he assisted at the ordination of two elders and eleven deacons, and must have seen that the American Church was moving towards a great position in that country. On May 27, he embarked on board a merchant ship for Dublin, and after a voyage of twenty-nine days, he reached that city. It may cause some surprise that Dr. Coke landed in Ireland instead of making his way to London. But Mr. Crookshank tells us that an arrangement had been made by Wesley that either he or Dr. Coke should visit Ireland once a year. Anxious that the position in America should be understood by Wesley, and knowing that the time for holding the Irish Conference was drawing near, Dr. Coke made up his mind to land in Ireland and explain the state of affairs in America at once. Bearing these facts in mind we can understand the note in Wesley's *Journal* on Tuesday, June 26, 1787. Wesley says: 'We were agreeably surprised with the arrival of Dr. Coke . . . who gave us a pleasing account of the work of God in America.'[1] It is clear that, on landing, Dr. Coke gave a cheerful description of the progress of Methodism in America to Wesley and other listeners. But later in the day it appears from an entry in his *Diary*, that Wesley had a private conversation with Dr. Coke. The significant words, 'within to Dr. Coke' appear in that book on June 26, 27 and 30. The interview on the last date, took place early in the morning. Later in the day Wesley made the following entry in his *Journal*: 'I desired all our preachers to meet me, and consider the state of our brethren in America, who have been terribly frightened at their

[1] *Journal*, vii., 294.

own shadow, as if the English preachers were just going to enslave them. I believe that fear is now over, and they are more aware of Satan's devices.'[1] Evidently he did not understand the position of the American Methodists at that time.

There is an entry in Wesley's *Journal* that precedes the note we have just quoted, that makes an irresistible appeal. On Thursday, June 28, we find this record: 'I had the pleasure of a conversation with Mr. Howard, I think one of the greatest men in Europe. Nothing but the mighty power of God can enable him to go through his difficult and dangerous employments. But what can hurt us, if God is on our side?' Two of the greatest admirers of John Wesley at that time were Robert Raikes and John Howard, and John Wesley stands out clearly as one of their principal supporters in the work they accomplished. There seems to be a law of Nature that the most reliable judge of the hard worker is the man who himself works hard.

John Wesley's description of John Howard makes us long to know more about him. We wish to see him as he appeared in the eyes of a man whom we can trust. It is fortunate that our desire can be gratified. In our volume entitled *John Wesley the Master Builder*, we have given a description of Alexander Knox, of Londonderry. He was a man who thought for himself, and whose opinion demands respect.[2] When Henry Moore was preparing his *Life of John Wesley*, wishing to know more about John Howard, he wrote a letter to Alexander Knox, and received the following reply:

'In the course of Mr. Howard's tour through Ireland, in the year 1787, he spent a few days in Londonderry, where I then resided. I earnestly wished to see him, but bad health confined me to the house and I thought I would not be gratified. Such were my thoughts when I was told a gentleman had called to see me. It was Mr. Howard. I was delightfully surprised. I acknowledge it as one of the happiest moments of my life. He came to see me because he understood I was Mr. Wesley's friend. He began immediately to speak of him. He told me that " he had seen him shortly before in Dublin; that he had spent some hours

---
[1] *Journal*, vii., 295.
[2] See *John Wesley the Master Builder*, 175-6.

with him, and was greatly edified by his conversation. I was encouraged by him to go on vigorously with my own designs. I saw in him how much a single man might achieve by zeal and perseverance, and I thought why may not I do as much, in my way, as Mr. Wesley has done in his, if I am only as assiduous and persevering? I determined I would pursue my work with more alacrity than ever." I cannot quit this subject,' continued Mr. Knox, 'without observing that excepting Mr. Wesley, no man ever gave me a more perfect idea of angelic goodness than Mr. Howard; his whole conversation exhibited a most interesting tissue of exalted piety, meek simplicity, and glowing charity. His striking adieu I shall never forget. "Farewell, sir," said he, "when we meet again may it be in heaven, or farther on our way to it." Precious man, may your prayer be answered.'

Alexander Knox's letter was helpful to John Wesley's biographer, but it must be remembered that Henry Moore had also met John Howard, and had been able to form his own opinion of his high character. We find the record of their interview in Mrs. Richard Smith's *Life of Moore*, which contains extracts from his *Autobiography*. We avail ourselves of his description of his meeting with John Howard, and will give it in his own words:

In the beginning of the year 1789, Mr. Howard called at Mr. Wesley's house, in the City Road, London, in order to take his leave of him previously to his again flying to the continent at the call of mercy. Mr. Howard carried his last quarto upon the jails under his arm, in order to present it to his friend; but Mr. Wesley was on his way to Ireland. We were then residing at the City Road, and Mr. Howard favoured us with his company for upwards of an hour.

He delightfully called to mind the former days when he had first heard Mr. Wesley at his seat in Bedfordshire, and well recollected the discourse which made the first impression on his mind. 'Whatsoever thy hand findeth to do, do it with thy might, for there is no work, nor device, nor knowledge, nor wisdom in the grave, whither thou goest.' *Ecclesiastes* ix. 10. 'I have,' added Mr. Howard, 'but one thing to do, and I strive to do it with my might. The Lord has taken away whatever might have been an incumbrance; all places are alike to me, for I find misery in all. He gives me continual health; I have no need to be careful for anything. I eat no animal food, and can have all I want in the most inconvenient situations. Present my respects and love to Mr. Wesley; tell him I had hoped to have seen him once more: perhaps we may meet again in this world, but if not, we shall meet, I trust, in a better.'

We hung upon his lips delighted: such a picture of love, simplicity, and cheerfulness, we have seldom seen. Taking his leave, Mr. Howard said, 'I think I have gained a little knowledge concerning the plague; I shall therefore, after visiting the Russian camp, pass into the Turkish, and from thence by Constantinople, to Egypt.' 'So he purposed,' adds Mr. Moore, 'his heart being enlarged with the love of God and man. But while this angel of mercy was ministering to the sons of war, in the hospital of the Russian camp, God said, "It is enough, come up hither, enter thou into the joy of thy Lord."' [1]

John Wesley's affection for the Methodists of Ireland is well known to the readers of his *Journal*. In 1787 his visit to Ireland began on April 6, and ended on July 11. It was a time of spiritual prosperity in the Dublin Society in which there had been an increase of more than two hundred members. In Sligo the increase in the membership amounted to more than one hundred. In some other circuits the advance had not been so great, but no one can read the list of the members throughout the island without seeing that Methodism was making a strong advance. It is no wonder that Wesley saw that he had arrived at a time of great opportunity. In the seventh volume of his *Journal* we are able to follow him from circuit to circuit. It is pleasant to read his description of the welcomes he received from a loving people. Those descriptions stand out all the more clearly when we read Mr. Crookshank's records of this memorable visit to Ireland.[2]

On Thursday, July 5, the members of the Irish Conference assembled in Dublin. The next day the Conference began its sessions, which ended 'as usual' on the following Tuesday. We have no particulars in Wesley's *Journal* of the business transacted, but we read Wesley's comment with satisfaction. He says: 'We had no jarring string, but all, from the beginning to the end, was love and harmony.' On Wednesday, July 11, he took 'an affectionate leave' of his loving people at the morning service, and having finished all his business, he went on board the *Prince of Wales*, one of the Parkgate packets, accompanied by several of his friends who were sailing for England. In the morning, about four o'clock, he awoke, being roused by an uncommon noise. He tells us that he found that 'the ship lay beating upon a large rock about a league from Holyhead.' The captain rose from his sleep, ran upon the

[1] *Life of Henry Moore*, 272.
[2] See Wesley's *Journal*, vii., 258-99; Crookshank's *History of Methodism in Ireland*, i., 426-39.

deck, and seeing how the ship lay, cried out, 'Your lives may be saved, but I am undone!' Then Wesley did what those who knew him expected he would do. He gathered his friends together and 'went to prayer.' He tells us that 'presently the ship ... shot off the rock and pursued her way, without any more damage than the wounding a few outside planks.' In the afternoon the little band of Methodists came in safety to Parkgate, and in the evening went on to Chester.

John Wesley remained in the north of England until Monday, August 6. We think that one reason of his lingering was that the Conference of 1786, held in Bristol, in answer to the question, 'When and where is the next Conference to be held?' had replied, 'At Manchester on the last Tuesday in next July.' In its zeal it had gone even further. It had agreed that all succeeding Conferences are to be held in the following order:—viz. first, in London; secondly, in Leeds; thirdly, in Bristol; fourthly, in Manchester. In *John Wesley the Master Builder* we have mentioned that in 1765 a Conference had been held in Manchester, and we expressed the opinion that Wesley discovered his mistake in summoning it. He seems to have overlooked the fact that 'the model deed,' on which many of the preaching-houses were settled, did not recognize Manchester as a town in which the Conference could appoint preachers to chapels. He remembered that fact afterwards for no Conference was held there until 1787. When the *Deed of Declaration* was prepared, in 1784, it contained a clause which gave the Conference power to appoint 'the place of holding the yearly assembly at any other city, town, or place than London, Bristol, or Leeds, when it shall seem expedient to so do.' It will be admitted that the *Deed* removed a great difficulty out of the way of the Conference.[1]

It is not easy to follow the proceedings of the Manchester Conference of 1787. In John Wesley's *Journal* the information is scanty in spite of the additional help given by the *Diary*. The 1862 edition of the *Minutes of Conference*, however, carries us back to the days when Methodist preachers had often to risk their lives when they preached in the open air. In answer to the question, 'Who have died this year?'

[1] See *Summary of Methodist Law and Discipline*, 379. Fifth edition.

we read: 'Thomas Lee, a faithful brother, and a good old soldier of Jesus Christ.'[1]

With the assistance of the *Minutes* it is also possible to get a little light on the business that was transacted at the Manchester Conference. For the last time we see that the names of the preachers in America appear under the questions: 'What preachers are admitted this year? Who remain on trial? Who are admitted on trial?' The answers reveal the progress that was being made in the American Methodist Church. Seventeen American preachers were admitted into 'full connexion' with the English Conference, nineteen remained 'on trial,' and thirty-five were admitted 'on trial.' Another important fact comes into view when we turn over the pages of the *Minutes* of this Manchester Conference. In 'Europe' the membership of the Methodist Church numbered 62,088; in America the number was 28,299. The total number of persons under the care of Methodist preachers and class-leaders, at that time, was 90,387. It must be remembered that, in addition to the class members, great crowds of people attended the Methodist services in both countries who did not place themselves under the care of class-leaders. That fact must be kept in mind when we attempt to estimate the influence of Methodism during the closing years of Wesley's life.

The *Minutes* of the Manchester Conference of 1787 contain valuable information on important subjects, but we miss the side-lights on interesting facts which brighten the records of some of the early Conferences over which John Wesley presided. We must be content with recording the following facts. The question was asked: 'Are there any directions to be given concerning Kingswood School?' This reply was given: 'Let the number of boarders be reduced as soon as possible to ten, and the number of preachers' sons be raised to thirty.' That question was followed by another which will be understood by those who are acquainted with some of the difficulties of that time. It was asked: 'Are there any directions to be given concerning preachers to whom we are strangers?' The answer was: 'Let no person that is not in connexion with us preach in any of our chapels, or preaching-houses, without a note from Mr. Wesley, or from

[1] See *John Wesley the Master Builder*, 115-16.

the Assistant of the circuit from whence he comes, which note must be renewed yearly.' We will close our selection of questions by producing one that may cause some surprise: 'What can be done to prevent the heavy burdens and expenses which are needlessly thrown on the Conference?' This reply was given: 'Those circuits that do not provide for their preachers (except Scotland, Ireland, and Wales, and a few small circuits in England) shall have no more preachers sent to them for the time to come than they will provide for.'

In the latest edition of John Wesley's *Journal* there is a footnote taken from his *Diary* which shows the interesting fact that, on Friday, August 3, 1787, John Wesley, at a very early hour in the morning, ordained four of his preachers in Manchester. There is some uncertainty about the name of the fourth, but we know that he then ordained Duncan McAllum and Alexander Suter for Scotland, and James Wray for Nova Scotia. The next morning the ordinations were completed. On Monday, August 6, he left Manchester by coach. He met with two accidents, but reached Birmingham at seven o'clock in the evening. He says: 'Finding a large congregation waiting, I stepped out of the coach into the house, and began preaching without delay, and such was the goodness of God that I found no more weariness when I had done than if I had rested all the day.'[1]

---

[1] See *Journal*, vii., 307-8. For the ordinations in Manchester, see *Proceedings of the Wesley Historical Society*, ix., 150.

XXI
THE CHANNEL ISLANDS

ON Thursday, August 9, 1787, we see John Wesley, Thomas Coke and Joseph Bradford on the pier at Southampton. They are looking for a ship that would take them to the Channel Islands. They found two 'sloops' that were nearly ready to sail. The captain of one of them promised to sail the next morning, but his ship did not leave the port until the Saturday of that week. John Wesley availed himself of the delay to preach in the evening in 'Mr. Fay's schoolroom,' to a small but deeply serious congregation. It is difficult to identify that schoolroom, but we know that he preached there again in the early morning and the evening of the next day. Then, on Saturday, August 11, he and his two companions went on board the *Queen,* a small sloop that was sailing for the Channel Islands.

At first the wind was 'tolerable.' Then it grew foul and blew a storm. To the relief of all on board, the captain put his ship into Yarmouth harbour. Taking advantage of the opportunity, Dr. Coke preached that evening in the market-house to 'a quiet and tolerably attentive congregation.' The storm continuing, the next morning John Wesley preached in the same place to a much larger congregation. Then he and his companions went to church. At four o'clock Wesley preached in the market-house which was 'more than filled,' and in the evening Dr. Coke preached there again. Wesley's comment on the work of that Sunday was: 'We have now delivered our own souls at Yarmouth, and trust God will suffer us to go on to Guernsey.' There were, however, further delays. The fair wind with which they set out from Yarmouth on the Monday soon changed, and in the afternoon it was blowing so hard that they were glad when the captain determined to shelter the ship in Swanage Bay. Wesley must have been reconciled to the decision. He knew that there was a little Methodist Society there, and he welcomed the opportunity of seeing its members. He had not been in Swanage for thirteen years. The news of his landing was soon noised abroad, and we can picture the gladness of the little band of Methodists when they heard of his unexpected arrival. In the evening he preached in the Presbyterian meeting-house to a large congregation, and afterwards passed an hour 'very agreeably' with the Presbyterian minister. Then he and his companions went to the house of that pillar of Methodism in Swanage, 'old brother Collins.' He must have felt regret when he received a message from the captain of the ship that he was about to sail. It was between eight and nine o'clock when Wesley and his companions left the port.

The next morning, as the boat sailed on with a fair wind, Wesley and his companions expected to reach Guernsey in the afternoon. But the wind again turned contrary, and they had to abandon their hope. We will give the result in Wesley's words. He says: 'We then judged it best to put in at the Isle of Alderney, but we were very near being shipwrecked in the bay. When we were in the middle of the rocks, with the sea rippling all round us, the wind totally failed. Had this continued we must have struck upon one or other of the rocks, so we went to prayer, and the wind sprung up instantly. About sunset we landed, and though we had five beds in the same room, slept in peace.'

At about eight o'clock in the morning of the following day Wesley went to the beach, and began an open-air service by giving out a hymn. A woman and two little children joined him and his companions. Before the hymn was ended 'a tolerable congregation' had assembled, all of whom behaved well. Wesley says: 'Part indeed continued at forty or fifty yards distance, but they were all quiet and attentive.' His action was well-timed. When we consult the *Minutes* of the Conference held in Manchester in 1787, we see that Alderney makes its first appearance as a circuit. It is placed in connexion with Guernsey.[1]

It must have been a relief to the voyagers to watch the stilling of the storm and the clearing of the sky. The weather changed. Wesley and his companions went on board the ship, which was soon making her way to Guernsey. Those who have known the Channel Islands in far distant years will be interested in Wesley's description of the voyage and the

[1] *Minutes*, i., 197.

arrival. He says: 'Soon after we set sail, and after a very pleasant passage, through little islands on either hand, we came to the venerable Castle, standing on a rock, about a quarter of a mile from Guernsey. The isle itself makes a beautiful appearance, spreading as a crescent to the right and left, about seven miles long, and five broad, part high land, and part low. The town itself is boldly situated, rising higher and higher from the water. The first thing I observed in it was very narrow streets and exceeding high houses. But we quickly went on to Mr. De Jersey's, hardly a mile from the town. Here I found a most cordial welcome, both from the master of the house and all his family. . . . His gardens and orchards are of vast extent, and wonderfully pleasant, and I know no nobleman in Great Britain that has such variety of the most excellent fruit, which he is every year increasing, either from France or other parts of the Continent. What quantity of fruit he has you may conjecture from one sort only: this summer he gathered fifty pounds of strawberries daily for six weeks together.'[1]

John Wesley at once commenced his mission to the people of Guernsey by preaching, in the evening of the day of his arrival in the island, in a large room in the house of Mr. De Jersey. The entry in his *Journal* reveals his satisfaction with the service. He says: 'I preached at seven in a large room, to as deeply serious a congregation as I ever saw, on " Jesus Christ, of God made unto us wisdom, righteousness, sanctification and redemption."' The next morning, at five o'clock, he had another 'very serious congregation' in Mr. De Jersey's 'large room.' These services made a deep impression on him. They revealed the soundness of the work that had been done before his visit. In the evening of the same day he went to a 'room' that was situated near Fort George. He calls it 'our own preaching-house.' It was in St. Peter Port, the largest town in the island. He says: 'So many people squeezed in (though not near all who came), that it was as hot as a stove. But this none seemed to regard, for the word of God was sharper than a two-edged sword.' It is clear that he was delighted with the advance that had been made by Methodism in Guernsey. He must have regretted that his stay in the island could not be prolonged.

[1] Wesley's *Journal*, vii., 312-13.

On Friday, August 17, we see Wesley again in St. Peter Port. He spent a short time with the Governor of the island in the morning. In the afternoon he and his companions had a walk on the pier. It was the old pier that, after some years, gave place to the present structure. But his verdict on the old pier is worth recording. He declared that it was 'the largest and finest he had ever seen.' In the evening he preached in the open air. He stood near 'the house in the yard' and was surrounded with tall, shady trees. To a large congregation he proclaimed that 'God is a Spirit, and they that worship Him must worship Him in spirit and in truth.' As he watched the crowd he was convinced that 'many were cut to the heart, and some not a little comforted.' The next day, and on Sunday, he preached to large congregations. At his last service he took a solemn and affectionate leave of the people. He thought it was probable that he would not see them again; but he was mistaken.

We think that it must have been with some reluctance that John Wesley said farewell to his friends in Guernsey; but he knew that in Jersey his arrival was being eagerly expected. So, on Monday, August 20, with his companions, Dr. Coke and Joseph Bradford, he went on board a small sloop between three and four o'clock in the morning. She was a slow sailer. It took her seven hours to reach Jersey; and we detect a note of impatience in Wesley's description of the voyage. But, at last, the harbour was reached, and the voyagers made their way to Mr. Brackenbury's pleasant home. It was with gladness that Wesley greeted his old friend, and his young colleague, Adam Clarke. He was delighted with Mr. Brackenbury's house. He says: 'It stands very pleasantly near the end of the town, and has a large, convenient garden, with a lovely range of fruitful hills, which rise at a small distance from it. I preached in the evening to an exceeding serious congregation on (Mark) iii. ult., and almost as many were present at five in the morning, whom I exhorted to go on to perfection, which many of them, Mr. Clarke informs me, are earnestly endeavouring to do.' In the evening of this eventful day he says that he was obliged 'to preach abroad.' We presume that a crowd had gathered, and that it was necessary that the service should be held in the open air.

We are much interested in the events which happened

between the services on Tuesday, August 21. Wesley's record is as follows: 'We took a walk to one of our friends in the country. Near his house stood what they call the College.[1] It is a free school, designed to train up children for the university, exceeding finely situated, in a quiet recess, surrounded by tall woods. Not far from it stands, on the top of a high hill (I suppose a Roman mount), an old chapel, believed to be the first Christian church which was built in the island. From hence we had a view of the whole island, the pleasantest I ever saw, as far superior to the Isle of Wight as that is to the Isle of Man. The little hills, almost covered with large trees, are inexpressibly beautiful. It seems they are to be equalled in the Isle of Guernsey.'[2]

Wesley does not mention the name of his companion on this memorable excursion. But we see that, in the early morning, he had a conversation with Adam Clarke. After recording the fact he commences a new paragraph in his *Journal*, with the words, 'We took a walk to one of our friends in the country.' We have no hesitation in naming Adam Clarke as his companion in this delightful ramble.

As we watch John Wesley and Adam Clarke during this ramble in Jersey we are impressed by Wesley's vivacity. When we look at his companion we note, now and then, signs of weariness. If we remember that Wesley, at the time we have reached, had ceased to be troubled by mob attacks, we can understand the contrast. The fact was that Adam Clarke had gone through some of Wesley's early experiences, and needed rest. Let us see what had happend to him one evening at St. Aubin's in Jersey. He shall describe the event in his own words. After telling the story of a dangerous assault made on him at La Valle in Guernsey, he describes a narrow escape from mob violence which he experienced one evening at St. Aubin's, in Jersey. He says:

<small>A desperate mob of some hundreds, with almost all instruments of destruction, assembled round the house in which he was preaching, which</small>

<small>[1] In a footnote in the *Journal* we see that the name of the College was Saint-Mannelier, and that it was an old endowed school that was, in later years, united to Victoria College in St. Heliers, the principal town in the Island. As the present writer received the best part of his school education at Elizabeth College in Guernsey, and Victoria College in Jersey, he may be pardoned for lingering for a few moments in the presence of St. Mannelier.
[2] Wesley's *Journal*, vii., 317.</small>

was a wooden building with five windows. At their first approach, the principal part of the congregation issued forth, and provided for their own safety. The Society alone, about thirteen persons, remained with their preacher. The mob, finding that all with whom they might claim brotherhood had escaped, resolved to pull down the house, and bury the preacher and his friends in the ruins. Mr. Clarke exhorted the friends to trust in that God who was able to save, when one of the mob presented a pistol at him through the window opposite to the pulpit, which twice flashed in the pan. Others had got crows, and were busily employed in sapping the foundations of the house. Mr. Clarke, perceiving this, said to the people, 'If we stay here we shall be all destroyed. I will go out among them; they seek not you, but me: after they have got me, they will permit you to pass unmolested.' They besought him with tears not to leave the house, as he would infallibly be murdered. He, seeing that there was no time to be lost, as they continued to sap the foundations, said, 'I will instantly go out among them in the name of God.' 'I will go with you,' said a stout young man. As the house was assailed with showers of stones, he met a volley of these, as he opened and passed through the door. It was a clear full-moon night, after a heavy storm of hail and rain. He walked forward. The mob divided to the right and left, and made an ample passage for him and the young man who followed him to pass through. This they did to the very skirts of the hundreds who were assembled with drums, horns, spades, forks, bludgeons, &c., to take the life of a man whose only crime was proclaiming to lost sinners redemption through the blood of the cross. During the whole time of his passing through the mob, there was a death-like silence, nor was there any motion but what was necessary to give him a free passage. Either their eyes were holden that they could not know him; or they were so overawed by the power of God that they could not lift a hand or utter a word against him. The poor people, finding all was quiet, came out a little after, and passed away, not one of them being either hurt or molested. In a few minutes, the mob seemed to awake as from a dream, and, finding that their prey had been plucked out of their teeth, they knew not how, attacked the house afresh, broke every square of glass in the windows, and scarcely left a whole tile upon the roof. He afterwards learned that their design was to put him in the sluice of an overshot water-mill, by which he must have been crushed in pieces.[1]

The next Sunday Adam Clarke went to the same place. The mob rose again, and when they began to make a tumult, he called on them to hear him for a few moments. The leaders of the assault answered to his appeal and stilled the mob. They listened to him. When he had finished his address this cry rang out: ' He is a clever fellow; he shall preach, and we will hear him! ' He says that they were ' as good as their word.' He proceeded without any further hindrance

[1] See Etheridge's *Life of the Rev. Adam Clarke, LL.D.*, 93-4.

from them, and they never afterwards gave him any molestation. We wish that we could end the story at this point. But it is necessary to continue it by quoting another extract from Adam Clarke's description of the St. Aubin's riots. He says that the little preaching-house being nearly destroyed, he, some Sabbaths afterwards, attempted to preach out of doors. This was the result, which we give in his own words : ' The mob having given up persecution, one of the magistrates of St. Aubin took up the business, came to the place with a mob of his own, and the drummer of the regiment stationed at the place, pulled down Mr. Clarke while he was at prayer, and delivered him into the hands of the *canaille* he had brought with him. The drummer attended him out of the town, beating the " Rogues' March " on his drum, and beating him frequently with the drumsticks, from the strokes of which, and other misusages, he did not recover for some weeks. But he wearied out all his persecutors. There were several who heard the word gladly, and for their sakes he freely ventured himself, till at last all opposition ceased.'[1]

It is time to return to the ramble of John Wesley and Adam Clarke in Jersey. We expect that Alderney was mentioned in their conversation, and that Clarke, who had introduced Methodism into that island, was delighted to hear the news of Wesley's open-air service by the side of the sea. In Etheridge's *Life of Adam Clarke,* there is a full account of Clarke's first visit to Alderney. It is contained in a report which Clarke gave to John Wesley. He says : ' My design being made public, many hindrances were thrown in my way. It was reported that the governor had threatened to prohibit my landing, and that, in case he found me on the island, he would transport me to the Caskets (a rock in the sea, about three leagues West of Alderney, on which there is a lighthouse). These threatenings, being published here, rendered it very difficult for me to procure a passage, as several of my friends were against my going, fearing bad consequences; and none of the captains who traded to the island were willing to take me, fearing to incur the displeasure of the governor, notwithstanding that I offered them anything they could reasonably demand for my passage. I thought at last I should

[1] Etheridge's *Life of Adam Clarke, LL.D.,* 95.

be obliged to hire one of the English packets, as I was determined to go, by God's grace, at all events.'

Having waited a long time, watching sometimes day and night, Adam Clarke at last got a vessel bound for Alderney. He landed on the island a homeless man. But walking to the town he tells us that he took particular notice of a very poor cottage, into which he felt a strong inclination to enter. He opened the door, saying 'Peace be unto this house.' He found in it an old man and woman who, having understood his business, bade him welcome to the best food they had, to a little chamber where he might sleep, and to their house to preach in. He told them that he would preach that evening if they would procure him a congregation. They went out and spread the news of his arrival in the town. He says: 'Long before the appointed hour a multitude of people flocked together, to whom I spoke of the Kingdom of God. It was with difficulty I could persuade them to go away after promising to preach to them again the next evening.'

Tired with his journey, Adam Clarke sought for rest in his little room. He had been there for about twenty minutes when the good woman of the house appeared and entreated him to come downstairs and preach again, as several of the gentry, among whom was one of the Justices, had come 'to hear what he had to say.' He went at once, and found that the room was full. He held a service that lasted nearly an hour. In a letter to John Wesley, in which he described the service, he said that deep attention sat on every face while he showed the congregation their great need of a Saviour, and exhorted them 'to turn at once from their iniquities to the living God.' At the close of the sermon he told his audience his design in visiting the island. As the congregation rose to disperse, the Justice exchanged 'a few very civil words' with him. It is clear that he had been deeply impressed by the sermon, and we think that his influence may be detected in an event which afterwards occurred.

A little later in the week, while Adam Clarke sat at dinner, a constable made his appearance. He shall describe what he calls 'a singular thing.' In his letter to Wesley, he says:

'While I sat at dinner, a constable, from a person in authority, came to solicit my immediate appearance at a place called the Bray (where several respectable families live, and where the governor's stores are kept) to preach to a company of gentlemen and ladies, who were waiting, and at whose desire one of the large store-rooms was prepared for that purpose. I went without delay, and was brought by the *lictor* to his master's apartment, who behaved with much civility, told me the reason of his sending for me, and begged I would preach without delay. I willingly consented, and in a quarter of an hour a large company was assembled. The gentry were not so partial to themselves as to exclude several sailors, smugglers, and labourers, from hearing with them. The Lord was with me, and enabled me to explain, from Prov. xii. 26, the character and conduct of the righteous, and to prove that such an one was beyond all comparison more excellent than his ungodly neighbour, however great, rich, wise, or important he might be in the eyes of men. All heard with deep attention, save an English gentleman, so called, who walked out about the middle of the discourse.'

It is clear that Adam Clarke's visit to Alderney made a deep impression on all ranks of the islanders. On Sunday morning he preached, by invitation, in the English church. Then, in the evening, he preached in the large warehouse at the Bray to a much larger congregation. It was composed of the principal gentry of the island, together with justices, jurats, constables, and other inhabitants. He says: ' The Lord was again with me, and enabled me to declare His sacred counsel without fear.' When it became known that he was leaving the island on the following day many people expressed their unwillingness that he should leave them. They clustered around him and said : ' We have much need of such preaching, and such a preacher : we wish you would abide in the island, and go back no more.' But it would seem that their desire would not be gratified. He went down to the beach on the Monday morning. But ' the utmost of the flood did not set the vessel afloat,' so he returned to the town, and the people came together once more in the evening to hear him preach. He says : ' The vessel being got off the same night about twelve o'clock, I recommended them to God, promised them a preacher shortly, and setting sail, arrived in Guernsey in about twenty-one hours.'

We have watched Adam Clarke during his visit to Alderney with some anxiety. We have remembered that his physical strength had been lowered by the privations of his early life. We do not wonder that when he resumed his work in Jersey and Guernsey his health gave way. Etheridge says, 'he was brought to the brink of the grave.' Fortunately he was attended by a skilful doctor. He made a slow recovery. Shortly before Wesley's visit to the Islands he was able to go to England and visit some friends who nursed him with care. In the month of May he resumed his work in the Islands, and, in September, he was delighted to meet John Wesley in Jersey. Watching them during their walk in the country on that bright day, we have noted the contrast between them. John Wesley seems to have renewed his youth; Adam Clarke now and then reveals a sign of the weariness of a man who has not fully recovered the strength lost through sickness. No one had deeper sympathy with the suffering than Wesley; and we know that, after this walk, his concern for his friend was shown.

John Wesley's stay in Jersey was prolonged by the difficulty of finding a ship that would take him back to England. The weather changed and storms began to blow. We think that he was reconciled to his detention by the fact that he was staying in the house of his old friend, Robert Carr Brackenbury. If we had only the entries in Wesley's *Journal* which concern this visit to Jersey to guide us we should not be able to understand the feeling of the two men for each other. On August 23 this entry appears in Wesley's *Journal*: 'I rode to St. Mary's, five or six miles from St. Helier's, through shady, pleasant lanes. None at the house could speak English, but I had interpreters enough. In the evening our large room was thoroughly filled. I preached on "By grace are ye saved, through faith." Mr. Brackenbury interpreted sentence by sentence, and God owned his word, though delivered in so awkward a manner, but especially in prayer: I prayed in English, and Mr. Brackenbury in French.' We would gladly linger over this scene, which brings the perfect friendship of Wesley and Brackenbury vividly before us. The two men understood each other. In Marshall Claxton's painting of *The Death Bed of John Wesley*, in the background of the picture there is a man's face which is almost hidden by the large group that is watching the passing of the great evangelist. If the artist had known more about the principal friends of Wesley, we think he would have given Robert Carr Brackenbury a different position.[1]

It had been Wesley's intention to return to Southampton on August 27, but the weather in the Channel Islands compelled him to change his plans. He did not leave Jersey until August 30. Instead of sailing for England, he returned to Guernsey. Arriving there he was detained by great storms of wind. He resumed his work among the Methodists of the island. Then, on September 5, when he was visiting a friend he was told of a captain who had just come from France who proposed to sail in the morning for Penzance, ' for which the wind would serve, though not for Southampton.' Wesley changed his plans. The next day he and his companions went on board this ship. Adam Clarke was one of Wesley's comrades on the voyage. He tells us of an event which gives it a distinguished position in the stories of Wesley's travels. He says:

> Mr. Wesley was sitting reading in the cabin, and, hearing the noise and bustle occasioned by putting the vessel about to stand on her different tacks, he put his head above, and inquired what was the matter. Being told the wind was become contrary, and the ship was obliged thus to tack, he said, 'Then let us go to prayer.' His own company who were upon deck walked down, and at his request Dr. Coke, Mr. Bradford, and Mr. Clarke went to prayer. After the latter had ended, Mr. Wesley broke out into fervent supplication, which seemed to be more the offspring of strong faith than of mere desire, in words remarkable as well as the spirit, feeling, and manner in which they were uttered. Some of them were to the following effect:—' Almighty and everlasting God, Thou hast Thy way everywhere, and all things serve the purposes of Thy will. Thou holdest the winds in Thy fists, and sittest upon the waterfloods and reignest King for ever. Command these winds and these waves that they obey *Thee,* and take us speedily and safely to the haven whither we would be.' The power of his petition was felt by all. He rose from his knees, made no kind of remark, but took up his book, and continued his reading. Mr. Clarke went upon deck, and what was his surprise when he found the vessel standing on her right course with a steady breeze, which slackened not till, carrying them at the rate of nine or ten knots an hour, they anchored safely near St. Michael's Mount in Penzance Bay! On the sudden and favourable change of the wind Mr. Wesley made no remark: so fully did he expect to be heard, that he took it for granted he was heard. Such answers to prayer he was in the habit of receiving, and therefore to him the occurrence was not strange. Of such a circumstance how many of those who did not enter into his views would have descanted at large, had it happened in favour

[1] See *The Journal of John Wesley,* viii., 141.

of themselves! Yet all the notice he takes of this singular circumstance is contained in the following entry in his *Journal*:—'In the morning, Thursday (September 6, 1787) we went on board with a fair, moderate wind. But we had but just entered the ship when the wind died away. We cried to God for help; and it presently sprung up exactly fair, and did not cease till it brought us into Penzance Bay.'[1]

We can imagine the astonishment of the Methodists of Penzance when they saw John Wesley and his companions walking over the sands. Wesley says: 'We appeared to our friends here as men risen from the dead.' The news of their landing soon spread, and they were surrounded by a crowd of Methodists who welcomed their arrival with an enthusiasm that touched Wesley's heart. It was clear to him that he must not tear himself away from such a loving people. So he and his travelling companions stayed in Cornwall for nearly a week. In the evening of the day of their landing Wesley preached in Penzance. He says: 'Great was their rejoicing over us, and great was the power of God in the midst of the congregation while I explained and applied those words—"Whosoever doeth the will of God, the same is My brother, and sister, and mother."'

Wesley's record of this visit to Cornwall abounds in interest, but we will confine ourselves to the entry in his *Journal* on Sunday, September 9. He says: 'About nine I preached at the Copper-works, three or four miles from St. Ives, to a large congregation gathered from all parts, I believe with the demonstration of the Spirit. I then met the Society in the preaching-house, which is unlike any other in England, both as to its form and materials. It is exactly round, and composed wholly of brazen slags, which, I suppose, will last as long as the earth. Between one and two I began in the market-place at Redruth, to the largest congregation I ever saw there, they not only filled all the windows, but sat on the tops of the houses. About five I began in the pit at Gwennap. I suppose we had a thousand more than ever were there before. But it was all one; my voice was strengthened accordingly, so that every one could hear distinctly.'[2]

In trying to revive this wonderful scene we must forget the small 'Pit' of the present day. The services held there, once a year, still attract the attendance of crowds of Metho-

---

[1] Etheridge's *Life of Rev. Adam Clarke*, 102.
[2] *Journal*, vii., 325.

dists; but in its present shape it is a later construction. In our volume on *John Wesley the Master Builder* (200) we gave Wesley's description of a service he conducted at the Gwennap Pit on Sunday, September 14, 1766, to which he seems to make reference in the paragraph we have just quoted concerning the number of people who heard his voice at the later date.

After preaching in other places in Cornwall Wesley made his way, with his travelling companions, into Devonshire. On September 11 he was met by Methodists from Plymouth Dock who gave him a hearty welcome. He preached in the Dock chapel in the evening to an earnest, affectionate people. He stayed in Plymouth until September 13, when he set out early and dined at Exeter. His record of the condition of the Society there is encouraging. He says: 'In the evening we had a crowded congregation, that drank in every word. This Society likewise increases both in number and strength.' The next day he and his companions took the mail-coach, and in the afternoon came to Bath. He found abundance of letters waiting for him, but with the assistance of two of his friends he was able to answer them. In addition he preached several times in the City and was encouraged by the presence of large congregations, and the evident signs of improvement in the spirit of the people. He says that he left the Society in a better state than it had been for many years. He was much encouraged by the services he held on Sunday. The chapel was 'more than filled,' and he was cheered by the attendance at the sacrament of 'an unusual number of deeply serious communicants.'

On Monday, September 17, John Wesley left Bath and went to Bristol. He found that his brother had been there for some weeks. When Charles Wesley wearied of London he was accustomed to go to Bristol, where he found rest among his old friends. Fixing our thoughts on the meeting of John and Charles Wesley, we note the quickness of John Wesley's recognition of the approach of his brother's death. In earlier times it is clear that he had detected the ominous signs. He had watched the trouble coming on, and had given his brother advice, which had not been taken. It is clear that he saw that the shadow of death was approaching his brother, whom he loved with all his heart. He attempted to advise him, but found that his counsel was not welcomed. He gave up the task, and watched the coming of the shadow with deep regret.

John Wesley's visit to Bristol was influenced by the sickness of his brother, but again and again the sunshine found a way through the clouds. We note that on Friday, September 21, he went to Kingswood and spent the evening at the School. We have noted his anxieties about its condition in the years that were past, when he was tempted 'to end it or mend it.' It is a relief to read his note concerning its condition at the time we have reached. He says: 'I spent the evening at the School, and was much pleased with the management of it.' This was not the first time that the School had given him delight. Kingswood School had been one of John Wesley's ' calm retreats,' in which he had spent many hours, in his 'little room,' when he was preparing some of his best-known books for the press.

John Wesley made Bristol his headquarters until the second week in October. He preached at Temple Church, where his brother and the Kingswood colliers had been repelled from the Lord's Table forty-seven years before. He visited the Methodist circuits in the neighbourhood, and was much encouraged by their condition. Then on Tuesday, October 9, he reached London in time to preach to a large congregation in the evening. His stay there was brief. On October 15 he set out on a visit to country circuits from which he had been absent for many months. We watch him as he enters Oxford and preaches, on Tuesday, October 16, to ' a very quiet, deeply-serious congregation.' On the next day he preached again in the city of many memories. Half an hour before the service began there was a heavy fall of rain, but a large congregation assembled. His comment on the service causes many thoughts to arise in our mind. He says: 'I found great liberty of speech in enforcing the first and great commandment, and could not but hope there will be a great work of God here, notwithstanding all the wisdom of the world.' Between these entries in his *Journal* we find a record of his visit to Witney that is very suggestive. Following his reference to the service held at Oxford on October 16, there is this entry: 'The house at Witney would nothing near contain the people in the evening; it was well filled at five on *Wednesday* morning. I dearly love this people; they are so simple of heart, and so much alive to God!' In these sentences we have a revelation not only of the character of the Witney people but also of John Wesley. In his record of this journey he gives us an opportunity of seeing another congregation of the Methodists of those early times. On Thursday, October 18, he makes this entry in his *Journal*: ' We went on to High Wycombe. The work of God is so considerably increased here that, although three galleries are added to the preaching-house, it would scarce contain the people. Even at five in the morning, Friday, the nineteenth, it was thoroughly filled. Never before was there so fair a prospect of doing good at this place.'

John Wesley gave up the rest of the year to London and some of the counties that could be reached without serious inconvenience. The readers of his *Journal* will be impressed by the thoroughness of his work, and by the signs of the great advance of Methodism in England. But we must close this chapter by referring to an incident that links Methodism with the Evangelical party in the Church of England in the nineteenth century. On October 30, 1787, we find, in John Wesley's *Journal*, this entry : ' I went down to Miss Harvey's, at Hinxworth, in Hertfordshire. Mr. Simeon, from Cambridge, met me there, who breathes the very spirit of Mr. Fletcher.'[1] The student of Wesley's *Journal* will remember that the two men had met before in Hinxworth. On Monday, December 20, 1784, we find the following entry in the *Journal*: ' I went to Hinxworth, where I had the satisfaction of meeting Mr. Simeon, Fellow of King's College, in Cambridge. He has spent some time with Mr. Fletcher at Madeley, two kindred souls much resembling each other both in fervour of spirit and in the earnestness of their address. He gave me the pleasing information that there are three parish churches in Cambridge wherein true scriptural religion is preached and several young gentlemen who are happy partakers of it.'[2]

John Wesley's records of his meetings with Charles Simeon are brief but important. We know that he and Fletcher and Simeon were evangelical preachers. They preached the same doctrines and aimed at the conversion of their hearers. When Wesley wrote in his *Journal* the words we have quoted con-

[1] See *Journal*, vii., 337.   [2] *ibid*, vii., 39.

cerning the resemblance between Fletcher and Simeon he gave us the opportunity to understand the latter. It is no wonder that the friendship of Wesley and Simeon endured to the close of Wesley's life. The two men were true to each other and to the high standard they had set before them as ministers of the gospel of Christ.

XXII

THE DEATH OF CHARLES WESLEY

JOHN WESLEY spent the opening months of the year 1788 in London. On February 25 he writes these lines: 'I took a solemn leave of the congregation at West Street, by applying once more what I had enforced fifty years before: "By grace are ye saved through faith." At the following meeting the presence of God, in a marvellous manner filled the place. The next evening we had a very numerous congregation at the new chapel, to which I declared the whole counsel of God. I seemed now to have finished my work in London. If I see it again, well; if not, I pray God to raise up others that will be more faithful and more successful in His work!' There is a note of depression in this entry that arrests attention. To account for it we must remember that when he met his brother Charles in Bristol he received a shock from which he suffered for a long time. In London the brothers often met. Gradually his fears of Charles Wesley's sudden death lessened; so, on February 28, we see him stepping into the mail-coach in the evening. He reached Bath the next day in the early morning, and stayed there for a few days. But his brother was much on his mind. He hoped for the best, but his anxiety, though lessened, was not banished. In Thomas Jackson's *Life of Charles Wesley* there is a letter which John Wesley wrote to his brother from Bath. In it, after stating that he still believed that God had a little more work for his brother to do, he says: 'That is provided you now take up your cross (for that it frequently must be) and go out, at least an hour in a day. I would not blame you, if it were two or three. Never mind expense. I can make that up. You shall not die to save charges.'[1] It is well known that John Wesley did not approve of some of the

[1] Jackson's *Life of Charles Wesley*, ii., 438.

methods adopted by his brother's doctors; but it is clear that he admitted that progress towards recovery had been made.

During his visit to Bath the cloud that had rested on John Wesley in London began to move away. Those who have followed his career are aware that difficulties had arisen in the Society in Bath that had caused him some anxiety. But it is with a sense of relief that we read the records of this visit to the City. On Thursday, February 28, this is his entry in the *Journal*: 'I set out in the mail-coach, and the next morning came to Bath. Here I found a pleasing prospect. The congregations are larger than ever. The Society is, at length, at unity in itself; and consequently increases both in grace and number.' Then, on Sunday, March 2, he says: 'I preached at eleven, at half an hour past two and at half-hour past five. The first congregation was large, and so was the second, but the third was far the largest, filling every corner of the house. And the power of God seemed to increase with the number of the people, insomuch that in the evening, while I was applying " To me to live is Christ and to die is gain," the glory of the Lord seemed to overshadow the congregation in an uncommon manner. And I trust the impression then made upon rich and poor will not soon wear off.'[1]

On Monday, March 3, John Wesley made his way to Bristol. It was well that he had recovered his high spirits during his visit to Bath. In Bristol many of Charles Wesley's chief friends were to be found. On arrival in the city John Wesley was surrounded by crowds of people who were anxious to know the latest news concerning his brother. He was able to cause them to share his hopefulness. The excitement was lessened, and he had an opportunity to get much-needed rest. But he was soon at work. He found that the question that was then causing great disturbance in the city was the much-debated subject of slavery. Bristol occupied the chief place among the English towns that profited by the slave trade and in spite of the decision of the highest law court, ships still brought their cargoes of slaves to Bristol. They were landed and shut up in huts which stood by the river side, and were sold to eager purchasers. It is no wonder that Wesley's announcement of the subject on which he would preach on

[1] *Journal*, vii., 358.

Thursday evening caused great excitement in the city. We will give the result of his sermon in his own words. He says:

'On Thursday the house from end to end was filled with high and low, rich and poor. I preached on that ancient prophecy, "God shall enlarge Japhet. And he shall dwell in the tents of Shem; and Canaan shall be His servant." About the middle of the discourse, while there was on every side attention still as night, a vehement noise arose, none could tell why, and shot like lightning through the whole congregation. The terror and confusion were inexpressible. You might have imagined it was a city taken by storm. The people rushed upon each other with the utmost violence; the benches were broke in pieces, and nine-tenths of the congregation appeared to be struck with the same panic. In about six minutes the storm ceased, almost as suddenly as it rose; and, all being calm, I went on without the least interruption.

'It was the strangest incident of the kind I ever remember; and I believe none can account for it without supposing some preternatural influence. Satan fought, lest his kingdom should be delivered up. We set *Friday* apart as a day of fasting and prayer that God would remember those poor outcasts of men; and (what seems impossible with men, considering the wealth and power of their oppressors) make a way for them to escape and break their chains in sunder.'[1]

John Wesley remained in Bristol until Monday, March 17. His days were crowded with work. He went to Kingswood School, and to his great satisfaction, found everything 'in excellent order.' On Sunday, March 9, he preached at Kingswood to a congregation that 'crowded the house.' During that week he visited the classes in Bristol, and was disappointed with the small progress that had been made. They contained a little more than nine hundred members. His comment has its value in the present day. He says: 'I wonder that, with such preachers, there is so little increase. Dublin has outrun Bristol already, so will Manchester, Sheffield, and even Birmingham soon, unless they stir themselves up before the Lord.'

One of the most interesting events in this visit of John Wesley to Bristol must be recorded. He expected to preach in Temple Church. It had been the scene of many memorable events in his history, but he could only arrange to preach there on Saturday, March 15. He tells us why he was not able to take a Sunday appointment in that church. We know that he was leaving Bristol on the following Monday. Where was he preaching on March 16? We read in his *Journal* under the date Sunday, March 16, 1788:

[1] John Wesley's *Journal*, vii., 359-60.

'I was invited by the Mayor, Mr. Edgar, to preach in his chapel,[1] and afterwards to dine with him at the Mansion House. Most of the aldermen were at church, and a multitude of high and low, to whom I explained and applied that awful passage of Scripture, the history of Dives and Lazarus.' Only those who have watched the change of opinion in England during the later years of Wesley's life can understand the profound meaning of this event.

As John Wesley was leaving Bristol on Monday, March 17, he followed his usual custom and rose early in the morning. In spite of his anxieties he was hopeful that the most dangerous stage of his brother's sickness was passed. Yet he felt he must write to his brother before setting out on a long journey to the north. His last letter to his brother is headed, Bristol, March 17, 1788, between four and five:

'DEAR BROTHER,—I am just setting out on my northern journey, but must snatch time to write two or three lines. I stand and admire the wise and gracious dispensations of divine Providence! Never was there before so loud a call to all that are under your roof. If they have not hitherto sufficiently regarded either you, or the Lord God of their fathers, what was more calculated to convince them than to see you hovering so long upon the borders of the grave? And I verily believe, if they receive the admonition, God will raise you up again. I know you have the sentence of death in yourself. So had I more than twelve years ago. I know nature is utterly exhausted; but is not nature subject to *His* word? I do not depend upon physicians, but upon Him that raiseth the dead. Only let your whole family stir themselves up, and be instant in prayer, then I have only to say to each: "If thou canst believe thou shalt see the glory of God!" "Be strong in the Lord, and in the power of His might." Adieu!'[2]

Having written his letter John Wesley set out on his northern journey ' in a mild, lovely morning.' It would be pleasant to follow him in his visits to the midland towns. He

---

[1] The Mayor's Chapel stands on College Green and was used by the Huguenots when they were expelled from France by the Revocation of the Edict of Nantes.
[2] Thomas Jackson's *Life of Charles Wesley*, ii., 440; *Journal of John Wesley*, vii., 363.

met with encouragement nearly all the way. He was delighted with the change that had taken place in Wolverhampton. A 'new house' had been erected there. His comment will be understood by those who remember his experience at a former visit to the town. He says: 'What a den of lions was this town for many years! But now, it seems, the last will be first.' Glancing at the footnote in his *Journal* we understand his meaning. It is as follows: 'In those wild days Wesley had been struck by a stone flung by Moseley, a young locksmith, causing blood to flow down his face. The memory of the vicious act pursued him. He was afterwards soundly converted in "the new house," Noah's Ark Chapel, and continued a faithful Methodist until his death at the age of ninety.'[1] As to Birmingham, those who know it will rejoice to read Wesley's entry in his *Journal* on Saturday, March 22, 1788. He says: 'In the evening we had a Sunday congregation at Birmingham. Here there is a glorious increase of the work of God. The Society is risen to above eight hundred, so that it is at present inferior to none in England, except those in London and Bristol.'

Rejoicing in the light that came to him during this visit to the Midlands Wesley soon found himself in a darkened world. On Friday, March 28, he reached Madeley. His home was with Mrs. Fletcher. The memories of former days arose, when her husband used to join in giving him the hearty greeting. Three years had passed since Fletcher died. In the evening Wesley preached to a large congregation in the church on a text which revealed the trend of his quiet thoughts—'When Christ, who is our life, shall appear, then shall ye also appear with Him in glory.' On Sunday, March 30, he preached there again, but was 'distressed by the large concourse of people.' He tells us that it was too cold 'to stand abroad, and the church could in no wise contain the congregation. But we could not help it, so as many as could, got in, the rest stood without, or went away.' He preached on the 'Three that bear record in heaven.' In the afternoon he preached again in the church. He took for his text: 'This is the record, that God hath given unto us eternal life, and this life is in His Son.' It is clear that, during this visit, he was constantly thinking of his old friend, John Fletcher. It

[1] *Methodist Recorder*, April 3, 1902.

was a comfort to him to know that Mrs. Fletcher had received much help from the sermons he preached during this visit to Madeley. He was thankful that he had brought comfort to her, but he did not know that he himself would soon need to listen to the voice of the Comforter.

Wesley left Madeley on Monday, March 31, and reached Macclesfield on April 4, where he received a letter from London. It had been delayed on its journey. It contained the news of his brother's death, and of the funeral that was to take place on Saturday, April 5. It was impossible that he could reach London in time for the funeral. In his letter to Mrs. Charles Wesley, written on April 4, he says: 'Half an hour ago I received a letter from Mr. Bradburn informing me of my brother's death. For eleven or twelve days before I had not one line concerning him. The last I had was from Charles, which I delayed to answer, expecting every day to receive some further information. . . . If it had been necessary, in order to serve either him or you, I should not have thought much of coming up to London. Indeed, to serve you, or your dear family, in anything that is in my power, will always be a pleasure.' In a letter to the Rev. Peard Dickinson, who was stationed in London, he said: 'If Mr. Bradburn's letter of March 29 had been directed to Birmingham, where I then was, I should have taken coach on Sunday, the thirtieth, and been with you on Monday, the thirty-first.' It is clear that his absence from his brother's funeral caused him much regret. On Saturday, April 5, after writing his letter to Mrs. Charles Wesley, he seems to have given himself up to thinking of his loss. When we open his *Journal* at that date we find no record of his actions. It was a day of silence that was devoted to memories of the past.

Before John Wesley left London he had a conversation with his brother which comes now to our mind. It concerned the place of Charles Wesley's burial. So far as John Wesley was concerned he had made arrangements for his own burial. He was to be buried in the graveyard of the City Road Chapel. But he was uncertain of the choice his brother would make. The subject is of such importance that we will give the result of the conversation between the brothers in the words of Thomas Jackson, the well-known writer of the *Life of Charles Wesley*. Describing the funeral, he says:

'The funeral of this honoured minister took place on the fifth of April. His remains, by his own desire, were interred in the churchyard of St. Mary-le-bone, near his own residence in Chesterfield Street. The pall was supported by eight clergymen of the Church of England. . . . As a friendship of the most tender and confidential kind had through life subsisted between Mr. John and Charles Wesley, and they had been labourers together for half a century in carrying on a deep and extensive work of God, it was John's desire that their remains should rest together in the tomb which he had prepared in the ground connected with the Chapel in the City Road; but this Charles declined, because the ground was not consecrated. It was under the influence of this disappointment that Mr. John Wesley wrote the paper on the inutility of consecrating burying grounds, which he inserted in his monthly magazine. He thought that churches and chapels require no consecration but that which arises from the celebration of God's worship, and that burying-grounds are made sacred by the ashes of the pious dead, rather than by ceremonies of Popish origin which the New Testament never mentions.'[1]

There can be no doubt that John Wesley regretted the choice of a burial ground which his brother had made. It will be enough to say that in after years the churchyard of St. Mary-le-bone has been sacred in the eyes of Wesleyan Methodists. Numerous years have left their mark on the monumental tomb of Charles Wesley, but the Methodists have been its restorers when it was in peril. Only a short time ago their care for the tomb was shown. It now stands in its strength as a monument of the affection of those who made it possible to rescue it from danger.

But from the time when Charles Wesley made Bristol his home the Societies missed his inspiring visits. We have often wondered at the effect of his settlement in Bristol and London, not only on the other parts of the country, but especially on the minds of the preachers in London and elsewhere. Thomas Jackson gives a complete answer to our questionings :

'Some persons have thought that the part which Mr. Charles Wesley took in opposition to his brother's ordinations, and against the administrations of the Sacraments by any man

[1] Thomas Jackson's *Life of the Rev. Charles Wesley, M.A.*, ii., 445-6.

on whose head the hands of a bishop had not been laid, must have rendered him an object of dislike and jealousy among the Methodist preachers generally. But this is a mistake. Those who knew him best were convinced of his integrity and conscientiousness, and though they might dissent from his views of ecclesiastical order, they admired the man, whom they saw to be as generous as he was upright.' Mr. Bradburn, for instance, whose opinions concerning episcopal ordination were very different from those of Mr. Charles Wesley, was honoured with the personal friendship of this eminent man, and in return regarded him with the profoundest respect and admiration, as is manifested from the following letter, which he addressed to Mr. Bardsley, a brother preacher, a few days after Mr. Charles Wesley's interment:

'Mr. Charles Wesley died just as any one who knew him might have expected. I have had the pleasure and profit of his acquaintance and correspondence for years, and shall have a great loss of a true friend now that he is gone. I visited him often in his illness, and sat up with him all night, the last but one of his life. He had no disorder but old age. He had very little pain. His mind was as calm as a summer evening. . . . His general character was such as at once adorned human nature and the Christian religion. He was candid, without cowardly weakness, and firm, without headstrong obstinacy. He was equally free from the cold indifference of lifeless formality, and the imaginary fire of enthusiastic wildness. He never was known to say anything in commendation of himself, and never was at a loss for something good to say of his divine Master. His soul was formed for friendship in affliction, and his words and letters were as a precious balm to those of a sorrowful spirit. He was courteous, without dissimulation, and honest, without vulgar roughness. He was truly a great scholar, without pedantic ostentation. He was a great Christian, without any pompous singularity, and a great Divine, without the least contempt for the meanest of his brethren. He died, or rather fell asleep, on Saturday, March 29, 1788, in the eightieth year of his age. I preached his funeral sermon at West Street, and at the new chapel, on Sunday, April 6, to an inconceivable concourse of people, of every description, from 2 Sam. iii. 38: "A Prince and a great man is fallen this day in Israel." . . . Our chapels are hung in black around the pulpits, desks, &c., and all the people are in mourning.'[1]

On April 4, the day when John Wesley received the news of his brother's death from Samuel Bradburn, we notice another writer who was busy in London. She was one of John Wesley's chief friends. She was his niece, who sometimes accompanied him on his journeys. On the day named we see her sitting at a table in her home in London writing a letter to her uncle. The letter contains a full account of the sickness and death of her father. It was delayed on its journey, and did not reach John Wesley until about a week after the funeral had taken place. He was then in Manchester. It seems as if the letter had been posted soon after it was written, but had gone on its wanderings. We note that John Wesley, in acknowledging its reception, expresses his relief at its arrival. It is impossible to read the letter without seeing that it was written for John Wesley. It has the beauty of simplicity in it, and reveals in every sentence the depth of a daughter's love. There is one paragraph which we think we must reproduce. We have referred, in another place, to the fact of Samuel Wesley's action in becoming a Roman Catholic, and have described his father's sorrow at the event. Writing about her father's death Miss Wesley says: 'It was with great difficulty he seemed to speak. About ten days before, on my brother Samuel's entering the room, he took hold of his hand, and pronounced, with a voice of faith, "I shall bless God to all eternity, that ever you were born. I am persuaded I shall!"' Those who are familiar with Samuel Wesley's life are aware that, after being a Roman Catholic for a short time, he returned to the Church of England, and died a Protestant. It must have been with a sense of relief that John Wesley read these words.

He himself had written to his nephew Samuel on March 18 from Stroud, the day after he wrote his last letter to his brother from Bristol. 'Dear Sammy,' he said, 'I have long had a great concern for you, but never more than at present. Just now you are in a critical situation and every hour is of importance. Your father is, to all known appearances, just quivering over the grave, and ready to leave you, with all the

---

[1] *The Life of the Rev. Charles Wesley, M.A.*, by Thomas Jackson, vol. 2, 445-7.

first inexperience of youth, under your tuition. The time was when you would have taken my advice. But now Miss Freeman has taught you another lesson! Alas! what a fatal step was that! I care not for one *opinion* or another. I care not who is head of the Church, provided *you* be a *Christian*! But what a grievous loss is it to *you* to be cut off on any pretence whatever from that preaching which is more calculated than any other in England to make you a *real scriptural* Christian. O Sammy, I take upon me to say, if you had neglected no opportunity of hearing your father and me preaching, you would have been another man than you are now. But it seems the time is past! Your father is on the wing. You are not likely to see him long; and you know not that you will see me any more. Whether you do or do not, I earnestly advise you to make a friend of Mr. Dickinson. He is a sensible and pious man, and has a tender regard for you. I commit you to Him who is able to carry you through all temptations.'[1]

If we tried to estimate the depth of John Wesley's sorrow under this great loss from his *Journal* and *Diary* alone, we should be astonished to find no reference to his brother's death either in the one or the other. Moreover, after writing calmly to his sister-in-law to explain why it had been impossible to be present at the funeral, he continues his northern tour through Cheshire, Lancashire and Yorkshire into Scotland, and then slowly back to London again. The *Letters,* however, tell another story. Apart from several letters to his preachers about his brother's illness and death, there are in existence no less than sixteen letters written on this tour by John Wesley, either to his brother or to Mrs. Charles or to her children. Full of affection though they are, they do not tell us all. We get a deeper insight into his constant meditations on the theme of his brother's death when we turn to the texts from which he preached in those days. They are entered in the *Diary* without comment, save the note of exclamation occasionally that is the mark of a season of great emotion. Passing through a violent storm between Congleton and Macclesfield in the afternoon of April 4, he arrived at the latter place at four o'clock. What the *Diary* says is: '4 Maccles., letters, tea; 6 Jo. ix. 4! Within to

[1] *The Letters of John Wesley,* viii., 47. Standard edition.

A. Mather; 8 supper, conversed, prayer; 9.30.' The usual programme with bed at the usual time. He reads his letters over a cup of tea as soon as he arrives and learns the sad news. Then he goes out to preach, and his text is, 'I must work the works of Him that sent me, while it is day; the night cometh when no man can work.' Could anything be more characteristic than that?

Henry Moore has told us that a little before Charles Wesley died he prophesied that his brother would outlive him but one year, and says that although Wesley himself 'considered such an event as highly probable, he did not allow it to make the least alteration in his manner of living or in his labours. He often said to me during that year, " What ought I to do, in case I am to die this year? I do not see what I can do but to go on in my labour just as I have done hitherto." '[1] We are not surprised, therefore, that there is no suggestion of going back to London when he knows that the funeral is over. The next morning he rises at four o'clock as usual and over his prayers reads the ninetieth Psalm, lingering over the twelfth verse, 'So teach us to number our days, that we may apply our hearts unto wisdom.' We have not the texts for the morning and afternoon sermons, but in the evening it is: 'It is a fearful thing to fall into the hands of the living God.' The next day is Sunday and from four in the morning to 9.30 in the evening, it is a day of prayer and praise and preaching. Three texts stand out in the *Diary*, 'Let me die the death of the righteous, and let my last end be like his!' Then his spirit rises and ' Great was our rejoicing in the Lord ' in the afternoon, as he preached on the New Covenant, 'I will be to them a God and they shall be to Me a people.' It was in the evening that the climax was reached and the gloom disappeared altogether. He is with his brother in the Book of Psalms, 'Rejoice in the Lord, O ye righteous; for praise is comely for the upright.'

It was Charles who taught Methodists to sing at death,
> Rejoice for a brother deceased,
> Our loss is his infinite gain,

and it would belie the whole tradition if John Wesley allowed his head 'to hang down like a bulrush' when death came so near to him. The Sunday ends on the great cry of triumph.

[1] Moore's *Life of Wesley*, ii., 378.

A fortnight later he is at Bolton in Lancashire, but this time the 'sweet praises of Israel' are too much for him. He says nothing in his *Journal* of his feelings except to praise the children, the Sunday schools, and above all, the singing. 'The spirit with which they all sing, and the beauty of many of them, so suits the melody, that I defy any to exceed it, except the singing of angels in our Father's house.' This is unusually ecstatic; but we must turn to Tyerman to learn what happened. He attempted to give out, as his second hymn, the one beginning with the words, 'Come, O Thou Traveller unknown,' but when he came to the lines—
> My company before is gone
> And I am left alone with Thee—

the bereaved old man sunk beneath emotion that was uncontrollable, burst into a flood of tears, sat down in the pulpit, and hid his face with his hands. The crowded congregation well knew the cause of his speechless excitement; singing ceased, and the chapel became a Bochim. At length Wesley recovered himself, rose again and went through a service that was never forgotten by those who were present at it.[1]

It would be difficult to find a finer comradeship between two brothers, who differed widely in opinion and in temperament, but whose gifts were complementary to each other and were consecrated to the highest ends that man can serve. John Wesley continued to assist his brother's family in financial and other ways until his own death, and the same service was continued by the Methodist people through the profits of the Book Room until Mrs. Charles Wesley died in 1822 at the advanced age of ninety-six. The official record concerning Charles Wesley in the *Minutes of Conference,* 1788, was written by his brother. In answer to the question 'who have died this year?' Charles Wesley's name occurs fifth in a list of seven. '5. Mr. Charles Wesley, who, after spending fourscore years with much sorrow and pain, quietly retired into Abraham's bosom. He had no disease, but, after a gradual decay of some months,
> The weary wheels of life stood still at last.

His least praise was his talent for poetry, although Dr. Watts did not scruple to say that "that single poem, *Wrestling Jacob,* was worth all the verses he himself had written."'

[1] Tyerman, *The Life and Times of John Wesley,* iii., 527.

XXIII
A TRIUMPHAL PROGRESS

On June 26, 1785, John Wesley wrote, 'I am become, I know not how, an honourable man. The scandal of the Cross is ceased, and all the kingdom, rich and poor, Romanists and Protestants, behave with courtesy, nay, and seeming goodwill! It seems as if I had well-nigh finished my course, and our blessed Lord was giving me an honourable discharge.' In the closing years of his life this was increasingly true, not only of Ireland, of which he was then writing, but of England, Wales and Scotland too; for his journeyings continued almost to the very end. In his northern tour in 1788 the crowds were greater than ever. Now he was more frequently invited to preach in the churches, but sometimes he was glad to take his stand in the open air because neither church nor 'house' could contain the crowds. In one place after another in Yorkshire he records his joy at the attention of the great congregations and so through Cumberland across the border into Scotland. At Dumfries he said, 'Rich and poor attended from every quarter, of whatever denomination, and everyone seemed to hear for life. Surely the Scots are the best hearers in Europe!' This stay in Scotland was a short one (less than a fortnight) and given chiefly to Glasgow and Edinburgh; but it is full of praise, not only of his hearers, but of the beauty of the countryside.

In going up to the Scottish border he had preached more than eighty sermons in eight weeks, in fifty-seven different towns and villages. There is no slackening in his activity as he returns to Yorkshire through Northumberland and Durham. Newcastle was the centre for a fortnight crowded with movement and success. Then, whether he is preaching in the polite city of Durham, or to the 'lovely congregation at Stokesley,' or the 'plain people of Whitby,' or in elegant

Scarborough, it is the same story of unusual crowds and the word of power: 'Now is the accepted time, now is the day of salvation.' On June 23 he not only travelled all the way from Hull to York, but preached at four different places on the way. He spent his birthday this year at Epworth and there must have been an overwhelming crowd of memories in his mind as he sat down in his birth-place to write in his *Journal* his impressions about his fitness for the work of God after eighty-five years of life. He admits that he is not so agile as he was: 'I do not run or walk as fast as I did'; also there is some decay in memory. Still, he knows nothing of weariness, either in travelling or preaching, and he is able to write his sermons as well as ever.

The Conference met this year in London at the end of July and lasted nine days. 'And we found the time little enough,' he says, 'being obliged to pass over many things briefly which deserved a fuller consideration.' There were, indeed, difficult matters to be considered, of which the chief were separation from the Church and the trust deeds on which the chapels were settled. The probability that Wesley's long life was drawing to an end made both these questions vitally important and they will demand our attention later. However great the difficulties may have been in the Conference itself, there was unity and it 'ended, as it began, in great peace.' One of the preachers thought the work went very slowly, 'but what made amends for this was the love and gentleness which seemed to prevail through the whole.'[1] After three days' work over his papers and finishing his London work, Wesley preached on the Sunday morning at West Street and in the evening at City Road, setting out immediately afterwards by the mail-coach for Portsmouth, and so on to the West of England and South Wales. This was followed by a month of strenuous labour with Bristol as the centre, and then, during the winter months London became the headquarters for a series of preaching tours into East Anglia, Oxfordshire, Northampton, Kent and Sussex, Hertfordshire, Kent again, and in the new year, the Home Counties once more, setting out for his long tour to Bristol and Ireland at the beginning of March, 1789.

Tyerman has preserved from an old *Methodist Magazine*

[1] Valton's MS. *Journal* quoted in note Wesley's *Journal*, vii. 423.

an interesting story of Wesley's first attempt at extempore preaching.

On the last Sunday in the year (1788) he says he had an exceedingly large congregation in Allhallows Church, Lombard Street; and, concerning this, there is an anecdote worth relating. The sermon was for the benefit of forty-eight poor children belonging to St. Ethelburga Society. 'Sir,' said Wesley to his attendant whilst putting on his gown, 'It is above fifty years since I first preached in this church; I remember it from a particular circumstance. I came without a sermon; and, going up the pulpit stairs, I hesitated, and returned into the vestry, under much mental confusion and agitation. A woman, who stood by, noticed my concern, and said. "Pray, sir, what is the matter?" I replied, "I have not brought a sermon with me." Putting her hand on my shoulder, she said, "Is that all? Cannot you trust God for a sermon?" This question had such an effect upon me, that I ascended the pulpit, preached extempore, with great freedom to myself, and acceptance to the people; and have never since taken a written sermon into the pulpit.'[1]

On January 5, 1789, he sat for his portrait to Romney, and seemed chiefly delighted by the speed of the artist. So little time was wasted. 'Mr. Romney is a painter indeed,' he says. 'He struck off an exact likeness at once, and did more in one hour than Sir Joshua did in ten.' Certainly, the Romney portrait is a fine piece of work, but we should have liked to have had the chance of comparing it with the work of Sir Joshua. Unfortunately the Reynolds portrait has disappeared; it is thought that it perished in a fire at Dangan Castle, where Wellington's father, the Earl of Mornington, kept it. It is interesting to notice that both the portraits were connected with Ireland, for if his Irish kinsfolk, the Wellesleys, possessed the one, it was an Irish friend, Mrs. Tighe of Rosanna, who commissioned Romney to paint the other.

It is to Ireland that we must now turn our steps, for in 1789 he paid his last and twenty-first visit to Ireland. At an early period, several of his preachers expressed their regret that Wesley and his brother should go there so frequently and send so many preachers there; but his reply, full of true insight, was: 'Have patience and Ireland will repay you.'

He frequently seems to have set out on his travels by the Sunday night mail, which could hardly have won the approval of many of his strictly Sabbatarian followers of the early Victorian period. In this respect nineteenth-century Metho-

[1] Tyerman, *Life and Times of John Wesley*, iii.. 563.

dism was more narrowly severe than the Methodism of the eighteenth century. After a busy Sunday he says: 'At seven in the evening I took the mail-coach, and, having three of our brethren, we spent a comfortable night, partly in sound sleep and partly in singing praise to God. It will now quickly be seen whether they who prophesied some time since that I should not outlive this month be sent of God or not. One way or the other, it is my care to be always ready.'

We must not linger at Bristol, or Birmingham, or Shrewsbury by the way, nor share the discomforts of a stormy crossing. The same signs of eager interest in his visits are found everywhere. Landing at Dublin on the Sunday morning of March 29, with Joseph Bradford as his companion, he goes straight up to the new chapel and preaches 'on the sickness and recovery of King Hezekiah and King George.' This is a reference to the recovery of George III from his first attack of insanity, which saved the country from a Fox administration, which Wesley would have considered to be a calamity. It was the King's concern for morality as contrasted with the reckless and somewhat profligate entourage of Charles James Fox and the Prince of Wales that seems to have made Wesley so strong a supporter of the King and Mr. Pitt at this time. This was to be the year of the storming of the Bastille, but we shall find not a syllable about the French Revolution in Wesley's *Journal,* though we can well imagine what his comments might have been. 'Read Burke,' we find in the *Diary* for December 22 and 23, 1790, and there is little doubt that the *Reflections on the French Revolution* would be as likely to win his approval as *Taxation no Tyranny* did fifteen years before.

On the Monday morning Wesley began his preaching crusade and after a fortnight in Dublin, set out on a tour that took him to nearly every part of the island. Although he was assailed, as he says, with 'letter upon letter' on the subject of separation from the Church and the additional Sunday service which Dr. Coke had introduced at Dublin, personally he met with great respect and attention. Mr. Myles says he 'never saw the venerable evangelist more honoured by those who were not members of the Society than at this time. They seemed to think it a blessing to have him under their roof, and such a sacred influence attended his words that it was no ordinary privilege to have the opportunity of listening to his conversation.'[1] We shall have to consider the question in dispute at Dublin later, but meanwhile we will set out with Wesley upon his travels. His course was very much the same as that he had taken in 1787. First he travelled west to the centre of the country, then south and south-east and along the south coast to Cork and Bandon, then north through Limerick to Sligo and finally through Ulster back to Dublin.

Wesley continued to write up his *Journal* notes for more than a year after this date, and there is no slackening of interest in his clear, crisp comments, but there are several references to illness in the Irish round. Still, he kept his appointments regularly and kept rising at four in the morning for the most part. Occasionally, if a long journey had to be faced, it was an hour earlier, but sometimes he had to call upon Bradford to preach for him. Everywhere he seems to find signs of progress and again and again he repeats that he never saw such a congregation in some particular place before. The whole record must be read to appreciate the unabated energy and enthusiasm of the veteran. Very rarely is there a sign of opposition and there are several references to the friendliness of Roman Catholics. Near Limerick he reports that an 'uncommon flame' of revival had 'lately broke out,' and that some of the Societies had doubled in number, while others had 'increased six or even ten fold. All the neighbouring gentry were likewise gathered together, so that no house could contain them, but I was obliged to stand abroad. The people, as it were, swallowed every word, and great was our rejoicing in the Lord.'

Rain seemed to follow the preachers as they turned their faces to the north, but it was unable to diminish either the size of the congregations or the zeal of the evangelists. Like a good Irishman, C. H. Crookshank ignores the rain in his account of this campaign, but he is able to add details that are not found in the *Journal*. 'At Clones Wesley preached in the Danish fort to about four thousand people. One of the hearers was William Ferguson, who in the following year entered the itinerancy, and became a most devoted, exemplary and useful preacher.'[2] Ferguson was not the only young

[1] Crookshank's *History of Methodism in Ireland*, i., 451.   [2] *ibid*, 458.

man who heard the call to the hard toil of the Methodist preacher as Wesley continued his farewell visitation of the Irish Societies. From the beginning of his work in Ireland until his death no less than one hundred and thirty-seven men entered on the active work of the itinerancy, some of whom were amongst the most distinguished leaders of the Methodist Societies in the three kingdoms. Four of these were afterwards Presidents of the Conference in England. We read of an 'unwieldy multitude in the market-house at Enniskillen,' and it is natural to find great crowds in towns like Londonderry and Belfast, but it is the same story at small places like Ballymena and Tanderagee and Dungannon. At the last place he preached in the castle yard, 'it is a lovely place, and contained a huge congregation.'

Making all allowance for Wesley's optimistic outlook, the tour may, without exaggeration, be called a triumphal procession. It was closed by the Conference which met at Dublin on July 3, and ended on Tuesday, July 7. Most of the English preachers had now left the country and therefore the Conference consisted almost entirely of Irishmen. Wesley wrote of them in his *Journal,* 'I had much satisfaction with this Conference, in which, conversing with between forty and fifty travelling preachers, I found such a body of men as I hardly believed could have been found together in Ireland; men of so sound experience, so deep piety and so strong understanding. I am convinced they are no way inferior to the English Conference, except it be in number.' The increase in membership during the year was nearly one thousand eight hundred. Wesley attributed the increase to the unanimity of spirit among the preachers and to their resolve not to leave the Church. Mr. Crookshank adds, 'It is rather amusing to read the following minute—" Except in extraordinary cases, every preacher is to go to bed before ten o'clock." This year the first Pastoral Address was written. It was signed by Mr. Wesley, subsequently adopted verbatim by the British Conference, and consists of a statement of the increasing pressure that had come on the Contingent Fund, and an appeal for further assistance, urged on the ground of the increasing number and wealth of the Society.'[1]

On the Conference Sunday the Methodists crowded to St.

[1] Crookshank's *History of Methodism in Ireland,* i., 462.

Patrick's, where the Dean preached ' a serious, useful sermon and we had such a company of communicants as, I suppose, had scarce been seen there together for above a hundred years.' The following Sunday (July 12) Wesley preached his farewell sermon. We had better turn to C. H. Crookshank's account for the record of that memorable good-bye to Ireland:

At the conclusion he gave out the hymn beginning—' Come, let us join our friends above,' commented on its sentiments, and pronounced it the sweetest hymn his brother ever wrote. Having administered the Lord's Supper to several hundreds of the Society, he dined in the house of Mr. R. D'Olier, commended in prayer the family to the protection and blessing of the Almighty, and proceeded to the packet, accompanied by several members of the household and other friends, who were joined by a multitude at the quay. The scene was most touching as Wesley bade adieu to Ireland for ever. Before going on board, he gave out a hymn, and the crowd joined him in singing. He then knelt down, and asked God to bless them and their families, the Church, and especially Ireland. Shaking of hands followed, many wept, and not a few fell on the old man's neck and kissed him. He went on deck, the vessel moved, and then with his hands still lifted in prayer the winds of heaven wafted him from an island which he dearly loved, and the Irish Methodists ' saw his face no more.'[1]

Returning to England, Wesley found the same eagerness to hear that had been so manifest in Ireland. Probably many attended his services out of curiosity to see one whose labours had extended to all parts of the country for fifty years and who could not be expected to continue his wandering life much longer. We are impressed, too, by his reports of the crowds of Methodists who gathered at the Lord's Table. At Manchester on Sunday, July 19, he preached twice and, assisted by Dr. Coke, ' administered the sacrament to eleven or twelve hundred communicants.' A fortnight later at the Conference at Leeds, where he was assisted by three other clergymen, fifteen or sixteen hundred communicated. Some of the time between these two great festivals was spent at Otley in preparing for the work of the Conference. He was probably staying in that beautiful little town, at the home of his friend Elizabeth Ritchie, whose father, a retired ship's surgeon, had died there nine years before. He was far from well but managed to preach in several Yorkshire centres, notably in the drenching rain at Dewsbury. Here, he had lost the use of his preaching-house through an imperfect

[1] Crookshank, *History of Methodism in Ireland*, i., 463.

trust-deed and the unworthy action of his former book-steward, John Atlay.

Trust deeds and the warm subject of separation from the Church were the main themes for consideration at the Leeds Conference. What may be called the Conference sermon was preached by a layman, Dr. James Hamilton, and opposed the notion of Methodism becoming a 'separate people.' Wesley himself conducted all the business of the Conference as usual and preached every day during its sessions. More than a hundred preachers attended. The usual questions about preachers who were admitted on trial, preachers who had died, or withdrawn, where the preachers were stationed, what was the state of the finances, what the numbers of members in the Societies were all answered. This year no return of membership from Ireland was given presumably because it had already been made at the Dublin Conference. There was, however, an increase of over three thousand in Great Britain. It was resolved to build a new 'house' at Dewsbury and over £200 was subscribed in the Conference. Wesley and Coke opened the subscription with £50 each. No other preaching-house was to be built during the year.

Some of the questions and the answers to them, deserve to be given as they stand in the *Minutes*:

Q.20.—Are there any directions to be given to the Preachers?
A. 1.—Let the Rules of the Society be read in every Society once a quarter.
    2.—No person shall be admitted into the love-feasts without a Society ticket, or a note from the Assistant.
    3.—Every watch-night shall continue till midnight.
    4.—The money collected at the love-feasts shall be most conscientiously given to the poor.
    5.—It is advised that no Preacher go out to supper, or be from home after nine at night.
Q.21.—We are frequently reproached with the dress of our Preachers' children: how ought they to dress?
A. Exactly according to the rule of the Bands.
Q.22.—Are there any directions to be given concerning the books?
A. No books are to be published without Mr. Wesley's sanction; and those which are approved of by him shall be printed in his press in London, and sold by his book-keeper.
Q.23.—Are there any directions to be given concerning Scotland?
A. Only one Preacher is to come in future to the Conference from Scotland, except those who are to be admitted into full connexion.

The day the Conference ended Wesley set out for London in the afternoon, travelling seventy miles to Newark. His stay in London was short as he arrived on Friday afternoon and was away by mail-coach on the Sunday night for the West of England.

We must now turn our attention to his last visit to Cornwall, the county of so many difficulties and victories. He hurried on from Bristol to Plymouth, preaching at Taunton, Cullompton and Exeter on the way. There was a great audience at Plymouth, but a still larger one at Devonport (or Plymouth Dock as he calls it) on the Sunday. ' In the morning I believe we had not less than six hundred communicants, but they were all admirably well-behaved, as if they indeed discerned the Lord's body. But when I preached in the afternoon the house would not hold half the congregation. I chose the space adjoining the south side of the house, capable of containing some thousands of people. Besides, some hundreds sat on the ridge of the rock which ran along at my left hand. I preached on part of the Gospel for the day, " He beheld the city, and wept over it " ; and it seemed as if everyone felt

> His heart is made of tenderness,
> His bowels melt with love.'

He was up at two-thirty the next morning and after an early cup of tea, set out at three to cross the Hamoaze and begin his farewell visit to Cornwall. The *Journal* is as matter-of-fact as ever, with an occasional note of joy and wonder, but he must have received a royal welcome. Richard Watson says, ' When he was last in Cornwall Wesley passed through the towns and villages as in a triumphal march, whilst the windows were crowded with people anxious to get a sight of him and to pronounce upon him their benedictions ; yet he says not a word of it all! ' [1]

Neither at St. Austell, nor at Truro, could the chapel accommodate the crowds that gathered. At Falmouth he says, ' The last time I was here, above forty years ago, I was taken prisoner by an immense mob, gaping and roaring like lions. But how is the tide turned ! High and low now lined the street, from one end of the town to the other, out of stark love and kindness, gaping and staring as if the king were

[1] Watson's *Life of Wesley*, p. 160.

going by.' Watson must have forgotten this when he wrote, and Wesley himself is in error, for he had been at Falmouth in September, 1755 and August, 1770. In the High Street at Helston, he preached 'to the largest and most serious congregation I ever remember to have seen there.' St. Just provided 'a lovely congregation,' and neither at Newlyn nor Penzance, were the chapels big enough for his services. At Redruth he preached from the steps of the market-house to a 'huge multitude,' and his Saturday night comment is, 'I know not that I ever spent such a week in Cornwall before.'

On the Sunday morning (August 23) he was up at four as usual. It would seem from his *Diary* that the old man dressed and sat dozing before he wrote up his narrative. Then he took the morning service at Redruth and it is a sign of increasing weakness that he slept a little in the afternoon before his great service in the 'amphitheatre,' which is his name for Gwennap Pit. He supposed it would be his last service there, 'for my voice cannot now command the still-increasing multitude. It was supposed they were now more than five-and-twenty thousand.' The next day he returns to Marazion and Penzance, and on Tuesday to St. Ives. There, in the market-place, 'well-nigh all the town attended, and with all possible seriousness, surely forty years' labour has not been in vain here.' The same story continues in his rapid return journey from Land's End to Launceston. The same eager gathering of the people together at place after place, large or small. He cannot be charged with over-statement when he makes his last comment on Cornwall: 'So there's a fair prospect in Cornwall from Launceston to Land's End.' Indeed, the foundations of Methodism in the Duchy had been well and truly laid.

We cannot follow his journeys first with Bristol as the centre, and then from London during the remainder of the year. Nor can we share the triumphs of his last great tour of 1790, which lasted from March 1 to October 2, and took him as far north as Aberdeen, back to his last Conference at Bristol, and then home to London. He writes in his *Journal* on January 1: 'I am now an old man, decayed from head to foot,' and there are many signs of growing weakness in sight and speech as he travels on. Yet it is an amazing record. Everywhere people must have felt that it was their last opportunity of seeing England's greatest evangelist. The old days of criticism and fierce opposition seemed forgotten. Men and women of all classes and of every denomination of Christians seemed to combine to do him honour. In the last year of his life what he had said in 1785 was still more clearly demonstrated: 'I am become, I know not how, an honourable man.'

XXIV

PROBLEMS AND DIFFICULTIES

> Does the road wind uphill all the way?
> Yes, to the very end.

It must not be assumed that because Wesley enjoyed so many tokens of veneration and esteem in the last years of his life, that he was free from anxieties. 'The care of all the churches' seemed to increase as the Societies grew and multiplied not only in Great Britain, but across the Atlantic. At the Conference after his death the membership of the Society was returned as 72,476 for Great Britain and Ireland, 6,525 for the British Dominions in North America, and 57,621 for the United States. In spite of the Declaration of Independence all were counted as members of one Society. Both at home and abroad the growth was so marked that the figures lagged behind the truth. Indeed, a note was added to the effect that, in the West Indies, the increase was so rapid that only half the number was set down. Who should be the father of this great family when John Wesley died? John Fletcher had now been dead for some years, and there was no one who commanded the same universal esteem. Thomas Coke seemed to be the natural leader of the Methodists. In Wesley's absence he presided over the Conference in Ireland; he was a Bishop of the Methodist Episcopal Church; he was the inspirer of Methodist missions everywhere, and was destined to open a new chapter of Methodist activity in the East. Yet he never seemed to win Wesley's entire confidence and, although he became the Secretary of the Conference at Wesley's death, six other preachers were put into the chair of the Conference before his brethren entrusted Coke with that honour.

The very zeal with which Coke threw himself into every new enterprise, the generosity with which he flung his money as well as his service into the cause, a certain rashness both in utterance and action led him to be suspected of ambition. The impulsive Welshman sometimes provoked opposition by his mannerisms, but his truly Christian spirit of humble and fraternal love revealed itself in every crisis. Although an ordained priest of the Church of England he was more prepared to accept the actual situation of the Methodists in relation to the Established Church than Wesley was. As his biographer puts it, 'It was his conviction, strengthened by what from time to time he had witnessed in America, that unless some well-regulated union with the Church of England could be formed, the Methodist people would be better themselves, and would do more good to the world by becoming a Church made perfect as such, and thoroughly furnished unto every good word and work.'[1] We are not therefore surprised to find a certain restraint in Wesley's letters to Coke that have been preserved. In writing to others he complains occasionally that 'the doctor is too rash.' In writing to Asbury on September 20, 1788, about the founding of Cokesbury College at Abingdon, Maryland, Wesley says: ' But in one point, my dear brother, I am a little afraid both the doctor and you differ from me. I study to be little; you study to be great. I creep; you strut along. I found a school; you a college! Nay, and call it after your own names! O beware, do not seek to be something? Let me be nothing, and " Christ be all in all!"'[2]

These words were not altogether kind in their criticism of two such apostolic men as Coke and Asbury. Of all his followers they were nearest to him in the extent and influence of their labours. Asbury called this letter ' a bitter pill from one of my greatest friends.' The somewhat censorious tone may be due to the fact that in his later years Wesley was losing touch with the situation in America. It will be remembered that it was in 1784 that he had sent Coke across the Atlantic as superintendent of the Methodist Societies in America, with instructions to ordain Asbury as general superintendent, and at that Baltimore Conference the Methodist Episcopal Church was constituted. Three years later at another Baltimore Conference the name superintendent was changed to bishop and has been in use ever since. John Wesley did not approve

---

[1] Etheridge's *Life of Dr. Thomas Coke*, 255.
[2] *Letters of John Wesley*, viii., 91.

of this change of title, though he clearly intended Coke and Asbury to act as 'scriptural bishops,' and ordain others for the ministry. To add to his displeasure his own name was left off the Minutes of the American Conference and not restored until 1789. Moreover, John Wesley's desire that Richard Whatcoat should become joint superintendent with Asbury and Coke was ignored; it was not until 1800 that he was consecrated bishop. There were many signs in 1787 that the American brethren were not prepared to have their affairs ordered from England, even by John Wesley himself.[1]

We are not surprised to find Wesley writing to Richard Whatcoat on July 17, 1788: 'It was not well judged by Brother Asbury to *suffer,* much less indirectly to encourage, that foolish step in the late Conference. Every preacher present ought both in duty and in prudence to have said, " Brother Asbury, Mr. Wesley is *your* father, consequently ours, and we will affirm this in the face of all the world." It is truly probable the disavowing *me* will, as soon as my head is laid, occasion a total breach between the English and American Methodists.'[2] Further friction occurred in 1789 when Coke and Asbury signed a loyal address to George Washington after he had become President of the United States. Asbury was an American citizen, but when Coke returned to England he was severely taken to task by his brethren at the Bristol Conference[3] for declaring that civil and religious liberties had been transmitted to the American colonists 'by the providence of God and the glorious revolution.' It did not follow that because Coke was a British subject he was necessarily an enemy of the independence of America. Still, the war was too recent for the English Conference to take kindly to a statement to the effect that the Constitution of the United States was the 'admiration of the world,' and might become the 'great exemplar for imitation.' Neither John Wesley, nor his English preachers were republicans and Coke saw that he had made a mistake. Wesley's remark had been, 'I wish you to obey the " powers that be " in America, but I wish you to understand them too.'[4]

It is sad that these clouds gathered between John Wesley

---
[1] See Bangs' *History of the Methodist Episcopal Church,* i., 259.
[2] *Letters,* viii., 73.
[3] Not Leeds as in *Letters,* viii., 163; cf. Etheridge's *Life of Coke,* 196.
[4] *Letters,* viii., 164.

and his American 'superintendents' at the end of his life. Still, they were very transient clouds. Asbury understood the situation, and in his *Journal* for December, 1802, makes a remark that explains everything. 'I find the truth of an observation made by dear John Wesley to Dr. Coke, upon his going to Nova Scotia. The doctor said he did not think highly of the place. "That is because you have never been there," replied Wesley. "When you are there you will think and feel for the people."'[1] John Wesley's own experience of Georgia more than fifty years before, could give him but little real understanding of the problems and labours of Asbury in 1790. It is with special pleasure, therefore, that we find that one of Wesley's last letters was directed to Philadelphia. It was addressed to Ezekiel Cooper, who lived on until 1847, when he was the oldest Methodist preacher in the world. It is dated February 1, 1791. Wesley exhorts him to write a history of the work of God in America, and finishes his letter by saying: 'See that you never give place to one thought of separating from your brethren in Europe. Lose no opportunity of declaring to all men that the Methodists are one people in all the world and that it is their full determination so to continue,

> Though mountains rise, and oceans roll,
> To sever us in vain.'[2]

When the news of Wesley's death reached Asbury, he wrote a warm tribute in his *Journal* and said: 'For myself, notwithstanding my long absence from Mr. Wesley, and a few unpleasant expressions in some of the letters the dear old man has written to me (occasioned by the misrepresentations of others), I feel the stroke most sensibly; and I expect I shall never read his works without reflecting on the loss which the Church of God and the world has sustained by his death.'[3]

At home, Wesley's chief difficulties in the closing years of his life arose from the Trust Deeds upon which some of the preaching-houses had been settled, and the recurring problem of separation from the Established Church. We have seen what the difficulties over the trusts of certain chapels were in Chap. XIII, where the Birstall Chapel case was considered in some detail. Trouble of the same kind arose now at

[1] Tipple's *Heart of Asbury's Journal*, 501.
[2] *Letters*, viii., 260.
[3] Tipple's *Heart of Asbury's Journal*, 313-15.

Dewsbury, North Shields, and some other places. An amicable settlement was made at Birstall in the end, but Dewsbury was a more obstinate case. It was originally in the Birstall circuit, being five or six miles away, and the same tenacious Yorkshire characteristics were found there. In 1787 it was the head of a circuit. Three years before this date plans had been made for building a new chapel there, but some of the leading Methodists wished to have some say in the appointment of their own preachers. John Heald, a local maltster, wrote to Wesley's Book Steward, John Atlay, to know whether the trustees would have the power to make an appointment if the Conference failed to do so and would the trustees be able to reject a preacher who had been found guilty of immorality. Also the question arose whether the chapel would become the property of the trustees if the Conference failed to fulfil its duties. Atlay replied on behalf of Wesley, agreeing to these conditions; the question of ownership of the property remained open. In all deeds, property had been held on trust for Wesley and his helpers, and on the new model deed was held for the Conference.

Immediately after Atlay had written his letter, the Deed of Declaration was executed and the names of John Atlay and William Eels were not to be found among those who formed the Legal Hundred. They did not leave Wesley at once as John Hampson did, but began to make plans for their future. The draft of the trust-deed was presented to the Manchester Conference in 1787, but it contained clauses which gave the trustees powers that Wesley had never contemplated. In particular, it gave them the right to judge the conduct of preachers of whom they did not approve. Alexander Mather tells us that the trustees were self-elected and that neither Wesley nor the Dewsbury preachers had been consulted by them. It was to Mather that the draft was presented at Manchester, and he objected strongly to the clauses in question, pointing out that the ministers must be tried by their peers. The Conference appointed a deputation of five preachers to meet the trustees at Dewsbury on August 14, but the trustees would not give way, although Mather and his colleagues went as far as they could in the way of compromise.[1] It became evident later that Atlay was encouraging the

[1] Mather's *Supplement to Dr. Coke's State of the Dewsbury House*, 7.

trustees in their opposition at the time, though he did see that such powers given to trustees would endanger the whole itinerant plan[1] and that he himself might be excluded from the Dewsbury pulpit.

A further vain attempt at a peaceful settlement was made in February, 1788, and the business had to be referred to the London Conference of that year. Atlay, who was present, declared that if he were to go down to Dewsbury he could settle matters with the trustees. By this time, however, Mather had become aware of his double dealing and his offer was not accepted. The Conference deputation that did go met with no success, and on August 19, Atlay wrote to Wesley to inform him that he had accepted the invitation of the Dewsbury trustees to be their minister and must therefore resign his position as Book Steward.[2] He did not go to Dewsbury until September 24, and spent the interval in making a misleading return of the value of the stock at the Book Room. Wesley withdrew his own preachers and Dewsbury was put, for the next three years, into the Bradford circuit. The new chapel passed into the hands of the trustees and the work of Methodism was begun again in the town by the assistants from the neighbouring circuits preaching in the streets of Dewsbury in turns. John Pawson, who was then at Leeds, said, ' This is pain and grief to me. To preach in opposition, Methodists against Methodists, is painful beyond expression. I believe all might have been prevented by loving, prudent preachers.'

Possibly that might be true. Neither the tact of Mather nor of Wesley himself was perfect in this case, and it is clear that Dewsbury had suffered at the hands of some weak preachers. The obstinacy of the trustees was strengthened by Atlay, and he secured the help of William Eels, who was also disaffected. Eels had been overlooked by the 1788 Conference when appointments were made and was actually in Dewsbury when Atlay arrived.[3] Between them they succeeded in taking over nearly the entire congregation with them. Later Eels went to North Shields to take charge of a chapel about which a similar dispute had arisen. Fortunately there were two preaching-houses at North Shields, one of

---
[1] *Letters*, viii., 52-3. [2] *ibid*, 84.
[3] Tyerman's *Life and Times of John Wesley*, iii., 558.

which had adopted the Conference plan. After months of dispute Wesley ordered the Newcastle preachers to cease to supply the Milbourn Place Chapel unless it were settled on the 'Methodist plan.'[1] Here again Pawson thought his leader was too hasty. It is interesting to note that Pawson was called in to effect a reunion at Dewsbury after Wesley's death. Atlay had then given up his task and Eels died shortly afterwards. This problem has occupied our attention too long, but it comes up again and again in Wesley's letters, and caused him untold anxiety. An appeal was made at the 1789 Conference for subscriptions for a new chapel at Dewsbury, and £208 was raised there and then. The next month, Wesley sent an appeal to all the preachers. In September he wrote a pathetic appeal for support to the Methodist people throughout the country, 'for the love of God, for the love of me, your old and well-nigh worn-out servant, for the love of ancient Methodism, which, if itinerancy is interrupted will speedily come to nothing.'[2] A year before his death he shows his sense of the importance of this subject by begging the trustees at Trowbridge to settle their chapel on the model deed. 'I have only one thing in view,' he says, 'to keep all the Methodists in Great Britain one connected people. But this can't be done unless the Conference, not the trustees, appoint all their preachers.'[3]

He suffered equal anxiety during the closing years of his life because it seemed probable that his death would lead to disputes and divisions among his followers over the complete separation of Methodism from the Church of England. Neither he nor his brother Charles had much doubt that a complete separation would take place, but they feared that a separated Methodism would become a dry and formal sect. Charles was less in touch with the preachers and with the Societies in his later years than his brother, and his fears for the future were not relieved by the confident assurance that John Wesley had that every cautious step of irregularity had been taken under the guidance of the spirit of God. Moreover, Charles grew more conservative as he grew older, whereas in many respects John Wesley became more openminded. Still, the last word that we have from Charles

---

[1] *Letters*, viii., 131, April 11, 1789; cf. W.H.S. *Proceedings*, iv., 223-30.
[2] *Letters*, viii., 169.   [3] *ibid*, 205.

Wesley on the subject seems to imply that he had come round to his brother's view about the necessity for ordinations for Scotland and America: 'I leave America and Scotland to your latest thoughts and recognitions,' he writes on April 9, 1787, 'only observing now, that you are exactly right. Keep your authority while you live; and after your death *detur digniori*, or rather, *dignioribus*. You cannot settle the succession. You cannot divine how God will settle it.'[1] Charles Wesley once said: 'All the difference between my brother and me was that my brother's first object was the Methodists and then the Church: mine was first the Church and then the Methodists. Our different judgement of persons was owing to our different tempers, his all hope and mine all fears.'[2]

The American ordinations seem to mark the real separation from the Church of England, since all the Methodist irregularities which had taken place before that date could have been condoned by sagacious and liberal leaders of the Church of England. Such leadership would never have forced the necessity of the American and Scottish ordinations on Wesley. Of course, he did not admit that his action involved separation and explained the situation with characteristic ingenuousness. In his letter to the American Societies which is appended to the *Minutes* for 1785, he describes the Church of England as 'the best constituted national Church in the world.' Owing to the independence of the United States, he says: 'Our American brethren are now totally disentangled both from the State and the English Hierarchy.' That was his reason for refusing 'to entangle them again' with a national Church; the same argument applied to Scotland. He therefore prepared a liturgy for the use of the American Methodists, 'little differing from that of the Church of England,' according to Wesley. A careful examination of the liturgy, however, reveals many very drastic changes. There are also considerable alterations in the form for administering the Sacraments. The *Thirty-Nine Articles of Religion* are reduced to twenty-five. Many psalms are left out and many parts of others, 'as being highly improper for the mouths of a Christian congregation.' This was issued

---
[1] Tyerman's *Life and Times of John Wesley*, iii., 523.
[2] *Letters*, viii., 267.

in 1784 and the travelling preachers in America were advised to use it on the Lord's Day, reading the Litany only on Wednesdays and Fridays, and praying extempore on all other days.

Wesley explains carefully in the 1786 *Minutes* that his action in ordaining elders to administer the Sacraments in America and Scotland was not a separation from the Church. It soon became clear that further steps in that direction were necessary in England also. When Hanby and Joseph Taylor, two of his Scottish 'elders' returned to England in 1787, Wesley ordered them to put off their gowns and bands and refrain from administering the Sacraments. Taylor yielded to Wesley's request but Hanby considered it to be his duty to meet the needs of the people by administering the Lord's Supper. As both men were in the Nottingham circuit, difficulties soon arose. Hanby would not yield and Wesley's last extant letter was written to a clergyman in Lancashire to say: 'I do not approve of Mr. Hanby's baptizing children.'[1] It seemed possible that Hanby might be expelled, but Wesley died a few weeks after this letter was written. The judgement of his brethren on Hanby may be seen in the fact that he was the fourth President of the Conference after Wesley's death. How illogical was the position that Wesley had taken can be seen from the fact that on August 6, 1788, he ordained Alexander Mather, a presbyter, when he had been appointed to Wakefield, and on February 25, 1789, he ordained Henry Moore and Thomas Rankin deacons, and two days later presbyters, when they were stationed in London. These ordinations for the English work differed entirely from those that had preceded them. His edition of the Prayer Book for the Americans had, however, been issued in 1786 (with slight changes), as *The Sunday Service of the Methodists in His Majesty's Dominions*, and in 1788 as *The Sunday Service of the Methodists*.

Clearly the Methodists were moving to the same position in England that they already occupied in America and Scotland. It seems as though Dr. Coke was forcing the pace. When the subject was discussed at the 1786 Conference, we are informed by John Pawson that 'Dr. Coke thought that our public services in the large towns ought to be held in

[1] *Letters*, viii., 279.

church hours, and was freely speaking in the Conference upon that subject, and urging its necessity from the fact that nearly all the converted clergymen in the kingdom were Calvinists. Upon hearing this, Mr. Charles Wesley, with a very loud voice, and in great anger, cried out, " No," which was the only word he uttered during the whole of the Conference sittings. Mr. Mather, however, got up and confirmed what Dr. Coke had said, which we all knew to be a truth.'[1] It was a difficult matter to persuade the Methodists either to attend the preaching of or receive the Sacraments from clergy whom they could not regard as satisfactory spiritual guides. John Wesley argued and pleaded with them in vain. In 1788 he himself was ' constrained to confess, that the far greater part of these ministers I have conversed with, for above half a century, have not been holy men—not devoted to God—not deeply acquainted either with God or themselves.' Still, he hoped that the use of his form of the Book of Common Prayer might unite the Methodists to the Church rather than separate them from it. The conclusions of the discussion at the 1786 Conference were that services should be allowed in church hours

1. When the minister is a notoriously wicked man;
2. When he preaches Arian, or any equally pernicious doctrine;
3. When there are not churches in the town sufficient to contain half the people; and
4. When there is no church at all within two or three miles.[2]

These conditions did not apply to Dublin, which was soon to become a storm centre in this controversy. It was in the spring of 1788 that Coke found that many of the Methodists were in the habit of attending Dissenting chapels on the Sunday morning. He therefore arranged to hold services in the Whitefriar Street Chapel during Church hours on three Sundays out of the four. On the fourth the Methodists were invited to go to St. Patrick's Cathedral and receive the Sacrament.[3] This gave great offence to the Rev. Edward Smyth and his brother and some of the wealthy members of

[1] From Tyerman's *Life and Times of John Wesley*, iii., 478.
[2] *Minutes*, i., 193.
[3] Crookshank's *History of Methodism in Ireland*, i., 442.

the Dublin Society. Smyth was a clergyman, the nephew of an archbishop, who had become a Methodist, and was now preaching at a proprietary chapel called Bethesda, which his brother William had first built at his own expense. Probably the Smyths feared that the Bethesda congregations would be affected by the Whitefriar Street services. The Dublin assistant, Henry Moore, appealed to Wesley, who said: 'The Doctor is too warm. We must have no more service at Whitefriar's in the Church hours.' Ten days later he wrote again, agreeing to Dr Coke's arrangement.[1] It was inevitable that the question should come up at the Conference and we are not therefore surprised to find in the *Minutes* for 1788 that

> The assistants shall have a discretionary power to read the Prayer Book in the preaching-houses on Sunday morning, where they think it expedient, if the generality of the Society acquiesce with it; on condition that Divine Service never be performed in the Church hours on the Sundays when the Sacrament is administered in the parish church where the preaching-house is situated; and that the people be strenuously exhorted to attend the Sacrament in the parish church on these Sundays.

This was the situation when Wesley arrived in Dublin on his last visit to Ireland after a stormy voyage on the morning of Sunday, March 29, 1789. He was ill, but went straight to the Whitefriar Street Chapel and preached. Afterwards he administered the Lord's Supper to about five hundred communicants and called on the junior minister, William Myles, to assist him. Mr. Myles was not ordained, and the following week Wesley was attacked for his action in the columns of the *Evening Post*. Also he received 'letter upon letter' concerning the additional Sunday services. Indeed, a three months' newspaper controversy followed. At the close of his tour Wesley wrote to one of his preachers in Scotland and said: 'Dr. Coke has raised a storm almost in every part of this kingdom by talking of leaving the Church.'[2] He modified this a fortnight later when he wrote from Chester to Henry Moore (who was still at Dublin): 'Not anything which Dr. Coke has said or done, but the vile, wilful misrepresentation of it, had set all Ireland in a flame. But I am in hope it is now in a great measure quenched. It has brought a flood of obloquy upon me.'[3] Nearly a year later

---

[1] *Letters*, viii., 58-9.   [2] *ibid*, 150.   [3] *ibid*, 152.

he was to be found writing from the same place to the same correspondent: 'Is the Society in Dublin quiet or no? Are a majority of the people for retaining or for abolishing the eleven o'clock service? Surely Dr. Coke is not well in his senses.'[1]

Wesley had such a magnificent reception everywhere in Ireland on his last tour that it was a pity that he could not escape from these rebukes about leaving the Church. In the end he had to issue public manifestos on the subject. He reviewed the history of the whole question. He denied that he had left the Church. He claimed that Archbishops Potter and Secker agreed with him, though Archbishop Potter had said: 'These gentlemen are irregular; but they have done good, and I pray God to bless them.' He admitted his irregularities, but all the time he was denying that the Methodists had left the Church, he was defending the Methodist services in Church hours. When he was in Cork in May, 1789, he wrote his well-known Korah, Dathan and Abiram sermon and published it in his magazine twelve months afterwards. His text was: 'No man taketh this honour unto himself, but he that is called of God, as was Aaron.' He shows the difference between the office of the prophet and that of the priest. The Methodist preachers were not priests, he said; they were God's extraordinary messengers who had been called to stir up the regular ministry. He begs them to be Church of England men still. He denies his own inconsistency, but defends himself by saying: 'I say, put these two principles together, first, I will not *separate* from the Church; yet, secondly, in cases of necessity, I will *vary* from it; and inconsistency vanishes away. I have been true to my profession from 1730 to this day.'

It almost seems as though Wesley's sentiment got the better of his logic in this case. His preachers saw the matter more clearly. Most of them and most of the chapels were licensed under the Toleration Act. Yet they had not the legal rights of Dissenters, since they were not Dissenters. Several cases of persecution arose from this anomalous situation. A small minority of the people might desire to keep the Methodist Societies within the fold of the Established Church, but the great majority wished to receive the Sacraments from their

[1] *Letters*, viii., 216.

own preachers. There seemed every likelihood of a great division on this issue at Wesley's death. In the end peaceful counsels prevailed and by the Plan of Pacification of 1795 the will of the majority prevailed. It is interesting to observe that during the last decade of the century the membership of the Societies was increasing at a rate that had never been known before. So Wesley was wrong in his fears; the Methodists were separated from the Church and their success was greater than ever.

XXV
A PEACEFUL CLOSE

WESLEY wrote in his *Journal* on the first of January, 1790, 'I am now an old man, decayed from head to foot. My eyes are dim, my right hand shakes much, my mouth is hot and dry every morning, I have a lingering fever almost every day, my motion is weak and slow. However, blessed be God, I do not slack my labour. I can preach and write still.' That gives the note of the remaining fourteen months of his life. He gave up keeping his accounts in July, saying that he had kept them exactly for eighty-six years and was satisfied that he had carried out his own injunctions of his famous sermon on the use of money. Towards the end of October his *Journal* came suddenly to an end, but he kept up the terse entries in his *Diary* to within six days of his death. Henry Moore, who was living in the same house with him at that time, as assistant at City Road, was greatly surprised when he read the above extract from the *Journal*. He had not imagined the weakness to be so great. 'He still rose at his usual hour, four o'clock,' he says, 'and went through the many duties of the day, not, indeed, with the same apparent vigour, but without complaint, and with a degree of resolution that was astonishing.' Still, throughout the year we find signs of growing feebleness. The great crowds must often have found it impossible to hear what the old man was saying. Sometimes there were lapses of memory in public, sometimes he failed to see the print either of his Bible or hymn-book. In September he wrote to Robert Carr Brackenbury: 'My body seems nearly to have done its work and to be almost worn out. Last month my strength was nearly gone, and I could have sat almost still from morning to night. But, blessed be God, I crept about a little, and made shift to preach once a day.'[1]

Bodily weakness, however, did not prevent him carrying out

---
[1] *Letters*, viii., 237-8.

his usual programme. We find him this year as far north as Aberdeen, as far west as Haverfordwest, in the Isle of Wight, in East Anglia, in Kent and in Sussex. Most of his journeys were done in his own chaise, but on one occasion one of his horses died on the road and he had to take a post-chaise to get to Stockport. He travelled by coach to Norwich, but in some of his East Anglian journeys the coach failed and he had to hire as best he could. From Swaffham to Kings Lynn, in the middle of October, he rode in an open, single-horse chaise. 'The wind with mizzling rain, came full in our faces, and we had nothing to screen us from it, so that I was thoroughly chilled from head to foot before I came to Lynn. But I soon forgot this little inconvenience, for which the earnestness of the congregation made me large amends.' A week before at Colchester, according to Crabb Robinson, he had to be supported in the pulpit by two of his preachers as he preached, and his voice was scarcely audible. A week later he closed his *Journal* for ever. When we remember these facts, it is the indomitable spirit of the man, rather than his physical toughness that arrests our attention. We must not think of him as an object of pity. His bright conversation, his fresh complexion, his neat appearance were unchanged. Crabbe the poet, who heard him preach at Lowestoft about the same time, was charmed by his reverend appearance, his cheerful air and the beautiful cadence he gave to the lines

> Oft am I by woman told,
> Poor Anacreon! thou grow'st old.[1]

Certainly we can trace no decline in his enthusiasm for his great cause, nor in his alert and inquisitive mind during these months. One reason why Wesley's *Journal* deserves to stand side by side with the *Diaries* of Pepys and Evelyn is because he had as much interest in curiosities and odd happenings as either of them. It is an ill-assorted trio in other respects, for Wesley was a much more distinct and interesting personality than the latter and, though quite as human, certainly more godly than the former. There are at least three entries in his *Journal* for 1790 that might have come straight from the pages of Evelyn or Pepys. At Northwich he found 'one of the most extraordinary phenomena I ever saw or heard of: Mr. Sellers has in his yard a

[1] See Tyerman's *Life and Times of John Wesley*, iii., 628-9.

large Newfoundland dog and an old raven. These have fallen deeply in love with each other, and never desire to be apart. The bird has learned the bark of the dog, so that few can distinguish them. She is inconsolable when he goes out, and, if he stays out a day or two, she will get up all the bones and scraps she can, and hoard them up for him till he comes back.' At Bristol, 'William Kingston, the man born without arms,' came to see him. It is true that he came as an inquirer for salvation, but Wesley shows a boy's keen interest in his unusual visitor. ' He is of middling height and size, has a pleasing look and voice, and an easy, agreeable behaviour. At breakfast he shook off his shoes, which are made on purpose, took the tea-cup between his toes, and the toast with his other foot. He likewise writes a fair hand, and does most things with his feet which we do with our hands.'

John Wesley, at eighty-seven, seems more enthusiastic over this deformed man, who used his feet instead of his hands when he drank tea with him, than some of us might have been even when we were young. A fortnight later we find a still more thrilling entry in the *Journal*. It is Bristol Fair and some one apparently takes the old man down to the Fair to see its chief wonder. ' I was desired to see a monster, properly speaking. He was as large as the largest lion in the Tower, but covered with rough hair of a brown colour; has the head of a swine and feet like a mole. It is plain to me it was begotten between a bear and a wild boar. He lives on fruit and bread, chiefly the latter. The keeper handles him as he pleases, putting his hand in his mouth and taking hold of his tongue; but he has a horrible roar, between that of a lion and a bull.' After that vivid account it is almost depressing to read the explanation of the zoologist that it was probably an Indian sloth-bear, Melursus ursinus. But Wesley saw more than the sloth. ' At the same time I saw a pelican. Is it not strange that we have no true account or picture of this bird? It is one of the most beautiful in nature, being, indeed, a large swan, almost twice as big as a tame one, snow-white and elegantly shaped. Only its neck is three-quarters of a yard long, and capable of being so distended as to contain two gallons of liquid or solid. She builds her nest in some wood, not far from a river, from which she daily brings a quantity of fish to her young. This she carries in her neck (the only pouch she has), and then divides it among her young; and hence is fabricated the idle tale of her feeding them with her blood.'

We cannot follow the eager, enthusiastic old man in his itinerary. He spent January and February in and about London, and set out as usual on March 1 on his long journey. After visiting Bristol he went up into the Midlands to Birmingham, preaching to crowds at place after place. Shropshire, Staffordshire and Cheshire saw him for the last time. On Easter Day at Manchester: 'We had about one thousand six hundred communicants. I preached both morning and evening, without weariness, and in the evening lay down in peace.' Wicked Wigan he found wicked no longer, while Bolton's 'lovely house' had 'one of the loveliest congregations in England.' It was a long journey through Yorkshire and over the border as far as Aberdeen, but the chaise travelled well. On Tyneside as he went north he preached on May 9 to several thousands of people in the open air. Newcastle was again a port of call on the return journey, with the note about the Orphan House: 'In this and Kingswood house, were I to do my own will, I should choose to spend the short remainder of my days. But it cannot be; this is not my rest.' So he presses on to York and Lincoln, with a characteristic comparison between the two cathedrals; then back to his native Epworth for a last visit, preaching in the market-place on 'How shall we escape if we neglect so great salvation?' to such a congregation as was never seen in Epworth before.

Passing through Sheffield, Derby, Nottingham and Leicester to London, he is in Bristol on July 19 to prepare for his last Conference, which opened in the 'New Room' a week later. Here the *Journal* fails us altogether and the terse abbreviations of the *Diary* give us no information about the subjects under discussion there. Charles Atmore said, 'Mr. Wesley appeared very feeble; his eyesight had failed so much that he could not see to give out the hymns; yet his voice was strong, his spirit remarkably lively, and the powers of his mind and his love towards his fellow-creatures, were as bright and as ardent as ever.'[1] Joseph Sutcliffe, who was that year

[1] See Tyerman's *Life and Times of John Wesley*, iii., 618.

received into Full Connexion, says: 'About 150 preachers were present; and assuredly it was a friendly meeting of the brethren. Mr. Wesley, amidst his sons, looked fresh and lively, and likely to run out his course for years to come. . . . A long table being placed across the chapel, which had no pews, Mr. Wesley sat in a chair at the head of the table, and about twenty venerable men in the benches ten on each side. Mr. Mather conducted the whole business, and Mr. Valton was the secretary with his small quarto ledger.' Another preacher speaks of Wesley's sermon on Colossians ii. 6, and says that the preachers were much affected and edified and went back to their circuits 'greatly strengthened in our attachment to each other, to our venerable father in the gospel and to the cause of our God and Saviour.'[1] There can be no doubt about the affection of the preachers for one another and for the cause; nothing else could explain the remarkable unity and progress of the Connexion after the death of their leader. Turning to the *Minutes of Conference*, apart from the usual questions about the ministry and the stations of the preachers, finance and the settlement of all chapels on the Model Deed seem the most important subjects of consideration. Collections were again made for Dewsbury, and not only was it laid down that 'all preaching-houses are to be settled on the Methodist plan,' but as a later instruction to a special Conference building committee it was stated that not a stone must be laid 'till the house is settled after the Methodist form, verbatim.'

We may be quite sure that much time was given to prayer and praise and meditation on the message of the gospel. Preachers were forbidden to preach three times on the same day to the same congregation, and not to preach oftener than twice on a week-day, or oftener than three times on the Lord's Day. It appears from the *Life of Adam Clarke* that Wesley was really afraid that some of his preachers were in danger of shortening their lives by excessive labour. The illnesses of Adam Clarke himself, for whom he had a particular affection, caused him great anxiety. In June he had written to Mrs. Clarke suggesting that her husband should go to a circuit where there could be 'much rest and little work.' It is hard to imagine where that could be, when we consider the

[1] *Wesleyan Methodist Magazine*, 1843, p. 181.

size of the great 'rounds' of that day. All he could think of was that Adam Clarke and his wife should spend September 'in my rooms at Kingswood, on condition that he shall preach but twice a week and ride to the Hot Wells every day.'[1] In the end he went to the difficult and responsible post of superintendent at Dublin and Wesley had many forebodings on the subject. Three weeks before his own death he writes to him: 'I will desire Dr. Whitehead to consider your case and give you his thoughts upon it. I am not afraid of your doing too little, but too much. I am in continual danger of this.'[2] With him, as with all his best preachers, the sense of duty was stronger than any self-pity or self-indulgence. It was more than a year before Adam Clarke recovered.

After the Conference Wesley set out on a tour through South Wales. In three weeks he preached at twenty different places between Gloucester and Pembroke and then returned to spend a month in and about Bristol visiting the Societies. On September 27 he said good-bye to the west and wrote in his *Journal*: 'I left Bristol; about eleven I preached in the Devizes, and in the evening at Sarum. I do not know that ever I saw the house so crowded before with high and low, rich and poor, so that I hope we shall again see fruit here also.' He makes similar remarks on the day following about Winchester (or Winton as he calls it). We feel that in these last tours many came out of curiosity to hear Wesley preaching, knowing that they might not have another opportunity. He had become a national figure and all sorts of people wished to see him. This had the advantage of giving us such impressions as the boy Walter Scott remembered when he heard Wesley at Kelso in 1784, and also those valuable sidelights from Crabb Robinson's *Diary* and the *Life of Crabbe* that came from the East Anglian tour of October, 1790. This tour was one of a series of what he used to call his 'little journeys,' made from London in the last three months of the year. From his *Diary* we find him also in the counties of Hertford, Bedford, Huntingdon, Northampton, Oxford and Buckingham, as well as in Kent and Sussex. Much time also was given to the Societies in and about London, and his routine seems to be as strenuous as ever.

It is fortunate that for the last weeks of Wesley's life we

---

[1] *Letters*, viii., 220.   [2] *ibid*, 261.

have the charming account of Elizabeth Ritchie, whose affection and veneration for John Wesley, was almost equalled by his esteem for her. Ten years before this he feared she was dying of consumption, and wrote to John Valton, when she went to the Hot Wells at Bristol: 'I send you herewith one of our Lord's jewels, my dear Miss Ritchie; such an one as you have hardly seen before.'[1] She recovered from her serious illness and, with her 'twin soul,' Hester Ann Rogers, did much to brighten the closing years of Wesley's life. It was a very happy coincidence that they were both living in the preacher's house at City Road in these closing days. James Rogers had been appointed to London at the Conference of 1790 as Wesley's helper there, while his wife had the oversight of the busy house at City Road Chapel, where so many Methodists were found day by day. We have seen how Wesley stayed with Miss Ritchie at Otley, while he was preparing for his last Leeds Conference. Now in November, 1790, she came on a visit to London, hoping that she would be in time for 'dear Mr. Wesley's visiting the classes, as she would be sorry to miss that fortnight of his fatherly instructions.' He was delighted to see her and pressed her to stay at the chapel-house. She consented the more readily as her friend, Hester Ann Rogers, was far from well and very glad of Miss Ritchie's help. She soon found, as she says: 'Sufficient business on my hands.'

Again and again we find in the *Diary* at this time 'E.R. read,' or 'prayed Miss R.' Sometimes we have the fact noted that E.R. read Belisarius, or a sermon or Bruce. Her account is: 'The preacher who had usually read to Mr. Wesley being absent, he said to me, " Betsy, you must be eyes to the blind." I therefore rose with pleasure about half-past five o'clock, and generally read to him from six to breakfast-time. Sometimes he would converse freely, and say, " How good is the Lord to bring you to me when I want you most! I should wish you to be with me in my dying moments. I would have you to close my eyes." When the fullness of my heart did not prevent reply, I have said, "'This, my dear sir, I would willingly do; but you live such a flying life, I do not well see how it is to be accomplished." He would close the conversation by adding, " Our God does all things well: we will leave

---

[1] *Letters*, vii., 17.

it in His hands."' He paid a visit in January, 1791, to his sister-in-law in Chesterfield Street, but the only one of his relations who had any sympathy with his work was his niece Sally. He wrote to her fairly often and said, with some pathos to her, in a letter dated October 5, 1790: 'Let me have the comfort of one relation at least that will be an assistant to me in the blessed work of God.'[1] He did his best to bring Sally Wesley and Elizabeth Ritchie together, but now the two women whom he regarded as the saints of Methodism were more to him than any of his kith and kin.

The last months were not without incidents of importance. It was on October 7 that he preached his last open-air sermon at Winchelsea. 'I stood under a large tree on the side of the church,' he says, 'and called to most of the inhabitants of the town, "The Kingdom of heaven is at hand; repent, and believe the gospel." It seemed as if all that heard were, for the present, almost persuaded to be Christians.' On February 1, 1791, he wrote to Ezekiel Cooper, of Philadelphia.[2] It was on February 23 that he preached his last sermon. 'On Wednesday morning,' says Miss Ritchie, 'Mr. Rogers went with him to Leatherhead to visit a family who have lately begun to receive the truth. They had the honour of this almost worn-out veteran in his blessed Master's service delivering his last public message beneath their roof. Oh, that all that heard may take the solemn warning, and so embrace the blessed invitation he gave them from "Seek ye the Lord while He may be found, call upon Him while He is near," as to meet our dear departed friend at God's right hand.'[3]

The next day he returned as far as Balham, staying the night with his friend, Mr. Wolff. While he was there he wrote his letter to William Wilberforce, which is perhaps as well known as any letter he ever wrote, and was the last of all. He had been particularly moved in reading that week the account of a negro slave named Gustavus Vasa, and was particularly roused by the discovery that nowhere in the West Indies was the oath of a negro admitted as testimony against the word of a white man. His passion for justice and liberty finds vigorous expression in this last letter. He says:

Dear Sir,—Unless the divine power had raised you up to be an *Athanasius contra mundum*, I see not how you can go through your

[1] *Letters*, viii., 239.   [2] *ibid*, 260. See p. 322.   [3] See *Journal*, viii., 134.

glorious enterprise in opposing that execrable villainy, which is the scandal of religion, of England, and of human nature. Unless God has raised you up for this very thing, you will be worn out by the opposition of men and devils. But if God be for you, who can be against you? Are all of them together stronger than God? O be not weary of well doing! Go on in the name of God and in the power of His might, till even American slavery (the vilest that ever saw the sun) shall vanish away before it.

This was his last word to his fellow-countrymen. He went home on the Friday morning to die. As soon as he arrived his friends saw that he was very ill, with a high temperature, and he lay most of the day dozing. He continued in much the same state throughout Saturday, but seemed rather better on the Sunday morning. He was able to talk a little and began to repeat those fragments of Scripture and verses of hymns that were afterwards cherished in Methodist reminiscences. It was a joy to him when Miss Ritchie and his niece prayed with and for him. Then he passed into delirium, but he was still either meeting classes or setting out to preach. The ruling passion of his life was with him every moment. Then he recovered full consciousness and, although he knew that he was coming to the end of his long career, he sat up in his chair and talked a little. He was worse on the Monday, but refused to have the opinion of any other physician than his friend, Dr. Whitehead. Most of that day he slept and spoke very little. The night was restless, but on the Tuesday morning he began to sing his brother's hymn: 'All glory to God in the sky,' and struggled through two verses of it. This fine hymn is a prayer for world-peace and has come back into popularity since the Great War. It adds to its wealth of meaning when we remember that it strengthened the heart of John Wesley in his last hours. His last letter was a passionate denunciation of slavery and the last hymn of his brother's that was on his lips ended with the prayer for peace.

> Thou only art able to bless,
> And make the glad nations obey,
> And bid the dire enmity cease,
> And bow the whole world to thy sway.

The secret of English nineteenth-century philanthropy is revealed clearly here. The Evangelicals have sometimes been blamed for the evils of the life in mines and factories and slums in the dark days of the early part of the nineteenth century. One wonders what the condition of England after the Industrial Revolution would have been had there been no Evangelical Revival to temper its effects.

The death-bed of John Wesley is, however, no place for controversy. Whatever may have been the limitations of his followers, there is no question about the purity of his motives and the breadth of his philanthropy. After singing, he tried to write, but found that it was beyond his power. Miss Ritchie said to him, 'Let me write for you, sir; tell me what you would say.' 'Nothing,' he replied, 'but that God is with us.' Then a little later he astonished them all by singing with a strong voice two verses from a hymn of Dr. Watts that he dearly loved: 'I'll praise my Maker while I've breath.' Later on he returned to it more than once, saying: 'I'll praise,' but when he could go no further, he begged those who were present to 'pray and praise.' After sleeping a little he said to Miss Ritchie: 'Betsy, you, Mr. Bradford, pray and praise.' She says in her moving account of the scene: 'We knelt down, and truly our hearts were filled with the divine presence; the room seemed to be filled with God.' Several of his friends came in at intervals and questions were asked about the future, but he was quite content to leave the business of the Methodists in the hands of God. He knew that he had made, in his Conference, the best arrangements he could think of for carrying on his work.

Wesley himself had once said: 'Our people die well.' The Methodists were greatly interested in death-bed scenes, which seemed to carry them almost on to the streets of the celestial city. The modern sentiment on this subject is quite different. Yet even the sophisticated Christian of the present day, may pause a little and wonder when one of God's saints goes home. Claxton's familiar picture of the Death Bed of Wesley groups twenty spectators in that little room. It was painted in 1844, and must not be accepted as an accurate representation of the scene. Still, most, if not all, of the people represented there, were present at some time or other by his death-bed. They tried to get him to give them a farewell message. For a time he failed and then, says James Rogers, 'He cried out so loud as to be heard by all in the room, "The best of all is, God is with us!"' When Mrs.

Charles Wesley came, he thanked her as she pressed his hand and affectionately endeavoured to kiss her. Some one moistened his lips with water and instinctively he said : 'We thank Thee, O Lord, for these and all Thy mercies; bless the Church and King; grant us truth and peace, through Jesus Christ our Lord, for ever and ever.' It was his usual grace after meat. His brother's wife and the rest were forgotten. He was a little child again in the Epworth nursery, saying his grace exactly as his mother had taught him.

We must quote the last paragraph of Miss Ritchie's account :

On Wednesday morning we found the closing scene drew near. Mr. Bradford, his faithful friend, and most affectionate son, prayed with him and the last word he was heard to articulate was, 'Farewell!' A few minutes before ten, while Miss Wesley, Mr. Horton, Mr. Brackenbury, Mr. and Mrs. Rogers, Dr. Whitehead, Mr. Broadbent, Mr. Whitfield, Mr. Bradford, and E.R. were kneeling around his bed, according to his often expressed desire, without a lingering groan, this man of God gathered up his feet in the presence of his brethren. We felt what is inexpressible; the ineffable sweetness that filled our hearts as our beloved Pastor, Father and Friend entered his Master's joy, for a few moments blunted the edge of our painful feelings on this truly glorious, melancholy occasion. As our dear aged Father breathed his last, Mr. Bradford was inwardly saying, 'Lift up your heads, O ye gates; be ye lift up, ye everlasting doors, and let this heir of glory enter in.' Mr. Rogers gave out

> Waiting to receive thy spirit,
> Lo! the Saviour stands above :
> Shows the purchase of His merit,
> Reaches out the crown of love.

I then said, 'Let us pray for the mantle of our Elijah'; on which Mr. Rogers prayed in the spirit for the descent of the Holy Ghost on us, and all who mourn the general loss the Church Militant sustains by the removal of our much-loved father to his great reward.

We need not linger over any account of the thousands who gathered to look, for the last time, at the face of the man to whom they owed so much when he was alive, nor over the funeral service that took place a week later at the early hour of five in the morning. It has been said recently that no Englishman of any period is better known to us than Dr. Johnson. The person who made that statement must have forgotten John Wesley for the moment. The record of his life for fifty-five years lies before us like an open book. For the larger part of that time we have an hourly record of his activities, with significant expressions of his state of mind. We recognize in him a mind of transparent honesty, that is never inclined to suppress or exaggerate the truth. Esteem for the purity of his motives and for the complete devotion of his life grows with the years. No recent biographer makes the mistake of thinking that ambition was a dominant motive in the life of Wesley. The masterful autocracy of an eighteenth-century father of a family is there, but the paternal affection and humane consideration for all his children is there also. His preachers, whom he addressed as Sammy, or Tommy, especially in his later years, gave him an almost unbounded veneration. These men were no weaklings but, for the most part, men of strong common sense and sturdy individuality. Only the great qualities of a Wesley could have commanded such implicit obedience and such whole-hearted support. We may disagree with many of his opinions and smile at some of his eccentricities, but it is very difficult to discover real blemishes of character in the man.

> Whatever records leap to light, he never shall be blamed.

It must always be remembered that he had been searching passionately for twenty years for God's plan of life for him before he found it. He was nearly thirty-five when his real life-work began, and from that moment to the end he never swerved from the path laid down for him in the providence of God. He never claimed Christian perfection for himself, although he preached it as the goal of the Christian life; yet surely John Wesley has an exalted place on the roll of the saints. It is there that we would prefer to leave him. Macaulay has spoken of his genius for government as being second only to that of Richelieu. His shrewd, practical mind lives in the wonderful organization of world-wide Methodism to-day, but the soul of the loyal disciple of his Lord is greater than any contribution he may have made to Church government. In the fellowship of the saints he is in the best company that we can know.

SOLI DEO GLORIA.

INDEX

Aberdeen, 85, 132, 143, 189, 223, 256, 317, 333, 335.
Abergwilly, Palace of, 92.
Abingdon (America), 320.
Abraham, John, 132.
Act for further relief of Protestant Dissenting Ministers and Schoolmasters, 150.
Adams, John of Massachusetts, 46.
Adams, Samuel of Massachusetts, 35, 46.
Adams, Thomas of Osmotherley, 86-7.
Africa, 108, 133.
Alderney (Channel Isles), 281, 286-8.
Aldersgate Street (London), 262.
Alexandria (U.S.A.), 243.
Allen, Beverly, Elder in U.S.A., 241.
Allen, Dr., visited by Coke in U.S.A., 237.
Alley, Mary, an African slave in Antigua, 128.
Allhallows Church (Lombard Street), 96, 310.
Alnwick, 190, 194.
America, 20, 22-4, 26-7, 31-3, 41-4, 46-7, 49-52, 54-9, 63-5, 71, 83, 89, 97-8, 108, 113, 121-4, 126, 143, 163-4, 171, 197-9, 208, 220-6, 228-33, 235, 237, 239-40, 242, 244-6, 249-51, 256-8, 262, 264-6, 270-71, 273, 278, 326-7.
American Episcopal Church, 223-5, 229.
American Revolution, 33, 52, 121.
Amsterdam, Wesley's visit to, 202.
Anderson, Sir William, rector at Epworth, 156.
Annapolis (Maryland), 226, 243.
Antigua, 22, 43, 127-9, 241, 257, 263, 266, 268.
Appeal from Protestant Association to the People of Great Britain, 151.
Arbroath, 144.
Armagh, 56.
Arminian Magazine, 116.
Arminians, 75.

Asbury, Francis, 23-6, 28, 43, 55, 64, 83, 123, 199, 200, 208, 216, 220, 225, 229, 233, 235-41, 243-4, 249, 271, 320-2.
Ashgrove (U.S.A.), 54-5.
Ashton, a Dublin Methodist, 54-5.
Athlone, 143.
Atkinson, Myles, vicar of Kippax, 140.
Atlantic, 32-3, 50, 71, 121, 127, 171, 319-20.
Atlay, John, book-steward, 74, 315, 323-5.
Atmore, Charles, 64, 218, 335.

Baildon (Yorks.), 179.
Balaam, 66.
Ballingarane, 54-5.
Balham, 339.
Ballymena, 313.
Baltimore, 25, 236-8, 249, 271.
Bandon (Ireland), 312.
Banff, 85.
Baptists, 200, 227.
Bardsley, Samuel, 62, 303.
Barnard Castle, 140.
Barrett, Judge, protects Asbury, 225.
Barrett's Chapel, Coke preaches there, 236-7.
Barrington, the Hon. Daines (son of Viscount Barrington), 169, 170.
Barrow (i.e. Barton-on-Humber), Barton-on-Humber, 189. [189.
Bassett, Judge, protects Asbury, 225.
Bath (Somerset), 104, 119, 138, 146, 149, 161, 165, 171, 248, 292, 296-7.
Bath and Wells, Bishop of, 223.
Batley, 182, 185.
Baxter, John, pioneer missionary in W. Indies, 127-9, 241, 263, 267-8.
Baynes, Mr., master at Kingswood School, 119.
Beale (vicar of Bengeworth), 172.
Beard of New Mills, host of Wesley, whose daughter was given to finery in dress, 84.

INDEX

Bedford, 337.
Bedfordshire, 275.
Beer, G. L., on American Revolution, 50.
Belfast, 143, 313.
Bengeworth (Worcestershire), 153, 172.
Benson, Joseph, 37-9, 60, 68, 122-3, 126, 133, 144, 155, 214, 217.
Bethnal Green, 72, 96.
Beverley, 177.
Bible Christians, 83.
Bingley, 139, 153.
Birling (Kent), 167-8.
Birmingham, 23, 172, 190-1, 245, 298, 300-1, 311, 335.
Birstall, 42, 62-3, 131, 176, 192-6, 203-4, 206-7, 322-3.
Black, William, Missionary to Nova Scotia, 126-7.
Blackwell, Ebenezer, friend of Wesley, 118, 191.
Blair, Andrew, 149, 247.
Boardman, Richard, 23-5, 43-4, 54.
Bolingbroke (U.S.A.), 237.
Bolton (Lancs.), 84, 173, 307, 335.
Book Room, 74, 324.
Boroughbridge, 155.
Bosanquet, Mary (Mrs. John Fletcher), 36, 60, 62, 182, 185.
Boston (Massachusetts), 33-4, 44, 46, 59, 100-1, 244.
Boyer, Caleb, 241.
Brackenbury, Robert Carr of Spilsby, 87, 141, 184-5, 198, 202, 216-7, 283, 289-90, 332, 342.
Bradburn, Samuel, 214, 301, 303-4.
Bradford (Wilts.), 205.
Bradford (Yorks.), 177, 324.
Bradford, Joseph, Wesley's travelling companion, 149, 173-4, 214, 219, 280, 290, 311-2, 341-2.
Brecknock, 174.
Brecon, 91-2, 210.
Bretherton, Rev. F. F., 22-3, 43.
Bridgend, 174.
Bridgnorth, 185.
Brigden, Rev. T. E., 87.
Brigg (Lincs.), 87.
Briggs, Miss, grand-daughter of Vincent Perronet, 248.
Brislington, 113.
Bristol, 32, 40, 43-5, 62, 69, 71, 74, 80-3, 90, 97-100, 102, 104-5, 107-8, 113-4 117, 119, 126, 129, 134, 145-6, 148, 152, 161, 163-5, 169, 171-2, 184, 188, 193, 196, 202-8, 212, 220, 230, 232, 234, 253, 260, 268, 277, 292-3, 296-300, 302, 304, 309, 311, 316-7, 334-5, 337.
Bristol, John, 146.
Broadbent, John at Wesley's death-bed, 342.
Broadmead Chapel, Bristol, 71.
Brown, Rev. James, vicar of Kingston, near Taunton, 91, 93.
Buckingham, 337.
Bunhill Fields, 82.
Bunker Hill, 59.
Burke, Edmund, 45, 49, 63, 80,
Buxton, 201.   [311.

Caen Wood, 158.
Calm Address to the American Colonists, 70-1.
Calm Address to the Inhabitants of England, 98, 100.
Calvinists, 66, 74-5, 78, 113, 176.
Camberwell, 180.
Cambridge, 63, 88, 294.
Cambridge (U.S.A.), 237.
Camden (New York), 54-5.
Camelford, 197.
Campbell, Sophia, the coloured teacher, 128.
Canada, 245.
Canterbury, 78, 222, 246.
Carmarthen, 174.
Carolina, 20.
Caskets, The, 286.
Castletown (Isle of Man), 110.
Catcott, Alexander, vicar of Temple Church, Bristol, 172.
Catholic Relief Act, 150, 156.
Chancellor, Samuel, Trustee of City Road Chapel, 95.
Chancery Lane, 209.
Channel Islands, 88, 160, 198, 216, 280-1, 290.
Charlestown (South Carolina), 45, 270.
Chatham Dock, 127, 165.
Cheshire, 83, 129, 184, 187, 305.
Chester, 84, 174, 218, 246, 277, 329, 335.
Chesterfield, Earl of, 103.
Chew, a Methodist preacher in U.S.A., 122.
Chowbent, 84.
Christ Church (Oxford), 134.
Church of Alexandria, 229.
Church of England, 19, 96, 106, 130, 159, 162-4, 199, 200, 212, 220-1, 223, 225, 228-30, 232, 234, 240, 250-1, 264, 294, 304, 320, 325-6, 330.

INDEX

City Road Chapel, 90, 95, 108, 116, 132, 134-5, 137, 142, 145, 147-50, 158, 161, 167-8, 173, 207, 214, 216, 232, 301-3, 309, 332, 338.
Clara (Ireland), 53.
Clarke, Dr. Adam, 115, 204-5, 216, 283-8, 290, 336-7.
Clarke of Antigua, 268-9.
Claxton, Marshall, 289, 341.
Claxton of St. Vincent, 268-9.
Clones (Ireland), 312.
Clulow, William, Wesley's solicitor, 209-10, 212, 215.
Cockermouth, 155.
Coke, Dr. Thomas, 91-3, 117, 132, 134, 142, 149, 178, 180, 183, 192, 200, 203, 209-12, 214-5, 228-33, 235-41, 244, 246, 249-51, 260, 265-73, 280, 290, 311, 314-5, 319, 321-2, 327-30.
Cokesbury College (U.S.A.), 320.
Colchester, 333.
Cole, Le Roy, elder in U.S.A., 227, 241.
Collins of Swanage, 281.
Colne, 84.
Compassionate Address to the Inhabitants of Ireland, 129-30.
Concord, Battle of, 50.
Conference, Annual:
29. Leeds (1772), 22-3.
30. London (1773), 30-1.
31. Bristol (1774), 41-4.
32. Leeds (1775), 60-7. Benson suggests ordination of 'suitable preachers.'
33. London (1776), 88-90.
34. Bristol (1777), 113-6.
35. Leeds (1778), 131-4.
36. London (1779), 143-4. A short Conference.
37. Bristol (1780), 161-3, 176. Charles Wesley alarmed at movement from the Church of England.
38. Leeds (1781), 176-80. Size of Conference reduced.
39. London (1782), 192-6. Birstall Chapel case.
40. Bristol (1783), 203-6. Wesley ill during part of Conference, cf. 212.
41. Leeds (1784), 89, 212-9. *Deed of Declaration.* Fletcher's appeal for peace. See references to this 'eventful' Conference, 220, 228-30, 232, 253.
42. London (1785), 252-7.
43. Bristol (1786), 254, 262-6, 327-8.
44. Manchester (1787), 182, 277-9, 281, 323.
45. London (1788), 309, 324, 329.
46. Leeds (1789), 315-6, 325, 338.
47. Bristol (1790), 317, 335-8. Wesley's last Conference.
48. Manchester (1791), 319. Membership returns.
Conferences in America:
Philadelphia (1773), 23-6.
Fluvanna (Virginia), (1779), 227-8.
Baltimore (1784). Third in the year, 236-9, 241-3.
Charleston, Mecklenburg County & Baltimore (1787), three held by Dr. Coke, 271-2.
Coke and Asbury ordained at Baltimore as General Superintendents, 320.
Baltimore (1787), 320-1.
Conferences in Ireland:
Dublin (1778), 130-1.
Dublin (1782), first regular Conference. Dr. Coke in charge, 192.
Dublin (1783), 'a little Conference,' 201.
Dublin (1787), 276.
Dublin (1789), 313-5. Wesley's last visit to Ireland.
Conference Journal, 215, 217, 219.
Conference, Ecumenical Methodist (1891), 244.
Congleton, 43, 83, 107, 305.
Congress (U.S.A.), 89, 122.
Connecticut, 26-7, 221-2.
Constantinople, 276.
Contingent Fund, 313.
Cooper, Ezekiel, 322, 339.
Cork, 54, 109, 129, 143, 312, 330.
Cornwall, 32, 44, 69, 90, 94, 117, 131, 134, 160, 164, 291-2, 316-7.
Court of King's Bench, 137.
Coventry, 142.
Cowland, William, Trustee of City Road Chapel, 95.
Cowper, William, 124.
Crabbe, George, 333, 337.
Crabb, Robinson, 333, 337.
Creighton, Rev. James, 29, 149, 214, 231-2.
Cromwell, James, Elder in America, 241, 263.
Crook, John, 'Apostle of Methodism in the Isle of Man,' 109, 132, 175.

INDEX 347

Crookshank, Rev. C. H., author of *Methodism in Ireland*, 32, 117-8, 129, 133, 191, 273, 276, 312, 314.
Cruger, Henry, M.P. for Bristol, 45, 171.
Cullompton, 316.
Cumberland, 308.

Dall, Robert, preacher in the Isle of Man, 132.
Darlington, 140.
Dartmouth, Earl of, 72, 98, 105, 124-5.
Dartmouth, vessel, 33-4.
Dawgreen, near Birstall, 194.
Dawson, John, 142, 147.
Declaration of Independence, 319.
Deed of Declaration, 210, 211, 213-7, 219, 248, 253-5, 277, 323.
Deed of Union (1932), 219.
De Jersey, Mrs., of Guernsey, 282.
Delamotte, Charles, 189, 261.
Delaware, 235, 237, 242.
Demas, 66.
Derby, 156, 201, 335.
Derbyshire, 83.
Derryaghy (Ireland), 56.
Devizes, 104, 337.
Devon, 69, 138, 292.
Devonport, 316.
Dewsbury, 314-5, 323-5, 336.
Dickens, John, deacon in U.S.A., 241.
Dickinson, Rev. Peard, 149, 166, 301, 305.
Dodd, Dr. 102-3, 111, 166.
Doddridge, Philip, 63.
D'Olier, R. of Dublin, 314.
Dorset, 88.
Dorchester (U.S.A.), 226.
Douglas (Isle of Man), 109-11, 175.
Dover, 78.
Dover (U.S.A.), 235.
Downes, John, 48.
Downs, Sheriff, 122.
Dublin, 53-4, 56, 117, 129-30, 152, 191, 247, 273-4, 276, 298, 311-2, 315, 328-30, 337.
Dublin Bay, 247.
Dudley, 172.
Dumfries, 308.
Dunbar, 141.
Dundee, 85, 132, 144, 256.
Dungannon, 313.
Dunkeld, 144.
Dunleary (Kingstown), 53.
Duplex, John, trustee of City Road Chapel, 95.

Durham, 160, 308.
Dying Avowal (Toplady), 77.

East Anglia, 309, 333.
Easterbrook, Rev. Joseph, of Bristol (Temple Church), 172.
Edgar, Alexander, Mayor of Bristol, 299.
Edinburgh, 36-8, 61, 73, 85, 141-2, 153, 155, 189-90, 256, 308.
Eels, William, 323-5.
Egerton, Rev. W. H. (Rector of Whitchurch, Salop), 22.
Egypt, 276.
Elles, Reuben, member of a 'Presbytery' appointed at the Fluvanna Conference, 227, 241.
Embury, Philip, 54-5.
Enniskillen, 313.
Epworth, 156, 181, 188-9, 309, 335, 342.
Etheridge, Dr. J. W., author of Lives of Coke and Adam Clarke, 91, 93, 229-31, 235, 237, 239, 243, 268-71, 286, 289.
Europe, 58, 108.
Evans, Rev. Caleb (of Broadmead Chapel Bristol), 71-2.
Evelyn, John, the diarist, 333.
Evening Post, 329.
Exeter, 137-8, 145, 196, 292, 316.

Fakenham (Suffolk), 181.
Falmouth, 316-7.
Fenwick, Michael, 155.
Ferguson, William (of Ireland), 312.
Findlay, Mrs. G. G., 63.
Finningley, 156.
Fishguard, 117.
Fletcher, John (of Madeley), 20-2, 29-30, 40, 48, 60-1, 64-5, 67-8, 71-2, 90, 94, 113, 115, 117, 119, 139, 177-8, 182, 185-6, 218, 230-1, 257-8, 262, 294-5, 300.
Floyd, Mr. of Halifax, 173.
Fluvanna (U.S.A.), 228.
Folgham, John, trustee of City Road Chapel, 95.
Forres, 141.
Foundery, 70, 73-5, 77, 81, 95, 132, 134, 249.
Fox, Charles James, 311.
France, 101, 119, 121, 126, 129, 145, 197, 290.
Franklin, Benjamin, 51.
Franklin, Miss ('now Mrs. Parker'), of Fakenham, 181.
Frederica, 261.

Freeman's Journal, 152.
French Revolution, 311.

Gaffney, James (of Ireland), 133.
Gallatin, Colonel, 135.
Garrettson, Freeborn, 226, 235-7, 240-1, 263.
Gatch, an Elder in U.S.A., 227.
Gayer, Edward, clerk to the Irish House of Lords, 56.
George III., 36, 47, 72, 89, 122, 150, 311.
Georgia, 27, 46, 90, 100, 171, 189, 260-2.
German (Isle of Man), 110.
Gibson, Edmund, Bishop of London, 67.
Gibson, Joshua, curate at Epworth, 156.
Gilbert, Francis, 22-3, 43, 128.
Gilbert, Grace, 22-3.
Gilbert, Mary, 22-3.
Gilbert, Nathaniel, 22, 43, 127-8, 245, 269.
Gill, William, Elder in U.S.A., 241.
Glamorganshire, 68.
Glasgow, 74, 308.
Gloucester, 206, 337.
Gloucester, Dean of, 125.
Gloucestershire, 129.
Gordon, Lord George, 157, 166.
Gordon Riots, 150, 156-8, 166.
Grant, Sir Lodovick, 141.
Grassington, 154.
Gravesend, 266.
Great Yarmouth, 181.
Greenwood, Charles, trustee of City Road Chapel, 95, 119.
Grimshaw, Rev. William, 195.
Guernsey, 45, 260, 280-4, 288-90.
Gumley, Mrs., friend of Charles Wesley, 168.
Gwennap, 131, 180, 291-2, 317.

Haggerty, John, Elder in U.S.A., 241.
Hagley Park, 190.
Halifax, 36, 64.
Hall, Martha, 80.
Hall, Westley, 80.
Hamilton, Dr. James, 315.
Hammet, William, 266, 268-9.
Hamoaze, The, 316.
Hampson, John, junior, 323.
Hanby, Thomas, 62, 256, 327.
Handel, G. F., 170, 187.
Harford, Joseph, 45.
Harper, Joseph, 182.
Harris, Howell, 30, 68.

Harrison, Rev. A. W., 78-9.
Hartley, rector of Staveley, 155.
Hartley, Joseph (U.S.A.), 226.
Harvey, Miss, of Hinxworth, 294.
Harwich, 202.
Hatton, Thomas, 22.
Haverfordwest, 174-5, 333.
Hawes, Robert, 74.
Hawes, Thomas, chaplain to Lady Huntingdon, 77.
Hawkins, Sir John, 72.
Haworth, 36, 84, 139, 153.
Heart of Asbury's Journal, 239-40.
Heald, John, 323.
Helston, 94, 180, 317.
Heptonstall, 36, 153.
Herefordshire, 160.
Hertfordshire, 294, 309, 337.
Hey, William, 179.
High Wycombe, 294.
Hill, Rowland, 76.
Hilton, John, 114, 116.
Hinchcliffe, John, Bishop of Peterborough, 51.
Hinkhouse, Dr. Fred. J., 51-2.
Hinxworth (Herts.), 294.
Holland, 202, 233, 271.
Holme, Rev. Edward, of Birling (Kent), 167.
Holy Club, 96.
Holyhead, 174, 201, 247, 249, 276.
Hopper, Christopher, 39, 214.
Horbury, 194.
Horsley (nr. Newcastle-on-Tyne), 39.
Horsley, Samuel, Bishop of St. David's, 115.
Horton, John, at Wesley's deathbed, 342.
Hot Wells (Bristol), 337-8.
Howard, John, 274-6.
Huddersfield, 36.
Hull, 88, 177, 309.
Humane Society, 118.
Hunt, Alfred Leeds, 106-7, 186.
Hunt, Dr. William, 44, 46-7, 49.
Huntingdon, 337.
Huntingdon, Countess of, 68, 77.

Indians, 35, 261.
Industrial Revolution, 34.
Ingham, Benjamin, 39, 261.
Ireland, 19-20, 23-5, 29, 32, 42-3, 45, 53-4, 58, 60-1, 65, 74, 88-9, 109, 126, 129-31, 133, 140, 150-2, 160, 173-7, 185, 191-2, 201, 204-5, 212, 215, 245-6, 248, 253, 273-6, 279, 308-10, 314-5, 319, 329.

INDEX 349

Ireland, James, of Brislington, 113, 115.
Isle of Man, 109, 132, 155, 160, 174-5, 245, 284.
Isle of Scilly, 160.
Isle of Wight, 160, 245, 284, 333.
Ivey, Richard, Elder in U.S.A., 241.

Jackson, Thomas, 76-7, 103, 118, 162-3, 169, 251-2, 256, 296, 301-2.
Jaco, Peter, 132.
Jeffreston, near Pembroke, 112.
Jenkins, vicar of Maryborough, 53.
Jersey, 260, 283-4, 289-90.
Jesus College (Oxford), 92.
Johnson, Dr. Samuel, 70-1, 80, 342.

Keighley, Joshua, 266.
Kelso, 337.
Kemp, Richard, 95.
Kent, 75, 309, 333, 337.
Kent County (Delaware, U.S.A.), 124.
Kershaw, vicar of Leeds, 140.
Kidderminster, 185.
Kilgour, Bishop of Aberdeen, 223.
King, John, 24-5.
King, Peter, Lord Chancellor, 233.
King's Lynn, 333.
Kingston (near Taunton), 91, 93.
Kingston, William, 334.
Kingswood, 139.
Kingswood colliers, 172.
Kingswood School, 61, 66, 119, 203-4, 219, 278, 293, 298, 335, 337.
Kippax, 140.
Knox, Alexander, 274-5.

Lambert, Jeremiah, Elder in Antigua, 241, 263.
Lambeth, Archbishop's chapel at, 223.
Lancashire, 84, 109, 129, 160, 184, 187, 201, 305, 307.
Land's End, 317.
Lane's Chapel (U.S.A.), 237.
Latimer, *Annals of Bristol,* 45, 97-8, 104, 171.
Launceston, 317.
Lavington, Bishop of Exeter, 196.
Laws, Dr., consulted by Wesley, 55.
Leasowes, 191.
Leatherhead, 339.
Lee, Thomas, 155, 278.

Lee, *History of American Methodism,* 227.
Leeds, 22, 42, 60, 62, 131, 140, 143, 148, 178-9, 188, 206, 212, 220, 253, 277.
Leeward Isles, 245, 260.
Legal Hundred, ch. xv., 228, 247, 323.
Leicester, 335.
Leinster, 129.
Leipzig, 137.
Lewes, Miss, of Bristol, 62.
Lewisham, 147.
Lexington, 50, 53.
Lightwood, James T., 138.
Limerick, 54, 109, 129, 312.
Lincoln, 335.
Lincoln College (Oxford), 97.
Lincolnshire, 40, 87-8, 141, 160, 187.
Lindsay, Robert, 215.
Lisburn, 56.
Liverpool, 44, 84, 107-10, 126, 131, 143, 173-4, 201, 246.
Lloyd, David, 115.
Lloyd, John, merchant of Charlestown, U.S.A., 45.
Lockwood, author of *The Western Pioneers,* 22, 43.
Lodge, Henry Cabot, 33.
London, 29-30, 32, 36, 44-5, 47, 53, 68-70, 74-5, 81-2, 86, 88, 94-6, 102, 104-6, 111, 114, 116-8, 124-5, 132, 134, 137, 142-3, 147-8, 156, 158, 164-9, 173, 180-2, 184, 188, 191, 196-7, 200-3, 207, 209, 212, 223, 249, 252-4, 258, 262, 273, 277, 293-4, 296-7, 300-2, 304-6, 309, 316-7, 335, 338.
Londonderry, 43, 74, 274, 313.
London Packet or *New Lloyd's Post,* 78.
Lovely Lane Chapel (U.S.A.), 239.
Lowestoft, 333.
Lowth, Robert, Bishop of London, 118, 164, 228.
Lurgan, 59.
Lutheran Church, 240.
Lutherans, 27, 199.
Lytteltons, family seat of, 190.

McAllum, Duncan, 132-3.
Macaulay, T. B., 343.
Macclesfield, 83, 106-7, 186-7, 247, 301, 305.
Macdonald, James, 217.
Maclardie, Aeneas, 187.
McNab, Alexander, 146-7, 149.
Maddox, Mr., a London lawyer, 209.

INDEX

Madeley, 22, 30, 40, 67, 113, 139, 185, 294, 300-1.
Mallett, Sally, 182.
Malton, 177.
Manchester, 84, 172-3, 184, 201, 219, 277, 298, 314, 323, 335.
Marazion, 317.
March, Miss, of London, 41.
Markham, William, Archbishop of York, 186, 222.
Marlin, John, first Methodist preacher to the Isle of Man, 110.
Maryborough, 53.
Maryland, 20, 24-5, 27-9, 97, 100, 123, 226, 237, 242, 320.
Marylebone, 168, 302.
Massachusetts, 27, 33-4, 46.
Mather, Alexander, 149, 306, 323-4, 327-8, 336.
Maxfield, Thomas, 92.
Maxwell, Lady, 189.
Mecklenburg County (U.S.A.), 271.
Methodist Episcopal Church, 199, 235, 240, 257, 263, 273, 278, 319-20.
Methodist Magazine, 116, 216, 309.
Methodist Recorder, 64, 181.
Mingo Mattaw, 261.
Minutes of Conference, 24, 30-1, 37, 42-3, 62-4, 66, 89-90, 113-5, 130-3, 143, 146, 158-9, 162-3, 165, 178, 192-3, 205, 209-10, 215, 228, 230, 241, 253, 256, 263-4, 267, 273, 277-8, 281, 307, 315, 326-7, 336.
Mississippi, 101.
Model Deed, 193-4, 323, 325, 336.
Mohawks, 35.
Moister, author of *History of Methodist Missions,* 128.
Monmouthshire, 160.
Monthly Review, 72.
Moore, Henry, 21, 91, 149, 196, 199, 210, 274-6, 306, 327, 329, 332.
Moravians, 199.
Moray, Skinner, bishop of, 223.
Morning Post, 75, 78-9.
Mornington, Earl of, 170, 310.
Mount Vernon, home of Washington, 244.
Munster, 129.
Murray, James (Lord Mansfield), 157.
Myles, William, 130-1, 149, 160, 178, 195, 311, 329.

Nattrass, Rev, J. Conder, 181.
Nelson, John, 42, 193.

Netherlands, 57.
Nettleton Court, 262.
Newark, 316.
New Brunswick, 126.
Newbury, 69.
Newcastle-on-Tyne, 38-9, 73, 86, 141-2, 144, 155, 193, 308, 325, 335.
New England, 33, 53, 57, 100-1.
Newfoundland, 27, 198, 245, 260, 266, 268.
Newgate, 96, 103, 135, 157, 166.
New Hampshire, 27.
Newington, 119.
New Jersey, 25, 27, 57, 242.
New King Street Chapel (Bath), 138, 149.
Newlyn, 317.
Newmarket (Ireland), 54.
New Mills, 83.
Newport (Mon.), 68, 113, 174.
New Room (Horsefair, Bristol), 98, 115, 137, 196, 203, 206, 335.
Newton, Sir Isaac, 63.
New York, 20, 25, 27, 54, 100, 171, 222, 235.
New York Christian Advocate, 24.
New York State, 54.
Nind, Mr., the Papermaker, 74.
Norfolk, 182.
Norfolk (U.S.A.), 25.
Norfolk, Duchess of, 252.
North, Lord, 34, 49, 56, 59, 98, 100, 105.
Northampton, 63, 309, 337.
North Carolina, 27, 55.
North Shields, 323-4.
Northumberland, 187, 308.
Norwich, 94, 181, 228, 333.
Notes on the New Testament, 194.
Nottingham, 88, 202, 327, 335.
Nova Scotia, 27, 126, 241, 260, 279.

Oglethorpe, General, 171, 261.
O'Kelly, James, Elder in U.S.A., 241.
Oldham, 64, 187.
O'Leary, Father, 152-3, 173.
Osgood, Professor, 50.
Osmotherley, 86.
Otley, 73, 139, 153-4, 314, 338.
Otterbine (Otterbein), Rev. Philip (Lutheran), 240.
Oxford, 91-2, 96-7, 111, 134, 145, 165, 169, 210, 232, 240, 293, 309, 337.
Oxfordshire, 73.

Paramore, John, publisher, 249.
Parkgate, 60, 246, 276-7.

INDEX

Pateley Bridge, 73, 153-4.
Paulton, 248.
Paustoobee, 261.
Pawson, John, 132, 176, 205, 256, 324-5, 327.
Peace of Paris, 121.
Pebworth, 153, 172.
Pedicord, Caleb (U.S.A.), 226.
Peel (Isle of Man), 110-1, 176.
Pembroke, 112, 174, 337.
Pembrokeshire, 68.
Pennington, William, 54.
Pennsylvania, 20, 26-7, 57, 100, 242.
Penzance, 94, 180, 290-1, 317.
Pepys, Samuel, 333.
Perronet, Charles, 48, 90.
Perronet, Miss, 81.
Perronet, Vincent, 124, 135, 182, 248, 257.
Perth, 144.
Peterborough, John Hinchliffe, Bishop of, 51, 223.
Petersburg (U.S.A.), 25.
Petre, Bishop of Ross, 223.
Philadelphia, 23, 25, 46, 122, 235.
Philip of Spain, 57.
Pigman, Ignatius, Deacon in U.S.A., 241.
Pilgrim Fathers, 101.
Pilmoor, Joseph, 24-5, 43-4, 54.
Pine, William, of Bristol, 74.
Pitchcombe, 153.
Pitt, William, the Elder, 33, 101, 311.
Plan of Pacification, 331.
Plato, 71.
Plessey (Newcastle-on-Tyne), 155.
Plymouth, 145, 316.
Plymouth Dock, 69, 196, 292, 316.
Pocklington, 177.
Portsmouth, 98, 165, 309.
Portugal, 129.
Potomac, River, 243-4.
Potter, John, Archbishop of Canterbury, 330.
Presbyterian Ministers, 200.
Preston, 58.
Price, Dr. Richard W., 72.
Prickard, John, 133.
Priestley, Dr. Joseph, 179.
Prince George County (U.S.A.), 226.
Proceedings of the Wesley Historical Society, 213.
Protestant Episcopal Church of U.S.A., 199, 220-1.
Provoost, Dr., a presbyter of American Episcopal Church, 223.

Public Advertiser, 151-2.

Quakers, 27, 52.
Quarterly Review, 230.
Quebec, 101, 260.
Quebec Act, 46.
Queen Anne, 67.
Queen Anne County (U.S.A.), 226.

Raikes, Robert, 274.
Raithby (Lincs.), 184.
Rankin, Thomas, 22-3, 25-6, 28, 43, 52-3, 126, 132, 142, 205, 214, 327.
Rathcormack (Ireland), 126.
Redmire, 39.
Redruth, 291, 317.
Reed, Nelson, Elder in U.S.A., 241.
Reflections on the French Revolution, 311.
Reformed Dutch Church in U.S.A., 199.
Rehoboam, 57.
Revenue Act, 34.
Reynolds, Sir Joshua, 310.
Rhode Island, 27.
Richardson, Rev. John, 142, 149, 153.
Rigg, Dr. J. H., 64.
Risley (Derbyshire), 156.
Ritchie, Dr., 153-4.
Ritchie, Elizabeth, 109, 153-4, 314, 338-42.
Road (Somerset), 92.
Robinson, Beatrice, 154.
Roe, Charles of Macclesfield, 107, 186.
Rogers, Hester Ann (née Roe), 247, 338, 342.
Rogers, James, 149, 247, 338-9, 341-2.
Roman Catholics, 150-2, 158, 199.
Romney, 310.
Rosanna (Ireland), 310.
Ross, John, Bishop of Exeter, 196, 223.
Rotch, owner of the *Dartmouth*, 34-5.
Rules of a Helper, 146.
Ryle, John, of Macclesfield, 83.

St. Asaph, 51.
St. Aubin's, 284, 286.
St. Austell, 316.
St. Christopher, 268-9.
St. David's, 175.
St. Eustatius, 268-70.
St. Gennys, 197.

St. Helier, 289.
St. Ives, 291, 317.
St. John's (Antigua), 128, 267.
St. Just, 94, 317.
St. Luke's Church (Old Street), 135.
St. Margaret's Church (Rood Lane), 135.
St. Michael's Mount, 290.
St. Peter Port, 282-3.
St. Sepulchre's Church (Holborn), 135.
St. Swithin's Church (London Stone), 200.
St. Thomas's Church (Southwark), 200.
St. Vincent's, 268-9.
St. Werbergh Church (Bristol), 104.
Salisbury (Sarum), 32, 164, 337.
Saughton Hall, 189.
Saunderson, Hugh, 37-8, 155.
Saunderson, Joseph, 63, 132, 215.
Saunderson, Nicolas, 63.
Saunderson, William, 63.
Savannah, 261.
Scarborough, 177, 309.
Scotland, 19-20, 36-7, 42, 67, 81, 85-6, 132, 138, 140-1, 144, 155, 167, 176-7, 184, 187, 189, 212, 223, 230, 256, 260, 265, 279, 305, 308, 315, 326-7, 329.
Scott, Sir Walter, 337.
Seabury, Samuel, delegate from American Episcopal Church to England, 222-3.
Secker, Thomas, Archbishop of Canterbury, 330.
Serious Advice to the Inhabitants of England, 125.
Sewell, Mary, a class-leader in Norfolk, 181.
Shadford, George, 22-6.
Shaftesbury, 32.
Shaw Hall, 109.
Sheerness, 165.
Sheffield, 156, 180, 298, 335.
Shenstone, William, 191.
Shipley, Jonathan, Bishop of St. Asaph, 51.
Shoreham (Kent), 81, 124, 135, 182.
Shrewsbury, 172, 311.
Shropshire, 22, 335.
Simeon, Charles, 294-5.
Simpson, David, of Macclesfield, 106-7, 186-7.
Skinner, Bishop of Moray, 223.
Slavery, 241-2, 297, 340.
Sligo, 276, 312.

Smith, Richard, Mrs., 275.
Smith, William, of Newcastle-on-Tyne, 39, 73, 144, 155.
Smith, William, Mrs. (Jenny Vazeille), 40, 141.
Smollett, Tobias, *History of England* quoted, 139-40.
Smyth, Rev. Edward, 130, 145-6, 328-9.
Snowdon, 173.
Society for the Propagation of the Gospel, 222.
Socinians, 66.
Somerset, 94, 258.
Southampton, 280, 290.
South Carolina, 27, 45.
Southey, Robert, 152.
South Petherton, 91-3, 117.
Spain, 129, 145.
Spitalfields, 125.
Staffordshire, 129, 335.
Stamp Act, 33.
Staten Isle, 222.
Staveley (Yorks.), 155.
Stevens, Abel, author of *History of American Methodism*, 23, 25, 28, 42, 199, 225, 227, 239, 241.
Stillingfleet, Edward, 163.
Stockport, 333.
Stokesley, 308.
Stormont, Lord, 166.
Strawbridge, Robert, 25-6, 28, 123.
Stroud, 202, 304.
Suffolk County (U.S.A.), 46.
Sussex, 32, 309, 333, 337.
Sutcliffe, Joseph, 335.
Suter, Alexander, 279.
Swaffham, 333.
Swaledale, 39.
Swanage, 280.
Swanlinbar, 29.
Swansea (vessel of), 171.
Sydney, author of *England and the English in the Eighteenth Century*, 157.

Tabernacle, Whitefield's, 134.
Talbot County (U.S.A.), 22.
Talgarth, 30.
Tanderagee (Ireland), 55, 313.
Taunton, 64, 69, 82, 91, 93, 117.
Taxation no Tyranny, 70-1, 311.
Taylor, Thomas, 41, 133.
Taylor, Joseph, 256, 327.
Telford, Rev. John, 169,-70, 250.
Temple Church (Bristol), 164, 171-2, 293, 298.
Tennant, Thomas, 132, 142.
Thames, 96.

Thirty-nine Articles, 326.
Thomas, Barnabas, 245.
Thompson, George, vicar of St. Gennys, 197.
Thompson, William, 149.
Thurlton (Norfolk), 181.
Tighe, Mrs., of Rosanna (Ireland), 310.
Tipple, Dr. E. S., author of *The Heart of Asbury's Journal*, 239-40.
Tiverton, 137-8.
Todmorden, 153.
Tolbooth, 37-8.
Told, Silas, 135.
Toleration Act, 138.
Toplady, Augustus M., 76-7, 111.
Townshend, Charles, 34.
Tract Society, 183.
Trevecca, 30, 68.
Trowbridge, 325.
Truro, 316.
Tuckaho (U.S.A.), 123.
Tudor, Owen, 175.
Tunbridge Wells, 124, 182.
Tyerman, Luke, author of *Life and Times of Wesley*, 22, 71, 75-6, 118, 147, 163-4, 178-9, 183, 211, 307, 309.

Ulster, 32, 311.
United States of America, 101, 121, 198, 200, 220, 228-9, 237, 241, 271-2, 319, 321, 326.
Upperthorpe (' Overthorpe '), 188.
Utrecht, 202.

Valton, John, 146, 149, 336, 338.
Vasa, Gustavus, an African slave, 339.
Vasey, Thomas, 228, 231-3, 235, 239.
Vaughan, Admiral, 72.
Vazeille, Jenny (Mrs. William Smith), 40, 141.
Vazeille, Mrs. (i.e. Mrs. John Wesley), 144.
Versailles, Treaty of, 197.
Virginia, 20, 24-9, 42, 55, 97, 100, 221, 237, 242-3.

Wakefield, 194.
Wakeley, author of *Early History of American Methodism*, 54-5.
Wales, 38, 44, 68, 91, 111-3, 145, 160, 167, 169, 174-5, 177, 212, 220, 279, 308, 337.
Wandsworth, 128.
Wapping, 167.
Warrener, William, 266, 268.

Washington (U.S.A.), 244.
Washington County (U.S.A.), 54.
Washington, George, 47, 129, 243-4.
Waterford, 53-4. [321.
Waters, William, 25.
Watson (or Adams), of Osmotherley, 87.
Watson, John, 132.
Watson, Richard, 73, 316.
Watts, Isaac, 307, 341.
Webb, Captain (or Lieutenant), 22-5, 123, 164-5.
Wednesbury, 83, 172.
Wellington, Duke of, 170, 310.
Wells (Norfolk), 181.
Wensleydale, 39.
Wesley, Charles:
  His attitude to the American War, 53.
  Benson suggests that Charles should join his brother John and Fletcher of Madeley in ordaining preachers, 60.
  John writes to him concerning Mrs. John Wesley, 74; see also 76.
  Attempts to save Dr. Dodd, 103.
  Appointed to the City Road Chapel, 132.
  Travels with his brother to Bristol, 134.
  Opposes a licence for the New Room (Bristol), 137.
  Dispute of Charles with the preachers about City Road Chapel, 142, 148.
  Travels with his brother to Wales, 145.
  Travels with his brother to Bath to settle disturbance, 147.
  Protects James Murray (after Lord Mansfield) at Westminster School, 157.
  At the 1780 Bristol Conference, 161.
  On separation from the Church of England, 162-3, 249-51, 325-6, 328.
  His household in Marylebone (Chesterfield Street), 168-9.
  With his brother at Mrs. Blackwell's at Lewisham, 191.
  His rights as a trustee of chapels, 193, 195, 212.
  A member of the Legal Hundred, 214.

Controversy with Dr. Coke, 249-51, 260.
Informed by the Duchess of Norfolk that his son has joined the Roman Catholic Church, 251-2.
Meets his brother in Bristol, 292.
Illness of, and death, ch. xxii., 296-7, 301, 306-7.
Wesley, Mrs. Charles, 307, 342.
Wesley, Charles junior, 169, 301.
Wesley, John:
1773—Faces the question of the future of Methodism and asks Fletcher to succeed him, 19-22. A similar problem in U.S.A., 22-9. In Ireland, 29; at Conference and in tours from London, 30-2.
1774—An operation and then the northern tour, including Scotland, 36-40; at Bristol Conference, 40-4; in Wales, Cornwall and Bristol, 44-7; in London and neighbourhood, 47-8.
1775—On the war in America, 52-3, 56-9, 70-2; in Ireland where he was laid aside by illness, 53-9; at Leeds Conference, 60-8; in Wales and the West of England, 68-9; in London, 70-2.
1776—Attacks on his character and teaching, 74-80; arrangements for City Road Chapel, 81-2; Bristol, the North of England and Scotland, 82-8; at Conference in London, 88-90; to West of England, where he meets Dr. Coke, 91-5.
1777—London and Bristol, 96-101; writes his *Address to the Inhabitants of England*, 99-101; visits Dr. Dodd in prison, 102-3; Bristol and then London, 104-6; North of England and the Isle of Man, 106-11; Midlands, Wales and the Bristol Conference, 111-16; London and Bristol, 117-20.
1778—Interviews the Earl of Dartmouth, 124-6; in Ireland, 129-31; at the Leeds Conference, 131-4; the Midlands and London, 134-6.
1779—On licences for Chapels, 137-8; Bath, the North of England and Scotland, 138-43; at Conference in London, 143-4; Wales and the Bath difficulty, 144-9.
1780—Catholic Emancipation, 150-3; the North of England and Scotland, 153-6; the Gordon Riots, 156-8; on licences for Chapels, 158-61; at Conference in Bristol, 161-3; Bristol and London, 163-6.
1781—In London, 167-71; Bristol, the Midlands and Wales, 171-5; the Isle of Man and Yorkshire, 175-7; at the Leeds Conference, 177-80; Cornwall and the Home Counties, 180-2.
1782—London, Bristol, the North of England and Scotland, 183-90; at the London Conference, 192-6; Cornwall, London, 196-7.
1783—Illness in London, 201; in Ireland and the Midlands, 201-2; journey to Holland, 202; at the Bristol Conference, 203-6.
1784—Difficulties of American Methodism, 208-9, 220-44; appointment of the Legal Hundred, 209-15; at Conference in Leeds, 215-9.
1785—In Ireland, 245-9; at Conference in London, 252-7; loses Vincent Perronet and John Fletcher, 257-8.
1786—On Foreign Missions, 259-62; at Conference in Bristol, 262-6; question of Ordination, 204-6.
1787—In Ireland; meets Coke and Howard there, 273-7; at Conference in Manchester, 277-9; ordaining more preachers there; in the Channel Isles, 280-91; Cornwall and the West, 291-3; Oxford and London neighbourhood, 294-5.
1788—Bath and Bristol, 296-300; hears of his brother's death, 301; in Cheshire and Lancashire, 305-7; Scotland, 308; at the London Conference, and in the Home Counties, 309.

INDEX 355

1789—Sits for the Romney portrait, 310; pays his last visit to Ireland, 310-4; at Manchester and the Leeds Conference, 314-6; his last visit to Cornwall, 316-7.
1790—Failing strength, 332; interest in curiosities, 333-5; London to Aberdeen, 335; last Conference at Bristol, 335-7; South Wales and Home Counties, 337-8; last open-air sermon, 339.
1791—His last sermon and his last words on slavery, 339-40; last illness and death, 340-3.

Wesley, Mrs. John, 73-6, 144.
Wesley, Samuel, junior, 169-70, 251, 304.
Wesley, Sarah, 77, 301, 304, 339, 342.
Wesley's *Sermons*, 244.
West Indies, 319, 341.
Westminster, 50, 125.
Westminster School, 157.
West Street Chapel, 30, 48, 81, 135, 145, 161, 168, 296, 303, 309.
Wharfedale, 154.
Whatcoat, Richard, 228, 231-3, 235, 239, 271-2, 321.
Wheeler, Charles, 95.
Whiston, William, 63.
Whitby, 308.
White, Dr., a presbyter of American Episcopal Church, 223.
White, George, vicar of Colne, 84.
White, Judge, of U.S.A., 124, 225.
Whitehaven, 37, 109-11, 155, 175-6.
Whitehead, Dr., 337, 340, 342.

Whitfield, George, Wesley's 'travelling companion,' 180, 247, 342.
Whitworth, Abraham, 24-5.
Wigan, 84, 335.
Wilberforce, Samuel, 26, 29, 220-4, 339.
Williams, Robert, 24-6, 54-5.
Willis, Henry, Elder in U.S.A., 241.
Wilson, vicar of Otley, 154.
Winchelsea, 339.
Winchester (Winton), 337.
Witney, 293.
Wolff, George, of Balham, 339.
Wolverhampton, 300.
Wood, James, 214.
Wood, Vice-Chancellor, 195.
Worcester, 112, 172, 245.
Worcestershire, 129.
Word to a Freeholder, 45.
Wray, James, ordained for Nova Scotia, 279.
Wren, William, American preacher imprisoned, 226.
Wrigley, Francis, 132.
Wright, Richard, preacher in U.S.A., 24-5.

Yarmouth, 181, 280.
Yeadon, 187.
Yearbry, Joseph, preacher in U.S.A., 24-5.
York, 143, 177, 190, 309, 335.
York, Archbishop of (William Markham), 222.
Yorkshire, 36, 40, 73, 84, 87, 111, 139, 160, 179, 182, 184, 187, 213, 305, 308, 314, 323, 335.

Zion's Herald, 244.

www.ingramcontent.com/pod-product-compliance
Lightning Source LLC
Chambersburg PA
CBHW070011010526
44117CB00011B/1516